Shifting the Focus:
From Static Structures to the Dynamics of Interpretation

Current Research in the Semantics/Pragmatics Interface

Series Editors:
K.M. Jaszczolt, University of Cambridge, UK
K. Turner, University of Brighton, UK

Other titles in this Series:

TURNER (Ed.)	The Semantics/Pragmatics Interface from Different Points of View
JASZCZOLT	Discourse, Beliefs and Intentions: Semantic Defaults and Propositional Attitude Ascription
GEURTS	Presuppositions and Pronouns
JASZCZOLT (Ed.)	The Pragmatics of Propositional Attitude Reports
PEETERS (Ed.)	The Lexicon-Encyclopedia Interface
PAPAFRAGOU	Modality: Issues in the Semantics-Pragmatics Interface
LEEZENBERG	Contexts of Metaphor
NÉMETH & BIBOK (eds.)	Pragmatics and the Flexibility of Word Meaning
BRAS & VIEU (eds.)	Semantic and Pragmatic Issues in Discourse and Dialogue
GUTIÉRREZ-REXACH	From Words to Discourse: Trends in Spanish Semantics and Pragmatics
PEREGRIN (ed.)	Meaning: The Dynamic Turn
NEW! DOBROVOL'SKIJ & PIIRAINEN	Figurative Language: Cross-cultural and Cross-linguistic Perspectives

---

NEW!

KAMP & PARTEE (Eds.) **Context-Dependence in the Analysis of Linguistic Meaning**

Does context and context-dependence belong to the research agenda of semantics - and, specifically, of formal semantics? Not so long ago many linguists and philosophers would probably have given a negative answer to the question. However, recent developments in formal semantics have indicated that analyzing natural language semantics without a thorough accommodation of context-dependence is next to impossible. The classification of the ways in which context and context-dependence enter semantic analysis, though, is still a matter of much controversy and some of these disputes are ventilated in the present collection. This book is not only a collection of papers addressing context-dependence and methods for dealing with it: it also records comments to the papers and the authors' replies to the comments. In this way, the contributions themselves are contextually dependent.

In view of the fact that the contributors to the volume are such key figures in contemporary formal semantics as Hans Kamp, Barbara Partee, Reinhard Muskens, Nicholas Asher, Manfred Krifka, Jaroslav Peregrin and many others, the book represents a quite unique inquiry into the current activities on the semantics side of the semantics/pragmatics boundary.

Audience
Researchers and students of linguistics, philosophy of language, computational science and logic.

For further information on the CRiSPI series including sample chapters and details of how to submit a proposal go to:
www.elsevier.com/locate/series/crispi

SHIFTING THE FOCUS: FROM STATIC STRUCTURES TO THE DYNAMICS OF INTERPRETATION

Daniel Wedgwood
University of Edinburgh, UK

2005

ELSEVIER

Amsterdam – Boston – Heidelberg – London – New York – Oxford
Paris – San Diego – San Francisco – Singapore – Sydney – Tokyo

ELSEVIER B.V.
Sara Burgerhartstraat 25
P.O. Box 211, 1000 AE
Amsterdam, The Netherlands

ELSEVIER Inc.
525 B Street
Suite 1900, San Diego
CA 92101-4495, USA

ELSEVIER Ltd.
The Boulevard
Langford Lane, Kidlington,
Oxford OX5 1GB, UK

ELSEVIER Ltd.
84 Theobalds Road
London WC1X 8RR
UK

© 2005 Elsevier Ltd. All rights reserved.

This work is protected under copyright by Elsevier Ltd., and the following terms and conditions apply to its use:

Photocopying
Single photocopies of single chapters may be made for personal use as allowed by national copyright laws. Permission of the Publisher and payment of a fee is required for all other photocopying, including multiple or systematic copying, copying for advertising or promotional purposes, resale, and all forms of document delivery. Special rates are available for educational institutions that wish to make photocopies for non-profit educational classroom use.

Permissions may be sought directly from Elsevier's Rights Department in Oxford, UK: phone (+44) 1865 843830, fax (+44) 1865 853333, e-mail: permissions@elsevier.com. Requests may also be completed on-line via the Elsevier homepage (http://www.elsevier.com/locate/permissions).

In the USA, users may clear permissions and make payments through the Copyright Clearance Center, Inc., 222 Rosewood Drive, Danvers, MA 01923, USA; phone: (+1) (978) 7508400, fax: (+1) (978) 7504744, and in the UK through the Copyright Licensing Agency Rapid Clearance Service (CLARCS), 90 Tottenham Court Road, London W1P 0LP, UK; phone: (+44) 20 7631 5555; fax: (+44) 20 7631 5500. Other countries may have a local reprographic rights agency for payments.

Derivative Works
Tables of contents may be reproduced for internal circulation, but permission of the Publisher is required for external resale or distribution of such material. Permission of the Publisher is required for all other derivative works, including compilations and translations.

Electronic Storage or Usage
Permission of the Publisher is required to store or use electronically any material contained in this work, including any chapter or part of a chapter.

Except as outlined above, no part of this work may be reproduced, stored in a retrieval system or transmitted in any form or by any means, electronic, mechanical, photocopying, recording or otherwise, without prior written permission of the Publisher.
Address permissions requests to: Elsevier's Rights Department, at the fax and e-mail addresses noted above.

Notice
No responsibility is assumed by the Publisher for any injury and/or damage to persons or property as a matter of products liability, negligence or otherwise, or from any use or operation of any methods, products, instructions or ideas contained in the material herein. Because of rapid advances in the medical sciences, in particular, independent verification of diagnoses and drug dosages should be made.

First edition 2005

Library of Congress Cataloging in Publication Data
A catalog record is available from the Library of Congress.

British Library Cataloguing in Publication Data
A catalogue record is available from the British Library.

ISBN: 0-08-044577-2

∞ The paper used in this publication meets the requirements of ANSI/NISO Z39.48-1992 (Permanence of Paper).
Printed in The Netherlands.

Working together to grow
libraries in developing countries

www.elsevier.com | www.bookaid.org | www.sabre.org

ELSEVIER BOOK AID International Sabre Foundation

Current Research in the Semantics/Pragmatics Interface (CRiSPI)

Series Editors: K.M. Jaszczolt, University of Cambridge, UK and K. Turner, University of Brighton, UK

Editorial Advisory Board:
N. Asher, USA
B. Birner, USA
C. Casadio, Italy
M. Dascal, Israel
B. Fraser, USA
T. Fretheim, Norway
B. Gillon, Canada
P. Gochet, Belgium
J. Groenendijk, The Netherlands
Y. Gu, PRC
A. Kasher, Israel
M. Krifka, Germany
S. Kubo, Japan
C. Lee, Korea
S. Levinson, The Netherlands
T. McEnery, UK
F. Nemo, France
P. Pelyvas, Hungary
J. Peregrin, Czech Republic
A. Ramsay, UK
R. Stalnaker, USA
M. Stokhof, The Netherlands
J. van der Auwera, Belgium
R. van der Sandt, The Netherlands
K. von Heusinger, Germany
G. Ward, USA
H. Zeevat, The Netherlands

The aim of this series is to focus upon the relationship between semantic and pragmatic theories for a variety of natural language constructions. The boundary between semantics and pragmatics can be drawn in many various ways; the relative benefits of each gave rise to a vivid theoretical dispute in the literature in the last two decades. As a side effect, this variety has given rise to a certain amount of confusion and lack of purpose in the extant publications on the topic. This series provides a forum where the confusion within existing literature can be removed and the issues raised by different positions can be discussed with a renewed sense of purpose. The editors intend the contributions to this series to take further strides towards clarity and cautious consensus.

Contents

Preface — xiii

1 Language and Meaning — 1
- 1.1 Pragmatics and the study of grammar — 1
  - 1.1.1 Competence and performance in theory and in method — 3
  - 1.1.2 Pragmatics and the dynamicisation of grammar — 7
  - 1.1.3 Focus and theory at the interfaces — 8
- 1.2 Semantics and the interpretation of natural languages — 12
  - 1.2.1 Fundamentals — 12
  - 1.2.2 Inference and semantics — 16
  - 1.2.3 Pragmatic contributions to propositional semantics — 17
  - 1.2.4 Pragmatics and the assumption of compositionality — 21
- 1.3 Consequences of compositionality: illustrations from domain restriction — 27
  - 1.3.1 A comparability restriction in exclusive readings — 28
  - 1.3.2 Domain restricting indexicals — 33
- 1.4 Semantics: what it means — 37
- 1.5 Summary — 38

2 Relevance Theory and Implications for Linguistic Structure — 41
- 2.1 Relevance Theory — 42
- 2.2 Some misconceptions about RT — 48
  - 2.2.1 RT as a reduction of Gricean pragmatics — 48
  - 2.2.2 Practical falsifiability — 50
- 2.3 A different perspective on language structure — 52
  - 2.3.1 Encoded meaning as constraints on inference — 52
  - 2.3.2 Inference in the course of processing — 55
- 2.4 Syntax: static structures versus instructions for interpretation — 57
  - 2.4.1 Static syntax is unnecessary — 58

viii *Shifting the Focus*

		2.4.2	Abstraction and the accessibility of the object of study	62
	2.5	Grammar from a parsing perspective		67
		2.5.1	Well-formedness without syntactic representations	67
		2.5.2	The argument from production and parsing	68
	2.6	Formal and informal analysis		70
	2.7	Summary		72
3	**The Hungarian Data**			**75**
	3.1	Overview		75
	3.2	The data		75
		3.2.1	The basic positions of the Hungarian sentence	75
		3.2.2	Immediately pre-verbal position	77
		3.2.3	The interpretation of focus	79
		3.2.4	Verbal modifiers	81
		3.2.5	Other PV elements	84
	3.3	The focus position: syntactic analyses		85
		3.3.1	'Single position' analyses	85
		3.3.2	The verb movement analysis	89
		3.3.3	Independent movement to multiple PV positions	91
	3.4	Summary: looking beyond conventional syntactic analysis		93
4	**Focus and Grammar**			**95**
	4.1	Overview		95
	4.2	The broader notion of focus		96
		4.2.1	The meaning of 'focus'	96
		4.2.2	Focus and the encoded/inferred distinction	98
		4.2.3	A dynamic, RT approach to English	102
		4.2.4	The general meaning of focus (and presupposition)	104
	4.3	The nature of 'focus position' foci		106
		4.3.1	There is no simple 'focus position'	106
		4.3.2	'Narrow' and 'broad' focus	107
		4.3.3	Exhaustivity: are there two kinds of focus?	110
	4.4	Encoded versus inferred exhaustive focus		112
		4.4.1	The case against inferred exhaustivity	113
		4.4.2	The significance of the argument	116
	4.5	Exhaustivity as an inference in context		116
		4.5.1	Exhaustivity as an unmarked reading	117

	4.5.2	Dependence on (psychological) context 118
	4.5.3	Alternatives emerge from context 119
	4.5.4	Different contexts; different kinds of exhaustivity 121
	4.5.5	Non-exhaustive narrow foci are linguistically marked 124
	4.5.6	The *it*-cleft translation 127
	4.5.7	Quantity implicature 130
	4.5.8	Quantity implicature in RT 132
4.6	The failure of encoded focus: the absence of exhaustivity 135
4.7	Narrow focus and the presupposition of eventualities 138
	4.7.1	The costs and benefits of presupposed eventualities 143
	4.7.2	Non-exhaustive narrow foci and eventualities 143
4.8	Summary 145

5 Focus and Quantifier Distribution   149

5.1	Overview 149
5.2	Quantificational projections and procedures 150
	5.2.1 Szabolcsi (1997b) 150
	5.2.2 Against the PredOp/Focus distinction 154
	5.2.3 The apparent difference 156
	5.2.4 Numerals, narrow focus and scalar implicature 159
5.3	Constraints on TP and QP 168
	5.3.1 The monotonicity constraint 168
	5.3.2 Witness set representations and information structure 170
5.4	Constraints on PV 171
	5.4.1 Proportionality and PV 172
5.5	The apparent counterexamples 177
	5.5.1 'Counterexample' 1: a complex determiner 178
	5.5.2 'Counterexample' 2: complex QNP-internal information structure . . . 179
	5.5.3 'Counterexample' 3: a different kind of proportionality 181
	5.5.4 Proportionals in PV and the idea of 'counting' 183
5.6	Contrastive focus on non-PV quantifiers 184
5.7	Summary 185

6 Dynamic Structured Meanings: Predication and Information Structure   187

6.1	Overview 187
6.2	Focus and predication 189
	6.2.1 Focus and focus frame as predicate and logical subject 189

		6.2.2 Main predication 191
		6.2.3 Basic inferences over main predicates 192
	6.3	Eventualities and structured meanings 194
		6.3.1 Eventuality-based semantics 195
		6.3.2 Herburger (2000): structured eventualities 197
	6.4	Making structured meanings dynamic: epsilon terms 199
		6.4.1 The creation of propositional forms 199
		6.4.2 The epsilon operator 201
		6.4.3 The epsilon operator with event variables 203
	6.5	Hungarian syntax and main predication 206
	6.6	Simple worked examples 210
		6.6.1 Topic>comment 210
		6.6.2 Narrow focus 213
		6.6.3 Two readings of main predicate verbs 215
	6.7	Summary 217

7 Verbal Modifiers and Main Predication   219

	7.1	Overview 219
	7.2	Verbal 'prefix' particles and resultatives 221
	7.3	Why the VM, not the verb, is the unmarked main predicate 229
		7.3.1 VMs as unmarked main predicates: empirical support 235
	7.4	Other VMs 236
		7.4.1 Bare nominals 236
		7.4.2 Adverbs 241
		7.4.3 Locatives 247
	7.5	Summary 252

8 'Aspectual Constructions' and Negation   255

	8.1	Overview 255
	8.2	The 'existential/evidential' and 'progressive' constructions 256
		8.2.1 The 'abstract operator' analysis 257
		8.2.2 The AspP analysis 258
	8.3	The main predication analysis 260
		8.3.1 Explaining the 'progressive construction' 260
		8.3.2 Explaining the 'existential construction' 265
	8.4	Negation 268

		8.4.1	Negation and main predication 271

	8.5	The homogeneity of negation 273
		8.5.1 'Constituent negation' 273
		8.5.2 Simple sentential negation 275
		8.5.3 Focus > *nem* > V 277
		8.5.4 Why *nem* is pre-verbal 279
		8.5.5 Negation and the interpretive relevance of lexicalisation 281
	8.6	Summary 282

9 Summary and Conclusions   285

9.1	Theoretical concerns 285
9.2	Empirical illustrations 286
9.3	Implications and further research 290

Bibliography   295

Index   307

PREFACE

During the final preparations of this book, it was made known to me that one anagram of *pragmatics* is *tragic spam*. In their more paranoid moments, pragmaticists might be tempted to feel that this is how their field is viewed from other areas of linguistics: at best deserving of pity for its relative lack of formal rigour and, like unsolicited email (or the temptations of cheap luncheon meat?), probably best ignored. Any such impression is doubtless increasingly wide of the mark, as the existence of the *CRiSPI* series testifies. On the other hand, it is one of my major contentions in this book that pragmatics is still typically not given nearly its due as a source of explanation of linguistic phenomena. Furthermore, once we begin to grant this, it brings significant consequences for our very conceptions of syntax and semantics, as well as for the role of pragmatics.

When I say 'pragmatics', I mean the kind of general inferential processes that are attributable to extra-grammatical cognitive domains: the kind of reasoning that is most often associated with the work of Grice, though I argue for a distinctly post-Gricean line. The overarching theme of the book is the necessity to establish the division of labour between the grammar and extra-linguistic factors, in particular inferential pragmatics, if we are to account with any accuracy for the ways in which the structures of natural languages relate to the interpretations that they convey—that is to say, if we are to 'do syntax and semantics' well. I argue that this requires active consideration of inferential processes, not wholesale abstraction away from them, and that to do this properly requires a radical perspective on linguistic structure and its relationship to semantics. As I emphasise in the book, this does not entail a denial of the competence/performance distinction. On the contrary, the aim is to elucidate matters of strict linguistic competence. There is no contradiction between holding this objective and the claim that meeting it successfully requires active consideration of factors from performance and from extra-linguistic kinds of competence.

The book opens with two chapters of theoretical discussion, which point to the quite fundamental assumptions of conventional forms of linguistic analysis that are responsible for the marginalisation of pragmatics and the consequent loss of crucial information to theories of linguistic competence. These chapters purposefully take a strong line—at the very least, I hope to show that evaluation of the fundamentals of linguistic theory is of more than abstract philosophical interest: the basic value of the work that linguists produce is at stake. It behooves us to question whether received wisdom about the relationships between semantics, pragmatics and syntax provides a suitable basis for meeting the objectives of research within any of those domains. The discussion is concerned with the implicit assumptions revealed by common practice in linguistic analysis as much as with the explicitly stated assumptions of existing frameworks (though I take issue with both).

The key questions underlying this discussion are the following: (1) Given that the data with which linguists work is inevitably filtered through the extra-linguistic cognitive capacities that are involved in the use of language, how are we even to delimit the object of study of theories of syntactic and semantic competence—never mind produce realistic models—unless we make an active effort to account for these extra-linguistic factors? (2) What kind of theory is required to give the analyst access to all potentially significant extra-linguistic factors? For the reasons outlined in the opening chapters (see in particular sections 1.1.1 and 2.4.2), I do not find the usual answers (to the extent that these questions are usually considered) at all convincing. These answers often amount to little more than justifications for ignoring the issue. One of the major aims of this book is to not only argue, but also demonstrate, that this can only distort our model of grammar.

My own response to these questions is that we should make two major changes to the way linguistic data are usually analysed. The first is to recognise the need to invoke general processes of pragmatic inference as an integral part of analysing the relationship between linguistic structure and propositional meanings (in the manner of Relevance Theory). The second is to adopt an incremental processing-based view of linguistic structure (in the manner of Dynamic Syntax), so that the analyst has access to crucial influences on the construction of meanings that stem from the linear presentation of linguistic expressions.

Such conclusions are unashamedly radical in the context of most contemporary linguistic analysis, so naturally the need for them and the positive consequences of them require some persuasive demonstration. This is why Chapters 3–8 leave broad theoretical discussion behind and provide repeated illustration of my arguments through extensive linguistic analysis. This is based on a fairly well-known phenomenon, previous analyses of which have had a considerable impact on the formal literature on syntax and semantics: the so-called 'focus position' of Hungarian (along with some other, grammatically related matters). The idea is to demonstrate empirically both the unsustainability of analyses based on conventional assumptions and the considerable potential of dynamic and pragmatically informed (but nonetheless formalisable) approaches to provide more genuinely explanatory analyses of linguistic phenomena.

Given this theoretical stance, I inevitably spend a certain amount of time in the following pages taking a critical approach to previous work on Hungarian. I hope that this doesn't convey an overwhelmingly negative impression, since the analysis in this book of course owes a huge intellectual debt to much of the work discussed in this way. In particular, the insightful and admirably clear work of Katalin É. Kiss and of Anna Szabolcsi provides the crucial point of departure for many of my arguments. My position more obviously draws on Sperber & Wilson's Relevance Theory (benefiting in particular from Robyn Carston's work within that framework) and the theoretical perspective provided by Dynamic Syntax (Kempson, Meyer-Viol & Gabbay

2001). However, it should be noted that my overall position is not central to either of these frameworks, so practitioners of them cannot be assumed to agree with all, indeed any, of my arguments in this book.

Other acknowledgements can be found in my Ph.D. thesis (cited here as Wedgwood 2003), from which this book sprang, via substantial changes. All of the people thanked there are implicitly thanked again, but some must be given special mention here also. First, the supervisors of that thesis, Ronnie Cann and Caroline Heycock, contributed hugely to the development of this work through many incisive but always constructive discussions of it and through their generous guidance and encouragement. The thesis was examined by Ruth Kempson and Jim Hurford, both of whom also provided very helpful feedback. Ronnie and Ruth, along with Ian Underwood, are also thanked for reading chapters that are new to the book and once again providing many useful comments and suggestions. Of course, no-one gets to claim credit for any remaining nonsense, which is indubitably all my own work, nor do the aforementioned people necessarily agree with all that I say in the following chapters.

I'd also like to re-state my immense gratitude to my Hungarian informants, especially Anna Babarczy and Ágnes Bende-Farkas. Many thanks to Cassie Mayo, for a great deal of time and effort helping with the technical side of producing a book, and to Lynda Hutchison for vital assistance with the index, as well as helping out in innumerable other ways. Thanks also to the CRiSPI series editors for their very attentive work on the manuscript and to the linguistics team at Elsevier. Financial support for parts of the preparation of this book came from an ESRC Postdoctoral Fellowship and a British Academy Postdoctoral Fellowship.

1

LANGUAGE AND MEANING

1.1 PRAGMATICS AND THE STUDY OF GRAMMAR

This book addresses issues at what would conventionally be thought of as the syntax-semantics interface, yet takes as its starting point the effects of inferential pragmatic principles. To many linguists this may seem a curious way to proceed. Standardly, syntax is thought of as an abstract system of knowledge, something to which linguistic processing refers, but essentially encapsulated from such processing. Formal semantics, for all its anchoring in an 'external' model, is also strictly part of a system of competence, typically based in the investigation of model-theoretic logical representations, whose compositional nature is related to the combinatory properties of syntax. Inferential pragmatics, on the other hand, inherently involves discussion of procedures that occur in the processing of actual utterances in context: by any definition (see Turner 1999 for a variety of positions on this), pragmatics is concerned with the *use* of language. The overall model assumed in most formal linguistic work can therefore be summarised as in Figure 1.1. While it is important to note that not every school of thought would accept precisely the schema in Figure 1.1[1], it seems fair to say that this general picture is at least implicit in the majority of syntactic and semantic approaches.

How, then, should consideration of inferential pragmatics, hence matters of contextualised language use, form the basis for explanations of the relationship between the 'competence' modules of syntax and semantics? Addressing this question at a theoretical level is the purpose of the present chapter; the whole book, including the extended case-study of the Hungarian 'focus position' in later chapters, is an illustration of the importance of the question and of some of the

---

[1] For example, Chomsky (1995a) remains sceptical about the possibility of interfacing syntactic analysis with an 'externalist' semantics. However, it is clear that the majority of researchers in what could be called 'Chomskyan frameworks' assume a fairly direct form of mapping from the structures of LF to logical semantic representations. Indeed, existing notions of LF and of 'syntactic scope' arguably make this kind of semantic interface an integral part of Principles and Parameters and the Minimalist Program. It is widely recognised that there is little 'syntactic' research today that is not effectively research on the syntax-semantics interface, discussing the production of different readings of word strings, rather than simple grammaticality versus ungrammaticality.

2 Shifting the Focus

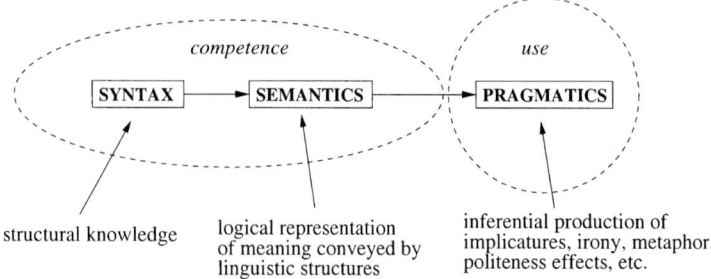

Figure 1.1: Outline schema of the commonly assumed structure of linguistic theory

consequences of addressing it.

The principal motivation for attacking structural matters via pragmatic theory is a problem with the picture of linguistic theory summarised in Figure 1.1, a problem so fundamental that it calls for a radical change of perspective on the integration of structural, semantic and pragmatic information. This problem is expanded upon throughout this book, but is worth stating in simple terms here at the beginning. It crucially turns upon the role of pragmatics in linguistic analysis and can be summarised as follows:

- what is accounted for by general principles of inference in communication need not be accounted for in the grammar

- there is considerable evidence in the recent pragmatic literature that extra-linguistic principles of inference make a significant contribution to the determination of propositional meanings associated with linguistic utterances

- this means that we must carefully distinguish between grammatically encoded and inferential contributions to meaning, in order to approach a realistic view of linguistic competence

- to achieve this, we require a substantially different approach to the analysis of linguistic competence to those commonly adopted; one that allows active consideration of inferential processes in order to take account of them

If the effects of inferences drawn in use are *not* accounted for, there is a real danger of attributing much more semantic material than necessary to direct grammatical encoding and of distorting our model of the grammar by positing otiose grammatical machinery to do this encoding work. The problem with the assumptions embodied in Figure 1.1 is therefore that the mechanisms that determine the grammar-meaning correspondence have no access to pragmatic processes and so cannot take this information into account. As such, these assumptions practically guarantee an over-complicated, inaccurate model of the grammar and of the meaning that it encodes.

This may appear not to be a valid conclusion, under conventional assumptions about the semantics-pragmatics distinction. These assumptions, adhered to in the supposedly 'radical' pragmatics of Grice and his followers as well as (at least implicitly) in most syntactic and semantic work, limit the domain of inferential pragmatics to inherently 'post-semantic' matters. That is, propositional meanings are delivered algorithmically by the grammar and pragmatic principles of communication serve only to manipulate these propositional meanings in context to produce cancellable conversational implicatures and 'non-literal' meanings like irony (as shown in Figure 1.1). If these assumptions were correct, it would not matter that the syntax-semantics interface has no access to pragmatic processes. However, more recent work in pragmatics, in what might be termed 'post-Gricean' approaches, such as Relevance Theory (Sperber & Wilson 1986/95), has concluded that such assumptions are wholly unsupported. There is, quite simply, no principled reason to assume that inferential pragmatic processes are restricted to non-truth-conditional, 'non-literal' domains. On the contrary, as outlined below, there is rich evidence—in addition to simple intuitive reasoning about the nature of communication—to suggest that principles of pragmatic inference must be involved in the mapping from linguistic forms to propositional representations of meaning. If this is the case, the conventional picture of abstract syntax interfacing directly with logical semantics is simply unsustainable.

If this observation is accepted—and I argue below (following Sperber & Wilson 1986/95, Carston 2002) that it must be—the consequences are profound. Semantics must be carefully re-evaluated, as linguistically encoded meaning can no longer be identified with the components of propositional representations. The possibility of heavily underspecified encoded semantics, to be enriched by pragmatic processes in context, and the likelihood of widespread procedural meaning, as opposed to declarative logical semantics, must be taken seriously. This much has been argued repeatedly in the Relevance Theory literature (see section 2.4), but with relatively little practical impact on work in semantics. Still more radical consequences follow for syntax, though these remain largely unexplored even by relevance theorists[2]. If what needs to be encoded by the grammar is quite different to what has been assumed hitherto, then the machinery required to effect this encoding may also be significantly different to that supplied by conventional approaches.

1.1.1 Competence and performance in theory and in method

The theoretical position outlined above might seem to entail the abandonment of one of the basic tenets of practically all formal approaches to language: the idea that linguistic theory must be concerned with matters of competence, rather than performance (or use); a distinction based on the need in linguistic analysis, as in any scientific endeavour, for a degree of idealisation away from the often chaotic observable data. After all, arguing that the analysis of grammatical structure and its encoded semantics must take account of pragmatic processes implies a perspective

---

[2]Rubovitz (1997) and Marten (2002) represent rare examples of work that does investigate the implications of relevance-theoretic pragmatics for syntactic analysis.

that cuts right across the division between knowledge of language and its use.

In fact, the position to be outlined in this chapter is most definitely not that of the stereotypical 'functionalist' who wishes to collapse the competence-performance distinction as an *a priori* move and denies the value of characterising linguistic structure out of its social context. On the contrary, the aim is to establish a coherent and fruitful theoretical context for investigating the nature of human linguistic competence and, where appropriate, characterising this in formal terms. How is this compatible with my stated aim of allowing issues relating to language use to influence the analysis of structure? Understanding that this represents no contradiction simply involves recognising that there is a difference between a model of competence and a mode of analysis that restricts itself to competence.

Anyone with the goal of characterising human linguistic competence must address the fact that the only data from which to work are by their nature imbued with traces of various performance factors—again, a situation with analogues in any field of science. Given this, the analyst must make decisions about which factors to ignore as simple unsystematic irrelevances, which to control for in the course of analysis and which to accept as integral parts of one's model of competence.

Uncontroversial examples of the first kind of factor include disfluencies and the relative pitch of different speakers' voices. These factors may reasonably be assumed to be 'noise' in the data; there is certainly no conceivable way that they could influence the systematic relationships between what an individual knows about linguistic structure and the meanings that individual associates with given structures. As such, the analyst may safely ignore such factors, making no reference to them in the process of formulating technical proposals within a theory of grammar.

Some other factors that clearly pertain to use at some level can unproblematically be accounted for within an abstract competence theory. For example, Japanese 'honorifics' and the *tu/vous*-type forms of address found in many languages are on the one hand inherently use-related, being licensed by certain socially-defined relationships between communicator and addressee, but on the other hand are naturally dealt with as a matter of abstract knowledge of language: it is part of the meaning of certain morphemes or lexemes that the communicator is expressing a certain attitude in relation to the addressee(s)[3].

There are many use-related factors that fall into neither of the above categories, however. In particular, there are many effects that arise through the inevitable interaction of any observable linguistic datum and the non-linguistic aspects of human cognition that go into its formulation and interpretation. Crucial factors of this kind are those that spring from the processes of reasoning which mediate between linguistic forms and what interlocutors perceive about the contexts in which they are used, thus helping to determine the particular meanings that given forms con-

---

[3]It should be noted, however, that this meaning is likely to be significantly underspecified: for example, *tu*-type forms can often express either friendly familiarity or disrespectful superiority, in different contexts, while *vous*-type forms can be taken to indicate either sincere respect, a disrespectful refusal to be familiar or a neutral expression of social distance (with a variety of subtle variations being found in different languages).

vey in given contexts. Such factors, far from being unruly 'noise', may well be determined by strict underlying competence principles, but not the kind of language-specific competence that should be captured in a model of mental grammar. It is reasonable to suggest that such factors could have significant effects on the relationship between an underlying linguistic form and the meaning that it is understood to carry—certainly there seems no *a priori* basis for ruling this out. If this is the case, then in order to obtain an accurate picture of what enters into *linguistic* competence—and I take this to be the only worthwhile goal of any formal linguistic theory (see section 1.2.1)—such factors must be controlled for, rather than ignored.

Controlling for some factor means understanding it, as far as possible, in order to identify where its effects on the object of study begin and end. Thus, 'abstracting away from' such a factor carries as a prerequisite a need to engage in an active process of addressing it. In this way, the outcome of a programme of research may be a 'competence' model, even though the process of formulating this involves direct consideration of 'performance' factors. Looked at in these terms, it is fairly clear that this is in fact the normal situation in science. For example, a physicist wishing to uncover some principles relating to the motion of some body might choose to imagine idealised conditions under which, say, friction simply does not occur[4]. Even in order to take this step at a very abstract level of theorising, it is very helpful if the physicist has some idea of what friction is and how it may affect things. As soon as the same scientist wishes to compare his or her theories with any actual data such knowledge becomes quite essential, either for the formulation of special experimental conditions that eliminate friction or for the ability to calculate its effects, in order to count them out in the analysis of results. This very simple analogy points up a crucial observation: without actively understanding and controlling for certain theory-external factors, it is not even clear what a theoretical model should account for. Certainly, a model should not 'account for the data'; at most, a model should account for that part of the data that is not attributable to factors that are external to the model but known to interact with it.

Seen in this context, linguistic theory often seems to proceed rather strangely. Syntacticians regularly seek evidence for a proposal concerning an abstract grammatical model directly from the intuitions of native speakers regarding categorical judgements of the grammaticality or acceptability of some linguistic expression—and rarely with even any systematic effort to consider the possible effects of different contexts. Yet through the very act of presenting the expression in question for interpretation by a human being, it comes under the influence of all kinds of extra-linguistic factors, including the other cognitive faculties of the interpreter. Semanticists, meanwhile regularly accept the existence of some recognised reading of some expression (according to some particular definition; usually truth conditions) as data to be explained in terms of compositional processes—which in turn may be taken as evidence for some grammatical machinery that maps onto these processes. Again, this ignores the many other factors that are inevitably present and quite possibly exerting a significant influence.

---

[4] See Jackendoff (2002, 33) for a related use of this analogy.

Pragmatic factors tend to be treated in one of two ways. On one approach, they are ignored as if they were mere 'noise', on the grounds that matters of performance are not the subject of grammatical theories, but rather the subject of theories that will eventually supplement models of grammar and semantics that are derived from the direct study of competence. On another, they are absorbed into the competence model (a charge that could be levelled at certain variants of Discourse Representation Theory, or heavily 'discourse configurational' syntactic analyses, such as Rizzi 1997). In other words, what does not happen is the kind of active controlling for external factors that one would expect in normal scientific research. The competence-performance distinction that is a necessary part of characterising the theory of language has thus been wrongly applied also in the process of deriving this theory. Linguists appear unwilling even to consider the possible significance of performance issues, unless they can be re-assigned to the domain of competence, just because of the desire to produce strictly competence theories[5]. But, as argued above, these things are not only compatible, they necessarily go together.

To summarise so far, a model of linguistic competence is the *output* of linguistic analysis. The desire to produce a true competence model does not in itself determine an approach to analysis that eschews all reference to factors from language use. What kind of factors should be admitted into analysis is in part a philosophical question, but it is also a practical one: if some factor demonstrably has a direct and significant bearing on the shape of the competence theory that is under construction, then efforts must be made to understand this factor and take it into consideration. If such a factor happens to come from extra-linguistic or 'performance' domains, the result of this analytical work will be no less a theory of linguistic competence. Hence, analysts wishing to characterise the contents of the space on the left-hand side of Figure 1.1 cannot safely turn their attention solely to this space.

There is undeniably more awareness of this than my broad-brush characterisation of the problem implies, at least in terms of linguists' avowed theoretical beliefs. Especially in the current period of concern for the role of grammatical 'interfaces' with other modules, many analysts would agree that extra-grammatical domains contain many insights of some significance for the theory of grammar. However, the 'external' factors that are considered in this way tend to be of very limited kinds: observations from logical analysis of meaning feeding back into the syntax that is presumed to convey this meaning, for example, or proposals for the alignment of syntax with very abstract characterisations of prosodic structure (which may themselves be based on syntactic structures; e.g. Reinhart 1995). The implications of pragmatic theory—theory that addresses truly extra-linguistic principles—remain largely unexplored, and apparently this is widely considered the proper way to proceed. My central contention is that pragmatic theory of the kind represented by RT is precisely the kind of matter that must be actively addressed in

---

[5]This way of thinking infects even some approaches that ostensibly pay considerable attention to pragmatics. For example, Asher & Lascarides (2003, 76) reject the Relevance Theory perspective of considering how interlocutors recognise each other's intentions on the grounds that they wish to develop a competence theory. This ignores the likelihood that the consequences of intention-recognition impact upon the domain of a model of linguistic competence.

the construction of competence grammars and that doing so has significant consequences for the nature of grammatical theory.

1.1.2 Pragmatics and the dynamicisation of grammar

If pragmatic theory is to be allowed to impact on the analysis of linguistic structure and its interpretation, how should this analysis proceed? One approach that is clearly not helpful in this regard is simply to produce complete representations of linguistic structure and representations of perceived meanings and map the one to the other. Instead, we require some more direct way of looking at *how* given structures come to convey the precise range of meanings that they convey—taking account, where appropriate, of context-dependent inferential processes. This is complicated by the fact that inferences drawn in context are not restricted to operating over the meanings of entire utterances, but may be drawn during the course of parsing. Therefore, if a grammatical framework is to facilitate discussion of how such inferences contribute to meaning, it must include a concept of partial representations, reflecting the time-linear nature of language use. This means that a 'dynamic' grammatical framework is required (in the sense of Kempson *et al.*'s 2001 Dynamic Syntax), if linguistic theory is to provide an accurate picture of how structure encodes meaning in natural languages. This nature of this kind of framework is outlined in sections 2.4 and 2.5.1.

A re-assessment of the picture in Figure 1.1 is arguably required for other reasons too. As Cann, Kempson & Marten (forthcoming) point out, semantic theory increasingly recognises the need to invoke the 'left-to-right' dynamics of communication, at least in the treatment of phenomena like anaphora (and hence in everything that interacts with such phenomena), yet syntax is still typically assumed to interface directly with semantics. This, argue Cann *et al.*, brings about a tension within linguistic theory: the usual conception of syntax as an abstract structural knowledge base seems to contradict its supposed position as the input to semantics, if semantics must take account of features of linguistic processing. One counter to this observation would be to assume, in the manner of DRT (Kamp & Reyle 1993), that static syntactic representations encode a good deal of procedural information that effectively underspecifies semantic content. However, as I argue below, the introduction of procedural semantics opens up a more generalised view of human language as a system for indicating how to construct meanings, rather than a direct means of encoding them. This perspective also provides a resolution to the problem outlined above of the need to integrate pragmatics with grammatical analysis. Multiple tensions between syntax, semantics and pragmatics all seem, therefore, to point in one direction.

Another important observation to make about the perspective I adopt in this work, before I proceed to outline it in more detail, is that, while decidedly unconventional, it is neither unprecedented nor alone among contemporary work. Many of the crucial assumptions that I have to outline are those of the 'cognitive pragmatic' framework, Relevance Theory (henceforth RT), as originally set out by Sperber & Wilson (1986/95). The more unconventional part of the present work lies in pursuing what I believe to be the logical consequences of RT for the relationship between linguistic structure and its interpretation (i.e. for what can no longer simply be called 'the syntax-semantics interface') and, in turn, for the nature of the grammar itself and the kinds of meanings it conveys. This connects to another existing (if young) framework, Dynamic Syntax (Kempson *et al.* 2001, Cann *et al.* forthcoming), whose perspective I adopt (though not its formalism, in the present work) because its aim of modelling syntax in terms of the incremental processing of utterances meshes with my aims of showing the influence of context-dependent pragmatic inference on the communication of meaning and of thereby deducing the content of linguistic semantics[6]. In its close integration of Dynamic Syntax assumptions with RT-based reasoning, this work is fairly distinctive, though it has a close relative in Marten (2002).

For all these precedents, the overall approach that I adopt is both sufficiently different to conventional approaches and sufficiently prey to various potential misconceptions that it is worth outlining it from the very most fundamental assumptions on which it is based (something that in any case would not go amiss more generally in linguistic analyses, if they are to have any scientific credibility). This also provides an opportunity to emphasise the point made above: that the intention is not to abandon the aims of competence grammars and formal semantics, but rather to build up a more coherent way of addressing these very aims than currently dominant models provide. This presentation of the theoretical approach begins below, in section 1.2. However, the idea behind this book is not only to present a somewhat radical theoretical stance but also to show in some detail, through an extended case study, how the analysis of linguistic data benefits from it and even demands it, given the degree to which conventional approaches have forced analysis in inappropriate directions. The choice of subject-matter for this 'case study' analysis is clearly an important matter. Therefore, I first offer some comments on the empirical domain that the analytical part of the book deals with and why this represents a particularly useful and significant source of illustration for the theoretical stance.

1.1.3 Focus and theory at the interfaces

The domain of information structure is an ideal one in which to investigate the relationships between grammar, semantics and pragmatics, being in many ways a quintessential area of theory 'at the interfaces'[7]. The present work is principally concerned with expressions of focus, which is probably the most studied area of information structure (though it is important to recognise that the term is used in the literature to cover a range of individual phenomena, whose connection to each other is in many cases a matter of on-going debate). By any definition, information-

---

[6] See Tugwell (1998) for discussion of other examples of dynamic approaches to grammar, in the relevant sense.

[7] This area is a notorious terminological minefield (Vallduví 1992, von Heusinger 2002). I use 'information structure' as a loose cover term for all phenomena involving the linguistic expression (whether direct or indirect) of meanings relating to the interlocutors' perspectives on the information conveyed. I prefer this to terms such as 'discourse relations', as I believe it emphasises that the primary concern here is with linguistic phenomena and their effects, whatever kind of explanation they eventually receive. Some analysts appear to reserve 'information structure' for specific kinds of syntactic expression of the relevant meanings. This is not my use of the term, though given my choice of empirical data, this is unlikely to cause serious confusion.

structural phenomena involve meanings that are not straightforwardly extensional, but rather involve aspects of the interlocutors' perspectives on what is being said; what is new information versus what is already accessible, what is asserted versus what is presupposed, and so on.

To give a very simple example concerning focus in English, (1.1a) and (1.1b) appear to have the same extensional semantics, but they are clearly appropriate in different circumstances. Specifically, (1.1a) suggests that the matter of John seeing someone or something is 'given' information, or already 'under discussion' (as demonstrated in its felicity as an answer to the question *Who/What did John see?*), while (1.1b) indicates that the speaker takes Mary's being seen by someone to be the information that is already 'in play' (it is a felicitous answer to *Who saw Mary?*).

(1.1)   a.   John saw MARY.
        b.   JOHN saw Mary.

The involvement of interlocutors' perspectives on the information communicated means that information-structural meanings are inherently related to particular contexts: factors like previous discourse, knowledge derived from the physical environment and the speaker's assumptions about the addressee's knowledge state will clearly affect what the speaker can take to be 'known' or 'under discussion'. It is also commonly noted that the use of focus prompts a sense of contrast: typically, (1.1b) not only conveys that Mary was seen by John but also that other people the addressee may have had in mind didn't see Mary. Who these other people are is clearly dependent on the extra-linguistic context. Pragmatic theory should therefore have much to say about the information-structural meanings and how they relate to linguistic expressions. Nevertheless, many aspects of the interpretation of information structural phenomena can be captured in formal semantic terms and some can be shown to affect truth conditions. Hence, important theoretical questions immediately arise regarding the correct way to apportion the explanation of information-structural phenomena across the semantics-pragmatics divide. Given my stated characterisation of this distinction, this issue is necessarily wrapped up with that of how much of information structure is directly expressed in the grammar.

This question is made more complex by the array of strategies that different languages use to convey information-structural distinctions (see Vallduví & Engdahl 1996 for a compact overview). In a language like English, in which the relevant meanings are regularly conveyed by phonological means alone, it may be tempting to view information structure as a peripheral matter, the 'merely pragmatic' meanings being conveyed by 'merely phonological' means—i.e. not core syntax and therefore not indicative of the central properties of the grammar. In other languages, however, the expression of information structure seems to be a much more intrinsically grammatical matter, being clearly associated with syntactic or morphological forms. These languages make it impossible to relegate information-structure and its context-related meanings to extra-grammatical domains and demand active consideration of just how the grammar, its encoded semantics, general pragmatic principles and truth-conditional representations should interact. For these reasons, they provide excellent material from which to address the theoretical questions raised in the present chapter.

The particular information-structural phenomenon that constitutes the principal empirical concern of this book is a syntactic position in Hungarian that is commonly called the 'focus position'[8]. A very simple example of the use of this position is given in (1.2b), which may be compared with (1.2a), a so-called 'neutral' sentence, which does not, ostensibly, feature the use of the 'focus position'[9].

(1.2) a. János látta Marit.
János saw Mari-ACC
'János saw Mari.'
b. János MARIT látta.
János Mari-ACC saw
'It's Mari who János saw.'

At first glance, this appears to be a straightforward piece of grammatical encoding: a distinctive word order is associated with a distinctive interpretation, suggesting that the grammatical configuration behind the former encodes the latter. Specifically, an expression that inhabits the 'focus position' is typically said to be associated with an interpretation resembling that of the clefted expression in an English *it*-cleft construction, as shown in the translation of (1.2b). This interpretation is often called 'exhaustive' or 'exclusive' focus; "focus" because the expression in question is generally the newly asserted material in the sentence, and "exhaustive" or "exclusive" since it appears to be part of the meaning that the focused expression is the only one that makes the sentence true—hence (1.2b) appears to rule out the possibility that János saw Kati, or that János saw Zoltán, and so on. Structurally, the expression in the 'focus position' is immediately left-adjacent to the tensed verb and bears a pitch accent, while all material subsequent to it is unaccented (in contrast, the verb in a sentence like (1.2a) carries a prominent pitch accent and phrases subsequent to it also bear pitch accents; Rosenthall 1992).

In addition, if the sentence contains a so-called 'verbal modifier' (VM) element, such as the directional/aspectual particle *fel* in (1.3), then the position of this is affected by the use of the 'focus position'. As shown in the contrast between (1.3a) and (1.3b), a VM is usually immediately pre-verbal, but appears after the verb in the presence of a syntactically 'focused' expression.

(1.3) a. János felhívta Marit.
János up(VM)-called Mari-ACC
'János called Mari.'

---

[8] For the time being, I employ the traditional name for this position, but always in scare quotes, since my analysis will eventually show its encoded meaning to be something less specific than any kind of focus reading.

[9] At this stage, I use SMALL CAPS to indicate the expression that is taken to be 'in focus'. Later in the book, getting away from the idea that the position in question directly encodes any kind of focus, I drop this convention, except where it helps to clarify significant contrasts in interpretation.

b. János MARIT   hívta fel   / *felhívta.
    János Mari-ACC called up(VM)   up(VM)-called
    'It's Mari who János called.'

This apparently arbitrary structural reflex of the use of the 'focus position' seems to offer strong evidence for the idea that the construction as a whole represents a straightforward interaction of two conventional components of the grammar: an abstract syntactic component that determines the nature of well-formed strings and semantic principles that interpret the structures that it produces. Practically all contemporary analyses of the construction therefore assume that the syntax of Hungarian includes a dedicated pre-verbal position which encodes the semantics of 'exhaustive focus' (or some similar semantic formulation). That is, in the terminology of Chomskyan syntactic frameworks, expressions are said to move to the pre-verbal 'focus position', the effect of which is to supply the semantics of exhaustive focus at LF. There are various ways in the literature to account for the concomitant postposing of VMs; one popular proposal, for example, is that focus movement is accompanied by verb movement, leaving any VM 'stranded' to the right of the verb (as in Bródy 1990)[10].

However, as I argue in later chapters, this kind of approach crucially fails to take account of the processes of reasoning that addressees engage in in context. In Chapter 4, I show that the purely syntactico-semantic approach runs into significant empirical difficulties when a broader range of data is introduced and I proceed to argue that these data are accounted for under an approach that is opened up by the active consideration of pragmatic inference in the course of syntactic analysis. This necessitates radical underspecification in what is taken to be grammatically encoded, but this in itself proves to be advantageous in explaining a wide range of related phenomena. The 'focus position' phenomenon thus provides a clear-cut illustration of my central concerns: of how different modes of analysis deal with the interaction of syntax, semantics and pragmatics and of the theoretical issues that this raises.

A crucial question within this, taken up in some detail below, is the role of truth-conditional semantics in analysis. The Hungarian 'focus position' provides an unusually clear case study also in relation to this, illustrating how assumptions regarding the theoretical role of truth conditions have profoundly affected the nature of grammatical models. Anticipating slightly the discussion of Chapter 4, the crux of the matter is Szabolcsi's (1981) observation that use of the 'focus position', compared to the use of 'neutral' word order, can affect the truth conditions associated with a sentence, as shown in the fact that the two clauses of (1.4) are truth-conditionally incompatible (hence the felicity of conjoining them with *hanem* 'but, rather'), even though the latter would entail the former were the 'focus position' not employed.

---

[10] See Chapter 3, section 3.3 for more detail on this and other existing approaches to the 'focus position' construction.

(1.4) Nem PÉTER aludt a padlón, hanem PÉTER ÉS PÁL / hanem AZ EGÉSZ TÁRSASÁG
 not Péter slept the floor-on but Péter and Pál but the whole company
 'It isn't Péter who slept on the floor; it's Péter and Pál / it's the whole company.'

The fact that use of the 'focus position' can affect truth conditions has been taken as a reason to deal with its interpretation as a matter of grammatically encoded semantics. If it is correct to assume in this way that elements of truth-conditional meaning must be attributed to the grammar, examples like (1.4) effectively preclude any other approach, so this is obviously a crucial issue. Below, in section 1.2.2, I argue that there is no basis to such an assumption in the context of post-Gricean pragmatic theory. This clearly could have important consequences for the analysis of a wide range of linguistic phenomena. Thus, the domain of focus, as manifested in languages like Hungarian, proves once again to provide a particularly useful point of illustration for more widely significant theoretical matters. With this illustration to come in the form of the detailed analysis presented in subsequent chapters, it is time now to return to the broader theoretical issues themselves.

1.2 SEMANTICS AND THE INTERPRETATION OF NATURAL LANGUAGES

I begin this discussion of relevant theoretical issues with some truly basic assumptions, concerning the broadest aims behind the general enterprise of linguistic analysis. This is in order to bring out just how fundamental the problems that I identify with conventional approaches to syntactico-semantic analysis are. At a very basic level, the methods and assumptions that underpin such approaches are in contradiction with what would seem to be the overall aims that all linguists share. Having discussed these fundamental issues, I use the remainder of this chapter to illustrate in some more detail the basic problems with semantic theory and practice in the light of post-Gricean pragmatic insights. This is done as far as possible without reliance on any particular theoretical framework, since the key points do follow from fundamental properties of human language (including the crucial question of its relationship to other human cognitive faculties). The observations made nevertheless point in the direction of a certain view of the semantics-pragmatics relationship, which is essentially that of Relevance Theory. This pragmatic framework is set out at the beginning of Chapter 2 and adopted throughout the rest of the book as a basis for the pragmatic elements of the argumentation. Nevertheless, the most important observations motivating the approach taken in this book exist independently of any particular analytical framework, as argued below.

1.2.1 Fundamentals

Stated as far as possible in a theory-neutral way, I propose the following as a summary of the principal aim of analysing linguistic structure and its interpretation:

(1.5)   *What syntactico-semantic analysis is for:* Linguists study the structure of languages and the meanings they convey in order to gain understanding of the characteristic properties of human languages and of the ways in which they contribute to the communication of meaning.

I take this to be uncontroversial. Certainly, one may have various higher-level goals in mind—computational linguistic aims, for example, or addressing broader philosophical, psychological or evolutionary questions—but to the extent that these rely on linguistic analysis, the immediate aim must surely be to understand what language does and how it does it. After all, if this is not a precondition to one's eventual goal, one may safely dispense with linguistic analysis altogether and concentrate instead on invented logical systems exclusively. I therefore continue to take (1.5) to be a fundamental, generally accepted assumption and so proceed to investigate its implications and its relationship to existing analytical approaches.

The second part of (1.5) is the real point of interest here: the idea that we study linguistic semantics in order to understand how languages convey meaning and, as part of this, aim to isolate the elements of meaning that are directly associated with linguistic objects. This may seem so uncontroversial as to be uninteresting—this at least would explain why it is very rarely discussed in any explicit fashion—but I believe that this assumption demands an approach to analysis that is typically not in evidence in the linguistics literature.

What (1.5) demands is the identification of those parts of any perceived meaning that are directly conveyed by linguistic means. As emphasised above, this entails the separation of aspects of meaning derived directly from linguistic objects from aspects of meaning that come from other sources, such as general principles of cognition that may be involved in the process of human communication. Introducing a first terminological distinction from RT, (1.5) thus requires us to distinguish what is *encoded* in a language from what is *inferred* in the course of interpreting linguistic utterances. Along with other relevance theorists (see in particular Carston 1999), I take this encoding versus inference distinction to constitute the only cognitively interesting way of dividing semantics from pragmatics. Other distinctions (such as truth-conditional versus non-truth-conditional meaning) may have a role to play in analysis, but fundamentally we must distinguish the linguistic (encoded) from the non-linguistic (inferred) and it is an empirical question to what extent any other distinction matches up to this[11].

My contention regarding most contemporary approaches to syntax and semantics—and the main point of this chapter—is that they fail to address this distinction in any adequate way and as a result they inevitably fail to fulfil the aims expressed in (1.5). By failing (to a greater or lesser extent) to account for the degree to which inferential processes, as guided by general principles

---

[11] Given that distinguishing linguistically encoded meaning from non-linguistic meaning is effectively the fundamental aim of studying the interpretation of language (as expressed in (1.5)), it is telling that relevance theorists should even have to make this point. Similarly, Ariel (1999) advocates the drawing of a 'linguistic-extralinguistic distinction' as a basis for semantic analysis, a proposal that should be quite superfluous, if linguistic analysis as such has any motivation, yet apparently is not considered so.

of cognition, adapt and enrich encoded meanings, such frameworks maintain too close a match between perceived communicated meanings and what is encoded in the grammar. The result is significant overstatement of the degree of semantic detail that grammars must encode and a corresponding over-estimation of the amount and complexity of structural machinery required to account for semantic effects. This, inevitably, is to the detriment of such analyses, sometimes demonstrably, in terms of their empirical accuracy (as I show in particular with regard to conventional analyses of the Hungarian 'focus position' in the later chapters of this book), and always in terms of theoretical economy. Taking Occam's Razor to constitute another very fundamental assumption, it is clear that an analysis that shifts the burden of explanation from posited details of grammatical machinery to independently motivated general principles of cognition is to be preferred, other things being equal. Of course, other things must indeed be equal; a more heavily inferential account must be at least as empirically accurate and plausible as an 'encoding' account in order for this argument from economy to stand. One important purpose of the detailed study of Hungarian syntactic phenomena later in this book is to demonstrate how an approach that systematically works general inferential processes into grammatical analysis can be not only more parsimonious, but also more empirically accurate (over a wide range of phenomena) than approaches that more directly match perceived elements of meanings to linguistic structure.

Mention of cognitive principles and of cognitively interesting distinctions brings up another fundamental assumption, (1.6) (which is again formulated to be as theory-neutral as possible). This is perhaps slightly more controversial than (1.5), though it is, in principle, accepted in much formal work in linguistics.

(1.6)   *The cognitive context of linguistic analysis:* Human language is a product of the human mind; hence, linguistic competence must be viewed in terms of interacting mental capacities. Our formal models of different aspects of linguistic competence are intended to be reflections of facts about the organisation of relevant parts of the human mind.

(1.6) is intended to encapsulate (perhaps among other positions) the 'mentalist' viewpoint associated with Chomsky (1965) and those formal frameworks that follow Chomsky at least at this level of theorising. As with (1.5), I believe that something like this assumption is essential to any coherent approach to the analysis of human languages. Even if one's motivations are not limited to the rather abstract one of illuminating the nature of the human mind, the idea that understanding *human* language is important presupposes that consideration of the nature of language as a product of cognitive processes is also important. Again, we may happily stick to the analysis of artificial languages where this is not the case. Hence, to the (considerable) extent that human language is worth studying, it should be studied from a cognitive perspective.

As in the case of (1.5), this assumption carries significant consequences that seem not always to be taken account of in conventional approaches to linguistic analysis. The point that concerns me here is that viewing language in terms of its cognitive origins implies that *all* aspects of cognition that may be relevant to the workings of language should be considered carefully.

This brings us back to the point made above, in section 1.1.1: if some extra-linguistic aspect of cognition (in the sense of not being uniquely devoted to language) influences some part of how linguistic structure relates to the communication of meaning, then this aspect of cognition should be taken account of in order to produce accurate models of strictly linguistic competence. Yet, as suggested above and discussed below in more detail, conventional approaches to syntax and semantics regularly fail to consider sufficiently the impact of extra-linguistic cognitive principles on the interpretation of linguistic forms. If this is correct then the very analytical approaches that ostensibly pursue the strictest mentalist agenda systematically fail to apply it in key areas and thereby compromise the value of the analyses they produce[12].

A third key assumption regarding human languages and analyses of them is summarised in (1.7).

(1.7) *The social context of linguistic analysis:* Natural languages are used in communication between human beings and the only observable linguistic data exist in a (real or implied) communicative situation. Formal models of linguistic competence do not aim to model this social interaction, so should aim to avoid modelling those aspects of the data that stem from it.

As the latter part of (1.7) makes explicit, the point of mentioning the social, communicative context of language use is not to move out of the domain of modelling competence, but once again to ensure that this domain and its empirical basis are properly defined. I do not comment further on this assumption here, since I believe that the aspects of human communicative interaction that impact upon competence theory are most fruitfully viewed in terms of the cognitive strategies (hence other forms of competence) that underlie them. As a result, the previous assumption (1.6) in many ways encompasses the important parts of (1.7). Furthermore, the arguments of the following sections and the exposition of Relevance Theory in Chapter 2 provides further discussion of the significance of the communicative context of language use for theories of linguistic competence.

To summarise the most important points in this section, the two assumptions (1.5) and (1.6) are fundamental to any analysis of human language, yet aspects of conventional approaches to the relationship between syntax and semantics fail to remain compatible with even these very basic aims. More specifically, a tendency to equate perceived, truth-conditionally characterisable meaning in effect rides roughshod over the twin aims of identifying truly linguistic phenomena and of understanding language as a cognitive phenomenon. This tendency is manifested in—and to some extent attributable to—the assumption of a 'principle of compositionality', which

---

[12]In relation to the approach adopted in this book, it is important to note that a mentalist philosophy of science and other aspects of conventional approaches are not a package deal: dominant models in linguistics may give the impression that mentalism entails structuralism and even a commitment to a certain kind of architecture of the language faculty and perhaps a certain view on the innateness of universal principles of linguistic structure. This is not necessarily the case, nor does the rejection of any of these ideas entail a rejection of the study of language at the relatively abstract level of objects and processes of the mind.

is discussed in section 1.2.4. It is also connected to insufficient consideration of inferential pragmatic contributions to truth-conditional semantics, which forms the first point of discussion in the next section.

1.2.2 Inference and semantics

Having argued that pragmatic processes must be taken into account if they significantly affect the mapping from linguistic structure to meaning, it is time to illustrate some ways in which they do. This of course depends upon the question of what it means to affect meaning significantly; or, to put it another way, what constitutes significant kind of meaning. After all, there has never been anything controversial about the idea that the reasoning that language users employ in context has effects on what could broadly be termed the meaning conveyed by an utterance, through processes like 'conversational implicature', as illustrated in (1.8).

(1.8)   Mary: Is Pierre a good cook?
        John: Well, he's French.

This kind of example, well known from the 'Gricean' pragmatics literature, shows how meaning can be conveyed on the basis of information available to the interlocutors in context (including their assumptions about each other's beliefs): here, John does not say anything that could be taken to encode an answer to Mary's question, but she is able to infer that John at least considers it likely that Pierre is a good cook, on the assumption that she knows John to believe in the good reputation of French cooking (of course, it is also quite possible that Mary knows John to have a low opinion of French cooking, so that his contribution in (1.8) would communicate something quite different about Pierre).

From the point of view introduced by Grice (1975), which remains highly influential, the implicature conveyed in (1.8) is typical of pragmatically conveyed meaning in that it constitutes a kind of meaning that exists above and beyond 'what is said', or the 'literal' meaning of the utterance. In this case, the pragmatically supplied meaning is not part of the mapping from linguistic structure to linguistic semantics, so could not be considered a significant kind of meaning in terms of my arguments of the previous section.

What is commonly accepted to be a significant kind of meaning is truth conditions. The starting point for many semantic theories is the fact that language users have intuitions regarding the ways in which the meanings associated with different sentences are logically related to each other, in terms of entailment, contradiction and so on. These relations appear to provide some systematic indication of the 'essential' meaning of a sentence, and they are defined in terms of truth values, making the truth conditions attributed to a sentence the key characterisation of its meaning. Correspondingly, one common way to define the distinction between semantics and pragmatics is to associate the former with truth conditions and the latter with what remains, or, as in Gazdar's famous (1979) formulation, 'pragmatics = meaning − truth conditions'. If 'semantics' is taken to correspond to what is linguistically encoded, then this reasoning leads to the assumption, already mentioned in section 1.1.3, that all contributions to truth-conditional meaning are traceable to the grammar.

One might say that the defining characteristic of post-Gricean (as opposed to 'neo-Gricean') pragmatic approaches is the rejection of this view (see Carston 2002 for an extensive overview of the issues and various responses to them). The crucial point missed in the above reasoning is that logical relations like entailment and contradiction are defined over characterisations of meaning (propositions), whereas sentences are linguistic objects that, in one way or another, convey meaning. To speak of one sentence entailing another is to make an unspoken assumption that the relationship between a sentence and an associated meaning representation is direct. From a post-Gricean point of view, this is to pre-judge the very issue that should be of interest to linguists: *how* linguistic structures come to convey different kinds of meaning[13].

As such, there is a kind of self-fulfilling prophesy in comments such as Nunberg's (2002, 673) assertion that "it's unlikely that anything we [linguists] could tell philosophers about the structure of English would help them to decide whether the bearers of truth-values are sentences or propositions". Having in effect adopted the philosophical assumption that sentences (i.e. outputs of the grammar) should be associated with truth-conditional meaning, conventional analyses of linguistic semantics are bound to support the idea that sentences—as opposed to propositions conveyed by contextualised utterances—carry truth values. Once this assumption is dropped, however, and the different contributions of encoding and inference are considered, it is quite possible for linguistic analysis to provide evidence relating to such philosophical questions.

This kind of evidence, introduced in the following section, takes the form of demonstrations that what can be deduced to be the linguistically encoded meaning of some expression falls short of what would be required to achieve full truth-conditionality. Furthermore, the inferential processes required to plug the gap between encoded and truth-conditional meanings appear to be based in the same kinds of communicatively-oriented reasoning in context that allow for the derivation of uncontroversially pragmatic phenomena like the implicature in (1.8). This kind of evidence therefore supports the arguments of the previous sections to the effect that an accurate characterisation of syntactic and semantic competence depends upon active consideration of pragmatic processes.

1.2.3 Pragmatic contributions to propositional semantics

Carston (2002) offers a recent overview of easily identifiable forms of systematic underdetermination of truth-conditional content in natural language, all of which necessitate the involvement of inferential reasoning in context to establish the proposition that is conveyed. These include the

---

[13]Throughout this book, I follow the convention of representing propositions using sentences in single quotes. That is, 'John loves Mary' should not be taken to be a natural language sentence but rather the proposition that I assume to be indicated unambiguously enough, for practical purposes, by the sentence *John loves Mary*—although of course it is a central aim of mine to argue that this cannot be assumed as a simple mapping, irrespective of context, especially with more complex sentences.

underspecification and overspecification of conceptual content by linguistic material, illustrated in (1.9a) and (1.9b), respectively; the unspecified scope of logical elements such as negation, as in (1.9c); and the lack of encoding in a full sentential utterance of necessary constituents of the semantic interpretation, as in (1.9d).

(1.9) a. The north island is some distance from the south island.
       b. Her face is oblong.
       c. She didn't butter the toast in the bathroom with a knife.
       d. He is too young.

These forms of underdetermination stand in addition to the widespread use of indexical elements and the existence of ambiguous forms in natural language, both of which have always been recognised to necessitate reference to the context of utterance—indeed, as RT emphasises, saturating reference and resolving ambiguity in context can only be achieved through inferential processes aimed at recovering the speaker's communicative intentions. In other words, these important aspects of interpretation fall naturally under precisely the kind of general reasoning strategies that inferential pragmatic theories use to deal with other, indisputably pragmatic phenomena. An example of the latter is the 'conversational implicature' that makes Mary's statement interpretable as a coherent answer to John's question in (1.10).

(1.10) John: Would you like some salad?
        Mary: I don't eat rabbit food.

A chain of reasoning involving access to assumptions about Mary's likely intentions and to culturally salient attitudes is required to understand from this exchange that Mary is saying (i) that she considers the salad that she is being offered to be more suited to consumption by rabbits than by humans and (ii) that therefore she doesn't want any of the salad (also, presumably, that Mary wishes to be seen to show a disdainful attitude to such foods, which may lead inferentially to the recovery of further implications in certain contexts). This much seems quite uncontroversial, and is uncontroversially a matter of pragmatics. What is less commonly recognised (outside of RT) is that assigning the correct reference to John's use of the NP *some salad* also requires access to and inference over assumptions about the speaker's intentions. It may well be the case that Mary would not refuse (or ridicule) some kind of salad other than the one she has been offered by John, but this has no bearing on her choice of response. So even though there is nothing in John's question encoding the specific meaning 'some of this salad that I am offering you at the moment', this seems quite clearly to be what she understands to have been communicated, and furthermore it seems clear that this is achieved on the basis of contextual information, such as what Mary can perceive about the physical environment and can assume about John's intentions. There seems no reason to assign a different cognitive or theoretical status to these two uses of context-dependent reasoning (implicature and reference assignment) yet this would seem to be necessary if conventional assumptions were to be maintained, such that propositional semantics precedes inferential pragmatics[14].

In fact, examples like (1.10) show not only that reference assignment resembles other kinds of context-dependent contribution to meaning, but that the two *cannot* be separated from each other. Consider the denotation assigned to the expression *rabbit food*. On the one hand, the rhetorical impact of Mary's utterance comes partly from the evocation of what rabbits actually eat, but on another level, what she denotes using the term *rabbit food* must be taken to include the salad that John is offering her (even though it is plainly food intended for humans, in reality)—otherwise, the inference that Mary does not want any of the salad would not go through. That is, it must be assumed that Mary is communicating that the salad in question is a member of the set of entities that are rabbit food, in order for her not eating rabbit food to license the inference that she won't eat the salad. The process of denotation assignment is therefore determined here by the nature of an implicature that is to be drawn. Meanwhile, in other, more straightforward cases, recognising what is referred to may be a precondition to drawing implicatures. It follows that neither of these context-dependent contributions to meaning can be given precedence; both are simply part of the general process of establishing the relevance of a particular utterance in a particular situation.

A striking illustration of how inferred meaning contributes to truth-conditional meaning is the now quite well known case of the enrichment of conjunction (Carston 2002, Chapter 3). This is particularly significant in that it concerns what is often thought of as a natural language equivalent of a logical connective. If inference informs truth-conditional interpretation even in relation to this, it may be expected to permeate most parts of the grammar-meaning relationship.

As well as expressing logical conjunction, *and* (like the co-ordinating conjunctions in many languages) can be used to express a temporal progression of events, as in (1.11a), which is generally understood as conveying that the first conjunct in the sentence is also chronologically the first eventuality of the two mentioned. This is seen also in (1.11b), which in most contexts would also communicate a causal relationship between the conjuncts. Other forms of temporal relationship are possible, however, such as simultaneity (1.11c) and temporal containment (1.11d).

(1.11) a. She gave him her key and he opened the door.
        b. She became an alcoholic and her husband left her.
        c. Mary was in the kitchen and she was listening to the radio.
        d. He slept deeply all night and dreamt that he was flying.

Carston rejects the possibility that *and* is multiply lexically ambiguous, given the variety of meanings involved in these examples (which do not exhaust the shades of temporal and causal

---

[14]See Larson & Segal (1995) for a statement of the conventional position that mechanisms for reference and disambiguation must exist separately to the inferential pragmatic principles that deal with matters like implicature. This is notably just a statement: there is no attempt to justify this distinction, despite the necessary involvement of reasoning over speaker's intentions in context in all these areas.

meaning; Carston 1988, 159) and the intuition that the reflection of temporal ordering and patterns of causation in the linguistic presentation of eventualities is likely to relate rather to properties of human cognition that to the encoded meaning of a single connective.

The difference between *and* in (1.11a,b) and *and* in (1.11c) is therefore not encoded, so must be inferred on the basis of contextual factors[15]. That the 'added' meanings in each case affect truth-conditional interpretation, rather than being cases of Gricean conversational implicature, can be demonstrated by embedding such an utterance under a logical operator like negation, as in (1.12).

(1.12)   It is not the case that she became an alcoholic and her husband left her, but rather that her husband left her and she became an alcoholic.

The fact that (1.12) is a coherent sentence demonstrates that the temporal/causal element of the conjunction contributes to the truth-conditions of each clause: a logical contradiction would arise if this were not the case (i.e. $\neg P \ \& \ P$). The conclusion must be that inferential processes, based in identifying the speaker's purpose in conjoining two particular clauses in a certain order, play an important part in determining the truth-conditional meaning.

This argument has come in for some criticism recently. King & Stanley (2005) argue that examples like (1.12) can be dealt with under more traditional assumptions. Their account rests on the idea that the two tensed verbs in each clause carry their own temporal indices. The two conjoined clauses may therefore contrast in their semantic content, given that semantic content is calculated relative to a variable assignment. However, as King & Stanley recognise, restricting the temporal variables within the each clause such that they are not only non-identical but encapsulate a temporal progression requires "a pragmatic maxim that affects semantic content". This seems to me already to contradict King & Stanley's aim of rescuing the idea of fully compositional semantic content (relative to reference assignment). In any case, as the examples in (1.11) show, there would in fact be a need for a whole series of 'maxims' of this kind, and presumably something like Relevance Theory would be required to select the appropriate one, in the course of interpretation. All King & Stanley really succeed in showing, therefore, is that the liberal use of indices and equally liberal positing of *ad hoc* pragmatic maxims can be used to provide a non-explanatory formalisation of any given case of context dependence[16]. This hardly detracts from the force of arguments like Carston's, to the effect that this context-dependence is rife in natural languages and that ultimately some general theory of intention recognition in context is required to deal with it.

---

[15] Such factors include the linguistic context, but are not limited to it: for example, a sentence like *Dorothy talked to her daughter and bought a dress in Marks and Spencer* could convey at least three states of affairs, depending entirely on the perceived extra-linguistic context: (i) two independent, unordered events (the interlocutors are interested in things Dorothy did that evening), (ii) a temporal/causal relationship (the interlocutors are interested in how Dorothy made a decision), or (iii) simultaneous events (in a discussion of the ways people behave with their mobile phones, for example).

[16] See section 1.3.2 below for some further comments on this kind of approach.

The examples given above are merely initial illustrations of the fact that contextualised inference can influence propositional meaning; though there is little in the RT literature to date that goes further than essentially lexical semantic issues like these, they do not necessarily indicate the limits of this influence. My aim in this book is to probe further into the implications of pragmatic contributions to interpretation and to show that these implications extend not only to semantic theory but also deep into grammatical analysis—as they must, given the conventional assumption that the output of the grammar maps onto representations of meaning. However, even the initial indications contained in this section are sufficient to call into question certain fundamental assumptions that underlie the majority of formal work on the semantics of human languages, which I turn to in the following section.

1.2.4 Pragmatics and the assumption of compositionality

While individual examples such as those in the previous section might receive a variety of analyses in different frameworks, the need for some degree of pragmatic influence on the semantic interpretations of utterances is recognised across a broad spectrum of approaches to pragmatics. Ariel (2002) goes so far as to state that

> All researchers, no matter how different their views on literal meaning or on the semantics/pragmatics division of labor, have come to recognize that coded meanings constitute only a very small core of the meaning actually conveyed by the speaker. It is quite clear that in addition to decoding the speaker's linguistic expressions, we perform a substantial amount of inferencing in order to reach the intended communicated message. [...] The question that has preoccupied researchers in semantics/pragmatics and literality, is how much inferencing should be allowed for just the semantic (or literal, or minimal) meaning to be generated. (Ariel 2002, 1003–1004)

While Ariel may be correct with regard to those researchers within linguistics who choose to address the question of the semantics-pragmatics distinction directly, it is not clear that this supposedly widespread acceptance of pragmatic influence on semantic meaning has had any significant effect on common practice in semantics. The overriding assumption in formal semantic work remains that some 'basic' kind of propositional meaning is to be derived more or less directly (*modulo* processes of reference assignment) from the output of the grammar. In other words, there remains a strong commitment to—or at least assumption of—the compositionality of communicated propositional meaning.

I take Pelletier's formulation in (1.13) to constitute an uncontroversial basic definition of compositionality.

(1.13)   *The Principle of Semantic Compositionality* is the principle that the meaning of an expression is a function of, and only of, the meanings of its parts together with the method by which those parts are combined. (Pelletier 1994, 11)

Pelletier points out that numerous variants of this very general principle have in fact been proposed in the literature, some being deliberate refinements, others perhaps differing less intentionally. I present the most general kind of formulation partly because I believe that even at this level the application of compositionality to natural languages is inappropriate, but partly also to point up how one particular notion of compositionality has been adopted almost universally in the semantics literature, despite being far from the only logically possible one and, I aim to show, demonstrably untrue, where natural languages are concerned.

It is also of course not the case that every semanticist, never mind every syntactician, would advocate the strong version of compositionality expressed in (1.13). However, it is clear from common practice in both syntax and semantics that some such presumption exercises considerable influence over both domains of enquiry. Semanticists will regularly appeal to compositionality as a reason to favour one possible analysis over another, while the increasing tendency in popular syntactic frameworks to incorporate semantic factors into the analysis of syntactic structure is testament to some underlying belief in compositionality, even if this often remains implicit. Moreover, one of the main points of the present section is to call into question any 'halfway house' or selective use of compositionality: many of the key methodological decisions that underpin most formal work in syntax and semantics depend upon a rather strong version of compositionality (see the quotation from Stanley & Szabó 2000 and surrounding discussion, below).

The presumption of compositionality in the study of natural languages is motivated primarily by the argument from the productivity and systematicity of language (Fodor & Pylyshyn 1988). We are able not only to produce but also to provide interpretations for an infinite number of utterances, including utterances of sentences that are entirely novel to us. This ability is clearly connected to the regularity with which individual words and ways of arranging those words contribute certain kinds of meaning. As Fodor (2001) puts it:

> There are, for better or worse, indefinitely many things that English allows you to say about pigeons and the weather in Manhattan. [...] English being compositional is what explains why so many of the sentences that you can use to say things about pigeons and the weather in Manhattan share some or all of their vocabulary [...] Barring idioms and such, this is the general case [...] Were this not so, we couldn't explain the familiar pattern according to which natural languages exhibit open ended clusters of semantically and syntactically related forms. [...] So that, in brief, is why compositionality is non-negotiable. (Fodor 2001, 6–7)

This argument is sound, as far as it goes. There are nevertheless several observations to be made, which together call into question the strong kind of 'principle of compositionality' that forms the basis of most formal semantic work.

First, the degree to which compositionality is 'non-negotiable' is limited. Logically, the strongest conclusion that can be drawn from productivity and systematicity is this: *to the extent that* a language conveys meanings productively and systematically, those meanings are compositional. Now, the extent of productivity and systematicity in the communication of meaning is an empirical matter, not the stuff of *a priori* principles. Nor is it necessarily an easily resolved empirical matter. The appearance of systematic structure-meaning correspondences can be deceptive: regularity in the uses a grammatical construction is put to should not be confused with systematicity in the encoding of meaning. The correspondences investigated in later chapters between certain word orders in Hungarian and meanings like 'exhaustive focus' constitute a case in point: I show that these correspondences are accounted for both with greater accuracy and more parsimoniously when it is recognised that the meanings in question arise from a combination of underspecified procedural semantics and inferences that are drawn in context according to standard pragmatic principles. Systematicity is an important feature of how languages convey meaning, as Fodor argues, but the *appearance* of systematicity is no guarantee that the analyst can safely match observed meanings directly with the grammatical structures that they are associated with.

Second, the *kind* of meaning that is productively and systematically conveyed by human languages is also an empirical issue. As Ariel (2002) notes (and practically any volume of formal semantics papers testifies), it is typically assumed that truth-conditional meaning is to be derived compositionally from the grammar. Even under strongly compositional assumptions, this does not have to be the case, as Pelletier observes:

> The Principle [of Compositionality] makes no assumptions about what meaning is, nor does it say how one can tell whether two expressions have the same or different meanings. It makes no assumptions about what the parts of a complex expression are, nor does it put any restrictions on what is the function on the parts and the mode of combination. (Pelletier 1994, 11)

The reasoning behind the conventional pairing of compositional and truth-conditional analysis, which is rarely if ever spelled out (notwithstanding general statements such as Montague's 1970 conjecture that human languages should be amenable to treatment as logical languages), appears to be a mixture of the theoretical and the methodological. The idea that understanding a sentence is knowing the conditions under which it is true constitutes one of the few concrete and practically workable definitions of meaning. Combining this with the perception that the argument from productivity and systematicity enforces a strongly compositional view of meaning, one ends up with the idea that languages must compositionally encode truth-conditional meaning. Moreover, logical representations of truth-conditional meaning, combined with a model-theoretic perspective, provide the means for capturing compositional processes; technical apparatus like the lambda calculus allows propositional meanings to be split into appropriately typed components that can be directly matched with the linguistic elements combined by the grammar.

The resulting picture is appealingly neat and opens up realms of theory that appear to hold great potential, in the shape of manipulations of logic of varying degrees of complexity. It is not obviously supported by even the most superficial facts of linguistic meaning, however. Consider again that most fundamental area of logic, propositional connectives. Examples like those in (1.11) and (1.12) show a linguistic connective, *and*, that radically underspecifies communicated propositional meaning by dint of the fact that it encodes no more than the logical connective &; *but*, on the other hand, encodes meaning that goes *beyond* the truth conditions of the sentence[17]. The Gricean strategy of assigning the non-truth-conditional content of *but* to 'conventional implicature' is no more than a way of avoiding the issue from a perspective that is committed to the composition of truth-conditions: this is truly systematic, encoded meaning, so bears no resemblance to conversational implicature. Rather than finding ways to assign this sort of phenomenon to some extra-semantic domain, we should simply make the empirical observation that not all encoded meaning—hence not all of linguistic semantics—is identifiable with truth-conditions, and take our theory-building from there[18].

In fact, as Fodor (2001) recognises, mismatches between full propositional meanings and the material available to encode meaning are endemic in human languages, which are highly elliptical, ambiguous and vague in relation to communicated truth-conditions, especially when compared to any logical language. To exemplify further, Carston (2002, 72) follows Jackendoff (1997, 51ff.) in pointing out how the truth of *Mary finished the book* and that of *Mary finished the beer* depend on quite different actions having taken place—hence different states of affairs holding in the world, which would have to be represented in a comprehensive specification of the truth-conditional meaning conveyed—yet this difference cannot be traced to the form of the verb or the structure of the sentence. In Chapter 2, I discuss an approach to language under which it is no accident that the forms of natural languages consistently fail to resemble those of invented systems for representing truth-conditional semantics: one in which natural languages are simply not assumed to be semantically compositional systems, but serve rather to provide a different kind of indication to reasoning human addressees of how to access an intended interpretation.

Fodor (2001) reaches the conclusion that the 'non-negotiable compositionality' that human languages appear to display is properly attributable to the meanings that languages convey (for Fodor, representations of the language of thought). Many linguists appear to find this hard to accept. Even among those who conform to the quotation from Ariel above, in recognising that not all conveyed propositional meaning is given in the grammar, it is common to assume

---

[17]Blakemore (1987), working within RT assumptions, argues that this kind of meaning should be treated as procedural meaning (see Chapter 2, section 2.4), indicating to the addressee how the propositions expressed should be interpreted in relation to each other and contextually relevant further assumptions.

[18]Neale (1999) offers an alternative approach to this kind of meaning, arguing that more than one proposition is expressed (roughly corresponding to 'what is said' plus what is conventionally implicated in a Gricean account), with different 'weightings' attaching to each proposition in different contexts. Even if some idea of encoded truth-conditional meaning is preserved in this way, the example of *but* still runs contrary to the (sometimes implicit) conventional definition of the semantics of an expression being the contribution it makes to the compositional derivation of 'the proposition expressed' by a sentence. Furthermore, one of the propositions expressed under Neale's approach (the one that corresponds to the Gricean conventional implicature) will be a statement about the relationship between the other propositions, in effect making the contribution of *but* a procedural meaning under another name.

that the structures of the syntactic component must at least closely resemble those of semantic representations—closely enough to justify the continued deduction of underlying syntactic structure from semantic considerations, and/or the deduction of encoded semantics of an expression from indications of the syntactic structure and perceived meaning of a sentence in which it appears. Indeed, this much is more or less implicit in the common conception of a syntax-semantics interface.

There is no reason to make this assumption, however. It is true that one might expect to find a close correspondence between the structure of human languages and that of the thoughts that they are taken to convey on the grounds that languages evolved at least in part in order to perform this communicative function. However, the same reasoning should also lead to the expectation that languages have developed to work in conjunction with the extra-linguistic faculties of reasoning which are inevitably involved in human communication. In any case, a 'close correspondence' between linguistic structure and the structure of thoughts could take many forms, depending on precisely how one conceives of the notion of the structure of a language (or the meanings it encodes) and even then the degree of closeness is an interesting empirical issue, not one to be pre-determined by one's analytical framework.

More importantly, one simply *cannot* sustain the assumption of a certain degree of syntax to 'language of thought' correspondence, once it is accepted that natural languages are not fully compositional. After all, it follows from this acceptance that languages contain means of conveying propositional meanings other than compositional encoding. If this is the case, there is in principle nothing to rule out an approach whereby a great deal of the communication of meaning works by these other means.

In this respect, I am in agreement with Stanley & Szabó (2000) and King & Stanley (2005), who recognise that the very possibility of pragmatic contributions to propositional meanings undermines the basis of conventional syntactico-semantic analysis. Their response is to attempt to deny this possibility, as they wish to maintain the conventional semantic view; nevertheless, their reasoning highlights the significance of the debate, showing that conventional semantic approaches cannot simply accommodate bits of syntactically unmotivated pragmatic enrichment where there seems to be strong evidence for it, but otherwise continue in a largely compositional vein. Stanley & Szabó's comments concern the analysis of quantificational phenomena, but clearly have wider relevance:

> Pragmatic approaches have an obvious advantage and an obvious disadvantage. The obvious advantage is that one can propose a syntax and semantics for sentences containing quantifiers that is extremely simple and does not involve covert expressions or covert semantic values. [...] The obvious disadvantage is that one has to abandon ordinary intuitions concerning the truth or falsity of most sentences containing quantifiers. This is worrisome because accounting for our ordinary judgements about the truth-conditions of various sentences is the central aim of semantics. Since these judgements are the data of semantic theorizing, we should be careful with pro-

posals that suggest a radical revision of these judgements. (Stanley & Szabó 2000, 240)

If one takes the central aim of semantics to be "accounting for our ordinary judgements about the truth-conditions of various sentences", then one must concur with Stanley & Szabó: the possibility of pragmatic contributions to truth-conditional meanings would throw a significant spanner into the works, where this putative research aim is concerned. However, as I set out in section 1.2.1, I take the central aim of linguistic semantics to be something else: the characterisation of how linguistic expressions contribute to meaning. To assume that sentences encode truth-conditions is to pre-judge this matter. Thus, evidence of pragmatic contributions to truth-conditional meaning is not 'worrisome' but merely something to be accounted for.

King & Stanley (2005) develop Stanley & Szabó's argument, claiming that pragmatic accounts, whereby "semantically interpreting the syntactic structure of a sentence relative to a context far underdetermines what is intuitively said by that utterance", leave the analyst reliant on 'unconstrained pragmatic processes', leading to "an unconstrained over-generation of predictions about what a sentence can be used to intuitively say, relative to a context". Once again, I believe that these authors are correct to observe that conventional approaches to semantics, even in their underlying assumptions, are quite incompatible with the observation that 'free' pragmatic processes (i.e. beyond the saturation of indexicals) can help to determine truth-conditional meaning—and their detailed discussion of the theoretical issues helps to make this clear. But, once again, I disagree with their argument that the correct response to this is to rule out such pragmatic processes. As I point out below, King & Stanley's idea of interpreting a sentence 'relative to a context' presupposes a stable, pre-determined kind of context that is shown by Relevance Theory to be an unsustainable notion. Furthermore, their preferred approach, which involves positing a silent indexical for every piece of context-dependent meaning, fails to obviate the need for exactly the kind of pragmatic processes that King & Stanley fear as being too unconstrained (see section 1.3).

Pragmatic influences on truth-conditional meaning should therefore be viewed as a very significant challenge to compositional analysis. However, the widespread assumption of the desirability of compositionality can make it difficult even to identify cases of such influence. Many illustrations of the non-determination of propositional meaning by natural languages can be obscured in the context of modern linguistic theory, which so commonly involves the use of silent structural entities precisely in order to maintain a compositional analysis. For example, Carston (2002, 71), citing Pelletier (1994), presents examples like those in (1.14) as evidence against truth-conditional compositionality.

(1.14)   a.   Every linguist knows two languages.
            b.   The philosophers lifted the piano.

The idea is that the ambiguity of these sentences (quantifier scope ambiguity in (1.14a); collective versus distributive readings in (1.14b)) constitutes counterevidence to the notion that truth-conditional meanings are always compositionally derived in natural languages: with no lexical or syntactic difference between the two readings of each sentence, there is no means by which to derive two different sets of truth conditions compositionally. Instead, what is encoded must be underspecified with regard to the propositional meaning conveyed, with inferential processes helping to determine the latter. However, many syntactic analyses do of course posit a syntactic difference between the two readings of (1.14a), through well-known processes such as covert Quantifier Raising and a notion of syntactic scope which translates into logical scope at the 'interface' level of LF. Similarly, the likes of Beghelli & Stowell (1997) and Szabolcsi (1997b) propose a covert syntactic basis for collective versus distributive readings. As Pelletier (1994) notes, it seems fairly clear that these forms of analysis are motivated by, rather than evidence for, a compositional approach to linguistic semantics. Pre-theoretically, what we have in each case is one sentence structure and two propositional meanings, but a commitment to compositionality is so widespread and unquestioned that there are few phenomena that have not received some form of analysis that allows this principle to be maintained, often at the cost of positing massive amounts of invisible/inaudible linguistic material[19].

In practice (even if not necessarily in professed theoretical stances), this raises compositionality to the status of an axiom in most formal linguistic work, meaning that there is effectively no empirical counterevidence that could ever be brought to the hypothesis that natural language is fully semantically compositional. Pelletier (1994), writing from a philosophical perspective, is brought to the exasperated observation that it is "really silly" to force oneself into positing multiple syntactic analyses for a single surface form merely in order to capture a semantic ambiguity. From the perspective of linguistics as a cognitive science, there is a more concrete reason to question the quasi-axiomatic presumption of compositionality. This is the simple observation that the meanings conveyed by natural languages are influenced by aspects of human communicative interaction that are undeniably extra-grammatical. In the absence of any strong evidence to the contrary, it is reasonable to assume that truth-conditional meaning is like any other meaning in this respect.

1.3 CONSEQUENCES OF COMPOSITIONALITY: ILLUSTRATIONS FROM DOMAIN RESTRICTION

Alongside the empirical evidence of section 1.2.3, I have argued that the assumption of compositionality—at least as conventionally construed, as holding over strings of words—is conceptually inappropriate to the study of natural languages because it encourages the complication of the grammar with technical apparatus that is posited only in order to ensure the encoding of se-

---

[19]It is worth noting that popular notions of universality at the syntax-semantics interface mean that such expansions of abstract linguistic machinery may come to complicate the proposed grammars even of languages that show little or no evidence of the phenomena that supposedly justify them—another reason to be particularly careful in attributing some meaning to grammatical origins.

mantic details which may be better dealt with through a combination of underspecified encoding and rich extra-grammatical inference. While the analytical chapters later in the book are intended to provide the main illustration of this argument, it is worth briefly considering some examples of this over-encoding, which I take from the literature on what can broadly be described as domain restriction for quantificational phenomena. This not only provides an initial illustration of how, according to my arguments, conventional compositional analysis leads to over-complication in the grammar, but also provides an opportunity to address a proposed semantic alternative to the idea that inference affects truth-conditional interpretation.

1.3.1 A comparability restriction in exclusive readings

First, an illustration of fairly conventional semantic practice from the literature on the same broad empirical domain that this book treats, focus. Following the likes of Jackendoff (1972) and Rooth (1985), Krifka (1991) discusses the nature of *only* as an 'association with focus' operator, in the course of which he comes to represent the interpretation of the sentences (1.15a) and (1.16a) as in (1.15b) and (1.16b)[20].

(1.15) a. John only introduced Bill to SUE.

b. $introduce'(j, s, b)$ & $\forall x \, [x \approx s$ & $introduce'(j, x, b) \rightarrow x = s]$

(1.16) a. John only INTRODUCED BILL TO SUE.

b. $introduce'(j, s, b)$ & $\forall P \, [P \approx \lambda x.introduce'(x, s, b)$ & $P(j) \rightarrow P = introduce'(x, s, b)]$

The symbol $\approx$ is used to represent 'comparability' and is introduced as part of Krifka's definition of the semantics of *only*. Hence, the interpretation of (1.15a) is roughly 'John introduced Bill to nothing comparable to Sue, other than Sue herself', while the interpretation of (1.16a) is roughly 'John introduced Bill to Sue and did nothing else comparable to introducing Bill to Sue'. Krifka explains that this comparability condition is a necessary part of the semantics of *only* (or possibly of the 'background' material with which it combines) in order

> [...] to capture contextual and ontological restrictions. For example, the first reading might be true even if John introduced more persons to Sue, but these persons are not contextually salient [...]. [(1.16a)] depends even more on this restriction; without it, it would express that introducing Bill to Sue is the only property John has, which of course cannot be true, as he has many additional properties, like being a man, or being identical to himself (Krifka 1991, 129).

---

[20] Once again, the SMALL CAPS here are meant to represent only the perceived extent of the focused part of the utterance in each case, making no claims about the way in which this is conveyed phonologically.

In other words, Krifka's ≈ condition fulfils the same kind of 'domain restricting' function as the 'C variable' that is used in many semantic analyses as a way of relativising certain parts of a representation to contextual factors (as combined with the ~ operator of Rooth 1992). The problem with the habitual use of such elements in representations of lexically or grammatically encoded semantics is that relativisation to context is a generalised phenomenon in communication, and one that falls out of any adequate theory of inferential pragmatics.

As discussed above in section 1.2.3, context-dependent elements are found throughout natural languages, interpretive operations such as reference assignment or establishing the truth-conditional contribution of conjunction being just as dependent on context (including such factors as the speaker's apparent intentions) as conversational implicature is. Must each and every one of these pieces of context-dependent meaning be assumed to follow from an individual encoded trigger? Surely not: it looks much more like there is a generalised process of actively seeking the contextualised meaning of an utterance, which will deal with each of the individual context-dependent expressions as well as generating conversational implicatures, which by definition have no specific encoded trigger (that is, there is no part of the utterance whose meaning is an instruction to generate a conversational implicature).

This is just what a theory of inferential pragmatics predicts. Theories of pragmatics, as theories of language use, are concerned with the actual process of interpretation. This process must begin with a desire on the part of the addressee to establish the meaning of the utterance. This cannot mean a desire merely to decode the information encoded in the linguistic forms used. Even according to the most conventional and formal of models, this information is recognised to be of little use on its own, thanks to the undeniable context-dependence of reference assignment: the very basic propositional content of an utterance cannot be established out of context. It is therefore necessarily the case, at a bare minimum, that an addressee's aim in interpreting an utterance is to recover some meaning that is relativised to the context. The process of interpretation is therefore geared up from the outset to recognising the contextual significance of employing some linguistic expression. It follows that putative elements of lexical meaning whose only function is to signal a need for contextualisation could serve no purpose—and this is the nature of contextual restrictions like Krifka's ≈.

Only need not carry any lexical restriction to the effect that it excludes just 'comparable' alternatives, because 'comparable' in this sense simply means 'contextually relevant' and contextual relevance is an overarching concern in interpretation, not something that hangs on individual lexical items. One thing that every analysis of *only* can agree upon is that *only* excludes alternatives to the item that it operates over. This minimal semantics is all that is required. The fact that *only* in practice only excludes contextually relevant alternatives is just a particular instance of the general process of establishing a contextually relevant meaning[21]. That is to say, the context-*in*dependent meaning of *only*, the meaning that Krifka introduces ≈ expressly to avoid,

---

[21] Roberts (1996) puts forward a similar point of view as part of an approach that derives the relevant effects from the addressee's inferring the current 'question under discussion'; see Chapter 4, section 4.2.2.

will simply never arise in a real communicative situation. Worries such as the observation that *only* may express a necessary falsehood, on its unrestricted interpretation, are misplaced, because the unrestricted interpretation will never be entertained as the contribution of *only* to a properly contextualised propositional interpretation. (1.16a) does not exclude John being a man or being identical to himself for the same reasons that *John* in the same utterance cannot mean just anyone who bears the name John, but must refer to some particular person who is identifiable to the addressee as being the relevant John in the context.

In other words, the cognitive and communicative conditions in which natural language expressions are interpreted suggest that encoded meaning *per se* does not carry truth values. It is a way of getting at representations that do, but these representations are always influenced by context. This is not merely a speculation from one view of pragmatics; it is a necessary conclusion, since, as the literature on RT points out (see in particular Carston 2002, Chapter 1), the encoded material of an utterance alone is rarely if ever propositional. This leads within RT to the assumption of *explicature* as the most basic representation of communicated meaning—a representation that is already an inferentially-derived enrichment of encoded meaning (though below I argue that the bare encoded meaning of whole sentential utterances—the 'logical forms' of RT—have no place in processing or grammar, owing to the need to consider the influence of incremental processing). This is of course anathema to any assumption of truth-conditional semantic compositionality, but when it comes to a clash between an antecedently assumed principle and reasoning from observable and significant factors concerning the conditions in which the process of interpretation takes place, it seems clear which has to give. All the more so when the principle in question forces the *ad hoc* adoption of entities whose effects are predicted by the alternative approach.

It is worth noting that the pragmatic reasoning required to restrict the application of an item like *only* may be minimal. In (1.17), the relevant 'comparable' alternative to *introduced Bill to Sue* is made clear by preceding dialogue, rendering a semantic restricting element like Krifka's ≈ quite superfluous, as long as one credits language users with any pragmatic abilities at all. In (1.18), the addressee (Tom) apparently has a little more active inferencing to do to reach the intended meaning, but in fact the set of events that he can take to be excluded are implicit in his own previous contribution, which discusses the causes of everyone arguing. Therefore, even in this case the 'comparable' alternatives to the *only*-phrase are effectively given in the context prior to the utterance that contains it [22].

---

[22] One way to respond to this point would be to view Krifka's comparability restriction as in effect an anaphoric element. This would be similar to Rooth's (1992) treatment of focus. It should be clear from the above discussion why this is no better, from a pragmatic point of view: the identification of relevant contextual information is a generalised pragmatic necessity that permeates the process of interpretation, not something to be attached to individual items like *only*, anaphorically or otherwise. This is not to deny that an important part of what *only* does is causing the addressee to manipulate elements of the context, to define sets of alternatives, and so on. This clearly happens, but *only* need not encode explicit triggers to make it happen—encoding unrestricted exclusive semantics is enough to make the addressee interested in what is relevantly excluded.

(1.17) Tom: What an embarrassing evening. Was it John who encouraged Julian to chat up Sandra?
Barbara: I don't think so. John only introduced Bill to Sue.

(1.18) Tom: Almost everyone ended up arguing tonight. Is this anything to do with John?
Barbara: I don't think so. John only introduced Bill to Sue.

[Tom infers: John didn't encourage Julian to chat up Sandra; John didn't get Ken to talk politics with Maggie; etc.]

That the context, not lexical semantics, is responsible for restricting of the exclusive effects of *only* is supported by the fact that 'wise guy' interpretations are possible, involving what, in the context, are not clearly 'comparable' alternatives, as in (1.19)[23]. The sardonic humour of Barbara's contribution here stems from the fact that she chooses to ignore the contextually relevant set of 'comparable things John might have done to help people get to know each other' and instead deliberately interprets Tom's utterance in a broader sense, as if Tom really had asserted that 'John did nothing else this evening but introduce Bill to Sue'. Countering this would-be assertion with the irrelevant things that John *did* do thus serves to emphasise how unhelpful he was.

(1.19) Tom: John's usually good at helping people get to know each other. This evening he only introduced Bill to Sue.
Barbara: That's not true—he also {drank an entire case of beer / stood and gawped at Sandra all night / just about managed to stand still and breathe}.

If *only* really did encode a comparability constraint, as in Krifka's analysis, this kind of 'non-comparable' interpretation should not be possible. A proponent of encoded domain restricting mechanisms might counter that 'wise guy' examples simply show manipulation of the *value* that is given to notions like 'comparable' or 'contextually relevant' in context and that the encoded constraint is thus still obeyed in such cases. While this is a possible way to maintain the lexical semantic analysis, it fails to account for the strong intuition that Barbara is being 'over-literal', in some sense—i.e. failing to apply some normal steps of pragmatic reasoning. Moreover, it exposes the decidedly odd status afforded to pragmatics by conventional semantic approaches. The use of context-related operators or variables implicitly recognises the need for sophisticated processes of reasoning involving world knowledge, recognition of speakers' intentions, and so on, since such reasoning is required to establish the particular sets of individuals or propositions that

---

[23]'Wise guy interpretation' is Ariel's term for what are, in effect, wilful misconstruals of the context in which the speaker expects the utterance to be interpreted. I do not share Ariel's (2002, 1032ff.) apparent belief that these interpretations reliably distinguish encoded from inferentially influenced meanings, since encoded meanings may in principle be too underspecified to surface even in this way, while it seems perfectly plausible that partially inferred readings that are contextually irrelevant but calculable could be the basis for 'wise guy' comments. However, such interpretations can help to show what is *not* encoded, in cases like that in the main text.

are considered to be relevant or 'comparable' in a given situation. Yet this strategy simultaneously constitutes a refusal to utilise such processes to their full potential—to do so would render such semantic entities superfluous. In effect, any semantic element of this nature constitutes an *ad hoc* instruction to the addressee to carry out a mental process that is already motivated by the very nature of communicative situations: that is, the process of establishing the point of a given utterance.

An analogy may be drawn to examples of 'loose use' (Wilson & Sperber 2002). A statement like *Holland is flat* may be reasonably considered to be true, despite the fact that even the smallest patch of land evidently contains some degree of unevenness, never mind an entire country. If *only* is to contain encoded material especially to ensure the contextual relevance of excluded alternatives, shouldn't the lexical semantics of *flat* contain something that triggers the determination of its particular interpretation (i.e. its degree of precision) in a given context? This certainly seems to be required by the assumption of truth-conditional compositionality (cf. Lewis 1979). Yet if the encoded meaning of *flat* includes its own contextualisation, then how can we account for the coherence (notwithstanding the annoyance) of a rejoinder such as *Of course, it's not literally flat*, which indicates that some underlying context-independent semantics is felt to exist? It seems much more straightforward—as well as more parsimonious—to assume, along with Wilson & Sperber, that the encoded semantics of *flat* is precise, while its contextualised meaning may be vague, to varying degrees. The same applies to *only*, except that the precise encoded meaning is less likely ever to be considered relevant. (On the potential proliferation of encoded context-oriented elements, see section 1.3.2, below.)

Krifka's use of an encoded comparability condition is a relatively insignificant instance of over-encoding: little of any real theoretical import hangs on this detail in Krifka's analysis. Like most existing discussions of encoding versus inference, it deals with the semantics of just a single lexical item. One might even argue that it is little more than a metaphor, standing for what could be cashed out in pragmatic terms under some future, fully explicit theory of language. However, it is indicative of a broader problem; one that has very significant effects on linguistic analyses and, thereby, on the nature and complexity of the properties that we ascribe to languages. It matters when theories propose the encoding of what may be explained inferentially, because each piece of putative encoding is a claim about the structure of some part of the mind and an extra burden for the lexicon or the syntax to deal with, often resulting in the presumption of some new piece of technical apparatus to carry out the job of conveying the meaning in question. The study of Hungarian syntax later in this book constitutes an extensive illustration of how profoundly decisions about the encoding/inference distinction can affect grammatical analysis, a more inferential view bringing about not only a vast simplification of what the grammar must deal with, but also motivating a radical perspective on the nature of the grammar itself. For all this, crucial aspects of the arguments involved rest upon exactly the reasoning applied above to Krifka's comparability condition. Even apparently innocuous cases of over-encoding are therefore worth avoiding.

1.3.2 Domain restricting indexicals

Krifka's comparability restriction on exclusive meanings is closely parallelled by the use of 'contextual variables' to effect domain restriction for quantification. The need for some contextual restriction on domains of quantification is clear from simple examples like the interpretation of *every bottle* in (1.20):

(1.20)   Every bottle is empty.

(1.20) is typically not taken to be an assertion that every bottle in the universe is empty, but rather that every member of some contextually identifiable set of bottles is empty. Furthermore, there may even be bottles that are evident in the physical context but which do not belong in this set and therefore there may exist full bottles even within a restricted context without an utterance of (1.20) being taken to express a falsehood—for example, if the conversation is about recycling beer bottles, the presence of a full bottle of water won't make a difference to the perceived truth value of the sentence.

From this basis, Stanley & Szabó (2000) proceed to develop an analysis whereby all common nouns are inherently associated with indices (more precisely, with a contextually determined function over contextually determined objects), such that the compositional semantics of *every bottle* does not denote universal quantification over the set of bottles, but rather universal quantification over the intersection of the set of bottles and some contextually determined set of objects. Stanley & Szabó are quite explicit about the theoretical connotations of such an analysis: domain restriction is thereby a matter of linguistically encoded semantics, not the result of general pragmatic processes. Indeed, the strategy of positing widespread indexical elements is proffered by Stanley (2000) as a way of rescuing fully compositional semantic analysis from the problems raised by post-Gricean pragmatics (see also the comments on King & Stanley 2005 in section 1.2.4, above). The success or otherwise of this approach is therefore of considerable theoretical import.

Being generalised across the category of common nouns, Stanley & Szabó's proposal is in some ways a good deal more palatable than Krifka's proposed restriction on a particular item (*only*). Furthermore, the use of indexicals, rather than the stipulation of notions like comparability, shows a welcome concern for the *process* of creating interpretations in context and lifts the approach out of the realm of the most naïve kind of compositional analysis, whereby observed meanings and structures are simply forced to reflect each other. Indeed, generalised indexicality is one way to characterise the view of language that I advocate below (see in particular Chapter 2, section 2.3), as a semantically underspecified system of signalling meaning. To this extent, Stanley & Szabó's approach reflects a number of the concerns of post-Gricean pragmatics. However, by assuming the indexicality of language to reside in lexical semantics, rather than emerging from the conditions in which natural language is interpreted, this approach inevitably fails to generalise enough and is ultimately prey to the same criticisms as Krifka's comparability restriction, because it is based in the same conventional but far from necessary assumptions about the relationship between encoding, inference and the communication of meaning. As such, it too can be taken as a demonstration of the more general incoherence of the compositional approach to linguistic semantics.

Just as in Krifka's case, Stanley & Szabó's (2000) principal argument against a pragmatic approach to domain restriction in effect depends upon the assumptions of a conventional compositional approach to truth-conditional meaning and as such fails to rule out post-Gricean approaches, which do not include such assumptions. Stanley & Szabó assume that an analyst who does not accept that domain restriction is lexically or grammatically encoded is committed to the idea that the sentence *Every bottle is empty* "expresses, in every context, the false proposition that every bottle in the universe is empty". They therefore imagine that any pragmatic explanation of more intuitively realistic truth-conditions would have to be based in Gricean reasoning over the fact that the speaker has uttered an obvious falsehood: "Thus, occurrences of [such sentences] always express false propositions, but they communicate true ones" (Stanley & Szabó 2000, 239). Rightly, Stanley & Szabó point out that such a situation would run contrary to intuitions concerning truth and falsity. They therefore reject pragmatic explanations of quantifier domain restriction.

The problem with this reasoning is the lack of any necessary psychological correlate to Stanley & Szabó's distinction between 'expressing' and 'communicating' a proposition. What Stanley & Szabó seek to eliminate through the use of encoded domain restricting variables is the stage of 'expressing' a false proposition, but, somewhat ironically, the very existence of such a stage is the product of compositional semantic assumptions, not those of a coherent pragmatic theory. As emphasised above (and discussed in terms of Relevance Theory below), the process of deriving propositional meanings is viewed in post-Gricean pragmatics as one that is permeated by context-dependent inference from beginning to end. The only reason one could have for assuming that the interpretation of linguistic utterances involves *two* stages of identifying propositional meaning, corresponding to Stanley & Szabó's 'expressing' and 'communicating', would be a prior conviction that the grammar compositionally derives propositions. The Gricean reasoning that Stanley & Szabó rightly find implausible is thus a consequence of their own, conventional assumptions and is in no way representative of all pragmatic approaches, as they imply[24].

In a way that again parallels Krifka's comparability restriction on *only*, the relationship between Stanley & Szabó's contextual indices and necessary pragmatic processes proves quite incoherent on closer inspection. The ability to provide a value for these indices would necessarily involve quite complex reasoning over the intentions and interests of other interlocutors, includ-

---

[24]It should be noted that Stanley & Szabó's (2000) argument rests on more than the mere assumption that truth-conditionally relevant aspects of meaning must be encoded (though it quite clearly originates in this assumption). In particular, they offer technical arguments, developed further in Stanley (2000), based on the binding of their putative contextual variables by higher quantifiers. See Breheny (2002), Carston (2002, 200) for counterarguments regarding the appropriateness of this kind of technical evidence in this theoretical context. My concern here, however, is simply with the way their admirably explicit discussion provides a telling illustration of some widespread assumptions with significant theoretical connotations.

ing assessments of the kind of attention each interlocutor will pay to different aspects of the perceivable physical environment—the mere existence of an indexical element will not help an addressee to identify whether *every bottle* in (1.20) means 'every beer bottle in my house', 'every large plastic water bottle in the Linguistics common room' or 'every oil bottle in the kitchen, with the exception of the twice-used chip oil'. At the same time, as virtually every kind of analyst agrees, the requisite kind of reasoning is also needed to account for conversational implicatures and other 'non-literal' effects[25].

My contention (alongside the likes of Bach 2000 and relevance theorists; see Carston 2002) is that any individual armed with such sophisticated powers of reasoning in context will infer appropriate domain restrictions on quantification—and other kinds of contextual restriction of propositional meaning—when presented with a lexical item or phrase that encodes no such restriction. Any such powers of reasoning must be based in the desire and ability of an addressee to establish the meaning intended by a communicator and this, in essence, is what the process of contextual restriction of quantificational domains is all about. With or without encoded indices, the addressee must in effect pose and then infer an answer to the question 'When you say *every bottle*, what exactly are you referring to?'. The point is that human interlocutors go through a parallel process of reasoning for each part of every utterance: relativisation of encoded meaning to context is a generalised interpretive process, not primarily a lexical semantic one (nor a matter of grammatical semantics; *pace* Pelletier 2003).

There are of course some plainly indexical elements in language and, as Carston (2002, 200) points out, inherently relational items like *local* and *friend* might require an indexical element in their semantics. But this use of indexicals to capture such specialised lexical meanings is quite different to a proposal that all common nouns (or noun phrases) must carry a covert indexical, in order to account for widespread context dependence. Indeed, the need to distinguish specifically indexical or relational elements is in itself an argument for avoiding the generalised use of indexicals. Furthermore, as Wilson & Sperber (2002) argue (see also Carston 2002, 203ff.), this strategy seems all too easily to reduce to absurdity: if one must propose an indexical for every element of meaning that may in certain contexts affect truth conditions, then even the simplest of utterances is likely to require a lengthy series of such indexicals, in order to cover all possibilities. For example, an utterance of *I've eaten* would normally be taken to convey the proposition

---

[25]The same point applies to King & Stanley's (2005) detailed arguments against the notion that encoded meaning often radically underspecifies what is taken to be the semantic content of a sentence. It seems to me that King & Stanley in effect succeed in demonstrating that a fully semantic analysis of a given interpretation is always possible, as long as one posits enough indexical material in the grammar (most of their strategies for avoiding 'strong pragmatic effects' involve the interaction of a set of meanings that are putatively encoded in or directly triggered by the grammar, but which themselves could be derived inferentially—including the evocation of alternative sets by focus). They do not show that strongly inferential accounts cannot be correct. In this situation, one must look to broader theoretical considerations to choose between the approaches. One important consideration must be the independent necessity for language users to be able to recognise each other's communicative intentions—in particular the fact that this is necessary simply to recognise 'the context', let alone to relativise the interpretation of any given piece of linguistic material to that context.

that the speaker has a certain kind and quantity of food at a certain time. This explains the use of this expression in the dialogue in (1.21). Under an approach that takes unspoken contributions to truth-conditional meaning to be attributable to covert indexical elements, there must clearly be at least a temporal indexical and an indexical for the thing eaten encoded in the linguistic expressions used.

(1.21)   Alan: Do you want to join us for dinner?
         Jill: No thanks. I've eaten.

However, as Wilson & Sperber point out, examples like those in (1.22) show that other kinds of information may be understood to form part of the proposition conveyed by *I've eaten*, or its negation, in different contexts. This would seem to call for further indexicals encoded in the grammatical representation of this expression, just to deal with such contexts. The list of necessary indexical elements can be expected to continue to grow as more contexts and different expressions are considered. Before long, the grammar and/or the lexicon will be packed with covert indexicals, hardly any of which will have any perceivable effect in any given utterance of a given expression (for example, Jill's contribution in (1.21) has nothing to do with her having eaten in a particular place, using particular utensils).

(1.22)   a.   I've often been to their parties, but I've never eaten anything [*implicitly*: there].
         b.   I must wash my hands: I've eaten [*implicitly*: using my hands, rather than, e.g. being spoon-fed.]

Stanley & Szabó's encoding of a domain restricting indexical for every common noun, which might already seem excessive, is therefore only the very tip of the iceberg. Given the apparent open-endedness of the set of non-overt contributions to propositional meaning in different contexts, it seems far more plausible, as well as being more parsimonious, to attribute these contributions to the inferential abilities of addressees rather than to silent linguistically encoded objects.

The issue of domain restricting indexicals illustrates a broader point regarding the relative statuses of semantic and pragmatic explanation. The literature on the semantics-pragmatics distinction contains references to 'pragmatic intrusion' into semantics, in reference to cases in which pragmatic principles must be considered before truth-conditional semantic representations can be established (Levinson 2000). What the above argumentation suggests is that, on a theoretical level, conventional conceptions of semantics regularly intrude into what should be thought of as the territory of pragmatics. The likes of Stanley & Szabó (2000), in resorting to such drastic measures as inserting covert contextual variables into every common noun denotation, highlight the nature of the problem: within compositional truth-conditional semantics this step is necessary, yet from a broader perspective it is quite unnecessary—and, as such, theoretically undesirable—because of the availability of independently motivated pragmatic principles that can produce the same results.

This kind of observation is crucial, because it shows that issues at the semantics-pragmatics interface have significant theoretical consequences. Such issues cannot be resolved simply by re-assigning individual phenomena one way or the other across the two domains, as they are traditionally defined. Instead, the whole notion that syntax and semantics work together to derive truth-conditional meanings compositionally must be re-assessed. Nor is this a matter of minor adjustment; as hinted above and illustrated at length in later chapters, the assumption of compositionality of truth-conditional meaning has driven linguistic analyses at least as much as it has received support from them. In doing so, it has significantly affected resulting models of linguistic competence, in ways that go far beyond the addition of indexical elements to lexical items. The reality of what is encoded in natural languages may therefore be radically different, if this assumption is dropped.

1.4 SEMANTICS: WHAT IT MEANS

In the previous sections, I have argued that both theoretical and empirical considerations militate against any form of analysis of a natural language whereby the grammatical mechanisms that combine words into well-formed strings translate into compositional derivations of propositional meanings. Furthermore, I have provided some initial, small-scale illustrations of how attempting to maintain any such approach leads to unnecessary and undesirable over-complication of the grammar itself. It is important not to throw the baby out with the bathwater, however: formal semantic notions of course remain of crucial importance—the issue is how semantic representations are created, and the precise roles that grammar and extra-linguistic reasoning each play in this process. Despite the impression given in most semantic work, a commitment to understanding this question does not entail a commitment to finding ways to make semantic representations reflect the perceived structural representations of sentences.

As noted above, in section 1.2.4, compositionality and truth-conditional semantics are in no way logically inseparable, despite the common assumption that it is desirable to maximise the compositionality of formal semantic analyses. The apparent psychological reality of truth-based relations like paraphrase and entailment and certain conclusions about the role of pragmatic theory suggest that it is compositionality, rather than conventional ways of representing the meanings that language users perceive, that should be abandoned. Certainly, some forms of semantic formalism can be expected to be more useful than others in allowing the representation of the process of building up interpretations, in tandem with pragmatic input—in Chapter 6, I introduce a novel combination of semantic techniques to give a transparent representation to the grammatical contribution to the interpretation of the Hungarian 'focus position'.

As Carston (2002) and others have pointed out, the conclusion that truth-conditional meaning and grammatically derived meaning are logically separate issues drives a wedge between two uses of the term 'semantics' which have not always hitherto been sufficiently differentiated. On the one hand, 'semantics' has traditionally referred to meaning as a whole; the kind of overall interpretation that might be rendered in truth-conditional terms. On the other hand, 'semantics' may be used to refer to meaning that is encoded in linguistic forms. The arguments presented above effectively show that these two uses of 'semantics' cannot be assumed to coincide. As mentioned above, I generally reserve the term 'semantic' for linguistically encoded meaning, though this will be argued to be regularly quite different in character to what is expressed in conventional semantic representations. Where the more general sense of 'semantic' as pertaining to overall meaning is intended, I often employ the less loaded term 'interpretive'.

This usage is intended to clarify my preferred, post-Gricean conception of the semantics-pragmatics distinction. While it may be potentially confusing to remove the term 'semantics' from its associations with denotations and truth conditions, there is one very good reason for choosing this move over the alternative: continuing to associate 'semantics' with denotations encourages the impression that pragmatics, as a separate, complementary discipline, is concerned with only non-truth-conditional meaning. This is of course precisely the idea that the post-Gricean approach aims do away with. With 'semantics' reserved for coding, 'pragmatics' can refer to all inferential processes, without implying anything about the nature of the meanings that are derived inferentially

Potentially the most confusing use of 'semantic' is then in the context of describing conventional 'semantic theory/analysis', where the definition of the word inevitably cuts across the definitions that I propose, given the very nature of the argument between post-Gricean pragmatic theory and the common assumptions of semanticists. In any case, I attempt to be quite explicit about these matters whenever they are crucial.

The idea of 'syntax' is also due for re-evaluation: once one abandons the idea that the structures of natural language grammars map directly onto truth-conditional semantic representations, different considerations affect the analysis of what these structures are and what they do. These issues are taken up in the latter part of the next chapter, where a truly radical view on the nature of grammar is advocated. This can be viewed as an attempt to follow through the consequences of a coherent, pragmatically informed theory of linguistic communication for the theory of grammar. First, it is time to give some substance to the broad claims made so far about the nature of such a theory. Chapter 2 therefore begins with an overview of Relevance Theory.

1.5 SUMMARY

This chapter has argued that some fundamental assumptions of conventional analytical approaches concerning the relationship between natural languages and the meanings they convey are in conflict with the most basic aims of linguistic science. That is, these assumptions obscure the distinction between what are truly linguistic contributions to meaning and what is derived from extra-linguistic sources, such as inferential reasoning in context.

For the sake of the theoretical discussion, the key assumption was identified as a strong version of compositionality, whereby truth-conditional meaning is necessarily traced directly to the grammar. However, it should be noted that any analysis that involves simply matching observed meanings (by some preconceived definition of observable meaning) with perceived linguistic structures is guilty in the same way of failing to attempt to distinguish what is truly encoded in the language from what may be derived by other means. In any case, frameworks claiming to adopt weaker versions of compositionality but maintaining a conventional notion of the syntax-semantics interface were argued to be incoherent: I am in agreement with some of the advocates of fully encoded truth-conditional semantics on the point that conventional syntactico-semantic analysis depends on a total lack of 'intrusion' into this interface of any pragmatic or other extra-linguistic factors. However, since there is considerable evidence for the widespread existence of this so-called intrusion, my conclusion is that the conventional conception of the syntax-semantics interface, as a direct mapping from one set of static structures to another, must be abandoned. As a result, arguments from the literature on post-Gricean pragmatics have implications not only for the definition of semantics but also for the theory and practice of grammatical analysis.

2

RELEVANCE THEORY AND IMPLICATIONS FOR LINGUISTIC STRUCTURE

Having argued that the inferential side of the construction of meaning cannot be ignored in the study of semantic competence, there is clearly a need for some theoretical framework with which to deal with the crucial inferential processes. At the beginning of this chapter, I give a brief overview of Relevance Theory[1], which I take to be the most well-grounded of available inferential pragmatic approaches, as well as the one most suited to pursuing my theoretical and analytical aims in this book. I include, in section 2.2, some comments on certain misplaced criticisms of Relevance Theory. As noted in Chapter 1, the basic thrust of my arguments is not dependent on the details of any one pragmatic framework, but rather stems from some very basic observations about the nature of human language and how the conditions of its use are germane to how it should be analysed. Nevertheless, the adoption of Relevance Theory is useful in allowing some more detailed discussion and in helping to locate my arguments in the context of existing debates about the semantics/pragmatics distinction. Moreover, Relevance Theory itself is developed from much the same fundamental observations about the use of language and what this implies for the nature of language. Indeed, many of my arguments of Chapter 1 regarding semantic issues openly echoed existing work in Relevance Theory (in particular Carston 2002).

Less commonly discussed within that literature is the issue of the implications of the 'post-Gricean' stance for the study of the linguistic structure that delivers the input to semantic interpretation: syntax. Yet the rejection of a simple, strongly compositional syntax-semantics mapping plainly has consequences for how one approaches syntax. A syntactic component that must map directly to truth-conditional semantics must be considerably more complicated than one that need not—and it may be expected to have a quite different form. Furthermore, once inferences

---

[1] For more thorough expositions, see Sperber & Wilson (1986/95), Sperber & Wilson (1987), Blakemore (1992), Wilson & Sperber (2004) and, most pertinently to my purposes, Carston (2002).

drawn in language use are accepted to influence propositional meaning, the question arises of how key inferences are triggered in the course of processing. One possibility that must be taken seriously is that important inferences may be triggered by the presentation of certain kinds of information at certain points during the incremental parse of a word string. If this is so, as the logic of Relevance Theory suggests it probably is, then the only kind of syntactic framework that will allow consideration of all the significant factors in the structure-meaning relationship is one that models structure in a dynamic way, in the sense of modelling the semantic contributions of partial representations of structure that arise during parsing. These points are discussed in the remainder of the chapter, starting in section 2.3.

2.1 RELEVANCE THEORY

Relevance Theory (henceforth RT), unlike some approaches to pragmatic issues, does not attempt merely to extend or supplement truth-conditional semantics. Instead it is based in reasoning about the cognitive principles that must underpin the interpretation of ostensively intended acts of communication, such as linguistic utterances, as they interact with the context in which they are produced. As such, RT rejects the idea that linguistic communication is essentially a matter of encoding and decoding, of simply matching forms to meanings, in favour of an approach that recognises that interpreting a linguistic act practically always involves a mixture of decoding and inference over the significance of the decoded information in its linguistic and non-linguistic context. RT is not an algorithmic, generative framework, therefore, but it does provide a way of reasoning about what the scope of encoding within a generative framework should be.

RT approaches the notion of context from a human cognitive point of view: not in terms of direct representations of external reality, but in terms of evidence about reality which is necessarily filtered through human communicators' perceptual and cognitive abilities. As such, it is fully in line with the assumption set out in (1.6). Any utterance is interpreted relative to the addressee's 'cognitive environment', which is defined as the collection of all the assumptions for which an individual is able to create a mental representation and which that individual is able to accept as true or probably true (with varying degrees of commitment), given available evidence. Such assumptions are said to be 'manifest' to the individual. Roughly speaking, this means they are accessible, being directly perceivable or inferable from other manifest assumptions, without the individual necessarily being conscious of them. Any pair of communicating individuals will share a certain cognitive environment, consisting of assumptions that are manifest to both individuals. When it is also manifest to the individuals that they share these assumptions, they are said to be 'mutually manifest' assumptions and to form a 'mutual cognitive environment'[2].

---

[2] Mutual cognitive environment is therefore a psychologically better motivated and more precise version of certain other concepts in the literature, such as the 'common ground' of Stalnaker (1974) and others. It also replaces the problematic notion of 'mutual knowledge' assumed by many pragmaticists (see Sperber & Wilson 1986/95, 15ff. for discussion).

The concept of a mutual cognitive environment is crucial to facilitating human communication, as it allows communicators to judge in what context their addressees will interpret a given utterance and, on the basis of this, to formulate utterances in such a way as to ensure that the intended meaning will be recovered[3]. The aim of an act of communication can also be defined in terms of cognitive environments: successful communication enlarges the mutual cognitive environment between individuals.

A given utterance is not interpreted against all of the assumptions in a mutual cognitive environment, since this will include many irrelevant assumptions and assumptions of different degrees of accessibility. Instead, communicators can be said to guide addressees to construct an appropriate context for the interpretation of an utterance, in the sense of accessing those assumptions that are involved in reaching a particular meaning (by forming premises for logical deductions, or restricting the context for reference assignment, for example). Sperber and Wilson propose that addressees are able to identify appropriate assumptions (and thereby approach the intended meaning of an utterance) and, in turn, communicators are able to anticipate how different utterances will be interpreted in context, on the basis of a single basic property of ostensive communication: the Communicative Principle of Relevance[4]. This states that every act of ostensive communication communicates a presumption of its own optimal relevance.

'Relevance' has a technical sense within RT, though this is intended to reflect the everyday definition of the word in many of its uses. It is a relative measure of the benefit:cost ratio involved in processing some piece of information, where the cost involved is mental processing effort and the benefit comes in the form of 'contextual effects'. The latter are of three kinds: the strengthening of existing assumptions (increasing the addressee's commitment to their truth), the contradiction (and elimination) of existing assumptions, or the creation of contextual implications (logical implications which arise only from the interaction of incoming and existing assumptions). Note that contextual effects are always derived from the interaction of 'new' information gained from the incoming utterance with 'old' (existing) assumptions from the cognitive environment. This is consistent with the intuition that information with which an individual has no prior point of contact is not relevant to that individual, while it is clearly a waste of effort to process information that has no new elements to it. When discussing this kind of relevance to an individual, the more recent version of RT (Sperber & Wilson 1986/95, 265) shifts to the notion of '(positive) cognitive effects', to avoid any inappropriate conception of context as a fixed set of assumptions; a purely formal object. The difference in terminology is largely symbolic, but is a useful reminder that the basis of utterance interpretation is to be sought in those aspects of

---

[3]This is not to say that this is always (if ever) achieved perfectly, or indeed that it is always achieved at all—it is one of the advantages of a pragmatic theory that eschews a simple coding model in favour of inferences over mutual assumptions that it correctly predicts that communication can sometimes break down. This happens when interlocutors fail to assess the scope of the mutual cognitive environment accurately.

[4]Also known as the Second Principle of Relevance. I follow here the terminology of the 1995 postface to Sperber & Wilson (1986/95); in the 1986 exposition, this is simply known as the Principle of Relevance. See below for the Cognitive Principle of Relevance, which was introduced in 1986 as 'the presumption of optimal relevance'.

human *cognition* that enable utterances to be related to contexts.

For something to be relevant to an individual at a given time it must have some positive cognitive effect in one or more of the immediate contexts (proper subsets of the cognitive environment) available to that individual at that time. The overall degree of relevance, however, is not simply a matter of richness of cognitive effects, because this is balanced by the effort involved in arriving at those cognitive effects. An assumption is relevant to an individual to the extent that it produces a high level of cognitive effects but also to the extent that it requires a low level of processing effort. The definition of the presumption of optimal relevance is given by Sperber & Wilson (1986/95, 270) in the form of the Cognitive Principle of Relevance, as follows.

(2.1)   *The Cognitive Principle of Relevance (presumption of optimal relevance)*

      a.   The ostensive stimulus is relevant enough for it to be worth the addressee's effort to process it.

      b.   The ostensive stimulus is the most relevant one compatible with the communicator's abilities and preferences.

In other words, two basic conditions are presumed to hold of an act of communication: it achieves at least enough relevance to be worth processing (i.e. it has some significant level of cognitive effects without demanding excessive effort); and it fulfils the communicator's intentions as efficiently as possible (requiring just enough effort to have the intended cognitive effects, and at the same time having the richest possible cognitive effects, given a certain level of effort).

Because, by the Communicative Principle of Relevance, every utterance communicates its own conforming to (2.1), addressees can use the notion of optimal relevance to guide them to a communicator's intentions. A given utterance must guide the addressee to the intended interpretation via the 'easiest' route, indicating the contextually most accessible assumptions that will interact with the addressee's current assumptions in such a way as to produce the intended cognitive effects. This means, in turn, that the addressee may stop at the first interpretation he arrives at which is consistent with the presumption of relevance and may assume that this is the intended interpretation (this means that no effort is wasted on comparing different possible interpretations; Sperber & Wilson 1986/95, 165ff.). Furthermore, the presumption of optimal relevance means that addressees can use the relative processing effort demanded by an utterance as a measure of how rich the intended set of cognitive effects must be. Thus, a relatively costly utterance must communicate that there are relatively rich cognitive effects to be gained from its interpretation. This argument is the basis of the relevance-theoretic analysis of, among other things, metaphor and irony, and will prove useful also in the analysis of the exhaustivity of Hungarian syntactic focus.

As should be clear from the above exposition, RT is a theory of utterance interpretation, of how addressees get from the words they hear or read to a recognition of what the communicator intended to convey thereby. This means that RT is not merely a means to explain away non-truth-conditional or 'non-literal' meanings. As mentioned in Chapter 1, section 1.2.2, RT argues that the same context-dependent reasoning is involved in establishing perceived propositional meanings and in deriving conversational implicatures. As Carston (2002) argues at length, this represents a crucial difference between RT and Grice's (1975) approach. Grice assumes a semantics-pragmatics distinction that is essentially identified with a distinction between 'what is said' (a linguistically conveyed propositional meaning) and 'what is implicated'. RT contains no such distinction, since 'what is said' contains the effects of inferential processes as well as encoded meaning. This means that the Gricean 'what is said' obscures the very object of the linguistic analysis of meaning (recall the arguments of Chapter 1, section 1.2.1 that useful analysis must aim to distinguish what is encoded from what is inferred).

In place of Grice's said/implicated distinction, RT introduces the notion of *explicature* to complement that of implicature. The term 'explicature' is intended to relate to 'explicit' information, in the sense of what is taken to be conveyed by the linguistic forms used, via inferential enrichment. This is distinct from implicature, which involves the interaction of what is conveyed as explicature with assumptions derived from the context alone. In other words, explicature is in a way 'what is said', but not in the Gricean sense, since explicature includes aspects of 'what is inferred'. Another way to define explicature is as a 'development of logical form' (Sperber & Wilson 1986/95, 182). 'Logical form', in RT, refers to a representation of meaning derived from the process of decoding alone; that is, prior to inferential processes. Given the RT line on the regular involvement of inference in determining conveyed propositional meanings, logical forms are rarely, if ever, propositional (never, according to Carston 2002, Chapter 1), but are rather skeletal, often highly underdetermined schemata, upon which inferential processes operate. While this may seem a somewhat radical claim to those accustomed to more conventional Gricean or formal semantic assumptions, it is quite consistent with the nature of natural languages. As Fodor (2001, 11) points out, human languages are characteristically "strikingly elliptical and inexplicit", relative to the thoughts they express[5]

Hence, the standard RT line is that logical forms are derived by decoding the linguistic forms used in utterances and explicatures are established in context through inferences drawn over logical forms and contextually relevant assumptions. Implicatures are different to explicatures in that they are drawn over explicatures (not logical forms) in interaction with contextual assumptions, but the nature of the inferential reasoning involved is just the same in the derivation of both explicatures and implicatures—that is, driven by the Principle of Relevance.

---

[5]Recognition of the underdetermination of propositional meaning by linguistically encoded material is what I take to be the defining characteristic of post-Gricean pragmatics and RT is of course not the only approach of this kind. The work of Récanati (e.g. 2002, 2004) notably takes a similarly radical post-Gricean line, though he argues that dealing with semantic underdetermination does not presuppose the strongly 'inferentialist' line of RT (that is, Récanati sees different kinds of pragmatic process involved in the derivation of what RT calls explicatures and implicatures). For the reasons expounded in this section and the next, I find RT to offer a particularly coherent overall picture of the process of interpretation, so this is the framework that I adopt and present here. Nevertheless, the essence of my arguments and analyses in this book would be compatible with a position such as Récanati's.

To give a simple example (discussed in detail in Wilson & Sperber 2002), Mary's utterance in (2.2a) can be assumed to encode something like the information in (2.2b). In the kind of context implied by the dialogue (2.2a), this will create an explicature along the lines of (2.2c). While this explicature probably in itself constitutes the most important part of the interpretation of this utterance, one may assume that it also carries implicatures such as (2.2d), which justify the effort of having to process the whole utterance, rather than a simple *No, thanks*. Note that the purely decoded material, approximated in (2.2b), is in this case propositional, but it clearly does not encapsulate the proposition to whose truth Mary is asserting a commitment. How does the addressee know this? Quite simply through the fact that the trivial information that Mary has eaten at some point in her life could not achieve a suitable level of relevance (i.e. it does not justify the effort required to process the utterance). This is why enrichment up to the explicature (2.2c) takes place[6].

(2.2)   a.   John: Would you like to stay for lunch?
    Mary: No, thanks. I've eaten.
 b.   There has been an event of Mary eating something.
 c.   There has been an event of Mary eating something that she considers lunch, on the day of the utterance.
 d.   Mary is turning down John's offer only on the grounds that she does not need to eat and not for any reason that might offend John (e.g. dislike of his cooking or company).

The derivation of explicatures from logical forms and of implicatures from explicatures should not be seen as a strictly linear process, in which logical forms feed into explicatures, which in turn feed into implicatures. RT is an approach to utterance interpretation as a whole, because it recognises the pervasiveness of the influence of contextualised reasoning. Enrichment processes that rely on judgements of relevance in context are part of the overall process of recognising speaker intentions, so it can easily be the case, for example, that recognising an explicature is dependent in part on the relevance of implicatures that it makes available. RT therefore allows for processes of 'mutual parallel adjustment' between explicatures and implicatures: in essence, addressees formulate hypotheses as to possible interpretations, using as a guide the 'least effort' principle embodied in the Cognitive Principle of Relevance, and assess these hypotheses according to whether they deliver sufficient cognitive effects to make the utterance optimally relevant.

---

[6]Note that this explanation does not rely on the addressee rejecting an encoded proposition on the grounds that it is obviously false (cf. Stanley & Szabó's 2000 comments on pragmatic explanations for context dependent meaning, discussed above in Chapter 1, section 1.3): the idea that Mary has eaten in her life is evidently true, but too irrelevant to be a plausible candidate for the intended interpretation. Though the encoded material happens to be propositional in form, it would not be correct to say, following Stanley & Szabó, that Mary's statement 'expresses' this proposition at any level. Without a suitable context to make this reading relevant (which is highly improbable, in this particular case), the irrelevant reading (2.2b) is simply not entertained as an interpretation in itself, any more than sub-propositional encoded material would be, given a different utterance.

A hypothesised explicature that fails to achieve optimal relevance on its own or by opening up relevant implicatures must be re-assessed and new hypotheses tested.

In this way, the recognition of communicative intentions, through the establishment of relevance, is a global process, affecting explicatures and implicatures together. No level of meaning has a privileged status that is comparable to 'the proposition expressed by a sentence' in more traditional semantic approaches. Of course, inference is not everything: it is obviously not the case that any meaning can be conveyed using any given linguistic material and in fact linguistic input can place rather strict constraints on inferential processes. However, coding and inference are seen to work in tandem throughout the process of interpretation, in contrast to the conventional perspective whereby inference provides a limited amount of embellishment to the encoding and decoding of propositional meanings.

The apparent 'messiness' of this view of interpretation may seem worrying to those used to the more algorithmic accounts of formal semantics (and of attempts to formalise pragmatics), but the relatively fluid distinction between explicature and implicature is reflected in the nature of communication and, arguably, is of relatively little theoretical import. Addressees are concerned with identifying an intended interpretation, not with compartmentalising different elements of this interpretation according to theoretical distinctions. From the analyst's point of view also, it may be difficult to determine whether a given piece of inferred meaning is strictly speaking explicature or implicature: the analysis of exhaustive focus in Chapter 4 of this book is a case in point. In fact, as I argue below, in section 2.5.2, the implicature/explicature distinction, taken in any strict sense, may be quite incompatible with the dynamic approach to interpretation that I advocate in this book. However, the explicature-implicature distinction is in any case arguably more expository than substantial and none of these observations affects the essential nature of the explanation of crucial linguistic phenomena in RT, as a post-Gricean framework. The importance of the notion of explicature is that it allows for discussion of inferential contributions to what is understood to be the meaning directly conveyed by the linguistic form of an utterance, providing a useful way of distinguishing this from what is actually encoded (which may be a good deal more abstract). But it is considerably more important (at least for the arguments that concern me here) that explicatures are derived according to exactly the same principles of inference that guide the derivation of implicatures. This recognition of the pervasiveness of context-dependent pragmatic inference in the process of utterance interpretation, and the related underdetermination of conveyed meanings by encoded semantics, has rather more significant consequences for broader linguistic theory than do the details of how (or whether) explicature should be distinguished from implicature.

What the reasoning behind RT demonstrates is that the central questions of a cognitive approach to pragmatics—how do people go beyond encoded meanings?, what is context and what is its role?, how do people use the resource of language to fulfil their particular aims?—cannot be answered in isolation from other aspects of the theory of language. An adequate theory of linguistic interpretation in context must be compatible with the analysis of the meaning that language encodes and—crucially—*vice versa*. The semantic content of linguistic expressions cannot be accessed by the analyst other than via the cognitive processes involved in some contextualised interpretive situation, so this semantic context must be viewed relative to the role that linguistically encoded meaning has in a broader theory of interpretation. Relevance-theoretic reasoning suggests that this role may be quite different to that which has traditionally been assumed. As Carston (2002, 206) puts it: "The balance has tipped, from encoded meaning with a few inferential additions when necessary, to pro-active pragmatic inferencing constrained by bits of encoding". Below, I argue that this change of perspective has more radical consequences for grammatical and semantic theories than have typically been recognised even within RT.

However, these arguments clearly depend upon an initial acceptance that a convincing and coherent case exists for adopting at least the basic perspective of a framework like RT. To this end, especially given the necessarily brief presentation of the framework in this work, it may be useful first to make clear some of the things that RT is not—contrary, in some cases, to relatively common beliefs.

2.2 SOME MISCONCEPTIONS ABOUT RT

2.2.1 RT as a reduction of Gricean pragmatics

It is important to distinguish RT from Grice's approach and the broadly 'Gricean' view of pragmatics which persists elsewhere in the pragmatics literature and which continues to form the primary point of pragmatic reference for most work in syntax and semantics. While there is no doubt that RT belongs to the 'radical pragmatics' tradition of highlighting the inferential contribution to meaning and that as such it owes a considerable historical debt to Grice's work, the actual explanatory mechanisms of RT and the drawing of the semantics-pragmatics distinction are significantly different to those of Grice and his followers.

RT is sometimes described as an attempt to reduce Grice's (1975) conversational maxims to one 'supermaxim' and has been criticised on the basis that this 'reductionism' is unrealistic (e.g. Roberts 1996). However, the theoretical status of Grice's maxims and the Principle of Relevance are quite different. Unlike the Gricean conversational principles (insofar as their status is clear from Grice's presentation of them), the Communicative Principle of Relevance is not a goal or an ideal that speakers aim for, but rather a description of an intrinsic property of utterances as ostensive acts of communication. This is deduced from a number of uncontroversial observations about communication, most importantly the fact that any such act of communication demands the attention of the addressee and in so doing carries the implication that it is worth making the effort to pay attention to it. It is not in the communicator's interests to waste effort on utterances that fail to get any message across, either because they simply don't carry any message of relevance to the addressee or because the addressee will not take the risk of investing processing effort, fearing inadequate rewards. A communicator manifestly wishing to guarantee that the addressee will make the effort to recover all of the intended meaning of an utterance must therefore be implicitly promising the addressee that this will not involve any wasted effort. Thus, the principle that an utterance carries a presumption of its own optimal relevance simply falls out from the twin facts that communicators want what they have to say to be understood and addressees want to know what communicators have to say, on the assumption that it is relevant in some way.

This contrasts with the Gricean maxim-based approach, which assumes co-operation towards some goal other than communication itself. Grice's (1975) overriding 'Co-operative Principle' states "Make your conversational contribution such as is required, at the stage at which it occurs, by the accepted purpose or direction of the talk exchange in which you are engaged". Apart from the question of why speakers should follow this instruction (and hence what this 'Principle' really represents), note the amount of interpretive reasoning that is already presupposed in this formulation. How do people know what is 'required'? How does one recognise 'the accepted purpose or direction of the talk exchange'? Grice's maxims, intended to provide the basis for the inference of intended interpretations in context, are only operable on the back of considerable amounts of prior context-dependent inference. RT explanations begin at a more fundamental level: the general cognitive cost-benefit trade-off that guides interpretation in RT itself allows for inferring 'the purposes of the talk exchange' (to the extent that it is relevant to do so) alongside other relevant aspects of the communicator's assumptions and intentions.

The charge of excessive reductionism is therefore misplaced. RT does not reduce the Gricean maxims to one maxim of similar theoretical status. Rather, it introduces a whole new form of analysis, which has its origins in fundamental considerations regarding the nature of cognition and communication, and which thereby has the power to explain what might be called 'Gricean effects' without resorting to a somewhat arbitrary-looking list of maxims. This is reductionism only in the positive sense that a set of vaguely motivated and disparate stipulations is replaced by a unified explanation in terms of general principles. In some ways, it is perhaps unfortunate that Sperber & Wilson's use of the term 'relevance' echoes Grice's (1975) 'maxim of relation' (="Be relevant"), as this may encourage the idea that the Principle of Relevance is nothing more than a Gricean maxim that is being made to do the work of all the others; beyond such superficial similarities, it is nothing of the sort[7].

The arguments above dispense with another misconceived objection to RT: that the Principle of Relevance entails a belief in 'speaker altruism' (Dessalles 1998), which might be considered

---

[7]While the accusation of reductionism fails to recognise important differences between Gricean reasoning and RT, Bach (1999) mistakenly denies an important similarity between the two approaches:

> the hearer may presume that the speaker's intention is identifiable under the circumstances. This leaves open, of course, the question of how the hearer, even when armed with that presumption, manages to figure out the speaker's intention. The basic shortcoming of relevance theory is that it provides no place for this presumption. It replaces the distinctive feature of rational communication with an *a priori* generalization about human cognitive processes. (Bach 1999, 79)

The formulation of the Principle of Relevance, far from being matter of *a priori* stipulation, is derived from precisely the presumption that Bach refers to here (see in particular Sperber & Wilson 1986/95, 60ff.). Reasoning from this presumption, RT also develops answers to the question that Bach here describes as left open.

unsustainable. It is in both communicators' and addressees' interests for communication to be successful and the implicit guarantee that this will not require excessive effort follows, being the only way for communicators to ensure an appropriate response from addressees. If one thinks of the addressee 'gaining' cognitive effects for minimum effort, the act of communication may seem weighted to the addressee's interests, but one might equally think of the communicator's aim being to 'plant' cognitive effects in the addressee's mind, along a path of least resistance. Both of these metaphors describe relevance-based communication, which may, on some other level, plainly be used for many purposes, whether generous or selfish, co-operative or misleading.

2.2.2 Practical falsifiability

Perhaps the most unpalatable part of RT to many formal linguists—and probably the main reason why it has had very little impact on syntactic and semantic practice—is the impression that it fails to constitute a usable analytical tool, because it fails to make falsifiable predictions. This is of course a very important issue and the accusation may seem fair. After all, RT discusses the interaction of individuals' cognitive environments, which are entirely internal cognitive objects and ever-changing ones at that. There is therefore no way in which relevance-theoretic explanations of linguistic phenomena are directly testable. Furthermore, neither cognitive effects nor overall mental processing effort are measurable, or even reasonably estimable, given current understanding of the mind or the brain. Even supposing an idealised model of a mutual cognitive environment, the Principle of Relevance cannot be shown uncontroversially to predict a particular path of interpretation, because of this uncertainty surrounding the key notions of psychological cost and benefit (Gazdar & Good 1982, Moore 1982, Bach & Harnish 1987): for example, is there more effort involved in processing extra linguistic material, thus favouring short utterances, *ceteris paribus*, or in recovering unspoken meaning, favouring longer, more explicit utterances? With such fundamental questions left hanging, any given analysis in RT inevitably involves a huge number of assumptions about processing effort and the content of cognitive environments which are based in little more than intuition. Given this, one might reasonably ask whether RT can be a useful part of a scientific approach to language at all—certainly one can understand why computational linguists and others seeking comparable levels of formal rigour might believe post-Gricean pragmatics to offer them little of practical use; perhaps at best an insightful description of some intuitively plausible generalisations.

Damning as this kind of observation may appear to be, at a quite fundamental level, I believe it misses an even more important and basic point; that which forms the overarching theme of this chapter and the last. That is, we need some way of understanding, and thereby identifying, extra-linguistic, context-dependent influence on the mapping from structure to interpretation, in order to strip this away and expose what a competence grammar must really account for. As I have argued throughout these chapters, there is every reason to believe that context-dependent reasoning plays a significant role in this mapping. Now, there is no avoiding the fact that such reasoning is dependent on a very complex set of factors, which, thanks to the very nature of the phenomenon, are very difficult to draw empirical generalisations over. In this situation, we must consider what our alternatives are. We may, as RT does, reason from what appears to be a sound set of assumptions about the aims and related behaviours of human interlocutors and thereby develop a set of general, cognitively plausible principles for explaining why and how interlocutors come to attach interpretations to utterances in the way they do—albeit principles that tend to require a host of ancillary assumptions to support any given application of them. Alternatively, we may, as linguistic theories have traditionally done, steer away from the messiness of inferred meaning and attempt to work only with the forms of the language. However, as I have argued above, the latter strategy is not really an option: it effectively constitutes condemning ourselves to producing inaccurate and unparsimonious models of linguistic competence, since we will fail to identify what our models actually need to account for.

There is arguably a certain irony in the desire within formal linguistics to avoid discussion of contributions to meaning that arise from beyond the grammar. Modern formal theories of linguistics are generally traced to the revolution in thinking that is commonly acknowledged to have followed Chomsky's (1959) review of Skinner (1957). The basis of this revolution can be roughly characterised as the rejection of the behaviourist—or, more broadly, empiricist—doctrine that only 'external', observable data could be admitted into explanation, in favour of an active attempt to uncover the structures of the mind that underpin human attributes such as language. In other words, this move reflected a recognition that what is interesting about language is the constraints that the organisation of the human mind puts on it; simply matching instances of 'verbal behaviour' to external stimuli neither identifies the underlying nature of linguistic ability nor explains it. However abstract the very idea of cognitive structures may be, we must be prepared to posit such objects if we are to understand and explain what is and is not possible linguistically.

In this theoretical context, the curious thing about the formal linguist's avoidance of inferential pragmatic theories like RT is the empiricist-like reasoning that seems to underpin it. Like the innate mental structures of a child (whatever these may be) in the explanation of language acquisition and the internal grammatical knowledge of an adult in the explanation of intuitions of grammaticality, the processes whereby interacting human beings infer each other's communicative intentions are a necessary and interesting part of any explanation of the derivation of linguistic meaning. There is a parallel to be drawn between the behaviourists' concentration on stimuli and responses and the limitation of formal linguistic investigation to linguistic forms and intuitions about meanings. Worries about the practical falsifiability of pragmatic theories do not justify compositional semantic assumptions (or the use of grammar-internal quasi-propositional representations like LF in most of its uses) any more than empiricist qualms about positing 'invisible' cognitive structure justify the treatment of language as a behaviour controlled by external circumstances. Unsustainable assumptions do not become sustainable through doubts about applying the alternative.

I use the phrase 'practical falsifiability' because the claims of RT are falsifiable, in principle;

the problem is that this would require things that are currently unavailable to us—notably some appropriate measure of processing effort and some means of verifying the existence and significance of cognitive effects. But even if these turn out to be impossible desires, the postulates of RT are not theoretically uninteresting; still less are they safely ignorable. In the absence of the means to test relevance-theoretic hypotheses objectively, one may still accept the existence of relevance-theoretic reasoning (or something akin to it) in linguistic interpretation as being, in effect, a conceptual necessity. As I have emphasised in this section, RT is more than a set of hypotheses adduced to account for certain pieces of data; it is rather the product of reasoning over fundamental aspects of what is involved in the production of meaning. Such factors cannot be merely abstracted away from in any theory that addresses questions of meaning—as all major syntactic, as well as semantic, theories now attempt to do.

In this respect, a pragmatic framework like RT that is derived from these factors might be viewed as a fundamental component of any broader theory of language; a set of considerations that any such theory must take into account. In other words, I contend that just as any spoken language can only be manifested through temporally ordered strings of pronounceable phones and just as meaning is constrained by what human beings are able to conceptualise, so the mapping from linguistic structure to interpretation necessarily involves the process of addressees attempting to recognise the intentions of communicators, using the relative costs and benefits of processing to guide them. A linguistic theory that fails to take into account such a fundamental consideration gives one little reason to take its results seriously, since it is simply not a theory of human language. And while a theory that rests on intuitively necessary but practically unfalsifiable assumptions is not ideal, one that fails to identify its *explanandum* correctly is of no use at all. Once again, note that this is not an argument against competence theories. All such theories must make some initial assumptions about the nature of the object of study, based on what are taken to be uncontroversial observations. The present argument merely advances RT as a set of extrapolations from uncontroversial observations, suggesting that it should therefore inform our initial assumptions in other areas of linguistic theory and whatever analytical frameworks we build on top of these assumptions.

2.3 A DIFFERENT PERSPECTIVE ON LANGUAGE STRUCTURE

2.3.1 Encoded meaning as constraints on inference

The conclusion drawn in section 2.1, following Carston (2002), was that the insights of RT demand something of a reversal of common assumptions about the relationship between encoded and inferred meaning in natural language. Rather than inference providing a degree of adjustment or embellishment to fully-formed meanings decoded from linguistic forms, interpretation should be viewed from start to finish as a heavily inferential process that is merely constrained by encoded material.

The consequences of adopting this view should not be underestimated. The very role of linguistic expressions is thereby changed radically, compared to conventional positions. Rather than being principally a *carrier* of meaning, directly translatable into a semantic form, a linguistic expression of any kind—whether a full sentence, a phrase or a word—becomes a *signal* to the addressee to construct a certain kind of interpretation. Thus, the 'meaning' of a whole utterance is not a proposition (or a set of propositions) but a trigger (or set of triggers) for inferences that lead to a propositional interpretation. In order to do this, linguistic expressions certainly must carry a good deal of meaning of one kind or another, but this is in the service of other processes. Accordingly, the meanings of smaller expressions must be thought of not in terms of the contribution that the expression makes to the truth-conditions of the sentence, as in the traditional compositional approach, but rather in terms of the way in which it helps to build a trigger for inferring an interpretation.

For example, the immediate contribution of a noun phrase will not be conceived of as a denotation of an individual, group or set type, but rather as an instruction to use relevance-based inferential processes to access some such denotation, plus a set of constraints on what this denotation may be, which act as a guide to these inferential processes. This perspective allows for a relevance-theoretic account of context-dependence in the conceptual content of such lexical items, as in Carston's (2002) notion of the creation of '*ad hoc* concepts'. Carston argues that the concepts accessed in interpretation, and assumed in truth-conditional renditions of meaning, rarely correspond directly to any encyclopedic definition of the conceptual content of the words that are taken to evoke them. That is, lexical contributions to meaning are regularly enriched by pragmatic inference in context. Hence, the use of *fish* seems to pick out a different kind of entity in each of the sentences in (2.3) (taken from Carston 2002, 325)[8].

(2.3)   a.   One by one, she prised the fish out of their shells.

      b.   We had some delicious fish in a mornay sauce.

      c.   The fish savagely attacked the young swimmer.

      d.   He smashed the glass bowl and the fish wriggled on the floor.

As Carston shows, similar points can be made with regard to all kinds of lexical item: consider the precise truth-conditions attached to *open* in *open a box, open the discussion, open one's mouth, open the door (with a key / by the handle)* or the interpretation of *happy* in *happy to admit, happy to announce* or *a happy child*. It is fairly clear that none of these is a case of ambiguity; that there is some common meaning to each use of each of these words. This common meaning is highly underspecified with respect to what must be true in the world to give a positive truth value to the proposition associated with any utterance containing these phrases. Establishing the

---

[8]Carston takes the idea of *ad hoc* concepts further than these examples imply, using it to account for, among other things, metaphorical use of language and suggesting that lexically encoded meanings may often be radically underspecified indicators of conceptual content—ideas that are clearly compatible with the view of language that I advocate here.

contribution of these expressions is therefore necessarily a matter of active inferencing; these are not mere Gricean adjustments made over and above a stable compositionally derived meaning.

Viewing linguistic expressions as constraints on, rather than carriers of, meaning is not necessarily far removed from conventional accounts, in principle. In conventional semantic analysis, the denotations of linguistic expressions are always established relative to an assignment function, which may be thought of as a way of formalising the contribution of context (Heim & Kratzer 1998, 242). There is a sense in which the semantic content of a linguistic expression under this view is indeed a constraint on the production of meaning, since it is the assignment function that ultimately creates a meaning (of a denotational kind), not the expression itself. For example, any linguistic expression whose semantic contribution is taken to be a predicate over a variable is effectively a constraint on a space of variable assignment functions. The kind of approach discussed above as that of Stanley & Szabó (2000) and King & Stanley (2005), in which silent variables are used liberally to capture context-dependence in the grammar, is particularly close to the idea of linguistic material as a set of constraints on interpretation. However, as argued above in relation to these works, dealing with the contribution of contextualised reasoning by simply assuming some process of the assignment of denotations is ultimately no more than a very important promissory note, standing for inferential pragmatic processes that demand investigation in their own terms. If such work can provide a generalised explanation of the origins and effects of context-dependence, this is surely preferable to an approach that necessitates the *ad hoc* presumption of new entities for each case of context-dependent meaning.

In any case, once one does consider pragmatic processes directly, further considerations open up which point to the unsustainability of the conventional semantic approach. For one thing, the foundational reasoning of RT suggests that the context of an utterance should not be viewed as a stable, pre-definable entity, yet this is what seems to be required if context is to be captured in terms of an assignment function. The RT conception of context is rather one of something constructed online as part of the process of interpretation itself; a limited sub-set of the set of mutually manifest assumptions, accessed partly in response to indications within the utterance as to what is relevant to the communicative act at hand (see in particular Sperber & Wilson 1986/95, 137ff.). To say that encoded meaning merely constrains active processes of inference in context therefore implies a much more radical stance than the conventional semantic line of relativising interpretation to an assignment function. The inferential processes in question cannot be so easily extricated from the process of semantic interpretation and dealt with as a promissory note, because they permeate this process in complex and varying ways. Accordingly, the semantic contributions of many linguistic expressions are likely to be much too radically underspecified to be adequately dealt with using conventional assignment functions—and may even be of a fundamentally different nature to the semantic objects of traditional approaches.

Nevertheless, for as long as the issue is taken to be the context-dependence of meanings that are decoded from static syntactic representations, the variable-rich strategy of King & Stanley (2005) might be maintained, for better or worse. While the unexplanatory notion of assignment function might be considered an inappropriate way to capture the complexities of context-dependent pragmatic reasoning and the extensive use of contextual variables somewhat unparsimonious, there may be no definitive counterevidence to this form of analysis, if the input to pragmatic inference is taken to be meanings derived from complete structural representations of sentences uttered. However, as the following section argues, the logic of RT suggests that this is not the correct assumption.

2.3.2 Inference in the course of processing

A point that is not commonly noted within the RT literature—but one with important implications, and particularly germane to the work presented in this book—is the fact that inferential pragmatic theory, as a theory of the actual process of interpretation, rather than of strictly competence matters, opens up the issue of what may be contributed via inference *in the course of parsing an utterance*. This question more than any other is crucial to the way in which matters of grammar versus pragmatics, encoding versus inference, are addressed. If the semantic contribution of an expression may be affected by inferences drawn mid-utterance, such that in some cases the association of a certain meaning with a linguistic expression actually stems from the time-linear processing of language itself, then the possibility of maintaining a conventional compositional semantic analysis, whereby complete syntactic structures map directly onto semantics, is simply removed. No amount of context-sensitive variables will save such an approach in this case, since the very structure that is assumed to map onto semantics, within which these variables must be found, would have to be underspecified until it is put to use.

Given the significance of this point, it is surprising how little work in RT has addressed the question of inference during parsing, or even asked whether RT as it stands is well formulated to deal with this. Some parts of the RT literature do make reference to such a possibility. Thus, Sperber & Wilson's (1986/95, 202–217) analysis of information-structural effects, taken up also by Breheny (1998), does make explicit use of the incremental ('left-to-right') presentation of information (see Chapter 4, section 4.2.3), while Carston (2004) states, as part of a general overview of RT, that

> [...] 'semantic' representations [...] are not recovered whole and then worked on by the pragmatic inferential system; rather, the mechanisms here (the parser and the pragmatic system) are performing on-line, millisecond by millisecond, so that very often pragmatics is making a hypothesis about an intended word-sense, or an indexical referent, or even an implicature, before the entire acoustic stimulus has been processed by the linguistic system.

Nevertheless, the majority of work in RT concentrates on the interpretation of entire sentential utterances and this seems to be more consistent with some of the theoretical constructs of RT, as Sperber & Wilson and others present it. The foundational work in RT generally appears to assume a fairly traditional (essentially Chomskyan) notion of the nature of syntax. That is, it is assumed that an autonomous syntactic module is responsible for deriving the surface forms of sentences and corresponding logical forms, though the latter will contain considerably more underspecified material than is usually presumed—RT 'logical forms' are intended to be nothing more than a minimal representation of what is encoded in the linguistic forms that make up a given utterance. These logical forms are taken to be the input to relevance-theoretic pragmatics, being involved in the very definition of explicatures (as 'developments of logical form'). In their potentially high degree of underspecification, RT logical forms may look quite different to those of other frameworks (e.g. the LF representations of the Minimalist Program), but they must nonetheless be taken to be representations drawn from whole, fully parsed utterances, for a single logical form must encapsulate not only lexically but also syntactically encoded meaning.

As Marten (1999, 174) points out (see also Marten 2002, 168), this leads to some problems within the theory, since at least some applications of RT by necessity take surface forms, rather than logical forms, as the input to pragmatic reasoning. This is true of the above-cited RT analyses that make reference to inference during parsing, for example, and in any case attention to surface forms seems more consistent with a pragmatic theory; that is to say, a theory of the process of interpretation in context. This process begins with actual linguistic forms, not abstract representations of them; the creation of a logical form for the whole utterance (even in the restricted RT sense) may involve a considerable amount of context-dependent inferencing, to resolve any structural ambiguities, for example. Furthermore, the order in which different expressions are presented to the addressee is in itself one way in which a communicator can manipulate the ways in which particular contextual assumptions are accessed and juxtaposed, and thereby provide a basis for the inferential recognition of intended meaning.

The most coherent view of the role of RT would therefore seem to be one in which the word-by-word parse of an utterance provides the initial input to relevance-theoretic processes of reasoning. This has important consequences. First, this approach allows for investigation of the possibility that inferential processes during parsing affect the 'semantic' interpretation of at least some linguistic forms: the situation which, I argued above, would definitively rule out the applicability of a strict principle of compositionality to natural languages. At the same time, this view of RT-style inference in parsing provides a way to make the traditional notion of syntax and its dubious interface with semantics unnecessary. For if parsing a linear string of words directly feeds interpretation, intermediate syntactic representations have no interpretive role.

This is of course a huge conceptual leap in the context of modern linguistic theory. It is a fundamental assumption of almost all major formal approaches to language that the structural principles of a language must be specified by a grammar that is encapsulated from all of the uses to which it may be put, and this is often held up as an indispensable part of any scientific investigation of the essential properties of human language. The analysis of Hungarian in the present work is intended to provide an empirical demonstration that dropping this assumption is both possible and highly desirable. The following sections discuss theoretical reasons to believe that an approach to structure and interpretation that eschews abstract syntactic machinery is not only consistent with the broader goals of formal linguistics but in fact more likely to capture the relevant features of human knowledge of language.

2.4 SYNTAX: STATIC STRUCTURES VERSUS INSTRUCTIONS FOR INTERPRETATION

The abandonment of semantic compositionality means that syntactic representations for natural language expressions do not function as the 'logical syntax' of the meanings that they are used to convey. In this section I take this one stage further, arguing, in line with Kempson *et al.* (2001), that the analysis of natural languages requires no static syntactic representations at all. That is to say, there is no real need or purpose behind positing 'the structure' of a sentence (under a given reading). This is not to deny that the grammars of natural languages contain purely structural elements; they plainly do, but this does not entail structural principles that are definable over complete sentences and are manifested only in the form of individual, static representations of constituent structure.

In the 'dynamic' approach that I advocate here, the surface structures of natural language are viewed instead as consisting of incrementally processed 'instructions' to the interpreter to build certain kinds of structured propositional form. Hierarchical constituent relations, to the extent that they are required, are expressed only in representations of the propositional form of the sentence—that is, in semantic representations of a certain kind[9].

The idea of syntax as a set of indications for building an interpretation also has important consequences for the kind of encoded semantics that might be posited. Under the dynamic conception of syntax it is natural to think of encoded meaning as including not only bits of declarative semantic meaning but also procedural meaning. Indeed, any meaning that originates in the grammar, rather than the lexicon, *must* be procedural, once the role of syntax is no longer that of a static structure whose combinatory properties map onto compositional semantics. This is, after all, the very nature of a system of instructions. Hence, many of the elements of meaning that spring from the words used might still be represented in fairly simple denotational terms, but any meaning that comes from the way those words are combined (as manifested in particular in word order) must be procedural, taking these lexically-derived meanings and indicating how they should be integrated into a semantic representation.

Lexically encoded meaning may also be procedural, however, as has been recognised within RT. For example, Blakemore (1987) analyses the semantic contributions of several discourse connectives in terms of procedural meaning. The meaning of *so*, for instance, is explicable in

---

[9]While Kempson *et al.*'s (2001) Dynamic Syntax formalism assumes the hierarchical representations of a standard predicate logic formalism, I deal with the focus-related phenomena treated in the present work using flatter, event-based representations, for reasons set out in Chapter 6. As mentioned there, other parts of the grammar undoubtedly require more hierarchical forms of representation and it remains a challenge for future research to accommodate the findings of this work into the Dynamic Syntax model.

relevance-theoretic terms as "an instruction to interpret the proposition it introduces as a logical consequence" (Blakemore 1987, 87). Kempson's (1988) analysis of pronouns (see also Wilson & Sperber 1993) as minimally restricted placeholder items that effectively encode the need to be substituted by some semantically contentful material, though still concerned with individual lexical items, brings procedural encoding a little deeper into the grammar. The formalism of Dynamic Syntax (Kempson *et al.* 2001, Cann *et al.* forthcoming) makes very explicit the ways in which lexically encoded procedural meaning can do much of the work more conventionally attributed to syntactic representations; in that framework, lexical entries contain both formulae of predicate logic and sets of formal procedures regarding how these formulae may be integrated into a semantic representation. A fully formalised version of the proposals presented later in this book would have to take a similar form.

The switch from static syntactic trees to dynamic 'instructions for interpretation' is no mere change of perspective or of terminology. Within logical formalisms, it may be the case that declarative and procedural modes of representation are essentially equivalent. This might be the case with the present notion of syntax encoding procedural meaning, were it not for the fact that this treats syntax as an incremental process, from a strictly parsing-based perspective. Crucially, this allows for the influence of performance factors on the characterisation of competence. As mentioned above, this means that the contribution of inferences drawn in the course of parsing can be considered; something that is simply inaccessible to frameworks that make the competence-performance distinction a part of their methodology as well as their objectives. Such inferences may be triggered directly by the procedures encoded in the grammar—i.e. by the *way* in which semantic information is to be integrated—as proves to be the case in my analysis of Hungarian. Far from being a mere change of perspective and of formal apparatus, then, the kind of dynamic approach that I argue for constitutes a radically different conception of the grammar; one that allows for considerable redistribution of the burden of grammatical explanation among the different components of linguistic competence, because it opens up whole new forms of explanation for structure-meaning correspondences in natural languages.

Having very briefly outlined a view of what linguistic syntax may be (and of the kind of meaning it may convey), I argue in the following section why this is not only theoretically unproblematic, in spite of the fundamental assumptions of most formal syntactic frameworks, but actually preferable on theoretical grounds to more conventional approaches.

2.4.1 Static syntax is unnecessary

In the broadest theoretical context, the initial motivation for considering the possibility that linguistic structure embodies a set of processing instructions rather than a static representation is the simple fact that this is a perfectly reasonable hypothesis, consistent with what is known about human cognition and communication, and as such its explanatory potential is worth investigating. It so happens that this possibility has generally been ignored within generative grammar, which has in effect meant that generative grammar has covered only a certain sub-part of the space of possible explanations for linguistic phenomena.

This is of course no mere accident; it has been argued repeatedly that assigning abstract syntactic structures to sentences and investigating the properties of these structures and the means of generating them is the only principled way to initiate a scientific approach to human knowledge of language. While such structures are recognised to be idealisations—and, at least initially, possibly quite unrealistic ones—it is claimed, by analogy to idealisations in the natural sciences, that only this approach can lead to working models of linguistic competence (Chomsky 1988, 6–8). The reason why this particular form of idealisation is taken to be necessary is based on two lines of reasoning; one put forward explicitly by Chomsky and his followers, the other not clearly compatible with any theories of linguistic structure, but stemming rather from the assumption (explicit or otherwise) of semantic compositionality.

The reason to be found explicitly argued in the literature is inherited by generative traditions from the American Structuralist school and amounts to no more than the belief that matters of interpretation are simply too chaotic and difficult to analyse to be admitted into the basic data of scientific enquiry. For Chomsky (1995b, 18,381), all aspects of interpretation—semantics and pragmatics—are in principle to be viewed as aspects of the use of language rather than part of a model of competence. The use of language, it is argued, is too little understood to provide even delimitation of the syntactic component. From a contemporary perspective, this position seems quite unsustainable. As Jackendoff (2002, 123) points out, a variety of different approaches to meaning have shown in recent decades that there is (at least in principle) much of scientific value to be said about the structure of meanings conveyed by natural languages. I would add that even pragmatics, which by definition deals with the use of language, has been given both a clear role within a mentalist approach to the language faculty and a sound basis from which to make explanatory claims about aspects of the relation between structure and interpretation, thanks to the reasoned approach to the role of inference in communication and cognition that underpins RT. Furthermore, as I argue in Chapter 1 and section 2.4.2, simply ignoring the 'difficult', even chaotic, parts of some domain of investigation is not the same as abstracting away from them in a scientifically responsible way. And if there are prior reasons to believe that these things impact on the object of study (as I have argued above is case with regard to pragmatics and the study of linguistic structure), they *cannot* be ignored.

Given these considerations, it seems unnecessary and undesirable to treat idealised representations of the abstract structure of sentences as the only domain of enquiry for generative theory. Insights gained from other components of the language faculty should be seen as being useful in delimiting the scope of syntactic theory, at the very least, and also quite reasonably as a prompt for wholesale re-assessment of the presumed nature of the grammar and of the syntactic component in particular.

This might appear to be a description of precisely the turn taken in the move from the 'Principles and Parameters' stage of Chomskyan theory to the Minimalist Program (Chomsky 1995b), in which the content of the syntactic component is in principle to be influenced heavily by the requirements of its interfaces with other cognitive modules. However, the fact that most Minimalist work simply accepts the vague characterisation of PF as the 'articulatory/perceptual interface' and LF as the 'intentional/conceptual interface' demonstrates that little serious effort is being made here to admit insights from anything but pure syntactic theory—and as such it is not clear that the Minimalist Program is founded on genuine 'conceptual necessities' at all, let alone the full range of conceptual necessities that such a framework should take into account (see Jackendoff 1997 for more detailed criticism of Chomsky 1995b along these lines). What remains is virtually the same dismissal of serious investigation of non-syntactic domains as characterised earlier Chomskyan theory[10].

Again, this leaves most unclear how the syntactic component itself is to be delineated as an object of study. Consider Chomsky's (1995b, 220) speculation that the suspiciously performance-related matters of information structure and "effects of adjacency and linearity" should be dealt with outside of syntax (somewhere within the phonological component). It is difficult to imagine how the study of syntax should proceed if adjacency and linearity (i.e. word order) cannot be taken as part of the evidential basis for this study, or what the highly abstract result of this study would consist in, were it possible. Certainly, this could not be considered in any sense a development of previous syntactic research and could not reasonably import any of the results thereof; and, of course, the vast majority of practitioners of syntactic analysis continue to assume that explaining word order phenomena is a central burden of generative syntactic frameworks (Minimalist or otherwise). Meanwhile, as is shown in Chapter 3, it is hard to see how information structure could be left out of this kind of model of syntax in a language like Hungarian. Moreover, the very fact that the syntactic component is taken to have a single point of interface with each of semantics and phonology rules out any possibility of taking account of a whole set of potentially significant interpretive processes: those that might take place on the basis of partial representations of meaning, during parsing[11].

The second reason for the characterisation of the syntactic component as a system of abstract structures lies in the apparent logic behind what the syntactic component must be—and this brings us back to the question of semantic compositionality, in spite of the professed commit-

---

[10]This is not to deny that some works have taken this aspect of the Minimalist Program more seriously than others. The likes of Reinhart (1995) and Neeleman & Reinhart (1998) are examples of real attempts to constrain the scope of syntactic theory by direct consideration of its 'interfaces'. Work on Hungarian that directly follows this line is to be found in Szendrői (2003). A major problem for this kind of approach is the question of how much of previous syntactic theory can be simply imported into the new framework, since the results of previous syntactic work were produced without the crucial new theoretical assumptions.

[11]Recent versions of Minimalism include multiple applications of 'Spell-Out', associated with different syntactic 'phases' (Uriagereka 1999, Chomsky 2001); an idea which could be seen as introducing a greater number of points of connection between observable linguistic structures and semantically significant representations (even though the theory retains just one level of LF). In some ways, this might be viewed as a way for this framework to ape some of the effects of incremental analysis while maintaining its strict competence-based perspective—however, a proper comparison of these approaches must await further research. This move too brings up the question of how much of the results of previous analysis can simply be imported into the revised framework (see previous footnote).

ment in many frameworks to syntactic principles that make no reference to semantics. There is arguably a problem with the very definition of the word 'syntax' in much of modern linguistics. The syntax of any system of representation is a set of structural principles that mediate between the elements of the system and the meaningful complex structures in which they may participate. This means that semantic representations have their own syntax, in the broader sense. This might be termed 'logician's syntax', and it may certainly be conceived of in hierarchical terms. The idea that human languages have a syntax of a similar kind does not follow inevitably from this; in fact, it would only follow straightforwardly under the Montagovian assumption of semantic compositionality. In an artificial formal language, or under an avowedly Montagovian view of natural language, the syntax of the language and the syntax of a representation of meaning can be conflated; semantics as such is a matter of interpreting the meaningful structure that this delivers (with respect to a model, for example). On this basis, it must be possible to assign static hierarchical structures to natural language sentences, since these structures are in themselves the means by which (inherently hierarchical) meanings are represented.

Under any other view of the relationship between the syntax and semantics of natural languages, the ability of human languages to convey structured representations of meaning provides no justification for the idea that strings of words in these languages correspond to abstract syntactic structures. To reason from the one to the other is to fail to account for the degree of abstraction inherent in the linguist's (as opposed to the logician's) concept of syntax. The surface characteristics of sentences may relate to all kinds of influences on meaning, as well as being determined in part by independent processing and phonological constraints, as is widely recognised within syntactic theory. Hence, no non-Montagovian generative theorist would suggest that the existence of structure in semantic representations in itself justifies the imposition of hierarchical syntactic structures on the linear word strings that are the superficial forms of sentences. Rather, LF (or some equivalent) is the level of representation at which meaningful compositional structure is expressed. But this means that the expression of logical form, which is essentially a matter of semantic representation, is the *only* level at which static structural representations are justified by conceptual necessity—even if it is accepted that the meaning encoded at this level is truly compositional. In a framework which includes representations of logical form (whether LF or any equivalent of it), it is quite unclear what justifies the assumption of static hierarchical representations at any other level of the grammar.

In this respect, the Chomskyan assumption that the same forms of computation are involved in the derivation of surface structures as those which are involved in creating LF representations seems quite unmotivated—still less the Minimalist idea that a surface structure is somehow built on an incomplete derivation of an LF structure (as determined by the location of Spell-out). There is one sense in which the surface form of a sentence is logically prior to its logical form, but this is not a matter of abstract computational 'knowledge': the only context in which it is truly necessary for surface forms to precede logical forms is in the actual process of parsing.

To summarise the general point of this section so far, the processes which *produce* representations of propositions may be quite different in character to a system that characterises the structure of a propositional form. It seems reasonable to suggest that these processes might take advantage of all the possible sources of signalling information that are made available by the conditions in which surface forms are realised—including, for example, prosody and linear presentation in real time—rather than only the properties of an abstract computational system.

There remain two further arguments for assuming static syntactic structure defined over sentences: the very concrete issue that constituent structure seems to be directly observable in natural languages and the more philosophical matter of which theoretical assumptions facilitate a scientific approach to the properties of human languages.

The latter argument is more complex; a reply to it falls out of the discussion in section 2.4.2. The former argument can be dealt with quickly: as Steedman (2000) emphasises, the accepted tools for establishing constituency, such as substitution, deletion and moveability tests, are not clearly indicators of purely structural, as opposed to semantic, or semantically influenced, properties. This problem is compounded by, or perhaps reflected in, the fact that no one constituency test is consistently reliable, as students in introductory syntax courses are always warned (usually provoking understandable disgruntlement and scepticism). The intuitive feeling that natural language sentences 'have structure' is therefore quite possibly no more than a reflection of structure in the meanings that languages convey, revealing nothing about the principles that determine how this is achieved. Perhaps because of such misgivings, few contemporary analyses in any major frameworks attach great importance to evidence from constituency (though it may be invoked intermittently to support or undermine the details of a given proposal). It is much more common to find essentially semantic evidence—the readings that some proposal does or does not make available, given certain assumptions about mapping to and from logical form—invoked in support of syntactic analyses. In effect, this amounts to the unspoken adoption of Montagovian assumptions, which are at odds with the avowed theoretical basis of many syntactic frameworks, a situation that in itself begs a re-assessment of the conventional conception of syntax and its relationship to semantics.

2.4.2 Abstraction and the accessibility of the object of study

Regardless of their merits in principle, efforts to characterise syntactic structure may be futile. Even if it is accepted that it is otherwise desirable to postulate a computational system that is responsible for both surface forms and logical forms and to investigate its properties, there are practical limitations on the construction of a theory, imposed by the nature of linguistic data, which may overwhelm any attempt to do so. It is uncontroversial within generative linguistics that characterisations of syntactic competence must involve considerable abstraction. To access the workings of any putative syntactic computational mechanism, one must control for not only the messiness of real world data (which includes the use of ungrammatical and incomplete forms, and so on) but also for the influence of non-syntactic elements of linguistic processing: those aspects of speakers' acceptability intuitions that are dependent on phonological, semantic or pragmatic factors.

Despite increasing attention being paid to this notion—not least because it is built into the Minimalist Program in a more explicit way than in previous Chomskyan frameworks—there is little rigorous discussion to be found, within the majority of the syntactic literature, of the possibility of explanations of given phenomena at different levels. This has deleterious consequences for the explanatory potential of syntactic theory itself, as I shall argue below. However, this issue of the practice of syntactic research should not affect the more general theoretical discussion, concerning how in principle syntacticians might identify the contents of a computational syntactic component.

The question, then, is not whether linguists access the putative syntactic level of representation accurately, but whether they ever could. It is not at all clear that it is possible to identify the syntactic component by direct means; that is, the only way to do so may be to investigate the other components of the grammar in order to eliminate their influence and 'see what is left'. If this is the case, it has consequences for the kind of perspective that must be taken on linguistic data.

The reason to believe that this is the case is the fact that there is rarely if ever any *a priori* way to distinguish which part of the language faculty accounts for a given phenomenon. The inadequacy of constituency tests for this purpose has been mentioned above. Meanwhile, speakers' intuitions, the primary source of data for the generative linguist, are notoriously unhelpful, and inevitably so—since it is in the very nature of (the relevant kind of) linguistic knowledge to be inaccessible to conscious reflection. This gap between speakers' intuitions and identifiably grammatical distinctions is well recognised:

> ...we may make an intuitive judgment that some linguistic expression is odd or deviant. But we cannot in general know, pretheoretically, whether this deviance is a matter of syntax, semantics, pragmatics, belief, memory limitations, style, etc. (Chomsky 1977, 4)

Rather than attempting to deny this problem, syntactic theorists simply take the line that the question of which component of the language faculty is responsible for a given phenomenon is an empirical one. That is, they place their faith in the idea that the boundaries and internal character of the syntactic component will become clearer as a result of amassing a suitably deep and broad body of syntactic research into a variety of grammatical phenomena. Any proposed model should make predictive hypotheses and standard falsificationist scientific procedure should lead to more and more accurate models. It is sometimes even suggested that this is not only an adequate way to proceed but necessarily the most theoretically responsible: a purely structural proposal represents a strong, testable and seemingly parsimonious hypothesis, so it might be argued that this approach should be pursued until the facts show it to be unsustainable.

The problem with this apparently fairly reasonable position is the theoretical status of the assumptions in question. The hypotheses tested by syntacticians typically do not and cannot have the form 'If phenomenon P in language L is accounted for by structural principle S_1, then it is correctly considered a syntactic phenomenon. Otherwise, it must be considered a semantic (or other kind of) phenomenon'. Instead, they tend to have the simpler form 'Phenomenon P in language L is accounted for by structural principle S_1', which if falsified can be replaced by an alternative hypothesis involving structural principle, S_2, S_3, S_4, ..., *ad infinitum*, without ever leading to the abandonment of the *assumption* that some principle of syntax rather than semantics, pragmatics or phonology must be involved. It is not clear what kind of evidence would be required to falsify this kind of background assumption, especially within the context of a constantly evolving framework such as those found in theoretical syntax.

In other words, it is not clear that syntactic theory alone bears the potential to delimit its own object of study. Nor should it need to: as emphasised above, there is much in what we know of the broader theoretical context which may guide the process of theory-building, if only one is prepared to investigate it. As for the more philosophical justification for purely structural approaches, boldness, simplicity and falsifiability cannot be the only motivations for advancing a particular hypothesis. Coherence with a broader context must be a constraint on the formulation of hypotheses. As already noted, one uncontroversial fact about the broader context of linguistic theorising is that the available data, whether in the form of attested usage or intuitive judgements, show only the final effects of grammatical knowledge, as filtered through a variety of 'performance' factors, each of which relates to the 'competence' principles of some other component of the mind. Since there are in fact a number of things we can say about these extra-grammatical factors, it would be irrational not to use such knowledge as we have at least to delimit the space of phenomena that require a structural explanation. This means being prepared to consider some matters of performance in the process of formulating hypotheses about competence, but there is nothing intrinsically undesirable about this, as argued above in Chapter 1, section 1.1.1. There is therefore no sense in which the desire to take a responsibly scientific approach militates in favour of exclusively structural analysis.

Analogies with other scientific pursuits are common in meta-theoretical discussions within linguistics; mathematics, theoretical physics and chemistry being favourite points of comparison (e.g. Chomsky 1988, 6–8). To bring out the combination of philosophical and practical issues faced by the theoretical linguist, I would suggest another analogy. Imagine an archaeologist researching some ruins left by an ancient civilisation in a now-rural area and hoping to establish the nature of the original buildings in as much detail as possible. These ruins, though preserving some discernible shape, are buried by centuries of soil deposits and the growth of vegetation, but due to some pesky environmental law the archaeologist is unable to remove the vegetation and dig up the ruins physically, so must resort to deducing what may be gleaned from the current state of the site and from such relevant knowledge as is available. On achieving some picture of the nature of the ruins, the ambitious archaeologist might wish to characterise the building technologies of the ancient civilisation in various ways (even in terms of a set of constraints on the construction of a complete building, if one liked), but the point here is that the whole analysis must *begin* with the influence of environmental factors in order to establish even what information may enter into the description of the underlying structure (let alone what it might tell us as part of any bigger picture). In order to understand the extent and basic shape of the buried ruins, our archaeologist might employ such knowledge as is available on matters like seismic activity or subsidence, rates of soil deposits under the local conditions, the nature of the locally available building materials, the depth of soil required for different kinds of local vegetation to grow and so on[12].

Of course, as an analogy to the linguist's attempts to discern underlying structures, this is decidedly imperfect—in ways that only make the syntactician's job harder. An archaeologist may have other important sources of information on which to work, such as the nature of comparable ruins that have previously been physically uncovered at other sites, whereas linguists never have *direct* access to any underlying, language-specific structure. Our situation is more like that of some hypothetical community of archaeologists in a universe in which tree-felling and digging is never possible: in this case, the *only* practical way to approach the underlying structures is via knowledge (or theories) of the ways in which these structures interact with their environments. On the other hand, linguists have the luxury of data regarding what is not possible, in the form of intuitive judgements—though these too are only indirect reflections of underlying structure. The analogy is close enough, however, to demonstrate the absurdity of dismissing 'environmental' factors from the process of analysis (as opposed to the form of resulting theory).

Imagine that our hypothetical community of entirely theoretical, spadeless archaeologists decided to home in on the underlying structures directly, positing systems of rules and/or constraints that would 'generate' their best guesses at underlying structures, *before* finding out (or at least without making any reference to) anything about erosion, soil deposits or plant growth. Certainly, such an approach would allow for the formulation of hypotheses that could be tested against the appearance of each known and any yet-to-be-discovered site. But could one credit it with much chance of eventually producing accurate models of their object of study? Surely not: it is too plain that presumed bits of buildings could be wrongly identified, with either great structural complexity remaining unknown, under the bland overgrown exterior, or all kinds of significant features being posited where in fact there is nothing but a mound of earth, some tree roots, or the effects of a landslide.

One might argue that, by the nature of the data themselves, theoretical linguists are somewhat less in the dark than these very unfortunate imaginary researchers. Nevertheless, the basic point surely carries over: in the absence of serious efforts to distinguish and account for the effects of interaction with the environment, there is a strong likelihood of confusing some environmental effects for parts of the underlying structure. Factors like the time-linear processing of

---

[12] Any sensible archaeologist would of course rule out from the beginning absurd conclusions such as some section of the ruin having the function of supporting a large shrub; an observation that I venture to suggest has some resonance regarding those syntactic and 'dynamic semantic' theories that regularly bring pragmatic factors into the formal structural description of languages, instead of seeking linguistically supplied triggers for independent pragmatic processes.

linguistic expressions and addressees' strategies for identifying the intention behind an utterance inescapably form a part of the environment in which observable linguistic data exist and as such the process of abstracting away from them should involve as far as possible understanding and accounting for them and their effects, not treating them as extraneous business that may simply supplement an independently established competence theory.

Jackendoff makes a related point in another context:

> One can't just "choose the strongest hypothesis because it's the most falsifiable" and then end up excluding phenomena because they're not "core grammar" (i.e. whatever one's theory can't handle). In order to draw a boundary properly, it is necessary to characterize phenomena on *both* sides of it, treating phenomena "outside of language" as more than a heterogeneous garbage can. (Jackendoff 1997, 157; emphasis in original)

Just as it is not explanatory simply to dismiss any phenomenon that does not fit one's theory as being outside core grammar, one should not accept that a phenomenon is explained, in any scientifically useful sense, simply because it *does* receive an account that is consistent with the mechanisms postulated within one's highly abstract model (*pace* Carr 1990). External factors must be allowed to impact on the scope of the theory—and the undisputed need for a degree of abstraction does not justify ignoring as many external factors as we can be reasonably sure of, if they demonstrably impact upon the process of relating forms to meanings.

As Jackendoff suggests, what is genuinely useful is when a convincing alternative explanation for phenomenon P is found using the tools of some non-syntactic theory. In this case, it is reasonable to assume (if only for the sake of satisfying Occam's Razor) that syntactic theory need not take on the burden of explaining P[13]. This implies that without much greater efforts to delimit the scope of any would-be computational syntactic component, using the insights of other linguistic sub-disciplines, syntacticians cannot even hope to define their object of study.

This is not the end of the argument, however, because of the particular nature of some key factors that influence the identification and interpretation of linguistic structure. As I have emphasised above, the time-linear processing of language is a factor that may be expected to influence

---

[13] The situation is complicated by the fact that there is nothing in principle to prevent some phenomenon being both grammatically encoded and independently explicable—an observation that represents a challenging problem for any kind of approach to linguistic theory and which not does help us to choose between them. It is clear, however, that a minimum criterion for attributing a phenomenon directly to the grammar is that it should be manifested quite consistently and not depend on particular contextual factors. My analysis of the Hungarian 'focus position' discusses semantic effects that are conventionally presumed to be grammatically encoded and shows how they simply fail to appear under certain subtle but significant conditions. This points up a further practical problem with the 'strong hypothesis' of purely syntactic explanation: for as long as one's structural proposals for a given language are internally consistent and broadly descriptively adequate, there is little motivation to investigate their realisation in a range of communicative contexts, though this may be the source not only of alternative explanations but also of crucial counterevidence.

the mapping from linguistic expressions to semantic interpretations, because of the opportunities that it opens up for triggering inferential processes at different points in a parse; processes that change, not only exploit, the context that many aspects of interpretation depend on. If this is the case, any formalism that is meant to capture the crucial relationships between linguistic structure and meaning must allow for direct reference to incremental processing. Otherwise, it simply affords no access to important elements of form-meaning correspondence, thus stifling both adequate description and appropriate further analysis. It is primarily for this reason that an approach based in assigning static structures to linguistic expressions is not only unnecessary (as argued above) but also inadequate for the analysis of natural languages.

2.5 GRAMMAR FROM A PARSING PERSPECTIVE

2.5.1 Well-formedness without syntactic representations

The kind of framework that I am advocating is one that, as in Dynamic Syntax, models grammatical phenomena through a certain kind of model of parsing. That is, incoming words are processed one by one and immediately slotted into the developing representation of a propositional meaning, rather than into a syntactic representation, on the basis of a combination of pre-determined parsing strategies, lexically encoded information (which may include significant amounts of procedural meaning) and contextually inferred information. This is consistent with the observation of section 2.4.1 that while semantic representations must have internal structure, there is no *a priori* justification for other levels of static structure which would map onto this. It also reflects the RT reasoning which suggests that the addressee's relevance-based attempts to establish the communicator's intended meaning pervade the process of interpretation, an idea that implies the conversion of each piece of incoming material directly to a representation of meaning which may be subsequently assessed for relevance, as may its combination (as a premise for further inference) with other lexically or inferentially derived bits of meaning. This leaves little room for intermediate kinds of representation that do not have immediate semantico-pragmatic significance, such as conventional syntactic representations.

In the relevant kind of dynamic approach to syntax, lexical items may encode, alongside more conventional semantic information, rich specifications of how the lexical item may be employed in constructing a propositional representation of meaning. In addition, strict principles of parsing may exist in a language that license transitions from one kind of lexical item to another only if a certain kind of structure is added to the incrementally expanding representation of meaning. In such ways, a concept of well-formedness can be defined that does not require reference to static structures defined over entire sentences (or, more or less equivalently, to an abstract derivation of such a structure). Instead, well-formedness results from the ability to construct a complete propositional meaning as a result of fulfilling all the requirements provided by the lexical items parsed and the parsing strategies that are available.

In Dynamic Syntax parsing is modelled as a goal-driven process, the overarching requirement being to construct a type *t* semantic object—that is, a proposition. This overarching requirement gradually expands into a richer semantic representation in the course of parsing. More detailed requirements are added by incoming lexical items and by language-specific parsing strategies—for example, a requirement to build a slot for an object of a certain semantic type, thus ensuring that the material already parsed must participate in a certain kind of semantic structure by the time the parse is complete. The denotational semantic material that lexical items also contribute must eventually fulfil such requirements and thus create a propositional representation with a certain internal structure. Well-formedness can therefore be viewed in terms of the ability of a given string to create a proposition according to prescribed parsing strategies without introducing any requirements that remain unfilled.

While my analysis of Hungarian in this book does not employ Dynamic Syntax as such, for reasons outlined below (section 2.6), it will become clear in Chapter 6 that my explanation of the 'focus position' phenomenon depends not only on the incremental presentation of information, but also on the notion of procedural requirements arising at certain points in parsing that must be fulfilled in order to treat the incoming string as well-formed. This limits certain word orders to being well-formed only on certain readings, thereby predicting the correspondences between word order and interpretation that are observed in the Hungarian clause.

In the spirit of Chapter 1, it is important to add to this notion of requirements in parsing the fact that the incremental construction of meaning must proceed according to principles of relevance in context. It follows that well-formedness may in effect also depend on the possibility of accessing contextual assumptions that make the possible meanings created by the required process of meaning construction relevant. This too plays an important part in my explanation of the Hungarian data. The crucial requirement is to fulfil a certain kind of predicative procedure; it is in the nature of this particular procedure that certain kinds of object can enter into it only if a certain kind of term to be predicated over can be drawn from the mutual cognitive environment of the interlocutors (as explained in Chapter 6). This accounts for the fact that the readings that license certain word orders in Hungarian are of a distinct information-structural kind.

2.5.2 The argument from production and parsing

To summarise the previous section, static, abstract representations of syntactic structure are otiose because the well-formedness of a natural language string can be viewed as the potential to trigger the construction of a suitable representation of meaning, given the availability of a certain extra-linguistic context. Following the Dynamic Syntax framework, I continue to assume for practical purposes that 'a suitable representation of meaning' means a full propositional form that can be taken as being in some sense the core meaning expressed by the utterance. This is certainly a simplification and brings up the question of what this propositional form relates to in terms of RT. It is not identical to the 'logical forms' of RT, since these are argued within RT to be often sub-propositional and, as argued above, are in any case seemingly static representations of the presumed decoded meaning of entire sentences/utterances, rather than the result of dynamic processing. The most obvious parallel from RT for the proposed propositional forms is to be found in explicatures. These are, after all, propositional meanings that are in some sense taken to be the basic meaning expressed by a given utterance in a certain context. However, explicatures carry the problem of being defined in relation to the non-dynamic logical forms of RT. Furthermore, it has been argued convincingly in the RT literature (see in particular Wilson & Sperber 1993; Carston 2002, 124ff.) that an utterance may have multiple explicatures, potentially causing trouble for a definition of well-formedness in terms of the derivation of a single propositional form, if this form is identified with explicature. I put these issues to one side in what follows. As argued in section 2.1, the notion of explicature arguably has a primarily expository role in RT and in any case I am more interested, in this book, in investigating the general implications of post-Gricean pragmatics than in rendering the internal details of RT perfectly compatible with other aspects of my analyses.

Irrespective of how these such issues are resolved, for present purposes the point remains that an alternative approach to the notion of well-formedness in natural languages is possible (and it is already applied in Dynamic Syntax). This removes the only reason to posit the static syntactic structures determined by a conventional grammar, when viewed from a parsing point of view.

However, there is another argument in the fundamentals of conventional theory for a syntactic level of representation, and for the abstract grammar that lies behind it. This is based on the observation that parsing provides just one perspective on language. As this argument runs, production and parsing utilise similar kinds of knowledge yet apply them in quite different, even quite opposite, ways. This in itself is said to demonstrate the need for the knowledge in question to be expressed in some form that is independent of either form of processing. That is, there must be an abstract generative grammar which determines questions of well-formedness independently of any processing issues.

Marten (2002) and Cann *et al.* (forthcoming) observe that there is another way to view this situation. One might argue that production and parsing appear to make reference to similar kinds of knowledge because the one is parasitic on the other. The argument for an independent and therefore static grammar relies upon the notion that production and parsing are completely independent of each other and as such in some sense of equal theoretical status. However, evidence from child language acquisition, as well as the basic logic of how linguistic structure relates to meaning (according to theories like RT), suggest that production is in some sense dependent on parsing. That is, in producing utterances, we refer to our knowledge of how to interpret them. Cann *et al.* (forthcoming) discuss how this need not make production an unrealistically complex process.

Arguments regarding production do not play any further role in the present work, whose aim is to show how a parsing-based approach, by admitting the insights of pragmatic theory into grammatical analysis, facilitates wide-ranging and explanatory analyses of linguistic phenomena that are simply not available to other kinds of approach. I take this in itself to offer important evidence as to the coherence and desirability of the general approach, and refer the reader to

2.6 FORMAL AND INFORMAL ANALYSIS

Given the stated aim of distinguishing encoded, hence truly linguistic, contributions to meaning from those that are inferred on the basis of extra-linguistic capabilities and context, the question arises as to how much of the process of interpretation should be subject to formal modelling. On the whole, work in pragmatic frameworks like RT proceeds on the assumption that aspects of interpretation that are attributable to general cognitive processes need not be represented as part of a formal linguistic analysis. Instead, inferential contributions to meaning tend to be discussed informally, though their effects might be shown in formal semantic renditions of the propositional meanings that result. This approach contrasts with many others within linguistics, in which the formalisation of an entire analysis—whether the derivation of syntactic structure or the details of how it maps onto meaning—is often taken to be an important research goal. In general terms, my approach to formalisation in the present work follows the assumptions of RT in this respect, though I present a good deal more in the way of formal representations than is commonly found in the RT literature, as befits my concerns with the connotations of RT for syntactic and semantic theory and practice. Given the general tendency to value formalisation in linguistic analysis, the decision not to formalise the whole process of interpretation perhaps requires some justification.

One significant factor is simple practicality: the analytical work in this book is intended primarily to illustrate a set of broad theoretical issues and although to do so it must be reasonably convincing both in descriptive and explanatory terms, the emphasis is not on developing a complete, polished account of the data. Furthermore, it is unclear at this stage precisely how the kinds of encoded procedural meaning proposed in my analysis of Hungarian should be formalised. The existing techniques of Dynamic Syntax constitute an appropriate general framework, but would require a good deal of adaptation to accommodate the particular proposals in question[14]. Rather than risk losing the theoretical morals of the bigger story amid a mass of formalism, much of it novel, it seems preferable to get the main points across informally, where this seems adequate, and to employ formal techniques merely to bolster this and demonstrate the potential for further formalisation. In the context of current linguistic theory, I believe that this is more useful than the provision of quasi-mathematical proofs.

More importantly, however, there are serious theoretical motivations to limit the scope of any formalism employed and, moreover, philosophical reasons to believe that doing so in no way compromises the value of the enterprise. The theoretical issues relate to the nature of inferential processes as the effects of extra-linguistic cognitive capacities. Important parts of my analyses depend on the fact that extra-linguistic processes are seen to influence interpretation in significant

---

[14]It is important to note, however, that Dynamic Syntax is in principle a formal framework; hence, my comments in this section should not be taken as representative of the opinions of researchers in Dynamic Syntax.

ways, and extra-linguistic processes should obviously not be formalised as part of the internal mechanisms of a language. For this reason, providing a fully formal representation of a pathway from some linguistic expression to its interpretation might misrepresent the nature of the processes involved, many of which may be logically independent of each other.

It should, of course, be possible to represent an act of interpretation as the interaction of different processes, all of which would ideally be formalised. However, the sheer complexity of human inferential processing in context and the objects it works with—the ephemeral assumption schemata of individual minds, themselves only inferable on any given occasion—make this an unrealistic aim, at least given contemporary knowledge of and access to cognitive processes. It therefore seems more useful to work with the informal principles of a theory like RT, which are at least founded in reasoning from the best evidence we have, including a number of genuine conceptual necessities. The use of such principles, for all that they inevitably contain an element of conjecture, facilitates a kind of linguistic analysis that takes account of important extra-linguistic influences on the structure-meaning relationship. As such, it points to more psychologically plausible analyses than are likely from approaches that limit themselves to fully formalisable factors. In this situation, there is no reason to suppose that it is necessarily formalisation that clarifies things best.

One response to the complexity and regular unfalsifiability inherent to inferential pragmatics is simply to ignore this whole area of study, as a number of formal approaches have regularly done. However, as argued throughout this chapter and the previous one, and illustrated in later ones, this is of little scientific value: attempting to associate linguistic structure directly with meaning may well yield hypotheses which, for all their formal rigour, have little connection to the ways in which linguistic structure actually encodes and conveys meaning. It is surely more interesting and useful to produce analyses of a high degree of plausibility, given everything we know or can reasonably infer about cognition and communication, than to produce fully formalised analyses whose connection to the realities of cognitive processes is unclear.

In any case, formal rigour is neither the only nor necessarily the best way to make progress in science, as Ludlow (1992) points out[15]. Using examples from the history of the physical sciences and even mathematics itself, Ludlow shows that progress tends to be made with less than perfectly rigorous frameworks and that the mathematically soundest approaches even appear sometimes to stifle scientific advances (Ludlow quotes numerous epoch-making natural scientists on their frustrations with contemporaries who insist on absolute formal rigour). If my arguments regarding the structure of linguistic theory are even partially correct, then the basis of linguistic analysis—certainly anything involving the issue of meaning—is considerably less certain than that of any of the physical sciences at the relevant points in history. An over-emphasis on formal principles therefore represents a potentially dangerous attempt to run before we can walk.

---

[15]Ludlow's motivation is rather different to mine: he appears to be defending the looser aspects of Chomskyan (Principles and Parameters) formalism against the more rigorous formal standards of HPSG and LFG. However, in essence Ludlow's arguments apply at least as well to my more general point about the limits of formalism.

Such a conclusion may seem particularly unhelpful from the point of view of the computational linguist, who can only implement fully formalised, or formalisable, analyses. However, as argued in Chapter 1, section 1.2.1, the results of approaches that forgo formal rigour in favour of compatibility with the conditions in which natural language exists should be of interest to any computational linguist who is truly concerned with the nature of human languages. Even when the most productive computational linguistic techniques are drawn from other domains (such as the use of heavily stochastic methods), a good theoretical model of natural language can provide vital information, notably in explaining the limitations of computational models. Therefore, the immediate needs of computational linguistics do not reflect or justify any presumed need for thorough formalisation in theoretical linguistics.

Formal representations as such are of course in many ways desirable—they can help to clarify proposals even when they are less than truly rigorous, as well as potentially enhancing the status of a scientific hypothesis by making it falsifiable (and transparently so). The important thing is to bear in mind the "other things being equal" condition that should come with such a statement. There is in fact a considerable amount of formal analysis in this book, from Chapter 6 onwards, including a certain amount of discussion of the formal techniques employed, since representing the particular procedural meanings that I identify requires a novel synthesis of existing semantic proposals (the less formally-minded reader should not be put off by this, as I provide prose explanations of the important facets of all key representations).

Given the dynamic nature of the approach taken, there is no formal equivalent of the 'logical forms' of RT. Instead, partial representations of meaning, as achieved at key points during parsing, are shown and the ways in which they can be developed up to a full proposition is also demonstrated in formal language. This proves to give a sufficient degree of formalisation to allow genuine predictive hypotheses to be made.

Overall, the aim is to clarify a theoretical position and to show both the problems that justify it and the value of the kinds of analysis that it facilitates. Part of this demonstration is showing how what is currently informally expressed pragmatic argumentation can be integrated with formal representations of the semantic contributions of linguistic objects and how this is part of the construction of propositional meanings. These representations may in many cases be radically underspecified, but nevertheless can be seen to encapsulate empirical predictions. The more formal sections of this work therefore serve in part as an 'existence proof': useful, explanatory proposals can be produced through the right combination of 'radical pragmatic' argumentation, processing-based analysis of structure and formalised representations of linguistically encoded material and its effects.

2.7 Summary

This chapter provides an overview of the post-Gricean pragmatic framework Relevance Theory, thereby providing a theoretical basis to the discussion of inferential reasoning in context which forms a key part of the argumentation in the book as a whole. This foundation is used to develop arguments introduced in Chapter 1, regarding the view that should be taken on the relative contributions of linguistically encoded meaning and inference to the derivation of propositional meanings. Above all, the perspective derived from many mainstream frameworks, that inferential pragmatic processes can only provide certain kinds of embellishment to, or manipulations of, linguistically encoded propositional meanings is argued to be inconsistent with both empirical evidence and reasonable assumptions about the nature of the broader process of interpretation.

Apart from embedding these arguments in the established framework of Relevance Theory, this chapter discusses in particular their implications for syntactic analysis. The post-Gricean view on semantics and pragmatics entails that aspects of the use of language must be considered in any attempt simply to identify which aspects of meaning the grammar must directly account for. Given this, the possibility must be admitted that crucial inferences are triggered by certain partial representations of meaning, during the process of parsing a linguistic string. This means that, *contra* most work in Relevance Theory as well as syntax, encoded meanings should not be defined over complete syntactic representations (such as LFs). Instead, the relationship between linguistic structure and interpretation should be viewed from a dynamic perspective, in the particular sense that the construction of propositional meanings should be modelled in terms of building partial representations during the incremental parse of a string of words. This is backed up by the observation that hierarchical syntactic representations are not logically necessary, on the perfectly plausible assumption that linguistic objects encode significant amounts of procedural information.

The scene is now set for the presentation of detailed linguistic analysis, to show the need for the theoretical approach advocated here and its ability to deliver truly explanatory accounts of complex and apparently problematic data. To this end, the following chapter introduces the empirical phenomena that form the basis of the extended illustrative case study in Chapters 4–8 and provides a brief critical overview of existing approaches to them.

3

THE HUNGARIAN DATA

3.1 OVERVIEW

The remainder of this book constitutes an extended case-study of a phenomenon which I use to illustrate the theoretical points set out in Chapters 1 and 2: the so-called 'focus position' of Hungarian. This provides unusually clear exemplification of how the adoption of compositional semantic assumptions has pushed previous analyses in a particular direction, producing a popularly accepted form of analysis that is shown in Chapter 4 to be simply unsustainable empirically. The phenomenon is interesting not only because it shows an apparent case of a pragmatic notion, focus, being signalled syntactically, but also because of the complex and seemingly arbitrary interactions between the use of the 'focus position' and the distribution and interpretation of certain other elements of the sentence. In this chapter, the basic data are introduced, following which a brief critical overview of previous analyses is provided.

3.2 THE DATA

3.2.1 The basic positions of the Hungarian sentence

Word order in Hungarian, a language with rich case morphology, tends to signal discourse-related meanings rather than grammatical relations. This aspect of the language has received considerable attention within theoretical linguistics and many proposals have been put forward to characterise the syntactic and semantic properties that lie behind the observed variation in order and interpretation (see É. Kiss 1987, 2002; Kiefer & É. Kiss 1994, Puskás 2000, Bende-Farkas 2002 for thorough overviews). Indeed, Hungarian has become one of the best studied, within mainstream generative syntactic frameworks, of what were once thought of as 'free word order' languages (as evidenced by the dominance of work on Hungarian in major collections dealing with the phenomenon, such as Abraham & de Meij 1986, É. Kiss 1995b).

The basic linear template of a simple Hungarian sentence is given in (3.1) (whose basic form is attributable to É. Kiss 1987). As usual, parentheses indicate optionality and the Kleene star indicates that the phrase may appear zero or more times[1]. A somewhat contrived example with each possible position in this template instantiated is given in (3.2)[2]

(3.1)   (T[opic]P*) (Q[uantifier]P*) (Focus) V (XP*)

(3.2)   Péter 'mindenkinek a 'bulira   küldött egy meghívót.
        Péter everyone-DAT the party-for sent   an invitation-ACC
        'It's the party that Péter sent everyone an invitation for.'

É. Kiss (1987) identifies the necessarily specific interpretation of expressions found in the Topic position, which relates intuitively to their 'topicality' and sentence-initial position, in the sense of being the starting point of an utterance and logical subject of some subsequent predicative material. The so-called Quantifier Position does not in fact host only quantifiers, though it is most commonly associated with a certain class of quantified NP, for some of which this is the only possible pre-verbal position (see example (3.6) below and Chapter 5). To some extent, this should probably not be analysed as a single position at all, in any significant sense. It may host either topic-like logical subject material or material that is part of the 'comment' of a 'topic-comment' sentence and it is only structurally definable in contradistinction to the Topic and Focus positions: phrases associated with this position will always follow any necessarily sentence-initial topic element (such as a specific indefinite topic) and precede the Focus position. If the sentence contains no focused expression in the Focus position, an item in the Quantifier Position will appear immediately preceding the verb, but will be prosodically distinguished from a focused expression by the fact that the verb in this case will carry a pitch accent, whereas it does not when it follows an expression in Focus (as (3.2) shows). The position here called Focus is very much the principal concern of this work, though the Topic and Quantifier positions enter the discussion in Chapter 5.

Within the theoretical literature, a common approach to the analysis of discourse-related meaning is to postulate specialised syntactic projections to which expressions move—an idea that to a certain extent has spread from the literature on Hungarian to the analysis of other languages (É. Kiss 1995b, Rizzi 1997). Hence, the majority of recent analyses postulate Topic and Focus projections that host expressions to be interpreted as topics and foci (see É. Kiss 2002). On the face of it, the 'focus position' of Hungarian provides particularly strong evidence for the need to employ this 'discourse configurational' approach, rather than an approach that seeks

---

[1] I omit here one arguably distinct position, which has no direct connection to my concerns: the usually sentence-initial position of an optional 'contrastive topic', which is distinguished from other topics by rising intonation and an apparent narrow scope reading. For a detailed analysis of these, and discussion of whether they have a distinct syntactic position, see Gyuris (2002), É. Kiss & Gyuris (2003).

[2] A prime is used to indicate a pitch accent on the following word; a convention common in the Hungarian literature, which I will employ only when prosody is germane to the discussion at hand. According to Rosenthall (1992), topics do carry a kind of pitch accent, but this is distinct from those elsewhere in the sentence and in any case never affects the points that I argue, so I do not mark it in this way.

to derive discourse-related meaning from the cognitive impact of different linear orderings (as in Downing & Noonan 1995, for example). This is because focused expressions syntactically interact in precise ways with the distribution of numerous other items, which apparently have no direct information-structural significance, but bear complex relationships to other facets of meaning, such as negation, aspect and quantification. This leads to the assumption that abstract, hierarchical syntactic representations must lie behind the template in (3.1). Analyses of this kind are briefly reviewed in section 3.3, although the existence of abstract syntactic positions of this sort is clearly incompatible with the kind of analytical approach advocated in the previous chapters.

3.2.2 Immediately pre-verbal position

For the time being, I treat the immediately pre-verbal slot in (3.1) as truly a 'focus position' and describe just this use of it. However, I eventually argue that this is an unsustainable view. For this reason, I adopt hereafter the neutral label 'PV' (for 'pre-verbal') instead of 'Focus'.

The PV position has a number of features that distinguish it from the other non-verbal positions. For one thing, it is notably the only non-verbal position in (3.1) that can be filled only once per sentence. This is not unconnected to its distinctive relationship to the tensed verb: an expression in this position is always strictly adjacent to the verb[3]. The strictness of this relationship is shown particularly starkly in sentences with the future auxiliary *fog*. In what tends to be called a 'neutral sentence'—one that contains no pre-verbal focus or negation—the infinitive of a simple verb like *lát* 'see' precedes the auxiliary, with an unmarked reading, as in (3.3a). Yet even this, the contentful part of the main verbal predicate, cannot intervene between a focused expression and the tensed auxiliary, being forced into a post-verbal position in the presence of a focused expression, as (3.3b,c) show[4].

(3.3)   a.   Mari látni   fogja Jánost.
              Mari see-INF will   János-ACC
              'Mari will see János.'
      b.   Mari a   'távcsővel   fogja {látni   Jánost   / Jánost   látni}.
              Mari the binoculars-WITH will   see-INF JánosACC   János-ACC see-INF
              'It's with the binoculars that Mari will see János.'
      c.   *Mari a   'távcsővel   látni   fogja Jánost.
              Mari the binoculars-WITH see-INF will   János-ACC

---

[3]The are two items that could be said to intervene between an item that is in other ways recognisably in this position and the tensed verb. These are the negative particle *nem*, whose distribution is accounted for in Chapter 8, and the 'emphatic' particle *is*, meaning roughly 'also,even'. The latter appears to be able to encliticise to practically any expression and thus can be seen as part of the immediately pre-verbal expression, rather than truly intervening between it and the verb. As such, the behaviour of *is* is not immediately relevant to any of my major concerns and it is not analysed further in this book.

[4]The considerable significance of such data in ways hitherto ignored is discussed in Chapter 6.

Intended: 'It's with the binoculars that Mari will see János.'

In addition, a syntactically focused expression enters into a compound-like relationship with the verb on a prosodic level, by carrying a pitch accent and always preceding a destressed verb (making focus+V analysable as a phonological word). Indeed, all post-focus material is typically devoid of independent pitch accents (hence the pitch accent carried by a focused expression has been called 'eradicating stress'; see Kálmán 1985b). This is intuitively closely connected to the information-structural interpretation of this material, which is always presupposed, in some sense, in contrast to the asserted focus.

Prosody is thus one major indicator that an expression is in the PV position, rather than any other linearly pre-verbal slot. Often there is another diagnostic available, since there is a family of items that (in parallel to the infinitive in (3.3)) unmarkedly appear before the verb in a 'neutral' sentence, but postpose in the presence of a focused expression in PV. These items can be given the generic term 'verbal modifier' (henceforth VM). (3.4), which involves a so-called 'verbal prefix' VM (shown in bold in these examples), illustrates how VMs obligatorily postpose in the presence of either a focused expression or sentential negation[5].

(3.4)   a.   Kati **meg**evett egy almát.
                  Kati VM-ate   an   apple-ACC
                  'Kati ate an apple (up).'

         b.   Kati evett **meg** egy almát.
                  Kati ate   VM an   apple-ACC
                  'It's Kati who ate an apple (up).'

         c.   Kati (***meg**)evett egy almát.
                  Kati VM-ate   an   apple-ACC
                  Intended: 'It's Kati who ate an apple (up).'

         d.   Kati nem evett **meg** egy almát.
                  Kati not   ate   VM an   apple-ACC
                  'Kati didn't eat (up) an apple.'

         e.   Kati nem (***meg**)evett egy almát.
                  Kati not   VM-ate   an apple-ACC
                  Intended: 'Kati didn't eat (up) an apple.'

Like foci, pre-verbal VMs cannot be separated from the verb by anything other than the negative particle *nem* or the enclitic *is* 'even,also'. They also bear a pitch accent and precede a destressed verb. They do not cause the destressing of post-verbal material, but this is unsurprising,

---

[5]To avoid the complex issue of the precise contribution of the prefix *meg*, I gloss it only as 'VM'. I also indicate the VM status of non-prefix VMs in glosses, where this is significant to the point of the example (see below). As the English translations indicate, a prefix-bearing verb in Hungarian is often less marked than an English verb-particle combination, being translatable with the bare verb or with the particle added, according to context.

since post-verbal material is not presupposed in these cases—typically, VMs appear pre-verbally in 'neutral' sentences, which are classic 'topic>comment' structures, in information-structural terms (i.e. following an initial topic, all subsequent material is newly asserted, non-presupposed 'comment').

Most kinds of expression can undergo syntactic focusing, including sub-phrasal items. If an item from within a noun phrase is focused, the whole noun phrase appears in the PV position and stress is shifted within this to indicate the item in focus, as in (3.5).

(3.5)   Péter egy használt ′autót   vett.
        Péter a   used   car-ACC bought
        'It's a used CAR that Peter bought [not a used caravan, for example].'

Certain quantifiers cannot be syntactically focused, however. For example, a universal quantifier cannot appear in the PV position even to force a contrastive focus reading, as (3.6) shows.

(3.6)   a. Minden gyerek **meg**ijedt / *ijedt meg.
            every child VM-feared   feared VM
            'Every child got frightened.'

        b. ′Minden gyerek **meg**ijedt, nem csak a   lányok.
            every child   VM-feared not only the girls
            'EVERY child got frightened; not just the girls.'

        c. *′Minden gyerek ijedt **meg**, nem csak a   lányok.
            every child   feared VM   not only the girls
            Intended: 'EVERY child got frightened; not just the girls.'

This constraint is illustrated in more detail and analysed in Chapter 5.

3.2.3 The interpretation of focus

As the examples above show, the interpretation commonly associated with syntactically focused expressions is roughly comparable to an English *it*-cleft construction. Considerable effort has been put into characterising this interpretation in precise truth-conditional semantic terms in the literature on Hungarian, on the grounds that such a characterisation would indicate the contribution of the use of the focus position to the meaning of sentences in which it plays a part—in other words, what is syntactically encoded in this position[6]. I have already offered arguments against this methodology and the overarching purpose of the present chapter is to illustrate that it produces unsustainable results. Nevertheless, it is worthwhile here to note the semantic consensus, in order to appreciate just what is to be explained.

---

[6]For example, Szabolcsi (1981, 1983, 1994), Kenesei (1986), É. Kiss (1998a), Vallduví & Vilkuna (1998).

Despite the usual reference to a 'focus position', practically all analysts accept the line summed up by É. Kiss (2002, 77) as follows: "Semantically, the focus is more than merely non-presupposed information; it expresses exhaustive identification from among a set of alternatives". The precise meaning of 'exhaustive identification' varies slightly according to different semantic characterisations, but it is generally accepted that syntactic focus encodes the fact that the focused expression denotes a proper subset of a (contextually given) set of possible occupants of a certain slot in the propositional translation of the sentence, and that this is the *only* subset of this set that can fill this slot and make the proposition true (a formulation derived from Szabolcsi 1994).

Various tests have been proposed to distinguish this 'exhaustive' reading from other forms of assertion. One test, already mentioned in Chapter 1, is due to Szabolcsi (1981). This involves the logical incompatibility of an exhaustively interpreted reference to an individual and co-ordination of that individual and another. Hence, the fact that (3.7) is a felicitous utterance, rather than a logical contradiction, is taken to show that a special, exhaustive form of focus is at work.

(3.7) Nem 'Péter aludt a   padlón, hanem 'Péter és   Pál.
       not Péter slept the floor-on but   Péter and Pál
       'It wasn't Péter who slept on the floor; it was Péter and Pál.'

A similar test (reported by É. Kiss 2002 and attributed to Donka Farkas) is illustrated in (3.8).

(3.8) a. János 'Pétert   mutatta **be**   Marinak.
           János Péter-ACC   showed in(VM)   Mari-DAT
           'It's Péter that János introduced to Mari.'
       b. Nem, 'Zoltánt   is.
           no   Zoltán-ACC   also
           'No, he also introduced Zoltán to her.'

The fact that adding a further individual is introduced to the dialogue as a contradiction to the original statement (3.8a) (i.e. by using *nem* 'no') shows that the original statement is taken to exhaustively identify the people introduced to Mari by János[7]. This contrasts with the infelicity of such a reply when PV focus is not employed, as shown in (3.9).

(3.9) a. János **be**mutatta   Marinak   Pétert
           János in(VM)-showed   Mari-DAT Péter-ACC
           'János introduced Péter to Mari.'
       b. #Nem, 'Zoltánt   is.
           no   Zoltán-ACC   also
           'No, he also introduced Zoltán to her.'

---

[7] I have not found this use of *nem* ... *is* to be consistently licensed by PV focus for all speakers in all contexts, however.

As discussed in Chapter 4, much has been made of the fact that PV focus can in this way affect the logical relations between sentences and hence can be seen as a truth-conditional aspect of meaning.

The association of syntactic focusing with this specific interpretation has led to the more general claim that languages encode two distinct kinds of focus: one the 'merely non-presupposed' kind and one the logical, exhaustive kind. These may be associated with separate syntactic features (É. Kiss 1998a) or 'information packaging' procedures (Vallduví & Vilkuna 1998). This approach fails to consider that pragmatic factors may determine the two readings, leaving a common underlying notion of focus. That non-presupposed status is not sufficient to trigger syntactic focusing is undeniably true: after all, the stress-bearing post-topical material in a 'neutral' sentence is newly asserted, not presupposed[8]. The idea of encoded exhaustive focus, on the other hand, is rejected in Chapter 4.

3.2.4 Verbal modifiers

As mention above, in section 3.2.2, there are certain items that may appear in the Hungarian sentence, the so-called verbal modifiers (VMs), which unmarkedly occupy an immediately preverbal position, but postpose in the presence of a pre-verbal focused expression or negation. A diverse set of expressions shows this syntactic behaviour and therefore a wide variety of expressions may be thought of as VMs. This variety causes problems for many an analysis: there is no obvious way to link the common syntactic behaviour of all the VMs to a single interpretive feature (see É. Kiss to appear for a detailed presentation of the considerable semantic diversity of only a subset of the VMs).

The verbal prefixes are the most frequently discussed kind of VM. The majority of these have directional meanings, though this does not suffice to characterise the whole class. For one thing, even these prefixes frequently appear in semantically opaque combinations, such as *beolvas* (lit. 'in-read') 'tell off', *feltesz* (lit. 'up-put') 'assume', *berúg* (lit. 'in-kick') 'get drunk' (in this respect, they parallel the contribution of English directional particles to 'complex verbs' such as *let down* 'disappoint', *take off* 'imitate', *put out* 'inconvenience'). There are also prefixes that are associated with no such directional or locative meaning, at least in a non-figurative sense, a common example being *meg*, which is generally simply described as a 'perfectivising' or 'telicising' prefix (if any underlying conceptual semantic content can be given to *meg* at all, it is necessarily highly underspecified, perhaps best approximated as 'to completion').

Other kinds of VM include bare (i.e. determinerless) nominals in various cases, case-marked adjectives acting as resultative secondary predicates, and locative full NPs in certain contexts. A selection of these is illustrated in (3.10)–(3.12). These all follow the syntactic pattern illustrated

---

[8] One recent analysis nevertheless attempts to reunite the two at an abstract level of syntax: Puskás (2000) proposes that all new information moves into FP, often as the result of a series of complex and string-vacuous movements. This is difficult to reconcile with the encoding of exhaustive identification in a special focus feature, which Puskás also claims to adopt.

in (3.4) (it is simply a convention of Hungarian orthography to write prefix+V combinations as a single word, while leaving other VMs separate from the verb—although this does serve to emphasise the 'complex predicate' nature of VM+V combinations; see below).

(3.10) accusative bare nominal:

    a. Pisti levelet írt.
       Pisti letter-ACC wrote
       'Pisti wrote a letter.'

    b. Pisti írt levelet.
       Pisti wrote letter-ACC
       'It's Pisti who wrote a letter.'

(3.11) resultative case-marked adjective:

    a. Ferenc pirosra festette a kerítést.
       Ferenc red-to painted the fence-ACC
       'Ferenc painted the fence red.'

    b. Ferenc a kerítést festette pirosra.
       Ferenc the fence-ACC painted red-to
       'It's the fence that Ferenc painted red.'

(3.12) locative:

    a. Péter a szobában maradt.
       Péter the room-in stayed
       'Péter stayed in the room.'

    b. Péter maradt a szobában.
       Péter stayed the room-in
       'It's Péter who stayed in the room.'

The word order of the (a) examples, with the VM in PV, is typically associated with 'neutral' sentences, meaning that the interpretation is of a 'topic>comment' kind (that is, with the VM and all subsequent material together creating a broad 'comment' of newly asserted material), and that post-verbal material is correspondingly stress-bearing. It should be noted that the same word order can in fact be used to create contrastive focus on the content of the VM itself, if post-verbal material is destressed. For exemplification of this and discussion of some putative theoretical implications, see section 3.3.1, below.

The more significant general observation, however, is that VMs tend to have a non-focused interpretation while maintaining apparently the same structural relationship to the verb as that held by syntactically focused expressions. Indeed, not only are VMs able to appear in PV on an unmarked reading; they must. The post-verbal appearance of a VM always prompts some form of marked reading, even in the absence of an explicit focused expression or negation in PV (where this is possible). Two principal kinds of reading are associated with this word order, depending on prosody, as demonstrated in (3.13). (3.13a) is thought of as a progressivising construction, given the normally perfective interpretation of prefixed verbs, while (3.13b), with all post-verbal material destressed, is usually termed the 'existential' or 'evidential' reading, and is also usually described as an aspectual construction (though this is shown to be inappropriate in Chapter 8, section 8.2).

(3.13) a. János 'nyitotta 'ki   az 'autóját,   amikor 'odaérkeztem.
           János opened out(VM) the car-his-ACC when   there-arrived.1SG
           'János was opening his car when I got there.'
       b. János 'nyitotta **ki** az autóját   kulcs nélkül.
           János opened out the car-his-ACC key without
           'János has opened his car without a key before.'

These constructions have in the past been analysed as involving silent VM-like or focus-like operators in the PV position, to account for the post-verbal appearance of the overt VM. In Chapter 8, I will show that no such elements are required to explain either the form or interpretation of such sentences, which follow from the dynamic analysis of PV effects that I develop in Chapters 6 and 7.

Intuitively, the distribution of VMs—in particular their adjacency to the verb in 'neutral' sentences—is related to their forming complex predicates of various kinds when in combination with lexical verbs. The non-compositional meanings associated with some VM+V combinations are one indicator of this, as is the fact that a VM+V combination may have a different argument structure to that of the same lexical verb appearing on its own. For example, É. Kiss (2002, 56) notes that *olvas* 'read' is intransitive or transitive, whereas *elolvas* (lit. 'away-read') 'read, finish reading' and *átolvas* (lit. 'across-read') 'read through, skim' are obligatorily transitive, and the non-compositional *beolvas* (lit. 'in-read') 'tell off' takes a dative argument. VM+V complexes can also be the input to morphological processes, creating words like *feltétel* 'assumption', from *feltesz* (lit. 'up-put') 'assume' (see É. Kiss 1987, 65 for a parallel example with a bare nominal VM). Evidence of a syntactic nature comes from co-ordination: as Bende-Farkas (2002) notes, examples like (3.14) (presented by É. Kiss 2002, 60 for different reasons), which shows that a prefix VM cannot 'scope' over co-ordination, can be taken as evidence for the complex predicate nature of the VM+V combination.

(3.14) a. *János **fel**hívta   Marit   és olvasta neki   a   versét.
           János up(VM)-called Mari-ACC and read   her.DAT the poem-3SG-ACC
           Intended: 'János called Mari and read out his poem to her.'

b. János **fel**hívta Marit és **fel**olvasta neki a versét.
János up(VM)-called Mari-ACC and up(VM)-read her.DAT the poem-3SG-ACC
'János called Mari and read out his poem to her.'

The fact that a VM seems to form a unit with the accompanying verb yet is syntactically separable from it is thought of as "a notoriously difficult problem of describing Hungarian syntax" (É. Kiss 2002, 56). Meanwhile, the fact that it is the presence of apparently unrelated elements like negation and foci that cause this separation seemingly gives support to the assumption that this must be accounted for in terms of abstract syntactic structure. In Chapters 6–8 it is shown that this situation is in fact predicted by an analysis based entirely in processes of interpretation (although the precise mechanisms involved in different kinds of complex predicate formation remain to be worked out).

3.2.5 Other PV elements

In addition to the clear VM items shown in (3.10)–(3.12), certain adverbs show VM-like behaviour, in requiring to be in PV, without necessarily showing a clearly contrastive reading. On the other hand, these may co-occur with other VMs, which are consequently postposed. These adverbs typically have some form of negative meaning, in a broad sense (they include *alig* 'hardly', *hasztalan* 'in vain', *rosszul* 'badly'); (3.15) gives an example.

(3.15) a. *János rosszul **meg**oldotta a házi feladatot.
János badly VM-solved the home assignment

b. János rosszul oldotta **meg** a házi feladatot.
János badly solved VM the home assignment
'János did the homework wrong.'

Some other adverbs appear either in PV or the 'Quantifier Position', but show a reading in PV that is unavailable in the latter, as shown in (3.16).

(3.16) a. Az őr részegen **le**csukta a foglyokat.
the guard drunkenly down(VM)-shut the prisoners-ACC
'The guard locked up the prisoners (while he was) drunk.'

b. Az őr részegen csukta **le** a foglyokat.
the guard drunkenly shut down(VM) the prisoners-ACC
'The guard locked up the prisoners (while he was) drunk.'
or:
'The guard locked up the prisoners (while they were) drunk.'

The relationship of adverbs to PV is discussed in more detail in Chapter 7, section 7.4.2.

Another class of expression that occupies PV, causing the postposing of any VM, is that of question words (i.e. the equivalents of the English *Wh*-words). As it is not my aim in this book to analyse the interpretation of questions, I simply assume for present purposes that these question words are a sub-species of focus and do not discuss them further in their own right. Though a simplifying assumption, this is essentially in line with the view of focus developed in later chapters (see also Tsiplakou 1998 for a dynamic analysis of Greek that reaches this conclusion about question words).

Another class of expressions sometimes claimed in the literature to be distinct from foci though found in PV involves certain quantified noun phrases; in particular, those featuring modified numerals, such as *kevesebb, mint hat N* 'fewer than six N'. However, these cases are shown in Wedgwood (2002) and in Chapter 5 to be also simply a sub-type of focus, once the interpretation of foci is analysed appropriately.

3.3 THE FOCUS POSITION: SYNTACTIC ANALYSES

3.3.1 'Single position' analyses

The traditional grammar view of Hungarian characterised it as having 'free word order', on account of there existing grammatical sentences with all possible permutations of subject, verb and object, on one reading or another (see É. Kiss 1987, 17 for references). Early generative analyses (e.g. Horvath 1981, É. Kiss 1987), breaking with this view, were instrumental in developing the notion of 'discourse configurationality': the idea that at least some languages in which word order is relatively free with respect to the signalling of grammatical relations have fixed syntactic positions whose inhabitants must bear a certain feature that corresponds to some aspect of discourse-related meaning (É. Kiss 1995b).

É. Kiss's consistent position, for example, has been that the Hungarian VP has a flat structure, while hierarchical structure is projected above the VP, including distinguished positions for topic and focus, and a number of other functional projections, to which elements from within the VP may move. É. Kiss's earlier (1987, 1994) work exemplifies what has been termed a 'single position' analysis of focus and VMs. That is, it follows the intuition described above, that foci, negation and VMs appear to compete for the immediately pre-verbal position that I have been calling PV. This is also supported by the observation of Jo (1995) that the kind of items that have the status of VMs in Hungarian are known to interact with the position of syntactically focused expressions in a variety of other languages[9]. É. Kiss's approach within this work is perhaps the closest within the syntactic literature to the one that I develop within a dynamic approach

---

[9] Jo's own analysis of this involves postulating a feature that can switch between two values, [+focus] and [+pred.comp.] (for 'predicate complement') according to the kind of expression that is to appear there; a technical innovation that is of little explanatory value within the terms of syntactic theory, but which is interesting in the context of the present work for its underlying mechanism of the resolution of underspecification by online inferential processes.

in later chapters. Though 'single position' approaches are now generally considered untenable by syntacticians, the evidence cited against them (see below) depends upon the assumptions of conventional syntactic frameworks, and is thus irrelevant to my approach.

É. Kiss (1994) identifies the crucial pre-verbal position as Spec,VP. The motivations for movement to this position are somewhat mixed. The primary one is the VP is said to be inherently associated with a feature [+F(ocus)], which É. Kiss links to the VP being the logical predicate of the sentence—an idea that in some ways prefigures the arguments of Chapter 6 of the present work. É. Kiss's (1994) explanation of why VMs typically get a different (i.e. non-exhaustive) interpretation to other expressions in PV is interesting from my perspective, since it is essentially an inferential pragmatic account. Exhaustivity is said to result from applying the [+F] interpretation to an expression that denotes an individual entity, whereas the effect of this feature on a non-entity is simply 'identification'. VMs being neither entity-denoters nor, in an important sense, semantically independent of the verb, the effect of a VM occupying Spec,VP is to produce non-exhaustive focus on the VM+V combination. The context of utterance may still force an 'individuated' reading of the VM, however, by setting it into contrast with the semantics of other VMs, hence the possibility of also getting a contrastive focus reading from a pre-verbal VM.

Many aspects of this account re-emerge in the analysis developed in the present work: notably, the determination of exhaustivity by context, not stipulation; and the linking of the location of the focus position to the fact that VM+V complexes (and VM-less verbs in sentences without PV foci) typically represent the beginning of the focused part of the sentence (broadly construed; i.e. the 'comment'), which is linked in turn to the notion of predication. There are problems with É. Kiss's technical implementation of this, however. Above all, it is not clear why the prosody and interpretation of post-verbal constituents should be different when different expressions occupy Spec,VP: the explanation of the interpretation of [+V] VMs suggests that the VM+V complex should be interpreted as parallel to a focused individual, which would leave all post-verbal material destressed and presupposed. In fact, post-verbal material is stressed and 'in focus' in most sentences containing a VM in PV. It is also unclear precisely how the VM percolates its [+F] marking to the main verb with which it forms a complex predicate in a sentence containing an auxiliary, such as (3.17), in which the main verb is an infinitive with a variable post-auxiliary position, yet the VM still appears before the tensed verb (cf. (3.3), above).

(3.17) János **fel** fogja {olvasni a verseit / a verseit olvasni}.
János up(VM) will read-INF the poems.3SG-ACC the poems.3SG-ACC read-INF
'János will read out his poems.'

Furthermore, É. Kiss (1994) relies on alternative or auxiliary explanations for the appearance in PV of certain other expressions. Certain items, such as some 'negative' quantifiers and adverbs, are said to bear no [+F] feature, but rather to move to Spec,VP to take scope over the

VP (an idea that clearly cannot carry over into a Minimalist analysis)[10]. The picture is further complicated by the notion that verbal prefixes are in fact also analysed as aspectual operators that have to be in Spec,VP to take the appropriate scope. Since focus itself is referred to as taking scope and possibly being an operator, Spec,VP appears to be in some sense an all-purpose 'operator position'—an idea that is proposed more explicitly in É. Kiss (1987, 52). The problem then becomes the basis on which different items should be declared to have 'operator' status; this begins to seems quite *ad hoc*, if all the different classes of VMs are to be included, while the explanation appears fragmented if not.

Whatever the virtues or problems to be found in the particular proposals of É. Kiss (1987, 1994), the whole idea of 'single position' analyses has since come in for other criticisms, which have led to the total abandonment of this approach in recent years by generative syntacticians. Farkas (1986) noted various objections early on; Piñón (1992) adds others.

Among these are the simple fact that under a 'single position' analysis the position in question, in hosting VMs, negation and exhaustively focused expressions, does not appear to relate to a consistent semantic interpretation, as would be required under a compositional view of the syntax-semantics interface. Though in principle there is no *a priori* reason to expect this kind of invariant interpretation for each syntactic position, outside of a strictly Montagovian analysis, this is a more or less implicit assumption of most generative work, as discussed in the previous chapters.

Piñón (1992) sees the ability to contrastively focus VMs, as in (3.18b), as an argument against the 'single position' approach. Again, this implicitly rests upon the assumption that all syntactic positions must relate to an invariant truth-conditional aspect of the overall interpretation of a sentence, the argument being that the VM in (3.18b) must be in a different position to that in (3.18a) in order to account for its different information-structural interpretation.

(3.18) a. Mari 'felment   a 'lépcsőn.
           Mari up(VM)-went the stair-on
           'Mari went up the stairs.'

      b. Mari 'felment   a lépcsőn, nem 'le.
           Mari up(VM)-went the stair-on not   down(VM)
           'Mari went UP the stairs, not DOWN them.'

Other challenges to 'single position' analyses of PV phenomena are more straightforwardly syntactic. Farkas (1986) concentrates in particular on evidence from co-ordination. As shown above in (3.14), co-ordination of the kind *[VM [[V XP] *and* [V XP]]] is not possible. Co-ordinating the VM+V combination, as in [[[VM V] *and* [VM V]] XP], is possible, in line with the idea that the VM+V combination is in some sense a complex predicate—an example is shown

---

[10]Note that more recent approaches, involving encoded exhaustivity, are no better equipped to deal with this kind of PV item, which can only be declared to be inherently [+Focus], in a syntactic sense, without producing the expected reading; see É. Kiss (2002, 90), for example.

in (3.19a). On the other hand, a pre-verbal focus can 'take scope' over a co-ordination, allowing the structure disallowed with VMs, [focus [[V XP] *and* [V XP]]], as in (3.19b).

(3.19) a. János [**össze**szedte és **össze**rakta] a széttépett levelet.
János together(VM)-picked and together(VM)-pieced the torn.up letter-ACC
'János collected and pieced together the torn up letter.'

b. János a Mari levelét [tépte **szét** tegnap este és rakta **össze** ma reggel].
János the Mari letter-3SG-ACC tore up(VM) yesterday evening and pieced together(VM) today morning
'It's Mari's letter that János tore up last night and pieced together this morning.'

Facts from ellipsis, as in (3.20), have similar implications.

(3.20) a. *János nem sokáig [tanulta a verset]$_i$, de meg e_i
János not long learnt the poemACC but VM
Intended: (??)'János hasn't been learning the poem long but he has [i.e. learnt it].'

b. Nem 'János [tudja a verset]$_i$, hanem 'Péter e_i
not János knows the poem but Péter
'It's not János who knows the poem, but Péter.'

In mainstream syntactic theory this must be taken as evidence for different syntactic structures and therefore most likely for a difference in the pre-verbal positions of foci and VMs. Note, however, that complex predicate formation is a semantic operation as well as syntactic (though in precisely what sense and to what extent this is true in either direction must be open to debate). The reasons why (3.14a) and (3.20a) are ruled out need not be purely a matter of abstract syntactic structure, therefore. It is worth noting in this regard that the English translations of (3.20a,b) differ in acceptability/grammaticality in parallel with the Hungarian grammaticality judgements, even though English clearly does not feature the same syntactic configurations (while the examples are due to É. Kiss 2002, the judgement on the English translation is my own—and if anything is understated).

Perhaps most damningly, Piñón points out that in any case not all PV items can be viewed as 'competing' with each other for a single underlying syntactic position. Negation, like foci, causes VMs to postpose, yet the negative particle *nem* can co-occur with pre-verbal foci, with different readings, depending whether it precedes or follows them, as in (3.21).

(3.21) a. Nem Ferenc ment **le** a lépcsőn.
not Ferenc went down(VM) the stair-on
'It wasn't Ferenc who went down the stairs.'
b. 'Ferenc nem ment **le** a lépcsőn.
Ferenc not went down(VM) the stair-on
'It was Ferenc who didn't go down the stairs.'

Like the other arguments presented above, this is genuinely problematic for any 'single position' account, in the strict sense, within the assumptions of conventional syntactic frameworks, but it does not preclude the possibility of a unified analysis of the PV phenomenon. The dynamic analysis that I develop in the later chapters of this book concentrates on the notion of how PV as a relationship between different items and the tensed verb, rather than an abstract position as such, contributes to different interpretations. This allows for the different characteristics of different PV items to have different effects, so that some may indeed be compatible with each other pre-verbally, while others exclude each other.

3.3.2 The verb movement analysis

The arguments against a single pre-verbal position for mutually exclusive PV elements being insurmountable within mainstream syntactic frameworks, separate positions for VMs, foci and negation have to be postulated in syntactic analyses. This requires some alternative explanation of the postposing of VMs in the presence of foci or negation. One highly influential proposal, to which a number of linguists still adhere is that of Bródy (1990, 1995), that V>VM order is caused not by postposing of the VM (or the VM failing to move) but by leftward movement of the verb, past the VM. In other words, the VM is in the same underlying position when pre-verbal in 'neutral' sentences and when post-verbal in 'non-neutral' sentences (whether this is considered to be its base-generated position or one that it moves to prior to V-movement). The explanation of post-verbal VM position is therefore somewhat parallel to the clause-final stranding of verbal particles in German main clauses, according to the V-movement analysis of V2 effects (van Riemsdijk 1982).

This analysis involves the assumption of an FP projection (as originally suggested for Hungarian by Choe 1989), that is associated with an exhaustive focus reading and hosts syntactically focused constituents in its specifier position. The verb is said to move to the head of FP to check a [+F] feature, which must be assumed to be associated with the verb somehow. This accounts for both the apparent postposing of VMs in the presence of focus and the strict adjacency of focus and verb. That is, (3.22) is derived as in (3.23) (ignoring here the means by which *János* comes to appear in T[opic]P).

(3.22) János Marit hívta meg.
János Mari-ACC called VM
'It's Mari who János invited.'

(3.23) [$_{TP}$ János [$_{FP}$ Marit$_i$ [$_{F'}$ hívta$_j$ [$_{VP}$ fel [$_{V'}$ t$_j$ [$_{NP}$ t$_i$]]]]]]

There are problems with the verb-movement approach, however. É. Kiss (2002) brings a theory-internal objection: whatever the precise analysis of the pre-verbal position of VMs (É. Kiss assumes them to be the specifier of an Asp[ect]P projection), they are generally considered to be incorporated into the verb in some way. Bródy's analysis therefore requires some process of 'excorporation' in order for the verb to move and strand the VM, and such a process is considered theoretically problematic. Alternatively, one could say that incorporation is somehow blocked by the presence of a focused constituent, but there is no clear motivation for this and it would in any case make for a much less elegant and general explanation. Koopman & Szabolcsi (2000) note a more straightforward empirical problem: the verb-movement account predicts that a post-verbal VM should always immediately follow the verb. While this may be the position of the postposed VM, which is generally preferred as close as possible to a finite main verb, it is not the only grammatical possibility: the VM may appear in any post-verbal position, as (3.24) shows (the judgements are due to É. Kiss 2002).

(3.24) a. Pétert   mutatta **be**   János Marinak.
            Péter-ACC showed in(VM) János Mari-DAT

        b. Pétert   mutatta János **be**   Marinak.
            Péter-ACC showed János in(VM) Mari-DAT

        c. (?) Pétert   mutatta János Marinak   **be**.
            Péter-ACC showed János Mari-DAT in(VM)
            'It was Péter that János introduced to Mari.'

This is particularly problematic in the case of sentences containing a tensed auxiliary. Recall from (3.17) that in the 'neutral' version of such sentences, the VM is found, as usual, to the immediate left of the tensed verb—hence to the left of the auxiliary, as in (3.25a). When a focused expression fills this position, a prefix VM is visibly not simply 'stranded' post-verbally, but must appear to the left of the main verb infinitive, as shown in (3.25b,c).

(3.25) a. Mari **be**   fog akarni   menni.
            Mari in(VM) will want-INF go-INF
            'Mari will want to go in.'

        b. *Mari fog **be**   akarni   menni.
            Mari will in(VM) want-INF go-INF
            Intended: 'It's Mari who will want to go in.'

        c. Mari fog akarni   **be**menni.
            Mari will want-INF in(VM)   go-INF
            'It's Mari who will want to go in.'

One way to deal with this would be to assume that (3.25c), rather than (3.25a), represents the underlying position of the VM—that is, that VMs always occur to the left of the main verb, prior to verb movement. This makes sentences with finite main verbs parallel to those with finite auxiliaries, in this sense, but it means admitting that the VM occupies a different position in 'neutral' and 'non-neutral' versions of the latter, which of course removes the basis of the verb-movement analysis. A special and apparently rather unconstrained process of 'VM-climbing' then has to be introduced to account for the pre-auxiliary position of VMs in sentences like (3.25a). If this is maintained alongside verb-movement with finite main verbs, then the analysis fails to reflect in a unitary fashion the simplest possible generalisation about the PV data: that VMs, foci and negation precede the tensed verb[11].

3.3.3 Independent movement to multiple PV positions

If neither a 'single position' analysis nor a 'VM-stranding' analysis is viable, the remaining mode of explanation within a conventional syntactic analysis is the idea that foci and VMs each move to different pre-verbal positions, but for some reason the one blocks the movement of the other. É. Kiss (2002) proposes that VMs move to AspP, which is projected above VP as an alternative to the projection of FP. While this may avoid the particular syntactic objections to the original 'single position' kind of analysis, it is clearly not highly explanatory (cf. Jo's (1995) mutable feature, mentioned above); indeed, it is essentially no more than a re-statement of the data in Minimalist vocabulary. Furthermore, É. Kiss's (2002) analysis of certain other phenomena appears to rely on the co-occurrence of FP and AspP (see É. Kiss 2002, 66, and Chapter 8, section 8.2.2 of the present work). In fact, the notion that an AspP projection could account for the behaviour of the whole disparate class of VMs is rather problematic, as É. Kiss recognises in more recent work (to appear) (see Chapter 8).

A quite different kind of account is offered by Dalmi (1998, 2000) and Szendrői (2003), who give a non-syntactic motivation for the movement of either focus or VM to a pre-verbal position. Both argue, though in different ways, that prosodic requirements lie behind the significance of the immediately pre-verbal position.

Dalmi's account postulates a set of 'operators', including exhaustive focus, negation and the EXIST and PROG 'aspectual operators' said to be responsible for sentences like those in (3.13), all of which are available via their respective functional projections in the pre-verbal field. She also assumes a constraint on phonological phrasing that requires some item to precede the verb and carry a pitch accent. If none of the aforementioned operators is instantiated, a

---

[11] Koopman & Szabolcsi (2000) reject the verb-movement analysis altogether and promote the 'VM-climbing' idea as one aspect of a highly abstract and complex system of syntactic machinery, involving a number of unconventional assumptions about constraints on syntactic models. This is intended to account primarily for ordering restrictions on sequences of post-auxiliary infinitival verbs; a matter well beyond the scope of this book, which is not obviously more than tangentially connected to the basic question of how PV items interact with each other and with the tensed verb.

VM incorporates into the verb to occupy the position that must carry a pitch accent. This is problematic in a number of ways. First, it is not at all clear that Dalmi's operators form a natural class, as she claims: simply calling something an operator does not capture any essential characteristic of either its contribution to interpretation or the reasons why this should relate to particular syntactic behaviours. The danger inherent in viewing the postulation of an operator as a form of explanation is discussed in more detail in Chapter 8, section 8.2 in relation to EXIST and PROG, and is also implicit in the discussion of the nature of PV focus in Chapter 4. Second (a theory-internal point), as Koopman & Szabolcsi (2000) point out, the fact that full XPs can be VMs, as in (3.12), casts doubt on the idea that VM position is the result of a 'last resort' process of the incorporation of syntactic heads.

In addition, the phonological side of Dalmi's account requires a number of *ad hoc* assumptions to make it work. For instance, the silent operators EXIST and PROG must be assumed to permit the pitch accent that otherwise must be pre-verbal to be shifted onto the verb itself. This is potentially not too damaging—the special interpretations with which they are associated could perhaps be said to justify such an operation—but there are of course VM-less verbs that allow for a pragmatically unmarked interpretation in which they themselves carry primary stress, as in a simple sentence like (3.26).

(3.26) Mari 'szereti 'Jánost.
Mari loves János-ACC
'Mari loves János.'

To account for these cases, Dalmi is forced to assume that such verbs appear with another silent operator in AspP, which shifts stress onto the verb.

Szendrői's (2001, 2003) analysis avoids most of these problems, as it effectively views the relationship between prosodic structure and PV effects from the opposite perspective: rather than a pre-verbal position having to be filled, the canonical position of the verb is associated with primary stress, and foci are forced by an interface requirement to move to acquire primary stress. This has the advantage of explaining the uniqueness of the syntactic focus position without recourse to any kind of stipulation of a syntactic nature: as there is only one location of primary, or 'nuclear', stress in each sentence, there can be only one expression bearing it as a result of movement. VMs are assumed to be *in situ* when pre-verbal. A functional projection is assumed to be projected to provide a landing place for any focus and this in turn triggers verb movement, which is argued to be required (for theory-internal reasons) to license the functional head. This yields the order focus>V>VM, ultimately in a comparable way to Bródy's feature-driven analysis. This means that Szendrői's account is of the kind described in section 3.3.2, requiring both verb-movement and 'VM-climbing' and thus losing a unitary analysis of the generalisation that VMs precede the tensed verb.

Szendrői's particular version of 'VM-climbing' has the curious status of a syntactic operation that exists not to allow the moved expression to take stress, as in the case of her account of focus movement, but in order to prevent another item from taking stress: specifically, the auxiliary verb (e.g. *fog* in (3.17)). Szendrői notes, following work by Komlósy (1992) that such verbs can bear primary stress only on a marked reading. It is not clear, however, why this should lead to the postulation of any special process to prevent them bearing stress. As shown in Chapter 8, section 8.2, the inability of such verbs to appear bearing stress in a 'neutral' sentence (i.e. with a 'topic>comment' reading) is attributable entirely to semantic and pragmatic factors. There is no reason to believe that the distribution of other items is in any way determined by this independently explicable matter.

In addition, as Szendrői (2003) recognises, the stressed based focus-movement analysis meets an empirical problem in the shape of sentences like (3.6b), repeated here as (3.27), in which contrastive focus that as usual carries the primary stress of the sentence fails to induce V>VM order.

(3.27) 'Minden gyerek **meg**ijedt, nem csak a lányok.
         every   child   VM-feared not only the girls
        'EVERY child got frightened; not just the girls.'

While this phenomenon requires some degree of *ad hoc* explanation in all frameworks, the stress-based analysis makes it particularly unexpected. In my analysis (see Chapter 5), this impossibility of the universally quantified NP in (3.27) occupying PV is predicted by the interpretive procedures associated with this position—procedures that are involved in the explanation of the use of PV for exhaustive focus in other cases. The exceptional status of (3.27) is thus forced by the grammar and not a puzzle for the analyst.

3.4 SUMMARY: LOOKING BEYOND CONVENTIONAL SYNTACTIC ANALYSIS

While the brief survey in the preceding section is far from comprehensive, it covers the main trends in the analysis of PV phenomena under mainstream syntactic approaches. It is clear that while each of these modes of analysis points to certain insights, none successfully explains the relation between VMs, syntactic foci, and items like the negative particle *nem*, even in terms of simply accounting for their mutual exclusivity in PV. Approaches that invoke phonological factors seem in some ways to offer potentially more coherent explanations, by relying not only on the tools of syntactic theory, but these fall short of producing a truly general account, requiring at least two main forms of explanation to cover the full range of relevant data, including auxiliary constructions and cases in which VM-less verbs take stress.

Even to achieve the degree of descriptive adequacy that they do possess, all of these syntactic accounts rely on a considerable number of highly abstract elements, many of which in effect exist just to encode semantic effects. The most obvious of these is the notion of focus itself, which is generally assumed to be encoded directly as an exhaustivity operator, via some specialised syntactic machinery. There is little discussion to be found of the differing impact of sentences containing syntactically focused expressions in different contexts (Szendrői 2003 is a notable exception in this regard), let alone whether this may at some level relate to the interpretation of other expressions, such as VMs and VM-less verbs. Indeed, this last question is not even entertained as a possible line of enquiry in most of these approaches, despite the fact that É. Kiss's early work (1987, 1994) gives reason to believe that it might be fruitful.

As argued in the previous chapters, I believe that the kind of limitations apparent in these analyses are to a great extent inherent in the assumptions of mainstream syntactic theory and in the relationship to meaning that it is assumed to bear. These assumptions encapsulate a view that is both too optimistic about the directness of the relationship between the syntactic structures and semantic formulae and too pessimistic about our ability to investigate a broader conception of interpretation in a rational way. Only by going beyond strict notions of compositional semantics and static representations of syntactic structure can phenomena like the interaction of PV elements in Hungarian be truly explained in a parsimonious fashion. This crucially involves investigating the boundary between encoded and inferred meaning, and thus ultimately relies on consideration of pragmatic theory to explain syntactic effects.

4

FOCUS AND GRAMMAR

4.1 OVERVIEW

As hinted in previous chapters, my analysis of the PV position of Hungarian eschews the idea that it is simply a dedicated 'focus position' of any kind. Nonetheless, the discussion in this chapter is limited to the use of this position to convey a certain kind of focus reading and to the relationship between this particular reading and more general ideas about focus. This use of PV is the one that is recognised throughout the literature, and therefore a good place to start in re-assessing the nature of the position. Furthermore, the illustration of key theoretical ideas using PV, as promised in the previous chapters, revolves around the analysis of exhaustive focus readings. Hence, a number of important points arise from consideration of this facet of Hungarian PV alone. Subsequent chapters broaden the discussion to show how the PV position can be conceptualised in new ways that make it more than a 'focus position'—resulting in an analysis with unusually wide-ranging application within the grammar of Hungarian.

The key theoretical point illustrated in this chapter is the distorting impact and ultimate incoherence of approaches to natural languages that assume the compositionality of truth-conditional meanings (and of near-compositional approaches, which I have argued to be incoherent in any case). The structure of the central argument, as set out in sections 4.4 and 4.5, can be summarised as follows:

- The compositional approach depends upon the assumption that any correspondence between a change in the syntactic structure of a sentence and a change in the truth conditions it expresses provides evidence for the encoding of the relevant contribution to truth conditions in the relevant part of the syntax.

- The use of the Hungarian 'focus position' can be shown to affect truth conditions through the addition of an 'exhaustive focus' reading.

- The compositional approach therefore predicts that the exhaustive focus reading must be directly encoded in the syntax of the 'focus position'.

96 *Shifting the Focus*

- It can be demonstrated empirically that this position does not encode the exhaustive focus reading: the syntactic structure in question can be employed without producing this meaning. Furthermore, assuming encoding of the exhaustive reading leaves many syntactic and interpretive facts about the construction unexplained.

- Therefore, intuitions regarding correspondences between truth-conditional meaning and syntactic structure do not provide a reliable basis for deducing the encoded content of the syntax.

- The case of Hungarian exhaustive focus therefore shows the fundamental assumptions of a compositionally-based approach to be unsustainable.

- Conversely, the possibility that extra-grammatical factors affect truth-conditional meaning must therefore be admitted, opening up whole new modes of analysis.

Filling in the details of this argument inevitably requires a certain amount of background discussion. The very idea of focus and its relationship to exhaustivity must be investigated and suitable terminology must be introduced to facilitate discussion of these matters. To this end, this chapter begins with some comments regarding the notion of focus, including very brief reviews of existing approaches to focus, where these make reference to some important or illuminating aspect of the phenomenon.

4.2 THE BROADER NOTION OF FOCUS

The kind of focus associated with the Hungarian PV position is generally argued not to be the same as that expressed by phonological means in English, nor anything that could be defined simply in terms of newness or any similar discourse-based definition. As such, one might not expect general 'theories of focus' to be of great use in approaching the PV phenomenon. Furthermore, my aim here is not to develop any general, cross-linguistic theory of focus, but rather to concentrate on what is useful for the analysis of the Hungarian PV position. However, it is also my aim to challenge the accepted view of the encoded semantics of PV, in the course of which I argue that there are more similarities between English focus-by-pitch-accent and Hungarian PV focus than are commonly recognised. It is therefore worth considering in broad outline what is usually referred to as focus, along with some of the main ideas emerging from the literature on focus which are of use in the description of focus readings in Hungarian and inform the subsequent discussion of the Hungarian data.

4.2.1 The meaning of 'focus'

The intuition underlying all work on focus is that utterances that otherwise appear to convey the same basic message in some sense differ in meaning according to indications of how the information in the utterance is structured; or, to put it another way, according to indications of the perspective that the speaker invites the addressee to take on different parts of the utterance. The analysis of focus in the existing literature typically begins with the observation that English sentences containing identical words identically ordered can carry different meanings according to the placement of certain pitch accents, which are taken to indicate which part of the sentence carries focus, in some abstract sense (usually thought of as a grammatical focus feature). For example, (4.1a–c) intuitively have different meanings, at least in the sense that they are felicitous in different kinds of context[1].

(4.1)   a.   John invited JILL.

   b.   John INVITED Jill.

   c.   JOHN invited Jill.

How to characterise the precise kind of meaning contrast involved is a matter of debate, but it is commonly approached by observing the different *Wh*-questions to which a given utterance would be a felicitous response. This is regularly a quite clear-cut matter, as (4.2) illustrates.

(4.2)   a.   Who did John invite?
             John invited JILL.
             #JOHN invited Jill.

   b.   Who invited Jill?
        #John invited JILL
        JOHN invited Jill.

The *Wh*-question test also indicates one of the most common intuitive and analytical observations about focus: the idea that it corresponds to the 'new information' in an utterance (here, that which is not included in the question to which the utterance provides a felicitous answer). However, there seems to be more to focus. Another common observation is that focus is associated with a sense of contrast: (4.1c) seems to suggest that John, rather than some other possible inviter or inviters, invited Jill, while (4.1b) seems to contrast the assertion that John invited Jill with some other possible relationship between the two participants (such as John excluding Jill from the event in question, or perhaps *merely* inviting her, contrasted with arranging to meet and accompany her somewhere). For some analysts, this intuitive sense of contrast is something inherent to the phenomenon of focus and should be accounted for in any analysis of it (e.g. Glanzberg 2005); others, such as É. Kiss (1998a), argue that the information-providing part

---

[1] Small caps on this occasion do signal the location of the primary, H*+L (falling) pitch accent, as this is assumed to equate to the location of any more abstract kind of focus in these particular examples (although a full discussion of English focus-by-prosody would have to include the possibility of 'focus projection' in the case of (4.1a); see Ladd 1996 and cf. example (4.4), below).

of focus readings is quite separate from any contrastive meaning, of which there are arguably various kinds.

While these introductory comments give some idea of the main ideas behind the treatment of focus as an individual phenomenon, the use of the word 'focus'—and a host of related terms from the domain of information structure—is notoriously variable in linguistic analysis. This in part reflects a variety of theoretical perspectives on the place of this kind of phenomenon in relation to grammatical modules. Within both 'formalist' and 'functionalist' literature, one may find information-structural properties treated either as being encoded in the grammar of certain (or even all) languages, or as being strictly extra-grammatical. Within approaches that locate these properties within the grammar, this may be a matter of the use of syntactic machinery, like features and projections (É. Kiss 1995b), or may involve the assumption of separate, specialised components of the grammar to deal with 'information packaging' (Vallduví 1992, Erteschik-Shir 1997; see section 4.2.2). 'Focus' may be strictly defined in semantic terms, as in Rooth's (1992) 'alternative semantics' approach; in 'formal pragmatic' terms, as in the 'discourse structure' approach of Roberts (1996) or the File Change Semantics approach of Vallduví (1992); or it may refer to more intuitive concepts such as 'newness' or 'assertion'.

There is one area of potential confusion arising from the uses of the word 'focus' that can be prevented from the outset: that caused by the use of the term 'focus' to refer to both a property of interpretations (and/or its syntactic encoding) and the phonological phenomenon of primary stress (where the latter may or may not be seen as a straightforward signal of the former). I shall reserve the word 'focus' for the interpretive domain, using unambiguously phonological terminology ('stress', 'pitch accent') when referring to prosodic phenomena[2].

4.2.2 Focus and the encoded/inferred distinction

Whatever one's precise definition of focus (discounting phonological definitions), it must have something to do with the perspective of the language user on certain parts of the information contained in an utterance. In this respect, the notion of focus is inseparable from the use of language—from context, in the broad, psychological sense employed in RT. It follows that the study of focus, more obviously than in many other aspects of the grammar, must involve careful consideration of precisely what is linguistically encoded and what derived from the application of general cognitive principles. The problem for any attempt to identify the encoded semantics of focus (assuming this is possible at all) is therefore parallel to the more general problem of determining the scope of syntactic theory, as discussed in Chapter 2. Attempting to match 'the semantic contribution of focus' directly with the linguistic phenomena that appear to express focus leaves open the real danger of assuming certain aspects of meaning to be part of the burden of the grammar, when they may be properly attributable to other factors, and/or of consigning some aspects of meaning to 'the pragmatic wastebasket' because of the limits of one's theory,

---

[2]For a comprehensive overview of different terminological distinctions within the study of information structure, relating to different theoretical perspectives, see Vallduví (1992), von Heusinger (2002).

rather than on any principled grounds.

However, this kind of direct matching of structures and observable semantic effects is the professed basis of some influential approaches to focus-related phenomena, as shown in the following description of an overall research programme from Rooth (1996, 275):

> We somehow modify our way of modeling the semantics of phrases so that phrases differing in the location of focus have different semantic values. We then state semantic and pragmatic rules for focus-sensitive constructions and discourse configurations in terms of such focus-influenced semantic values.

Rooth does here at least make reference to both semantics and pragmatics, though talk of 'pragmatic rules' implies some form of encoding, rather than active consideration of inferential processes. Given the inherently context-related nature of the very idea of focus, there is every reason to believe that the intuitive or logically representable effects of focus-related constructions are derived in part on the basis of inferences drawn over somewhat more basic, possibly procedural, encoded meanings. As in other areas of the grammar, the crucial question may not be how to construct rules to get from linguistic structures to observed meanings, but rather what kind of encoded meaning is necessary to trigger the inferential derivation of these meanings in appropriate contextual conditions.

The majority of existing approaches to focus in effect simply assume one or other of its observable effects to be its encoded meaning (this includes some procedural approaches; see below). In doing so, many of these approaches highlight significant aspects of the interpretation of focus-related phenomena, which are of descriptive use in the analysis that I propose in this chapter and in Chapter 6, but fail to identify what is truly attributable directly to the grammar, at least in the case of a phenomenon like Hungarian PV position.

One popular idea is that the fundamental function of any linguistic indication of focus is to partition a sentence into a focused part and a background part. This is found in a long-standing idea within the 'functionalist' literature that focused expressions convey the fact that they are the 'new' information in the sentence, while background expressions convey their own 'givenness' (see, for example, the papers in Downing & Noonan 1995). This throws up the question of what 'new' and 'given' really mean and how such ideas should be integrated into a more formal analysis of encoded semantics and its relationship to pragmatic inference.

One formalisation of these broad ideas may be found in Vallduví's (1992) 'information packaging' analysis, which uses File Change Semantics to model manipulations of a mental database (see also the closely related proposals of Erteschik-Shir 1997). Information-structural primitives like focus are given procedural semantics, in terms of operations to be performed on this mental database. Thus, a topic (or 'Link', in Vallduví's terminology) opens up an entry in the database, while a focused expression writes some information under the appropriate heading. This kind of approach undoubtedly models an important part of the process of interpreting information-structural phenomena, but it is unclear how it could be made to fit with the grammar of a language like Hungarian. Vallduví and Erteschik-Shir both envisage special post-syntactic 'information packaging' modules of the grammar, but this does not seem to be an option with Hungarian, where, as noted in Chapter 3, the structure of PV is inseparable from other, apparently 'core syntactic' operations. In any case, separating information structure from the rest of the grammar seems a quite *ad hoc* move and the assumption of a whole new component of the grammar is decidedly unparsimonious from a broader theoretical perspective. It seems preferable both for these reasons and in terms of creating a plausible model of processing to stick to the more conventional picture, with a single process of decoding the information provided by the lexicon and grammar—which, in a post-Gricean world, may subsequently be heavily enriched by inferential processes. Ultimately, the manipulation of a mental database remains an *effect* of focus-related linguistic phenomena; there is no particular reason to assume that this effect equates to the content of such phenomena.

Another approach that views the essential function of focus as being the introduction of a partition of the sentence, in this case of a more conventionally denotational semantic kind, is 'structured meaning semantics' (see von Stechow 1991a, von Stechow 1991b, Kratzer 1991, Rooth 1996 for overviews and discussion). Under this approach, focus induces a partition of sentence semantics into (i) the value of the focused item itself and (ii) a representation of the sentence with the focused item abstracted over. This can be thought of in terms of lambda abstraction, such that (4.3b) could be the representation of (4.3a) (see von Stechow 1991b, 44).

(4.3)   a.   John introduced B<small>ILL</small> to Sue.
          b. $< \lambda x\ [\text{introduce x to Sue}], \text{Bill} >$

The structuring of a focus-affected meaning in this way captures what is intuitively an important aspect of the interpretation of focus: the sense that the non-focused part of the sentence represents a unified 'background' to which the focus is somehow applied to create a complete meaning. This idea has intuitive connections to the idea of given versus new information, but also links to more conventional semantic notions, as Rooth notes:

> In the tradition of generative grammar, structuring as a semantics for focus was first proposed in Jackendoff (1972, 245), but it can be viewed as reconstruction of the notion that intonation can have the effect of dividing a sentence into a psychological predicate and psychological subject ... or a theme and rheme (Rooth 1996, 275)

The point need not be restricted to intonation. The idea of 'psychological predicate and psychological subject' and the potential for structured representations of propositions to reflect this will form an important part of my analysis of how the PV position in Hungarian comes to express a certain kind of focus, among other effects (Chapter 6). However, the order of explanation will be in effect the reverse of that found in structured meaning semantics: a requirement to perform a certain kind of predicative procedure, in combination with context-sensitive reasoning, results in the recognition of information-structural distinctions. That is, inducing the information-structural partition of the sentence is not taken to be the encoded function of the PV position; instead this partition itself emerges in the course of carrying out more basic encoded procedures, in the context of general principles of linguistic interpretation [3].

Two other approaches that are in many ways closely related to structured meanings semantics are also worth mentioning, as they highlight other important parts of the process of focus interpretation—though again they make the mistake of assuming these effects to be the encoded meaning of a focus primitive. These are the 'alternative semantics' approach of Rooth (1985, 1992) and the discourse-structural 'question under discussion' approach of Roberts (1996).

Rooth's analysis concentrates on the idea that a focused expression is something that is asserted in the context of a set of potential alternatives to it. Rooth uses the potential alternatives to a focused item primarily to help establish the domain of focus-sensitive operators like *only*, but the idea of interpretation from among alternatives intuitively also underpins the contrastive/exhaustive element to the interpretation of many foci, including those associated with the Hungarian PV position. The idea of a set of alternatives is closely linked to the idea of lambda abstraction since a representation like $\lambda x.\ introduce'(john', x, sue')$ extensionally denotes a set—hence the 'background' part of a sentence like *John introduced* BILL *to Sue* can be viewed as denoting a set. Despite this clear connection to structured meaning semantics, Rooth develops a slightly different form of representation, making the invocation and restriction of sets of alternatives the principal directly encoded effect of focus (see Rooth 1996 for some justification of the differences between his formalism and structured meanings, in terms of different predictions regarding the interaction of focus and certain operators).

From a pragmatic point of view, such an analysis seems to involve somewhat inverted reasoning. Alternatives to (the denotation of) some expression are invoked in the course of interpretation *to the extent that they are relevant*. The logic of RT suggests that a grammatically triggered evocation of alternatives is therefore unnecessary. If, as the result of other encoded meanings and contextual factors, certain alternatives are inferred to be relevant, they will be considered in interpretation, without any specially encoded instruction to do so. The crucial question is therefore what these other encoded meanings are that can trigger the inference that alternatives are relevant. This criticism is picked up below, in section 4.5.3.

Roberts (1996) also takes as a starting point the fact that abstracting over one argument in a sentence creates a set-denoting representation, but Roberts uses this in a different way. Noting that *Wh*-questions can be given a denotational semantics as sets of propositions, Roberts proposes that the effect of focus is first to induce lambda abstraction over the focused element and then

---

[3] Most versions of structured meaning semantics approach the partitioning of the sentence in an entirely compositional way, assuming syntactic (LF) movement to derive the lambda-abstractions required at the syntax-semantics interface. This kind of movement is obviously unavailable in the kind of dynamic account that I advocate in this work, but is in any case now widely recognised to be undesirable for theory-internal reasons, as it violates recognised constraints on syntactic movement (Rooth 1985, von Stechow 1991a, Kratzer 1991, Horvath 2000). Krifka (1991) gives a version of the structured meanings approach that involves *in situ* interpretation of focused expressions, via a complex set of mappings at the syntax-semantics interface.

to introduce a constraint that the resulting representation be congruent with the semantics of a 'question under discussion', which may be an overt preceding question in a dialogue or may be an abstract, inferred object (see also Glanzberg 2005). In effect, Roberts thus takes the well-known observation that different placements of focus are felicitous in reply to different *Wh*-questions (as exemplified in (4.2) above) and assumes this in itself to be the encoded semantics of focus.

The idea of a 'question under discussion' that is accessed by abstracting over the focused item is another intuitively significant part of the process of interpreting focus, being in effect one way of thinking about the 'background' information provided by the non-focused part of the sentence. Indeed, one might say that the difference between a representation of the 'background' to a focus, expressed through the use of the lambda operator, and a 'question under discussion' is merely one of perspective—albeit one that changes the nature of the analysis from a conventional syntactico-semantic one (in the case of structured meaning semantics) to one based in the abstract structure of a dialogue (in the case of Roberts' account).

It is notable that the intuitive idea of a 'question under discussion' could be paraphrased as 'what is currently relevant' (indeed, Roberts herself refers to a concept of Relevance, but this is a formal device, defined in terms of questions under discussion). Roberts' analysis therefore amounts to encoding in the expression of focus a stipulation that an assertion must be relevant. From the point of view of inferential pragmatic theory, this is to propose that an overarching principle of communication is encoded in a particular linguistic phenomenon, a move that plainly renders that phenomenon quite superfluous and does nothing to explain its existence or its particular effects.

4.2.3 A dynamic, RT approach to English

One existing account of information-structural interpretation that is much closer in spirit to that of the remainder of this chapter is Sperber & Wilson's (1986/95) RT analysis of how notions like 'topic' and 'focus' arise in the course of parsing an English sentence, which is developed further by Breheny (1998)[4]. This is inherently dynamic in approach and, at least in Sperber & Wilson's case, eschews the idea of grammatically encoded information-structural features, in favour of consideration of the cognitive effects of processing the elements of a sentence in a linearly ordered string, in conjunction with a very general, procedural notion of the function of primary stress.

The essence of the analysis is that phonological stress indicates information to which the addressee is intended to pay particular attention (Breheny draws an analogy to physical pointing as a way of making the purpose of an utterance manifest). Primary stress is thus associated with the main assertion of a sentence. In line with general RT reasoning, the role of other parts of the sentence is to construct the appropriate context for the interpretation of this assertion that will

---

[4]This basis of this analysis is Wilson & Sperber's earlier (1979) attempt to explain presupposition in terms of 'ordered entailments'.

produce the desired cognitive effects. This is not stipulated in any way, but follows from the assumption that inferential reasoning regarding the possible relevance of incoming lexical items is carried out during parsing (as Sperber & Wilson note, this is to be expected, given the potential it introduces for increasing the efficiency of parsing in the face of possible ambiguities). Given this, each word parsed can be expected to prompt an 'anticipatory hypothesis' about the logical form of the utterance. Thus, a person hearing the word *Jennifer* as the beginning of an utterance, having assigned a referent to the name, is likely to construct an anticipatory hypothesis along the lines of 'Jennifer did something', which in turn prompts the question 'What did Jennifer do?'; if the next word is *ate*, the hypothesis 'Jennifer ate something' is triggered. In a given context, either of these hypotheses may already have cognitive effects, or each may simply narrow down the context for the interpretation of the next item, in which case they are made relevant by virtue of reducing the effort required in interpretation. Sperber & Wilson refer to a hypothesis that achieves relevance though its own cognitive effects as a 'foreground implication', while a hypothesis that contributes to relevance merely by reducing the effort required to interpret subsequent items is a 'background implication'. The location of focus is then definable as the point at which a foreground implication is produced; where a relevant statement is produced, rather than simply the preparation for one.

As Sperber & Wilson note, this predicts the unmarked nature of phrase final focus in English: "The sense in which it is natural for focal stress to fall at the end of the utterance, and hence for the background to be recovered before foreground is the sense in which it is natural to raise a question before answering it, or to communicate a complex piece of information step by step" (1986/95, 211). As Breheny emphasises, the idea that a relevant proposition is established by the time a focus is encountered means that all context-setting material must be encountered before this point, so that post-focal material must be predictable in the context. This accounts for the fact that early stress-placement in English tends to result in a contrastive focus reading of the stressed expression, with post-focal material acting as presupposed 'background' to it.

While the basic approach to focus as an emergent property of inferential processes matches my assumptions, Sperber & Wilson's and Breheny's analyses of English focus clearly cannot carry over to the explanation of Hungarian PV focus, for a number of reasons. First, while expressions that appear after a PV focus are indeed predictable, presupposed material, primary stress is often followed by newly asserted material in Hungarian, since primary stress falls on the verb or VM in topic>comment sentences and this is often the second item in the sentence (following any overt topic). Second, as Sperber & Wilson recognise, their approach predicts that there should be something of a cline from topicality to focushood in many sentences, since there is no reason why an implication derived while parsing some sentence-medial item cannot contribute to relevance both by having some cognitive effects of its own and helping to construct the context for following material (this is implied in the way that each implication potentially sets up a question but also fills in some of the information sought by a preceding question). Yet Hungarian syntax requires that there be a clearer cut-off between what is considered to be 'in focus' and what is not. Post-verbal material in a topic>comment sentence (what É. Kiss 1998a calls 'information focus') has some intermediate status, it seems, but in this position it can have nothing to do with building context in advance of processing the primary-stressed expression. Lastly, Sperber & Wilson's and Breheny's work on English focus, like the approaches mentioned in the previous section, cannot be expected to reveal anything about why items such as VMs, VM-less verbs and negation interact with the position of syntactically focused items in the systematic way they do.

Nevertheless, this RT work provides a useful precedent, in investigating focus from the point of view of how linear processing in context influences the way different elements of a sentence affect each other's perceived information-structural status, and in thus deriving what other approaches tend to stipulate at some arbitrary level of semantic detail. The proposals that I outline in Chapter 6 do in fact bear a certain resemblance to Sperber & Wilson's and Breheny's approach to English, in the sense that the derivation of information-structural readings is shown to depend on the interaction between the location of primary stress—which coincides with a syntactic position in Hungarian—and the point in a linear parse by which a certain kind of meaning is conveyed. In the case of Hungarian, however, this is something rather more abstract than the 'foreground implication' used in Sperber & Wilson's account of English.

Returning to the topic of the present chapter, the first step in this analysis of Hungarian is to establish the true nature of the focus readings that are in fact found in the PV position. To this end, section 4.2.4 outlines some remaining issues regarding the idea of focus as a general phenomenon, which will be of use in analysing the more specific problem of the Hungarian foci.

4.2.4 The general meaning of focus (and presupposition)

Despite the reservations expressed here regarding the idea that focus directly induces some form of partition in the semantic representation of a sentence, I will use a basic division between focus and a 'presupposed' background for descriptive purposes throughout this chapter and the next. My proposals regarding the actual encoded content of the Hungarian position are delayed until Chapter 6, where the discussion moves beyond the expression only of focus. In the present chapter, the aim is primarily to show what is *not* encoded in the PV position, in spite of common assumptions. For these purposes, a general, pre-theoretical notion of focus will suffice. Such a notion will form a useful point of comparison for the nature of the focus readings found in the PV position. Alongside this, I set out here what I take to be an appropriate characterisation of the non-focused part of any utterance.

As shown above in (4.2), a common test for focus is the use of a context-setting *Wh*-question. In interpretive terms, the part of the answer that replaces the *Wh*-word is considered the focus, even though this may not be unambiguously signalled by pitch accent placement or any other overt indication. This is illustrated in the indicated foci of the English examples in (4.4), which may be phonetically identical.

(4.4) a. What did Mary eat?
Mary ate AN APPLE.

b. What did Mary do?
Mary ATE AN APPLE.

A 'context question' of this kind does not truly determine the context for interpretation, of course, since the context (as identified by RT) may involve all kinds of extra-linguistic information drawn from the interlocutors' mutual cognitive environment and is determined by the Principles of Relevance. A question may be thought of as making manifest the questioner's desire for a certain kind of information, and it is because of this rather direct connection to crucial elements of the mutual cognitive environment that felicity in response to a real or imagined question can indicate something about the information structure of an utterance. Note that this perspective avoids a good deal of trouble compared to any attempt to define 'the semantics of focus', which must be made to fit with a theory of 'the semantics of questions'.

The part of an utterance identified by the *Wh*-question heuristic as being 'in focus' is roughly definable as the asserted part of the utterance. In other words, the focus is (or at least is presented as being) the locus of information that updates the cognitive environment. It is important to note, however, that this 'updating' does not stop at adding information to a model of the universe, but works by triggering cognitive effects—which depend also on the context in which this update occurs. The rest of the utterance effectively serves to help construct the immediate context and is made up of 'presupposed' material.

The use of the word *presupposition* of course has an entire literature to itself, so I must make clear here what I mean by this. At least for the purposes of the analyses in this book, I take presupposition to be a purely pragmatic notion (thus broadly in the tradition of Stalnaker 1974). In RT terms, I use the word to refer to particular assumptions that manifestly have to be recovered from the cognitive environment in order to function as part of the immediate context for the interpretation of material asserted in the present utterance. As such, the prompting and identification of presuppositions occurs on the basis of the general relevance-based reasoning that, according to RT, underpins interpretation as a whole.

This is not to say that numerous phenomena often thought of as 'presuppositional' cannot be encoded, for example within particular lexical items. The important point is that presupposition should not be taken as necessarily a semantic notion, nor necessarily an encoded aspect of meaning[5]. Nor should the idea of pragmatic presupposition be thought of as merely a 'weak' (for example, cancellable) phenomenon, to be contrasted in this sense with a notion of 'real', semantic presupposition. Information that is inferred to be a *necessary* part of the context for interpreting some act of communication may not be cancellable without creating incoherence, so there is little empirical basis for such a distinction, which arguably originates in the ways

---

[5] See Herburger (2000, 13) for problems with using the semantic notion of presupposition in information-structural analysis.

in which semantics and pragmatics are conventionally kept artificially separated and linearly ordered—see also section 4.4.

Even material that is not highly salient to the addressee at point of utterance may be 'accommodated' (Lewis 1979) as presupposed material, since the RT definition of manifestness—and hence of what may be considered part of a cognitive environment—includes assumptions accessible via inferential processes that use other manifest assumptions as premises (see Chapter 2). Indeed, even information previously not accessible at all to the addressee may be accommodated at the point of utterance, since elements of the incoming utterance help to construct the immediate context for its own interpretation, by making particular assumptions manifestly relevant. This means that, in principle, a communicator can, for particular communicative reasons, present assumptions that may be quite new to the addressee as if they were presupposed material.

The fact that an utterance may be analysed as involving a presupposition (in a cognitive sense) even when the prior context does not contain salient material that relates to this presupposition illustrates the important RT argument that the context of an utterance is a set of assumptions constructed during processing, not merely a quasi-model-theoretic 'state of affairs' that is specifiable in advance of the utterance. It also shows the advantage of the RT notion of 'manifestness' (which includes contextually inferable assumptions) over simpler notions of prior knowledge, salience or accessibility in understanding the dynamics of interpretation: communicators are not restricted to utilising elements of a 'database' constructed by prior discourse, but may use a variety of means to indicate relevant assumptions—with a variety of resulting cognitive effects.

4.3 THE NATURE OF 'FOCUS POSITION' FOCI

4.3.1 There is no simple 'focus position'

While I argue below against the idea that exhaustive focus is encoded in the PV position, it is also true that a general definition of focus, in terms of 'new', updating information, will not suffice to characterise the foci that appear there. The *Wh*-question heuristic does not yield just those elements that appear as pre-verbal foci. A question such as (4.5a) demands a response with a 'topic>comment' structure, in which everything other than the topic provides the information sought by the questioner and hence is 'in focus' in the general sense. Yet the felicitous response (4.5b) shows no use of 'focus position'—the prefix VM *meg* remains pre-verbal and the post-verbal material will not be destressed[6]. Note that while the 'topic>comment' sentence (4.5b) contains what might alternatively be described as 'VP-focus', the Hungarian data would be unaffected by the use of a non-subject topic, as in (4.5c) (in answer to a question like 'What happened to the apple?'), so it is not the syntactic notion of VP, as [V+Object], that is significant

---

[6]In a genuine dialogue, the topical subject would not be repeated (but rather dropped completely, Hungarian being a pro-drop language). But the point is not to present a realistic dialogue: the function of the *Wh*-question is simply to indicate the information-structural constraints on the felicity of the declarative sentence that it precedes.

here[7].

(4.5) a. Mari mit   csinált?
        Mari what-ACC did
        'What did Mari do?'

     b. Mari megevett egy almát.
        Mari VM-ate   an apple-ACC
        'Mari ate up an apple'.

     c. Az almát   megette Mari.
        the apple-ACC VM-ate Mari
        'The apple, Mari ate it (up).'

What this shows is that an expression that, like *egy almát* in (4.5b), is part of a 'broad focus' does not appear in the pre-verbal 'focus position'. Instead, it appears after the verb, which is itself part of the broad focus. The use of the pre-verbal position is therefore clearly not necessary to signal what in the sentence is focused, in the general sense of the word.

4.3.2 'Narrow' and 'broad' focus

In contrast to (4.5a), a question like (4.6a), which contains the verb and therefore does not require anything akin to 'VP-focus' in the response, is typically answered with the expression that replaces the *Wh*-word in the pre-verbal 'focus position'—thus *egy almát* in (4.6b) appears pre-verbally, causing the VM *meg* to postpose and the verb stem to be destressed. That is, the 'focus' as indicated by the context-question heuristic now does coincide with the kind of meaning associated with the pre-verbal position[8].

(4.6) a. Mari mit   evett meg?
        Mari what-ACC ate   VM
        'What did Mari eat (up)?'

     b. Mari egy almát   evett meg.
        Mari an apple-ACC ate   VM
        'Mari ate (up) an apple.'

---

[7]The difference in the form of the verb between (4.5b) and (4.5c) is unconnected to the word order: the Hungarian verb has a 'definite conjugation' that is used whenever the direct object is definite.

[8]Again, this is not intended to be a realistic dialogue, in the sense that the most felicitous response to (4.6a) would be simply *egy almát*, with the remaining, background material elided. However, the question once again functions to indicate the kind of context that would make the assertion in (4.6b) acceptable—and native speakers confirm that, if required to supply a full sentence in response to a question like (4.6a), the use of PV is the only possibility. See also section 4.5.5

While one could contrive an argument to the effect that the PV expression in (4.6b) has a kind of exhaustive reading, there seems little in the question-answer sequence to suggest that exhaustivity is a specially added meaning here. The contrast between (4.5) and (4.6) suggests an alternative line of enquiry: that some notion of 'narrow' as opposed to 'broad' focus is somehow significant in the use of the pre-verbal position. It is hard to see how this could be encoded, however, since it is not clear how the distinction could even be defined in any rigorous fashion[9]. Perhaps for his reason the distinction has received remarkably little attention in the Hungarian literature, despite the suggestiveness of the contrast between examples like (4.5) and (4.6) (although see Szendrői 2003 for some related discussion and Horvath 2000 for arguments based around slightly different definitions of 'broad' versus 'narrow' focus). This is arguably also because of the general tendency to seek purely syntactic explanations for word order phenomena: if the assumption is that a syntactic explanation should be sought, only factors that are easily captured in syntactic terms are likely to be properly considered. Intuitively, the relevant broad/narrow focus distinction is an interpretive rather than a syntactically-defined one.

Close consideration shows that there is indeed no way to define a syntactic constraint on the 'breadth' of focus readings associated with use of the PV position—even though there is apparently a structural restriction on the size of expressions that may actually appear there. In terms of actual word order, it is true that nothing bigger or smaller than a simple NP may occur in the pre-verbal position. Hence if a sub-part of an NP is a narrow focus, the whole NP is 'pied-piped' into the pre-verbal position, with stress shifted rightwards within the NP if necessary to indicate the correct scope of focus (4.7a) (see Kenesei 1998, Szendrői 2003). Meanwhile, even a complex NP is too large for the pre-verbal position (4.7b)[10], necessitating alternative strategies, such as extraposition of any relative clause from within the NP, as in (4.7c), or some form of topicalisation-plus-reduplication strategy, as in (4.7d).

(4.7)   a.   Péter egy használt 'autót vett.
                Péter a used car-ACC bought
                'It's a used CAR that Peter bought [not a used caravan, for example].'

       b.   *(Azt) a nőt, aki a musicalt rendezte imádom.
                That-ACC the woman-ACC who the musical-ACC directed-3SG admire-1SG

       c.   (Azt) a nőt imádom, aki a musicalt rendezte.
                That-ACC the woman-ACC admire-1SG who the musical-ACC directed-3SG

---

[9]In section 4.7, I develop a technical definition (in terms of the presupposition of eventualities) of the kind of context that encapsulates the relevant notion of 'narrow focus', but this is not argued to be encoded as such, instead itself emerging from more general encoded factors (which are investigated in later chapters).

[10](4.7b) is impossible on the reading in which the whole complex NP is interpreted as a pre-verbal focus—e.g. given the kind of context suggested by the question 'Who do you admire?'. This word order would be acceptable if the NP were given rising intonation, and the verb a falling pitch accent, but this would represent a quite different interpretation (specifically, with the NP as 'contrastive topic')

d. A nőt,   aki a musicalt   rendezte,   őt   imádom.
   The woman-ACC who the musical-ACC directed-3SG PRO(3SG)-ACC admire-1SG

Intended in b,c,d: 'It's the woman who directed the musical that I admire.'

However, the syntactically-definable restriction on occupancy of the PV position does not suffice to define the limits on what size and complexity of expression may take on the relevant kind of focus *reading*. Examples like (4.8b) show that a VP-sized chunk may take on a reading in which the whole chunk is treated as parallel to a narrow focus, rather than having a 'topic>comment' reading, if part of this chunk is in the pre-verbal position (hence this kind of example is sometimes described as involving 'projection' of focus from the pre-verbal expression to the bigger chunk).

(4.8) a. János a   cikkeket   olvasta (el).
           János the articles-ACC read   VM
           'It's the articles that János read.'

       b. János a   cikkeket   olvasta, és   nem a   fürdőszobában énekelt.
           János the articles-ACC read   and not the bathroom-in   sang
           'What János did was read the articles (it's not that he sang in the bathroom).'

This may appear to contradict my suggestion that the narrow/broad focus distinction is relevant to Hungarian syntactic focus (and provide support instead for the conventional exhaustivity account). It is notable, however, that (4.8b) shows a marked reading, in the sense that a clear contrast with contextually accessible eventualities (generally made explicit, as in the clause in parentheses in (4.8b)) is required to make this reading accessible. The reading in (4.8a) is compatible with a far greater range of contexts, given this word order. At the same time, (4.8b) is not a normal case of 'broad' focus, as it requires not merely the context indicated by a question like *What did János do?* (cf. (4.5)), but a richer context containing some very restricted set of contextually accessible assumption(s) about what János did, which provides the point of contrast. This implies that there is good reason to maintain the idea that readings like (4.8b) represent some special process of reading a larger sized expression as if it were a smaller expression in PV, hence in some sense a narrow focus. It remains an interesting and potentially revealing observation that use of PV position is typically associated with 'narrow' foci, while a broad focus (as indicated by the context-question heuristic) is unmarkedly associated with a 'topic>comment' structure that does not involve the use of the PV position. The precise definition of 'narrow' and 'broad' also remains an interesting question, of course, but something akin to the semantic equivalents of 'NP-sized' versus 'VP-sized' seems to be suggested.

That (4.8b) is a possibility at all shows that the definition of the kinds of foci that may be associated with the PV position must make reference to some aspect of interpretation; it cannot be drawn in purely syntactic terms. Of course, some special syntactic operation of focus-feature

110 *Shifting the Focus*

projection or percolation could always be proposed, but, as Horvath (2000) points out with regard to Kenesei's (1995a) ideas along these lines, any such move is essentially *ad hoc* and as such only serves to undermine the whole approach of accounting for the pre-verbal 'focus position' by purely syntactic means.

Can the apparently significant broad/narrow distinction then be captured at an interpretive level? It is notable that foci involving the tensed verb are generally 'broad' and of a 'topic->comment' type, rather than of the kind that employs the 'focus position'. The significance of this is also suggested by the very fact that the way of signalling the use of the ' focus position' is a certain relationship to the tensed verb—this strongly implies that it is normal, in some sense, for the verb to stand outside of any syntactically focused expression. On an interpretive level, verbs and expressions containing verbs correspond to descriptions of eventualities. This suggests that the status of descriptions of eventualities in relation to the information structure of the sentence is an important factor in the characterisation of the use of PV. This idea is developed below, the notion of narrow focus being related to the (pragmatic) presupposition of a particular eventuality, which is seen to underlie also examples like (4.8b). This view is presented informally in this chapter (section 4.7) and given a degree of formalisation in Chapter 6, through a dynamic extension of neo-Davidsonian semantic representation.

The data reviewed above point to a dynamic account whereby the production of a certain kind of focus reading depends on inferences triggered by encountering certain expressions, like entity-denoting NPs, at the point in the parse where the verb would be expected in a 'topic>comment' sentence. Note that this leaves open the possibility of further kinds of inference being triggered if other kinds of expression are encountered (and/or if the context contains certain kinds of assumption) at this point in the parse, hence the possibility that the PV position may be not only a 'focus position'. This is the essence of the approach that I develop below and in Chapter 6.

For the time being, I continue to use the terms 'narrow' and 'broad' focus loosely for expository purposes, indicating roughly the difference between expressions that are 'up to NP-sized' and 'VP-sized', respectively—or rather the semantic values of such expressions.

4.3.3 Exhaustivity: are there two kinds of focus?

As stated in Chapter 3, exhaustivity is the property that is usually identified as being definitive of the occupants of 'focus position'. This is in line with the *it*-cleft-like reading that PV foci are typically said to have (as in (4.8a), above). The majority of recent analyses of Hungarian assume accordingly that it is exhaustivity, rather than any more general notion of focus, that is encoded in a pre-verbal 'focus position'. This may be expressed via the assumption that there exist two quite distinct kinds of focus, one of which involves exhaustivity and is related to the pre-verbal position. Alternatively, exhaustivity may be treated as a separate element of meaning that only indirectly relates to focus. The former position is given its most clear statement by É. Kiss (1998a) and Vallduví & Vilkuna (1998); the latter is explicitly argued by Horvath (2000). These positions may amount to the same thing, in the sense that they insist on the existence of two quite distinct concepts, whether or not the word 'focus' is applied to both. Many other analyses of Hungarian also refer to the exhaustive nature of pre-verbal foci, but without stating exactly what relationship, if any, holds between this and the more general notion of focus (i.e. that associated with the context-question heuristic).

The separation of exhaustive focus from other kinds of focus at the level of grammatical primitives allows for the correct association of certain word orders and interpretations by standard syntactic means, but it creates potential problems if there are shown to be connections between the two kinds of focus. If they share certain characteristics either at the interpretive level or in terms of the ways they are signalled linguistically, the assumption of separate grammatical primitives not only looks poorly supported, but potentially obscures the nature of the processes involved in relating word orders to interpretations. In particular, the possibility that the two notions of focus are somehow linked by inferential processes should be considered, but this is precluded by an analysis that posits separate primitives.

As Roberts (1998) points out, there are reasons to believe that the two kinds of focus are related both at the level of interpretation and in the linguistic properties associated with each in Hungarian. Adopting for expository purposes the terminology (but not the attendant theoretical stance) of É. Kiss (1998a), the crucial point of comparison is between exhaustive (PV) foci and 'information foci', the latter being expressions that form part of a broad focus or 'comment' (for example, *egy almát*) in (4.5b)). Exhaustive PV foci, just like 'information' foci, are necessarily 'in focus' according to the context-question heuristic—that is, they are a proper subset of the things that can be called 'focus' by any discourse-based definition (or a constituent part of one of these, in the case of an 'information focus' item). This is a strong indication that exhaustive foci are a special case of the more general notion of focus, rather than involving any separate grammatical primitive. In addition, both exhaustive and 'information' foci carry falling pitch accents in Hungarian (as is visible in Rosenthall's 1992 instrumental phonetic analysis; see also Kálmán 1985b). Exhaustive foci occupy the pre-tense position that always carries such an accent (whether this is on the verb stem, a VM or a pre-verbal focus), while in the case of 'information' foci the pitch accent surfaces on each post-verbal phrase (in contrast to the destressed post-verbal items that follow an instance of syntactic focus). Both of these observations suggest that the strategy of simply declaring the two kinds of focus to be distinct phenomena—and possibly assigning grammatical features on this basis—is over-simplistic. Making this distinction may facilitate a descriptively adequate derivation of many observed correspondences between word orders and interpretations, but it ignores all potential explanatory factors that have to do with what the two kinds of focus share.

To summarise this section, the general notion of focus, as identified by the *Wh*-question test, is not adequate, on its own, to characterise the foci that appear in the PV position, but at the same time the exhaustive reading usually associated with PV foci does not seem entirely separate from the more general idea of focus, either as an interpretive phenomenon or in terms of the way it is expressed in Hungarian. This points to the need for an account that can relate the two,

112 Shifting the Focus

supporting a partly inferential account over one that relies on grammatically encoded primitives to drive word order. One promising observation that might guide such an account is that PV seems to be in some sense associated with 'narrow' foci.

In section 4.5 I present a pragmatic analysis that explains the commonly observed sense of exhaustivity as the result of inferences drawn in certain contexts, which in turn relate to the idea of narrow focus. First, however, it is important to address the theoretical reasons why this kind of account has up to now been generally assumed, erroneously, to be inapplicable to the explanation of the exhaustivity of Hungarian pre-verbal focus. If this assumption were correct, then there would clearly be no point in presenting an analysis along these lines. This issues bring us to the crux of the illustration promised in chapters of how conventional theoretical assumptions have distorted the analysis linguistic phenomena like Hungarian PV. Accordingly, in section 4.6 I present strong evidence that the conventional position, involving the direct encoding of exhaustivity, is not only undesirable for the reasons given above, but also quite unsustainable empirically.

4.4 ENCODED VERSUS INFERRED EXHAUSTIVE FOCUS

As noted in Chapter 3, the first impression given by Hungarian 'focus position' data is that it must be dealt with in the syntactic component. In the context of conventional approaches to syntax and semantics, at least, this is strongly suggested by the combination of a distinctive word order, an interpretation that is apparently associated with it quite regularly and systematic interaction with other syntactic phenomena that seem quite arbitrary and meaningless. However, these observations alone are not sufficient to determine an encoded exhaustivity analysis even under conventional syntactico-semantic assumptions. These surface facts do not rule out the possibility that some more underspecified meaning is encoded in the syntactic position in question, leaving the exhaustive reading to be derived inferentially. As mentioned in the previous section, there are indeed other, equally superficial, observations that point towards this kind of account, in the shape of indications that information foci and exhaustive PV foci are related. To understand why such possibilities have been ruled out in the past requires reference to another assumption, that of the compositionality of truth-conditional meaning, as discussed in Chapter 1.

One useful thing about the literature on the Hungarian focus position, in this regard, is that it provides an unusually explicit statement of the importance of such underlying assumptions, given by Szabolcsi (1981). However much the theoretical frameworks employed in later analytical work may in principle differ from the strictly Montagovian approach adopted in Szabolcsi's paper, it would appear to have influenced subsequent work quite thoroughly, since its conclusions regarding the possibility of inferentially deriving the exhaustivity of pre-verbal foci have remained in effect unchallenged in subsequent formal analyses [11].

---

[11] As noted in Chapter 3, the earlier work of É. Kiss is something of an exception to the general lack of discussion of the possibility that inference is involved in creating the exhaustive reading. Kenesei (1986) and Szabolcsi (1994,

4.4.1 The case against inferred exhaustivity

Szabolcsi (1981) compares the possibility that exhaustive focus arises through pragmatic inference, as implicature, with the idea that it contributes via encoding in syntax to the compositional semantics of the sentences in which it appears. Her argument is couched in terms of explicitly (and strongly) stated Montagovian assumptions; that is, she identifies linguistic syntax with 'logician's syntax' as far as possible. Proposing (4.9) as the definition of the Fregean principle of compositionality that underpins Montague Grammar, Szabolcsi (1981, 141) is unequivocal about its applicability to natural language, stating, "I believe that the validity of [(4.9)] is beyond doubt and thus any grammar, whether organised to reflect [(4.9)] or not, may ultimately be required to satisfy it."

(4.9)   The literal meaning of an expression is uniquely determined by the literal meanings of its subexpressions and their mode of composition.

It is for this reason that Szabolcsi's argument may safely be seen not only as an important step in the development of analyses of Hungarian focus but also as a case study of the effects of treating the structure of natural language on a par with that of logical languages. This explicit statement of fundamental assumptions contrasts with the majority of more recent work in syntax and semantics. As argued in Chapters 1 and 2, this situation has led to much mainstream syntax embodying a somewhat incoherent vision of ostensibly Chomskyan syntax that is implicitly assumed also to perform the role of 'logician's syntax' to a great extent.

Szabolcsi's conclusion, that exhaustive focus must be a syntactically encoded property (at least in Hungarian), is reasonable given the assumptions about pragmatics that were available to her at the time. Indeed, she rightly criticises existing Gricean analyses of 'conventional implicature' (specifically, as formulated by Karttunen & Peters 1979) for the lack of a sufficiently clear theoretical underpinning that would allow its relation to other aspects of linguistic theory to be understood in a useful way (1981, 147). Therefore, while Szabolcsi (1981) provides the basis for illustrating my theoretical point, it should be borne in mind that it is not so much the reasoning in that work that is worthy of criticism, but rather the fact that this reasoning has not been subject to radical reappraisal in subsequent years, despite both philosophical and linguistic developments in the study of the semantics-pragmatics distinction[12].

1997b), É. Kiss (1998a) and Horvath (2000) can all be seen as examples of work on the syntax-semantics interface that accept the basic conclusions of Szabolcsi (1981) regarding encoding versus inference, though none clearly share the strict Montagovian assumptions of the latter. Much of the more syntactically-oriented work on Hungarian focus (e.g. Bródy 1990, 1995; Dalmi 1998) seems to adopt a similar position on what is encoded in the pre-verbal 'focus position', though not always explicitly.

[12]For one example of explicit evidence that an entailment from truth-conditional effects to grammatical encoding is still assumed to hold, see Seuren (1993, with respect to focus: 2004, 174ff.). Note that Seuren's 'generative semantic' approach in some ways constitutes a mirror-image of the parsing-based dynamic analysis that I advocate in Chapter 2, but—partly because of this orientation—denies itself the opportunity to take account of inferential contributions to propositional interpretations (see also Carston 2002, 205).

Szabolcsi's arguments rest on the twin premises of compositional semantics that truth-conditionally distinct meanings must relate to grammatical distinctions and that pragmatically derived aspects of meaning cannot interact with truth conditions. If these premises are accepted, it is always easy to resolve the question of whether some element of meaning is attributable directly to the grammar or to the operation of inferential processes: one simply has to demonstrate that this element of meaning can affect truth conditions in order to discount an inferential analysis.

Let us just remind ourselves where these assumptions spring from and why they continue, logically, to form part of any compositional analysis. First, the observation that sentences can intuitively bear certain logical relationships to each other—synonymy, entailment, contradiction—seems to justify the idea that sentences are direct bearers of truth-conditional meanings; these logical relations are defined in terms of truth values. Alongside this, the observation that sentences seem to build meanings out of their constituent parts appears to demand a compositional approach to linguistically conveyed meaning. Putting these observations together, it seems that the semantic content of the constituent parts of sentences must be defined in terms of their contributions to a truth-conditional meaning. This creates a closed system, with no room for non-compositional contributions to the truth-conditional meaning that is intuitively associated with a sentence and testable by investigating logical relations to the meanings of other sentences (a situation that is apparently reinforced by the Gricean restriction of pragmatic processes to defeasible implicatures). As Stanley & Szabó (2000) rightly observe, this latter conclusion is unavoidable: admitting the possibility of pragmatic contributions to truth-conditional meaning would undermine the whole compositional semantic enterprise, since it removes the ability to infer the semantic contribution of part of a sentence from its grammatical form and the truth-conditional meaning of the sentence as a whole (recall the discussion in Chapter 1, section 1.2.4).

The crucial question for Szabolcsi (1981) is thus whether the exhaustivity of PV focus can affect truth conditions. That it can is demonstrated by the fact that the relations of entailment and logical compatibility that hold between (the meanings of) focusless sentences do not necessarily hold between otherwise equivalent sentences that do contain the use of PV focus. As É. Kiss (1998a) points out, roughly the same effects are associated with English *it*-clefts. Szabolcsi offers the following examples (her (14) and (15), which I reproduce with Szabolcsi's notation, though I adapt the glosses and translations for the sake of explicitness and to show the parallel with the English cleft construction)[13].

(4.10) a. [$_F$ Péter] aludt a padlón
           Péter slept the floor-on
           'It's Péter who slept on the floor.'

---

[13]It should be noted that, in spite of Szabolcsi's notation, the verb-initial sentence (4.10b) is far from being pragmatically unmarked and, by my analysis and that of É. Kiss (2002), involves some focused material on any of its readings (see Chapter 8, section 8.2). The crucial arguments in this section are unaffected by this.

b. [$_F$ e] Aludt Péter a padlón
   slept Péter the floor-on
   'Péter slept on the floor.'

c. [$_F$ Péter és Pál] aludt a padlón
   Péter and Pál slept the floor-on
   'It's Péter and Pál who slept on the floor.'

Szabolcsi's argument proceeds as follows (1981, 149):

> It seems intuitively clear that it is not merely inadequate but pronouncedly false to infer [(4.10a)], as opposed to [(4.10b)], from [(4.10c)] i.e. that exhaustive listing is part of the truth conditions of [(4.10a,c)]. ...

To get away from merely intuitive evidence, Szabolcsi takes the argument further:

> ... suppose that above we were wrong and the truth conditions of [(4.10a,b)] are in fact identical, only their implicata being different. Then we would have to expect that the truth of [(4.11a)] is compatible only with the truth of [(4.11b)] and not with the truth of [(4.10c)], the later two being logically contradictory under any analysis.

(4.11) a. Nem [$_F$ Péter] aludt a padlón
           not   Péter slept the floor-on
           'It's not Péter who slept on the floor.'

        b. [$_F$ e] Nem aludt Péter a padlón
           not slept Péter the floor-on
           'Péter didn't sleep on the floor.'

Contrary to this expectation, (4.12) (Szabolcsi's (17b)—again with the gloss and translation adapted here—already presented above as (3.7)) shows the truth-conditional compatibility of (4.11a) and (4.10c) and therefore demonstrates that (4.10a) and (4.10b) have different truth conditions. According to Szabolcsi's (1981) compositional assumptions, this must be taken as concrete evidence against the pragmatic derivation of exhaustive focus.

(4.12) Nem [$_F$ Péter] aludt a padlón, hanem [$_F$ Péter és Pál] / hanem [$_F$ az egész társaság]
        not   Péter slept the floor-on but   Péter and Pál   but   the whole company
        'It isn't Péter who slept on the floor; it's Péter and Pál / it's the whole company.'

Consequently, Szabolcsi proposes a compositional analysis whereby a constituent placed in the pre-verbal focus position gains an 'exhaustive listing' interpretation, such that the propositional formula relating to a sentence like (4.10a) has the meaning "For every x, x slept on the floor if and only if x is Peter" (1981, 151; see Szabolcsi 1994 for a revision of this). In Szabolcsi's (1981) Montagovian approach, this form of composition is stated over the surface structure of Hungarian, but this kind of analysis is carried over implicitly into other approaches (including later work by Szabolcsi) in which the semantic effects of pre-verbal focus must presumably relate to LF rather than surface structures.

4.4.2 The significance of the argument

Szabolcsi's explicit consideration of grammatical encoding versus inference in exhaustive focus sets up a rare case of an empirical issue that directly tests not just a hypothesis within a certain framework, but a set of assumptions that are fundamental to a variety of frameworks. As pointed out above, the premises from which Szabolcsi (1981) works are intrinsic to any coherent approach that invokes or assumes compositional analysis at any stage and the conclusions she draws follow from these premises, in conjunction with undisputed Hungarian data. The status of these conclusions is therefore of broad theoretical significance. Should it be the case that there exists empirical evidence which shows them to be unsustainable, then it is not merely an individual analysis that fails, but the entire family of compositional approaches to truth-conditional meaning in natural languages.

In the following sections, I show that such evidence does exist. Radical reappraisal of the nature of grammatical structure and of the kinds of meaning it conveys must follow, in a way argued to be necessary on independent theoretical grounds in Chapters 1 and 2. The re-analysis of the Hungarian data in accordance with a suitably revised theoretical outlook is the business of subsequent chapters.

4.5 EXHAUSTIVITY AS AN INFERENCE IN CONTEXT

Section 4.3.3 introduced some initial reasons to suspect that the exhaustivity of Hungarian PV foci is not directly encoded. In this section and the next, more empirical evidence is presented that casts doubt on this common idea and ultimately shows it to be an impossibility. Section 4.6 presents evidence that exhaustivity cannot be encoded in the PV position (or in the English *it*-cleft), through constructed examples which show unequivocally that the exhaustive reading does not always arise when PV is used. First, the present, longer section considers the idea of exhaustive focus both in association with the Hungarian PV position and independently of it, using examples from English. Exhaustivity is shown to be part of the unmarked reading of narrow foci in both English and Hungarian, a fact attributable to simple inferential pragmatic processes that are in fact well known from the Gricean literature and which are shown to follow from the basic tenets of RT, which gives them a more solid and coherent theoretical basis.

Importantly, Hungarian pre-verbal foci prove to share all of the crucial characteristics of English narrow foci, whether the latter are expressed in the form of a cleft or using unmarked declarative word order. This points to the conclusion that Hungarian foci acquire an exhaustive reading through their narrowness, and the relationship to context that this implies, rather than as a direct result of appearing in the PV position. That is, the idea that exhaustivity is encoded in a pre-verbal syntactic position in Hungarian is at best redundant.

4.5.1 Exhaustivity as an unmarked reading

In order to approach the inferential relationship between focus and exhaustivity, let us begin with a simple English example—one that involves no special construction such as a cleft, but does have a narrow focus, as indicated by a context-question (for illustrative purposes, I concentrate throughout this section on the most straightforward cases of narrow focus, wherein a single NP is the only focused part of the sentence, further explanation of the exact role of 'narrowness' of focus being delayed until section 4.7):

(4.13)   *John*: What does Bob want?
        Mary: (Bob wants) a coffee.

Intuitively, Mary's statement communicates that a coffee is *the* thing that Bob wants, out of all relevant possibilities. Were the dialogue in (4.13) spoken across a table bearing cups of coffee, cups of tea and assorted food items, John would be entitled to assume that Mary is communicating that Bob does not want any tea or any of the food. This is confirmed by the intuitive feeling that if John were to give Bob a coffee only to be told by Mary *I never told you Bob wanted only coffee*, then John would have every right to feel that Mary had been either deliberately awkward or had failed to communicate efficiently in the original dialogue[14]. Thus, the intuitive understanding of the narrow focus in Mary's statement is that it is an exhaustive assertion of what may take the place of x in the proposition 'Bob wants x'.

Note that the utterance in question in (4.13) is a simple, unmarked declarative English sentence. This is not generally analysed as containing any encoding of exhaustivity and indeed there is no need to assume that there exists anything in the form of Mary's utterance to this effect. The fact that the context contains some manifest set of alternatives is all that is required for the assertion of one member of that set to be taken as excluding the others—in this case such a set, the selection of food and drink present on the table, is highly accessible from the physical environment and is obviously germane to the dialogue (i.e. via some readily accessible assumptions).

---

[14]Such situations can arise, of course, and it is one of the strengths of RT that it predicts both interpretations of them, including simple failure of communication. If it is manifestly the case that Mary is acting in a deliberately unco-operative manner, John may take assumptions about her attitude to him to be part of what is communicated by her latter statement. If, on the other hand, there is no such assumption manifest, it may be that communication has broken down due to the interlocutors' misjudging the nature of the mutual cognitive environment—for example, Mary may have considered it mutually manifest that only people's preferences in drinks were under discussion and that everyone present should be given food, but failed to realise that this assumption was not in fact manifest to John. As mentioned in Chapter 1, only a heavily inferential pragmatic theory with a psychological conception of context can explain how failures of communication are admitted by the same mechanisms that normally facilitate communication.

118 *Shifting the Focus*

The precise nature of the reasoning behind this claim is considered in section 4.5.7; for now it is sufficient to note that it is based upon the assumption that the communicator will not withhold any relevant information—and it is clearly relevant information to know when manifest alternatives to a focused item are in fact involved in the same eventuality. The following sections highlight some crucial features of such exhaustive interpretations and how these point towards an inferential approach to exhaustive focus in both English and Hungarian.

4.5.2 Dependence on (psychological) context

The pertinent notion of exhaustivity has little to do with model-theoretically definable truths. Exhaustive readings are only ever exhaustive with respect to contextually relevant sets of entities, whose membership depends upon contextually relevant assumptions[15]. Were John, in the same physical environment, to precede his question in (4.13) with a declaration that there isn't much tea left, it might be considered mutually manifest that only drinks are relevant to the discussion, in which case Mary's answer would be considered exhaustive only with respect to the set $\{coffee, tea\}$ and John would not understand her to have communicated that Bob doesn't want any of the available food.

As noted at various points above, this context-dependence of exhaustive readings is recognised also by those who would encode exhaustivity, or the invocation of alternatives, as in Rooth's (1992) adoption of the operator $\sim$, which prompts a search for a contextually-restricted set, or Szabolcsi's (1983) introduction of contextual indices into her semantic representations of what the Hungarian pre-verbal position putatively encodes. That the exhaustivity of Hungarian pre-verbal foci is clearly context-dependent in the same way as that of the English narrow focus in (4.13) can be illustrated with the following example from Szabolcsi (1983, 139):

(4.14)   [$_F$ Joseph Conrad] született lengyelnek.
         Joseph Conrad was-born Polish-DAT
         'It's Joseph Conrad who was born Polish.'

Clearly, it is extremely unlikely that any speaker would produce (4.14)—whether the Hungarian sentence or its English *it*-cleft translation—in order to communicate a belief that no-one other than Joseph Conrad has ever been born Polish. Rather, some relevant aspects of the context will make it clear that Conrad is asserted to be the only one of some particular restricted set of people to have been born with that nationality. The set in question might, for example, be any of 'great British novelists', 'British novelists of the nineteenth century', 'writers of English literature who were not first-language speakers of English', or indeed sets dependent on very particular conversational contexts such as the set $\{Joseph\ Conrad,\ Jasper\ Conran\}$. What will determine the

---

[15]Note that this does not rule out the possibility of certain sets that are manifest in any context acting as the set of alternatives to a narrow focus. One such set is the (infinite) set of numerals, which is manifest to all language users who can count. See below and Chapter 5, section 5.2.3.

actual set with respect to which the assertion of Conrad is taken to be exhaustive is entirely a matter of the interlocutors' mutually manifest assumptions, concerning such matters as (say) the speaker's depth of knowledge of English literature, the current relevance of the issue of writing in foreign languages, or (in the last example) the prior assumptions of the addressee regarding the ethnic background of a well-known fashion designer (assumptions which the communicator recognises as originating in confusion caused by similar-sounding names).

The point of such examples is to emphasise not only that the sets with respect to which exhaustivity is understood are dependent on context, but that the appropriate notion of context is necessarily a psychological one of the kind employed in RT, rather than merely a physical 'situation'. Since this crucial element in the generation of exhaustive meanings depends entirely on interlocutors' mutually manifest assumptions, it seems sensible to investigate just how much of the phenomenon of exhaustivity can be accounted for in terms of pragmatic theory alone, rather than adopting the semanticist's strategy of attempting to capture as much as possible from the outset in model-theoretic formulae and resorting to *ad hoc* contextual operators or variables where this fails. The above examples of what is in fact quite commonplace reasoning illustrate a point made in Chapters 1 and 2: highly sophisticated inferential abilities, which must be based in interlocutors' assumptions about each others' cognitive environments and intentions, are inevitably required to explain contextually restricted domains for interpretations like exhaustivity, whether or not one posits such technical apparatus as contextual variables. Give this, it behooves us to ask whether these inferential abilities might be sufficient to motivate as well as effect the restriction of domains, rendering such apparatus superfluous. The arguments of the following sections suggest that this is the case.

4.5.3 Alternatives emerge from context

The fact that consideration of sets of alternatives is involved in a given act of interpretation need not be introduced by any dedicated linguistic mechanism. A dialogue such as (4.13) shows clearly that sets of alternatives can be manifestly a part of the context in advance of a statement containing a focus. The context in which Mary makes her statement includes not only the physically present alternatives on the table, but also the assumptions made manifest by John's question. Depending on other aspects of the cognitive environment, these might include, for example, 'John would like to know which of the available items to pass to Bob' or 'John would like to know whether to make more tea'. Such contexts necessarily involve the manifestness of certain relevant sets (in the first case, the set of food and drink items on the table, in the second perhaps only the set of available drinks). In a cognitive environment in which such a set of alternatives is already manifestly relevant to the act of communication that is taking place, the addressee (John) cannot help but reason about any assertion in the light of this set. Hence no encoded, semantic-level mechanism, not even an anaphoric device (such as Rooth 1992 could be said to provide), is therefore necessary to bring these alternatives into play, nor to link them to the interpretation of Mary's assertion. It suffices simply that the addressee be able to recognise the asserted part of the utterance, as opposed to what is (pragmatically) presupposed, in order to ensure that the appropriate context is accessed and the appropriate inferences triggered.

Of course, not all instances of exhaustive interpretation occur in linguistic and extra-linguistic contexts like those in (4.13). But alternative sets are generated by contextual considerations alone even when the context is more obviously constructed on the basis of the incoming utterance itself, rather than largely determined in advance by factors like a preceding question and/or salient parts of the immediate physical environment. Consider a rather different dialogue, such as (4.15), in which there is no explicit *Wh*-question determining the narrow focus in Pete's statement.

(4.15)　　*Liz*: Someone should feed the tigers and the cheetahs. I wonder if Jake is around.
　　　　　Pete: Jake feeds lions.

Intuitively, one way of understanding Pete's contribution to the dialogue in (4.15) is as a kind of correction, conveying (at least) the message 'There's no point wondering about Jake, because he does lion-feeding, not tiger-feeding or cheetah-feeding.' This kind of corrective reading is a sub-type of exhaustive reading, as it clearly involves the exclusion of alternatives (see also section 4.5.4, below), yet Pete's statement is still in the form of a normal declarative sentence and there is no preceding *Wh*-question to which the evocation of alternatives could be attributed. Furthermore, there is no general cultural assumption that no-one could or would feed more than one kind of big cat which could be said to explain the exhaustive reading independently. Both the evocation of alternatives and the exhaustivity understood with respect to them emerge, in fact, from nothing more than the general process of the addressee seeking to recover the communicator's intentions on the basis of relevance-based reasoning. This proceeds roughly as follows.

Liz does not ask what animals Jake feeds, but Pete's contribution can still be read as containing narrow focus on *lions*—in confirmation of this, note that Pete's contribution could felicitously be changed to *It's lions that Jake feeds*, without changing the meaning greatly[16]. Liz's contribution makes manifest the assumption 'Jake feeds tigers', which has an entailment 'Jake feeds a kind of big cat'. Pete is able to treat the latter assumption as being itself mutually manifest, since it can be thus inferred from an existing manifest assumption. Therefore, when Pete produces a sentence of the form *Jake feeds x*, it may be understood as a presupposed (manifest) eventuality description, effectively creating a focus frame for the assertion of a particular kind of big cat.

Indeed, this is (in most imaginable situations) the *only* way in which Liz could make Pete's contribution relevant, once the whole sentence *Jake feeds lions* is processed. Given her own previous contribution and the hopes and intentions that it makes manifest, the only way in which

---

[16]Nevertheless, as RT predicts, there would be some kind of extra cognitive effects associated with the clefted version, since this would involve more processing effort from the addressee. The precise effects involved would of course depend on the context. To give a likely example, one could certainly imagine contexts in which Liz is known to have a mental block about which animals Jake feeds, in which case the cleft structure, which embodies a necessarily narrow focusing structure, emphasises the evocation of the presupposed eventuality description 'Jake feeds x' and can be taken to communicate Pete's exasperation at once again having to correct Liz on this score.

this sentence has immediate relevance is with respect to Liz's implicit assumption 'Jake feeds tigers and/or cheetahs'. Therefore, the context constructed by normal processes of relevance-based reasoning effectively associates the set of alternatives $\{tigers, cheetahs, lions\}$ with the manifest eventuality 'Jake feeds x'. No special mechanisms of 'focus semantics' are necessary; instead, an interpretation involving alternatives is simply a step in the chain of inference that leads to the optimally relevant interpretation of the utterance in question.

With this 'corrective' kind of example, it is also fairly clear on an intuitive level how the simple existence of a relevant set of alternatives leads to an exhaustive reading—it is hard to see how Pete's assertion and its concomitant evocation of alternatives could be relevant *unless* the assertion were intended to contrast with the alternatives—but this process is not always so obvious. More detailed discussion of the derivation of exhaustive readings by pragmatic principles alone is provided in section 4.5.7.

4.5.4 Different contexts; different kinds of exhaustivity

There are noticeable differences between the kinds of meanings invoked by the use of narrow focus in examples like (4.13) and (4.15). These illustrate an important theoretical point regarding the necessity to consider the origins of different interpretations, rather than merely attempting to characterise them in separate semantic representations.

These two simple examples involve the creation of quite different kinds of cognitive effect, despite the fact that (as shown in more detail in sections 4.5.8 and 4.7) these are prompted by the same basic inferential processes. In (4.13), there is an effect of strengthening the assumption 'Bob wants x' and, somewhat more significantly, there is likely to be some form of contextual implication—for example, to do with what John should do next, or whether John can afford not to make more tea. The most obvious cognitive effects associated with (4.15), on the other hand, involve the contradiction (hence intended elimination) of existing assumptions (and additional cognitive effects may well be triggered in the form of contextual implications). This is because the eventuality that Pete's assertion refers back to, 'Jake feeds x', manifestly relates in this context to beliefs and expectations held by Liz that contrast with the assertion that Pete makes.

As this description implies, the difference in meaning effectively originates in the particular role played by alternatives to the focus in a given context. The alternatives to a focus like that in (4.13) are not evoked as a salient part of the context: they are manifest in the context in the sense that they may be calculated, should their identity be or become relevant in some way (recall that the definition of manifestness includes what can be inferred from other manifest assumptions). Otherwise, they remain in the background, so to speak. Thus, in (4.13) Mary is understood to be communicating that Bob wants a coffee and it is inferable for the sake of any contextual implications that John might draw (for example, regarding what John should pass to Bob) that Bob doesn't want anything else; it is not taken to be a central part of Mary's meaning that, for instance, Bob doesn't want a sandwich (in the absence of further mutually manifest assumptions that might indicate this). That is, the exhaustivity of Mary's assertion can be thought of as in

122 *Shifting the Focus*

some sense 'incidental', although (as the discussion above makes clear) it is clearly a part of the interpretation. So the set of contextually available alternatives is not seen as the primary motivation for or the point of Mary's utterance, but it is an unavoidable part of the context of that utterance.

Exhaustive readings may involve still less salient sets of alternatives. This is likely to be true, for example, when the set of alternatives is one of the special cases whose existence is not dependent on a particular context. The (infinite) set of numerals, for example, is manifest to all numerate language users and does not change according to the assumptions manifest in a particular context (with the possible exception of the mutual cognitive environments of certain advanced mathematicians). If a numeral is narrowly focused, there will normally be some range of numbers, some sub-sequence of the infinite set, that forms the set of contextually possible alternatives to the focus, but the members of even such a relatively restricted range may be of extremely low salience: it may be quite large and/or open-ended and in any case does not have to be constructed in the course of processing, on the basis of context-dependent assumptions, as most other alternative sets must be. Precisely because of this relative independence from the context, the members of this kind of set are unlikely to be viewed as a central part of the message conveyed in a given context. Nevertheless, a narrow focus asserted against such an alternative set is interpreted as being exhaustive with respect to it, in the unmarked case. Consider (4.16).

(4.16)   The exam was failed by SIX students.

Such an utterance may of course be produced in the context of a highly restricted set of manifest expectations or prior beliefs, creating an alternative set of the nature of $\{five, six\}$, as when the communicator is correcting the addressee's mistaken belief that only five students failed the exam. In this case there is a clear parallelism to examples like (4.15). On the other hand, the addressee may manifestly have reasons to be interested in how many students failed the exam (hence the availability of the presupposed focus frame 'The exam was failed by n students') without having any prior expectations or beliefs about the actual number, other than the general range '0–[*the size of the class*]'. In this case, the involvement of alternatives is not felt to be a central part of the message conveyed—there is no particular expression of contrast with the other numbers in the given range—but the interpretation is nonetheless exhaustive. This is shown most clearly in the fact of the so-called 'scalar implicature' that *six* in (4.16) means 'exactly six', rather than 'at least six'. The relevance-theoretic explanation of scalar implicature is presented in section 4.5.8. What is of interest here is simply the fact that it occurs, and that it is clearly explicable as a kind of exhaustivity—the exclusion of all alternatives to *six*, which includes all numerals higher in the scale—even though the alternatives in question are not perceived to be a particularly salient part of either the context or the meaning of the utterance[17].

---

[17]Szabolcsi (1997b) takes the 'exactly six' reading to be a different kind of phenomenon to more obviously 'contrastive' or 'corrective' cases of focus on a numeral, at least in Hungarian. She analyses the former as not syntactically focused at all, but rather moved to a different pre-verbal position that has exclusively quantificational

Examples like (4.13) and (4.16), in which alternatives are merely an unavoidable part of the context, may be distinguished from cases like (4.15), in which it is precisely contrast with salient alternatives that makes the narrow focus relevant. This inevitably produces an impression that the sense of contrast is itself deliberately communicated. The important point here is that it is the role of alternatives in the process of recognising the communicator's intentions that determines what precise kind of exhaustive reading arises. As these examples show, this is a matter of the context in which alternatives are invoked; there is no reason to posit any differences in what is encoded.

This point is important because it exemplifies the potential dangers of any syntactico-semantic approach that attempts to match characterisations of 'observed meanings' directly with grammatical constructions (see Chapter 1). Attempts are sometimes made to identify sub-categories of focus according to the apparent impact they have in context, leading to the belief in some cases that, for example, 'contrastive focus' is different in kind to 'exhaustive focus' (see, for instance, É. Kiss 1998a) and to the proposal of other categories, whose theoretical status is not always clear, such as 'corrective sentences' (a category into which (4.15) would presumably fit). The temptation for the linguist faced with any such variety of meanings is to encode them separately, or at least to assume that one of them is necessarily encoded as such and the others derived somehow from it. This approach is apparently supported by observed tendencies for different constructions in different languages to be associated with different sub-types of exhaustivity. But these constructions must be analysed also in terms of the inferences that they tend to provoke, for one reason or another. Inferential pragmatic reasoning shows that such distinctions are at best descriptive labels for sub-categories of exhaustive reading, none of which is encoded as such.

This point also constitutes evidence against the kind of methodology advocated by Rooth (1996), which seeks to characterise 'the semantics of focus' (see section 4.2.2). Even assuming that one can somehow capture the necessarily context-dependent effects of focus within semantic representations, it turns out that one must ask not only 'what kind of focus?' but even 'what kind of exhaustive focus?'. Then, by characterising one kind or another semantically, one may do so at the expense of understanding more fundamental factors that link the different observed readings, as different facets of a single phenomenon. The following quotation shows the kind of problems that this causes for purely semantic methodology:

> it would be surprising if at least many of the things in the world's languages that we call focus did not turn out to have a common semantic and/or pragmatic core. ...Conceivably, ...the common core might turn out to be the weak semantics of the prominence feature [i.e. what is expressed by the use of primary phonological stress—DW] in English, with some constructions and morphemes expressing additional semantic content—such as existential presupposition or exhaustive listing—in

---

significance. The recognition that all such uses of numerals are effectively just a special case of exhaustive narrow focus therefore removes an unnecessary complication of the grammar. This issue is taken up in detail in Chapter 5.

addition to and in terms of the basic semantics. (Rooth 1996, 296)

Given the nature of Rooth's proposed semantics for English prosodic focus, this amounts to the idea that something could be added to the notion of 'assertion in the context of alternatives' to produce the exhaustive reading that is commonly associated with Hungarian pre-verbal foci. This seems very odd: exhaustive focus *is* assertion in the context of alternatives, so it is hard to see how any added element of meaning could possibly be considered to make this definition more precise. Moreover, consideration of the above examples shows that the supposed interpretive difference between the English and Hungarian focusing strategies is in fact spanned by the range of meanings associated with just one of them (i.e. with English narrow foci expressed in sentences of unmarked word order). The differences between what are really different kinds of exhaustive focus reading can be traced to the particular kinds of contextual relationship that the focus may bear to its alternatives. The identification of this contextual relationship is shown by the English data to depend on communicatively-oriented inferential processes, not on what can be encoded in different grammatical constructions.

4.5.5 Non-exhaustive narrow foci are linguistically marked

Overall, what the English examples (4.13) and (4.15) demonstrate is that exhaustivity represents an unmarked reading that follows automatically, by inference, once the information structure of an utterance is recognised to involve narrow focus—note that while the previous section shows different kinds of narrow focus reading to exist, none of these are non-exhaustive, other things being equal. This is further confirmed by the fact that special forms of signalling are generally required if the assertion of an individual entity is ever to be understood as non-exhaustive—as, for example, when a non-exhaustive reply is given to a *Wh*-question. Frequently, explicit phrases such as 'among others' are employed for this purpose; at the very least, special intonational signalling is required. A narrow focus asserted with the normal, falling pitch accent is typically taken to be exhaustive. If a speaker wishes to communicate that a narrow focus is non-exhaustive, the so-called rise-fall-rise tone is employed[18].

For example, imagine Mary's contribution in (4.13) uttered with a rise-fall-rise on the word *coffee*. This would communicate to John that Mary knows that Bob wants coffee, but also that there may well be other things (from among the contextually available options) that Bob also wants. Depending on other mutually manifest assumptions, John may derive other, more specific implications from this, such as that Mary expects that Bob wants something to eat, but doesn't know for sure; or that Mary does know of other things that Bob wants, but is for some

---

[18] Herburger (2000, 50ff.) argues that this pattern can be reduced to the assumption that a falling tone indicates 'closure' or 'completeness', while a tone which ends in a rise indicates a sense of the utterance remaining 'open' or 'unfinished' in its relationship to the context. This is consistent with the examples discussed in the main text. There is a clear sense in which an utterance which presents itself as 'incomplete' or 'unfinished' is more marked than one which is presented as a complete contribution to a discourse; see also the comments of Horvath (2000), quoted below. The argument here does not depend on such an analysis, however.

reason deliberately withholding this information from John (perhaps to invite him to guess, for example).

In addition, note that unless the context contains a quite rich set of assumptions that lead to such an interpretation, Mary is likely to employ not merely a marked intonation pattern, but an explicit explanation (e.g. *I know he wants coffee, but I don't know if he wants anything else*, or *He wants coffee, among other things*), in order to avoid the implication that her answer is exhaustive.

The crucial question, then, is whether Hungarian behaves in the same way. While consideration of the pragmatics of English examples suggests that exhaustivity should be considered an unmarked and inferentially derived element of meaning, this is not the view that is typically found in the literature on Hungarian 'focus position'. In most work on Hungarian it is assumed that the use of the PV position to express focus is necessarily a more marked option than any alternative word order (the term 'non-neutral' being commonly applied to sentences that show use of the PV position). That is, it is assumed that the use of the position must add something (such as an exhaustivity operator) to what would be the unmarked interpretation of the sentence. This is a natural enough assumption within an approach that views the existence of immediately pre-verbal expressions as the result of movement operations. Under such an analysis, a special syntactic operation appears to be associated with exhaustive interpretations, which in turn supports the idea that exhaustivity needs to be specially signalled. It is generally not questioned within syntactic analyses whether this view on exhaustivity is compatible with pragmatic theory.

Conversely, non-exhaustive foci are said to be associated with an unmarked, post-verbal syntactic position. However, there is clear evidence that Hungarian in fact resembles English in treating non-exhaustive narrow foci as a marked option that must be specially signalled. Indeed, the relevant facts in the two languages are strikingly similar, notwithstanding the complication of an apparent syntactic 'focus position' in Hungarian. Horvath (2000, 201) comes close to saying as much in her description of non-exhaustive answers to *Wh*-questions, such as (4.17) (Horvath's (24); capitals indicate phonological stress)[19].

(4.17) Kit hívtak meg?
       'Who did they invite?'

    a.   Jánost   hívták   meg.
         János-ACC invited-3PL VM
         'They invited JÁNOS (and nobody else).'

    b.   Meghívták   *(például   / többek között) Jánost.
         VM-invited-3PL   for.example / others among János-ACC
         'They invited JÁNOS for example / among others.'

Horvath notes (with an implicitly Gricean perspective) that

---

[19] See Roberts (1998) for further discussion and exemplification of non-exhaustive focus. Roberts notes that many speakers describe examples of this kind not merely as marked but as of marginal acceptability, if acceptable at all.

Since the pragmatically "normal" way of providing information e.g. in contexts like (wh-)questions (as in [(4.17)]) is to be maximally informative, any time a less than exhaustive identification of the relevant entities is provided, namely when Focus is left in situ, as in [(4.17b)], in Hungarian, the sentence sounds well-formed only if some explicit indication of the given information being incomplete/non-exhaustive is provided (e.g., by adding 'for example' or 'among others', or at least some rising intonation on the listed element(s) signaling the list being unfinished due to problems with recall).

To this extent, the Hungarian situation appears to resemble that in English (even down to the use of rising intonation to signal an 'unfinished' or 'incomplete' act of communication). Horvath attempts nevertheless to link the Hungarian facts to the existence of an 'exhaustivity operator' which is said to determine movement to the pre-verbal position. She argues that the necessity to signal non-exhaustivity in Hungarian indicates that a syntactically encoded strategy "takes precedence over leaving the choice of exhaustive vs. non-exhaustive interpretation open for pragmatics". But if this were the case, one would not expect explicit signalling of non-exhaustivity to be a necessary, marked operation also in English, which (as Horvath herself convincingly argues) does not have any kind of syntactic encoding of exhaustivity or focus. In any case, it seems odd to argue that the obligatory signalling of exhaustivity should necessitate the signalling also of non-exhaustivity—one would rather expect it to remove this necessity, as the latter is then redundant. These problems are easily avoided by recognising (as pragmatic principles in any case suggest) that exhaustive interpretations are the norm—as implied by Horvath's own reference to what is 'pragmatically normal'. Thus, Horvath's argumentation illustrates the dangers of conventional syntactic assumptions that fail to take into account the role of pragmatics.

In addition, the above discussion illustrates the problem of referring to 'neutral word order' out of context. It may be true that an utterance containing a narrow focus could be considered intrinsically less 'neutral' than one with a topic>comment structure (in the sense that the former requires a special context that contains quite detailed presuppositions about particular eventualities) and narrow foci are typically associated with the PV position. But a non-exhaustive narrow focus is far more marked, hence less 'neutral', than an exhaustive one, even if it shows no use of the immediately pre-verbal position, as in (4.17b).

While the unmarkedness of exhaustive narrow foci compromises the idea that special grammatical operations are required to produce them, the fact that non-exhaustive narrow foci appear post-verbally might still seem to constitute syntactic evidence in favour of the conventional analysis. It might be argued that even if non-exhaustivity is in some sense marked, the data show that the pre-verbal position cannot be considered simply the position of narrow foci—if it were, non-exhaustive narrow foci would be expected to appear there too. The fact that they do not might then be put down to the pre-verbal position being after all reserved for (or only licensed by) exhaustive foci.

This kind of reasoning would amount to pure stipulation of a syntax-semantics correspondence, disregarding the nature of the interpretations involved and other arguments concerning whether or not they should be encoded. How else might this correspondence be accounted for? One possibility is that the pre-verbal appearance of non-exhaustive foci is blocked for purely phonological reasons; an analysis that would clearly leave open the idea that the pre-verbal 'focus position' would otherwise be visibly the position of narrow foci as such. The rising pitch accent associated with non-exhaustive foci would effectively block the particular phonological relationship between pre-verbal expression and verb that is a necessary aspect of the PV configuration (as noted in Chapter 3, section 3.2.2). However, there is another side to the issue: since the arguments of this section show non-exhaustive foci to be marked both interpretively and structurally, one would ideally wish to identify a positive reason for their appearance post-verbally—despite the assumptions of certain syntactic accounts, there is no particular reason to treat the post-verbal domain as in some sense a 'default' position for all constituents. In section 4.7.2, I argue that post-verbal non-exhaustive narrow foci are nothing other than narrow foci which are presented as if they were involved in broad foci. This is, after all, the normal information-structural reading of expressions that follow a stressed verb that is the first post-topic element (since the verb usually introduces the 'comment' in a topic>comment sentence). There I argue that there are good interpretive reasons why a narrow focus presented in this way would be associated with a non-exhaustive reading. As a result, far from providing evidence in favour of the encoding of exhaustivity in the pre-verbal 'focus position', the post-verbal appearance of non-exhaustive foci turns out to support the dynamic perspective of the relationship between structure and interpretation, whereby interpretations arise on the basis of a left-to-right parse of the sentence.

4.5.6 The *it*-cleft translation

The cross-linguistic data of the previous section, from exhaustive and non-exhaustive narrow foci, suggest that there is a rather close parallel between narrow foci expressed in English sentences with unmarked word order (in which information structure is signalled only by phonological means) and narrow foci which appear in the immediately pre-verbal position in Hungarian. This runs against the common belief, most explicitly presented by É. Kiss (1998a), that interpretively Hungarian pre-verbal focus represents something significantly different to any notion of focus that is attributable to the use of pitch accents alone in English. As noted in Chapter 3, sentences containing pre-verbal foci are instead usually considered roughly equivalent to English *it*-cleft sentences[20]. This correspondence is implied also by the tests for truth-conditionality of meaning discussed in section 4.4.1, hence any evidence against it has repercussions for the assumption of compositionality that motivates the use of these tests.

The supposed correspondence between PV focus and *it*-cleft constructions is easily investigated. If it holds in the ways suggested in the literature, these two constructions should regularly

---

[20] Again, É. Kiss (1998a) states this particularly clearly, a parallel syntactic analysis for *it*-clefts being developed in É. Kiss (1999).

translate each other felicitously, being suited to use in the same kinds of context. Meanwhile, PV focus should not felicitously translate to the simple use of pitch accent to express narrow focus within unmarked word order in English, or *vice versa*. None of these predictions of the commonly accepted view is correct, as the following simple examples show.

First, consider the translation of the non-cleft English example (4.13), as in (4.18):

(4.18)   *John*: Bob mit   akar?
                 Bob what-ACC wants
         Mary: (Bob) egy kávét   (akar).
                 Bob a   coffee-ACC wants

As already seen in examples like (4.6) and (4.17a), the use of the PV position is obligatory in the only possible full sentence answer to this kind of simple *Wh*-question. However, the equivalent English example, (4.13), uses unmarked word order and furthermore an *it*-cleft would generally be quite infelicitous here.

While such examples run counter to the assumption of a close correspondence between PV and *it*-cleft constructions, they also hint at an explanation of why this assumption is commonly made. Recall that the normal way to answer a question like that in (4.18) would involve the elision of all presupposed material, as indicated by the parentheses used in the example. This means that the use of PV is very rarely encountered as an audible response to a *Wh*-question, even though native speakers recognise that any full sentence answer would have to involve this position in cases of narrow focus (as reflected in Horvath's use of the position in (4.17a)). As a result, explicit, observable use of the PV position tends to be associated with contexts in which the narrowness of the focus is not predetermined by a context-question. These are the kinds of contexts in which an *it*-cleft is more likely to be used in English, to disambiguate or emphasise the information structure of the utterance. Furthermore, these are also the kinds of context in which a narrow focus is more likely to result in a clearly contrastive reading (see section 4.5.4). Hence, it is not due to a special correspondence in encoded meaning that observable data involving the use of PV tend to be translatable with a cleft, but rather because of the coincidental 'invisibility' of PV structures in certain key contexts[21].

Note also that most syntactico-semantic literature deals in example sentences that are presented with no indication of context at all. This also encourages the association of PV foci with the *it*-cleft construction. As section 4.5.4 suggests, and the RT reasoning of section 4.5.8 explains, a strong sense of intended contrast is more likely to be understood in cases where the addressee must put significant effort into constructing important elements of the context, such as identifying potentially relevant alternatives to the item in focus. These are, of course, the kind of readings associated with English *it*-clefts (for reasons beyond the scope of the present work). Since the reader of a decontextualised linguistic example almost inevitably has to put extra effort

---

[21] Further support for this idea comes from Brunetti (2003), who independently comes to very similar conclusions regarding foci in a left-peripheral position in Italian.

into reconstructing a relevant context, it follows that decontextualised examples containing narrow foci will naturally tend to be translatable with a cleft. Thus common linguistic methodology tends to push the analyst's mind towards a certain reading of PV focus examples, but this should not be taken to represent the full of range of readings, let alone assumed to reflect the encoded semantics.

The translation of (4.15) (repeated as (4.19a)), provides a converse example: here a perfectly felicitous use of unmarked word order in English requires the use of the PV position in its Hungarian translation (no other word order would convey the same meaning). The Hungarian translation, (4.19b) (like (4.17) and (4.18)), therefore shows that PV focus cannot be associated directly with the English *it*-cleft; it demonstrably covers also instances of unmarked English word order. This further erodes any analysis whereby the former constructions are claimed to encode exhaustivity, in contradistinction to English unmarked focus by pitch accent.

(4.19) a. *Liz*: Someone should feed the tigers and the cheetahs. I wonder whether Jake is around.
Pete: Jake feeds lions.

b. *Liz*: Valakinek   meg kellene etetnie   a tigriseket és a gepárdokat.
someone-DAT VM should feed-INF.3SG the tigers-ACC and the cheetahs-ACC
Jake vajon   itt   van?
Jake whether here is
Pete: Jake oroszlánokat etet.
Jake lions-ACC   feeds

As noted in section 4.5.3, an *it*-cleft could be substituted for Pete's contribution in (4.19a), but the fact that it need not be shows that the contrastive meaning of the utterance is determined by inference in context and not by anything encoded in the cleft construction. While it is far from impossible for what is inferred in one language to be encoded in another (one need only consider the encoding of progressive aspect in English, or the wide cross-linguistic differences between personal pronoun systems), the possibility of recovering the interpretation in question by inference alone at least means that an analysis involving encoding should not be the only one, or even the first one, considered by linguists.

Moreover, evidence that there is no particular correspondence between the Hungarian PV position and the English *it*-cleft undermines entirely the arguments of section 4.4.1 and the compositional assumptions that underpin them. The tests for truth-conditionality proposed by Szabolcsi (1981) and others apply equally to PV and to *it*-clefts, as shown by É. Kiss (1998a, 1999), meaning that the compositional approach unequivocally implies that these two constructions share encoded exhaustive semantics and contrast in this way with English focus by pitch accent. Given these conclusions, (4.19) is unexpected, while (4.18)—in which PV is natural yet an *it*-cleft cannot be used—ought to be impossible.

4.5.7 Quantity implicature

According to Grice, inferential aspects of meaning are derived from the interaction of the encoded meaning of an utterance with the 'maxims' of communication that together instantiate the 'co-operative principle': "Make your conversational contribution such as is required, at the stage at which it occurs, by the accepted purpose or direction of the talk exchange in which you are engaged" (Grice 1975, 45). The particular maxims that are of current concern are the maxims of quantity, formulated as in (4.20).

(4.20)   1. Make your contribution as informative as is required (for the current purposes of the exchange).
2. Do not make your contribution more informative than is required.

Exhaustivity is arguably derivable from the first of these maxims since in effect it demands that communicators hold no useful information back. If it is informative (according to 'the accepted purpose or direction of the exchange') for the addressee to be told the identity of one object that fulfils a certain role with respect to a given eventuality, then it is presumably similarly informative, and therefore similarly 'required', to pass on the identity of any further objects that share this role. At the same time, Grice's second maxim of quantity effectively serves to ensure that only contextually relevant objects that fulfil the role in question are taken into consideration. For example, the utterance *It's Bill that I saw* will (in almost any imaginable context) be considered more 'co-operative' and felicitous than *It's Bill and the wall and the carpet and the dust on the mantelpiece* [etc. *ad infinitum*] *that I saw*, though the latter may be equally true in a given context. The latter utterance, however, gives more information than would be 'required' by a normal addressee for any normal purposes, and is therefore in contravention of the second quantity maxim.

Taken together, these maxims determine that if a communicator fails to mention all the contextually relevant objects that fulfil a role in which the addressee is interested, that communicator may be considered unco-operative. A context that produces narrow focus is one that makes clear that the addressee is (or should be) interested in the occupant(s) of a particular role. It follows that anyone obeying the first maxim of quantity will make any narrow focus exhaustive.

Notice that this reasoning has almost the status of tautology (a fact that also carries over to the RT re-working of quantity implicature discussed below): alternatives that are relevant in the context must be either asserted or assumed to be unassertable on the grounds of being false (in the role in question) precisely because of their relevance. The assertion of an object with no relevant alternatives would be trivially exhaustive—and clearly not because of any encoded instruction to interpret exhaustively (even given the existence, model-theoretically, of other possible but irrelevant alternatives). This further emphasises the points made above regarding the redundancy of any attempt to encode the exhaustivity of narrow foci and/or to define alternative sets by means of *ad hoc* contextual operators or variables: the relevance of an alternative, as determined by independent aspects of the current context, is what makes it worth mentioning if it is true and this in turn is what gives addressees the right to assume that unmentioned items are not true (or at least that the communicator does not mean to give the impression that their assertion would be true). Conversely, sets of alternatives are identifiable (*post hoc*, by the analyst) only on the basis of perceptions of what would have been worth mentioning, for independent contextual reasons.

While Grice's quantity maxims serve the purpose of conveying the intuitive basis of quantity implicature, the way in which they work illustrates one of the principal advantages of RT over Grice's approach. The quantity maxims—which are just two of nine maxims, grouped in four major categories—can be seen to deal each with one half of the problem of ensuring a relevant interpretation: the first maxim ensures that no information that would contribute to optimising the relevance of an utterance is omitted; the second blocks the mention of irrelevant information, which would cause unnecessary processing effort and therefore reduce the overall relevance of the utterance. This work is done in RT by the Principle of Relevance alone, and this deals with far more than quantity implicatures. Furthermore, the Principle of Relevance is derived from reasoning over basic assumptions about human cognitive priorities, in contrast to the specifically 'conversational' orientation of the Gricean maxims, which appear to be purposefully designed simply to plug certain gaps in the conventional code-based, truth-theoretic model of meaning and communication. It is noticeable that even the above discussion of the Gricean explanation of exhaustivity effects required crucial reference to the notion of relevance, which clearly calls for a theoretical basis to this notion.

In this sense, it is a general problem with Grice's framework that the number and nature of maxims seems somewhat *ad hoc* and the precise contribution of each rather vague. In the case of the quantity maxims, there is a clear problem determining what, even in principle, could be the definition of what is 'required' by any given conversational purpose (even if such a purpose is unequivocally recognised by all interlocutors). On the other hand, it is quite unclear what could be achieved by the so-called 'maxim of relation'—'Be relevant'—that is not already covered by the maxims of quantity.

Even abstracting away from the details of its implementation, Grice's approach rests on dubious assumptions. Communication is demonstrably not based on co-operation between interlocutors with some common purpose in mind. Being obstructive, offensive or deliberately misleading, and a host of other socially unco-operative acts, all involve successful communication, in the sense that an addressee recovers (at least) the message or messages intended by a communicator. The only common purpose that interlocutors need have is that of achieving communication, and this is not adopted as the result of following a string of stipulatory maxims, but rather follows from the reasons human beings have (and recognise in others) for paying attention to stimuli and making the effort to process them[22].

Grice's approach therefore seems quite inadequate on a theoretical level, though the quantity maxims do make clear the intuitive basis for an inferential explanation of the unmarkedness of exhaustive narrow foci. Happily, the notion of quantity implicature is easily subsumed within RT

---

[22] See Sperber & Wilson (1986/95) for more detailed criticism of Grice's framework.

and thereby given a sound footing in better motivated pragmatic principles.

4.5.8 Quantity implicature in RT

Unlike Grice, Sperber & Wilson (1986/95) derive quantity implicatures from general principles of inferential pragmatics (i.e. Relevance) rather than by invoking any specifically 'quantity'-based mechanisms[23]. I shall continue to use the term 'quantity implicature', purely as a descriptive label, to identify the particular cases of pragmatic reasoning under discussion, but it should be borne in mind that this term henceforth has no special theoretical status.

Sperber & Wilson do not discuss precisely the issue of exhaustive readings, but do cover the closely related notion of 'scalar implicature' (a sub-type of quantity implicature). This is exemplified by the common understanding of *some* to communicate 'not all'. This is such a regular aspect of the meaning of *some* that some neo-Gricean pragmatists (for example, Levinson 1987) take it to be a 'generalised implicature': an automatic part of the meaning of the word, in the absence of evidence to the contrary. Sperber & Wilson show that no such specialised information need be posited in association with this particular (kind of) word, since the meaning in question is produced by general relevance-theoretic principles, in appropriate contexts. They discuss the example of Mary's utterance in (4.21) (Sperber & Wilson 1986/95, 277).

(4.21)   *Henry*: Do all, or at least some, of your neighbours have pets?
         Mary: Some of them do.

Given the immediate context of Henry's question, Mary's utterance would normally be taken to communicate that not all of her neighbours have pets. Sperber & Wilson show that this follows from the second clause of (the 1995 version of) the Cognitive Principle of Relevance. Recall that this Principle (otherwise known as 'the presumption of optimal relevance'), is stated as in (4.22):

(4.22)   a.   The ostensive stimulus is relevant enough for it to be worth the addressee's effort to process it.
         b.   The ostensive stimulus is the most relevant one compatible with the communicator's abilities and preferences.

Clause (b) is the part that introduces the notion that relevance is optimised: out of possible utterances, *the most relevant one* should be chosen by the communicator, where relevance is understood in its technical sense, as a balance between cognitive effects and processing effort. This is necessarily understood relative to what the communicator can and will say (his or her 'abilities and preferences').

The presumption of optimal relevance has two main kinds of consequence. On the one hand, whenever an addressee is faced with an utterance that requires more processing effort than some

---

[23] Wedgwood (2002) contains a brief account of quantity implicature couched in terms of the original (1986) version of RT. This is effectively parallel to the 1995-style RT account given here.

alternative utterance, he is entitled to expect that the utterance produced carries richer cognitive effects than the alternative would have (and therefore the addressee will seek to identify these further effects). On the other hand, when a communicator chooses to produce an utterance that—by virtue of the information conveyed—is manifestly less relevant than an alternative utterance requiring similar processing effort would have been, the addressee is entitled to draw inferences about the communicator's lack of ability or willingness to communicate the alternative, since this is the only way to maintain the presumption of optimal relevance.

As it happens, the particular case of (4.21) can be explained from either direction, because of certain manifest possible utterances with which Mary's actual utterance contrasts. Although this is not mentioned by Sperber & Wilson, Mary's utterance is manifestly one that requires greater effort than an obvious alternative reply. This is because the form of Henry's question is such that the answers *Yes* and *No* are manifestly possible, given a suitable context. The fact that Mary puts Henry to the effort of processing her complete sentence instead of simply the word *Yes* shows that (at least in Mary's eyes) the relevant context must be one in which it is relevant to Henry to know not only whether pet-owners exist among her neighbours, but also whether or not it is the case that all of them come into this category (note that this is far from necessarily the case; Henry might easily be interested in the mere existence of animals in the area, given certain manifest assumptions). That is, a simple *Yes* would convey the message 'some and maybe all of Mary's neighbours have pets', so Mary's actual reply may be assumed to communicate more than this. The most relevant further cognitive effects in this case are those connected with her specification of *some* (and non-mention of *all*). The proposition 'some, but not all, of Mary's neighbours have pets' provides richer cognitive effects, since it provides information about a greater number of existing assumptions and therefore leads to a more extensive re-structuring of the mutual cognitive environment. It therefore justifies the relatively high processing effort required by Mary's utterance and is taken to be communicated by that utterance.

The explanation of (4.21) that is actually offered by Sperber & Wilson involves the second possible kind of inference. In the immediate context provided by Henry's question, it is manifest that Mary is producing the less informative of two possible positive replies (apart from *Yes*), which would each require essentially the same processing effort. That is, Mary chooses to say *some* where she might just as easily have said *all*, where *all* would have been manifestly more relevant to Henry, being more informative. Since Mary's utterance (as an act of ostensive communication) is nevertheless presumed to be the most relevant one compatible with her abilities and preferences, she thereby makes manifest that she is either unable or unwilling to produce the more informative utterance. Assumptions manifest in the context will point to which of these is the case and, if the former, which of two reasons apply: Mary may be unable to communicate something for lack of knowledge, or may be unable to communicate it because she knows it to be false.

Whichever explanation is preferred for the particular case of (4.21), the latter is more germane to the explanation of the unmarkedness of exhaustivity. As Sperber & Wilson argue[24]:

> Mary's answer in [(4.21)] is a case where the speaker has deliberately chosen to express a less informative proposition when a closely related, equally accessible and more informative proposition would have demanded no more effort, either from Mary or from the hearer. All such cases have a similar analysis. If the more informative proposition would not have been more relevant, there is no implicature. If the more informative proposition would have been more relevant, the utterance will be taken to implicate either that the speaker is unwilling or (more commonly) that she is unable to provide the more relevant information. In the latter case, the communicator's inability may be due either to her not knowing whether the more relevant information is true, or to her knowing it to be false. If either of these two possibilities is manifest and relevant, it will be treated as an implicature. (Sperber & Wilson 1986/95, 278)

This reasoning is straightforwardly applicable to the explanation of exhaustive readings. These too are cases where 'closely related, equally accessible' and manifestly more informative and more relevant propositions are contrasted with the proposition conveyed by the utterance actually produced. Thus, returning to the example (4.15), the reading 'Jake feeds lions, among other things, perhaps including tigers and cheetahs' is blocked for the same reasons that the reading 'it is true that some of my neighbours have pets, since all of them have pets' is blocked in (4.21): only the most informative manifestly possible assertion, relative to abilities and preferences, qualifies as the most relevant.

As Sperber & Wilson point out, the usual conclusion from this reasoning is that it is communicated that the communicator was unable to express the more informative proposition due to its being untrue, this being a more relevant assumption in most contexts than that the communicator is either ignorant of the facts or unwilling to communicate them (though these conclusions do of course also arise on occasion, given the existence of appropriate assumptions in the context). The overall effect of this process is that assertions tend to be understood as expressing the most informative possible proposition from among those manifestly available as relevant alternatives in the context. In other words, exhaustivity emerges as the usual reading of those assertions that are made in contexts that include manifest sets of alternatives, in the absence of evidence for lack of knowledge or unwillingness to pass on information on the part of the communicator. In general, such evidence may be provided by the communicator at the point of utterance, whence the structural markedness of non-exhaustive narrow foci, as outlined in section 4.5.5.

---

[24] Note that Sperber & Wilson consistently refer here to the assumptions regarding the communicator's willingness or ability as being 'implicated'. However, they point out elsewhere (1986/95, 257,298) that at least some kinds of so-called 'quantity implicature' may operate at the level of what is explicitly communicated, as is to be expected in RT.

It is clear that manifest sets of alternatives play a crucial role in the relevance-theoretic explanation, as they did above, in the discussion of the intuitive meanings of particular examples. Indeed, it can now be seen that the existence of such alternatives leads almost inevitably to exhaustive interpretations. This is related to the necessary context-dependence of alternative sets, as noted in section 4.5.2. Because alternatives are not mere truth-theoretic objects, but emerge only in relation to relevant assumptions in the context of utterance, they are by definition items whose assertion would increase the relevance any utterance.

Hence communicators do not provide exhaustive statements out of a specific desire or compulsion to be maximally informative as a co-operative strategy. Nor do they generally need to make a point of signalling exhaustivity by encoded means. Rather, the involuntary application of relevance-theoretic principles determines that assertions are typically inferred to be exhaustive among manifestly relevant possibilities. Communicators—who 'know' this, as relevance-based reasoners themselves—adjust their utterances accordingly[25].

4.6 THE FAILURE OF ENCODED FOCUS: THE ABSENCE OF EXHAUSTIVITY

So far in this chapter, my arguments have been limited to showing that exhaustive focus need not be encoded in the PV position, alongside primarily theoretical reasons to believe that it should not be. These arguments can be made using simple examples, the point being in most cases that some significant factor has been given too little attention in previous accounts or that some unsustainable theoretical assumption has tended to influence analysis. It is much harder to find clear-cut empirical evidence that the encoding of exhaustivity in the PV position is not only unnecessary but demonstrably incorrect. This is perhaps unsurprising: since the conventional analysis involving semantically significant syntactic movement is arguably a rather *ad hoc* response to the observed features of the 'focus position' construction, it can be expected to show a high degree of descriptive adequacy. However, such evidence does exist. Following observations of Horn (1981) concerning English (see also Vallduví 1992, 139ff.), I show here that the PV position cannot be simply a means of encoding exhaustivity. A little ironically, given the arguments of section 4.5.6, this evidence creates a parallel between the Hungarian PV and English *it*-cleft constructions, albeit a negative one: the same test rules out the possibility of encoded exhaustivity in both cases.

The basis of this evidence is the observation that any aspect of meaning that is truly encoded,

---

[25] This refers simply to the fundamental communicative behaviour of communicators' anticipating the meanings that their addressees will glean from their utterances and formulating utterances on this basis. It is important to reiterate this, however, since the talk in this section of communicators being 'unable' to express certain propositions 'because they are false' might otherwise lead to the impression that the RT explanation relies on a convention of truthfulness—which it emphatically does not (Wilson & Sperber 2002). Communicators are quite able to lie and mislead under this account, provided that they are able to maintain the right assumptions in the *mutual* cognitive environment to ensure that they communicate what they intend.

such that a given syntactic construction triggers a particular semantic effect, should not fail to appear whenever that construction is employed, regardless of context. This can be tested for by constructing a context that requires this aspect of meaning to surface in isolation in order to create a coherent discourse. If the crucial meaning is not encoded, but is rather inferentially derived on the basis of other factors, incoherence will be the result.

Horn (1981) creates such a test for the putatively encoded exhaustivity of English *it*-clefts, in the sentence (4.23a), which can be contrasted with (4.23b), in which the word *only* provides an explicit, lexical encoding of exhaustivity. If exhaustivity were encoded in the *it*-cleft construction, (4.23a) and (4.23b) should be equally acceptable, yet they clearly are not. The use of the cleft in (4.23a) proves insufficient to produce the exhaustive reading that, as (4.23b) shows, would create a coherent reading out of the connection of the two clauses by *but*.

(4.23)   a.   ??I know Mary ate a pizza but I've just discovered that it was a pizza that she ate.

   b.   I know Mary ate a pizza but I've just discovered that it was only a pizza that she ate.

Horn concludes that the exhaustivity of *it*-clefts must be due to what the Gricean tradition terms 'conversational implicature'—as opposed to 'conventional implicature' (which is essentially a form of encoding) or encoded truth-conditional meaning—but also speculates that the extra effort required in processing the special syntactic properties of a cleft is what makes the extra element of meaning, exhaustivity, more difficult to cancel with a cleft than with a focus expressed by phonological means alone, within unmarked word order. In effect, Horn thus sows the seeds of an RT analysis of the kind that I wish to promote.

It might be argued that the lack of parallelism with *only* merely shows that the kind of exhaustivity encoded syntactically is not identical to the effects of this lexical item. What is noticeable about (4.23a), however, is not simply the lack of parallelism between the cleft here and *only* in (4.23b): it is also highly significant that the reason (4.23a) is felt to contain an unacceptable conjunction is that the second clause is felt simply to repeat the information conveyed by the first—that the speaker is aware that Mary ate a pizza. This shows that there is *no* encoded truth-conditional difference between the ordinary declarative in the first clause and the *it*-cleft in the second. Such differences as do exist between these constructions in other contexts must therefore be differences in the perspective taken on the information conveyed in the course of processing, rather than differences in the information that is encoded.

Translating Horn's example into Hungarian shows that exactly the same point applies to PV foci: the sense of exhaustivity cannot be encoded in the construction, since this use of the construction fails to produce the exhaustive reading. (4.24a,b) are translations of (4.23a,b), respectively[26].

---

[26]The tense of the main verb has been changed to past to make the context still clearer—something which would also apply to the English examples (4.23a,b), according to my own intuitions, though I reproduce Horn's examples unchanged. Maintaining present tense in the Hungarian version would not alter the point at issue here.

(4.24) a. ??Azt tudtam, hogy Mari megevett egy pizzát, de most vettem
That knew.1SG that Mari VM-ate.3SG a pizza-ACC but now take
észre, hogy egy pizzát evett meg.
mind-to(VM) that a pizza-ACC ate VM

b. Azt tudtam, hogy Mari megevett egy pizzát, de most vettem
That knew.1SG that Mari VM-ate.3SG a pizza-ACC but now take
észre hogy csak egy pizzát evett meg.
mind-to(VM) that only a pizza-ACC ate VM

Another crucial aspect of Horn's examples, from my point of view, is that the exhaustivity of the English cleft and Hungarian pre-verbal focus fails to emerge just when the context prevents the clefted or pre-verbal item from being interpreted as a narrow focus. This is exactly as predicted in an inferential account of exhaustivity, as noted elsewhere in this chapter, but is quite inexplicable under a direct encoding analysis, under which the use of the relevant syntactic configuration should always map straight onto exhaustive semantics. In (4.23), the fact that *a pizza* fulfils the Patient role in the given event of Mary's eating something is already established—effectively part of a presupposed eventuality—by the time the second clause is processed. Consequently, any subsequent assertion of this NP as a narrow focus is redundant and therefore irrelevant. In (4.23b) and (4.23b), the word *only/csak* provides a new kind of narrow focus which is indeed asserted in the context of the presupposed eventuality 'Mary ate a pizza' (to the exclusion of the contextual alternative 'among other things') : note that *only* would be the locus of the main (probably quite exaggerated) pitch accent in this clause in any felicitous utterance of (4.23b).

To summarise section 4.5, the direct encoding of exhaustive semantics in constructions like the Hungarian PV position and English *it*-cleft is neither necessary nor desirable (given that the exhaustivity of narrow foci is independently predictable by pragmatic principles and demonstrably the unmarked case in both languages), nor empirically sustainable (given the absence of the exhaustive reading in carefully constructed test cases). As pointed out in section 4.4, this has theoretical and methodological implications well beyond the study of these particular phenomena: the logic of the compositional approach to the syntax-semantics interface demands that the exhaustive interpretation be encoded in the grammar, so the fact that this leads to empirical problems constitutes a challenge not only to an individual analysis but to some very fundamental and widespread assumptions. These implications have a broad theoretical reach, since few formal approaches are free of the influence of compositional semantics: for example, the demonstration that truth-conditionality of meaning cannot be relied upon to identify grammatically-encoded meaning has consequences for the methodology of many approaches, not all of which in principle include a strict assumption of compositionality. Clearly, such issues are significant for the theory of the pragmatics-semantics distinction as well as the syntax-semantics interface, supporting the post-Gricean position that inference is not limited to 'post-semantic' (i.e. non-truth-conditional) meaning, but instead pervades the process of interpretation, from the initial processing of linguistic input onwards.

Having demonstrated this important theoretical point, the remainder of this chapter ties up some loose ends. In particular, the notion of 'narrow focus', which has played an important role in the discussion of how exhaustivity is pragmatically unmarked, requires some clarification. Though a proper characterisation of the expressions that appear in the PV position must wait until the analysis in Chapter 6, the sense in which PV foci are narrow can be made a little more concrete through reference to the presupposition of an eventuality in which they participate. As section 4.7 shows, this idea helps to explain the connection between the relevant kind of narrow focus and the perception of the sense of contrast with alternatives which underpins the notion of 'exhaustive focus'. It also provides some indication of how of the less straightforward data—apparent cases of exhaustive broad foci and non-exhaustive, non-PV narrow foci—should be accounted for. This informal discussion partially prefigures the more technical analysis of Chapter 6, where the analysis moves beyond the focus-related use of the PV position.

4.7 Narrow Focus and the Presupposition of Eventualities

Having established that the exhaustivity of Hungarian PV foci can be attributed to purely inferential processes occurring in certain contexts, it is important to consider what the precise nature of these contexts is. I have argued that the creation of exhaustive readings is associated with narrow focus, on the grounds that narrow focus typically evokes contextually relevant sets of alternatives to the focused (asserted) item. This section investigates in more detail the nature of the relationship between narrow focus and alternatives (and, therefore, exhaustivity), taking into account also those exceptional contexts in which broader foci (those including the tensed verb) take on exhaustive readings. The connection between exhaustivity and narrow foci is argued to be the presupposition of a particular, identifiable eventuality—an idea that is picked up in Chapter 6 as the basis of a novel, dynamic form of neo-Davidsonian semantic representation (that is, one in which eventualities are explicitly represented), which is used in the explanation of several aspects of the pre-verbal position in Hungarian. That is, the crucial factor linking narrow focus to contextual alternatives, and therefore to exhaustivity, lies not in the focus itself—so not in anything expressible using grammatical primitives—but rather in the kind of context within which a narrow focus must be interpreted. This in turn must be understood in relation to fundamental principles of communication.

Recall what interlocutors aim to achieve by communicating, according to RT. The communicator aims to induce certain cognitive effects in the addressee, who aims to identify these as accurately as possible (based on the guiding principle that the effort demanded by the communicator's choice of ostensive stimulus will be optimally related to the richness of cognitive effects intended). The overall effect of this is to improve (by expanding or refining) their mutual cognitive environment. As Sperber & Wilson (1986/95) emphasise, this means that all genuine communication must involve the interaction of old and new assumptions, and cognitive effects are defined accordingly: existing assumptions may be strengthened or contradicted (and therefore eliminated) and/or contextual implications may be derived, the latter being conclusions drawn inferentially on the basis of both existing assumptions and newly communicated assumptions (and unavailable in the absence of either one of these).

A narrow focus itself effectively contributes only a single piece of information to the cognitive environment, typically of the nature of an entity of type $<e>$, contributed by an NP. This, on its own, does not constitute even a new assumption, much less a set of cognitive effects. In order to lead to cognitive effects, a narrow focus therefore requires a richly specified immediate context, allowing for the identification of the particular assumptions communicated by the assertion of this lone piece of information (and, in turn, their relationships to other existing assumptions).

At the level of an individual sentence, the immediate context required to make sense of a narrowly focused entity is of a particular kind. Each sentence conveys a certain eventuality (event or state). Therefore, if the asserted part of the sentence is only an entity, there must be a particular eventuality manifest in the context with respect to which this entity makes an assertion. Any explicit material that appears with a narrow focus—the typically unstressed material that one might call a 'focus frame'—helps to identify the eventuality in question. Hence the idea that the information structure of a sentence can be characterised in terms of 'focus and presupposition': the focus frame represents an eventuality that is presupposed by the assertive use of a single, simple phrase; i.e. by a narrow focus (see section 4.2.4 above for the appropriate conception of 'presupposition')[27]. Note that the information within a Hungarian NP that goes beyond the mere identification of an entity, case marking, can be viewed as purely procedural information that indicates how the entity is to be integrated into some eventuality, once the latter is recovered from the context.

The reason this kind of context is associated with the evocation of alternatives to the focused entity is essentially the relative specificity of the context provided by the presupposed eventuality. The discussion of examples (4.13) and (4.15) in section 4.5.1 already implies this: in each case, the recognition of a narrow focus leads to the identification of a manifest (incomplete) eventuality into which the focused item is to be integrated and this in turn calls up any expectations or assumptions that exist in the context with regard to this eventuality. These expectations or other related assumptions determine the possible range of alternatives to the item asserted as the focus. In fact, the very concept of a presupposed eventuality leads almost inevitably to the evocation of expectations or other assumptions concerning alternatives: a mentally represented eventuality is in essence a state of affairs conceptualised in a particular way (i.e. with particular details invoked, foregrounded or ignored; particular perspectives taken; anchored in particular spatio-temporal co-ordinates; and so on), so any eventuality that is mutually manifest as such must involve a clear shared conceptualisation of a state of affairs in the world. Given this level of detailed

---

[27] Recall (section 4.2.4) that, thanks to the possibility of 'accommodation', a presupposed eventuality need not always be pre-existing and salient in the context, though this will tend to be the case.

shared information, interlocutors could hardly fail to share a quite restricted set of assumptions about any given participant in such an eventuality.

With a case like (4.13), the very act of asking a *Wh*-question implies that it is relevant to establish which of any contextually possible alternatives plays a particular role in a particular eventuality: the question effectively establishes the eventuality in question and the set of alternatives (which may be more or less salient, see below) is determined by contextually manifest assumptions relating to this eventuality. Thus, the question in (4.13) makes clear that an eventuality of the form 'Bob wants x' is the eventuality with respect to which Mary's assertion is to be assessed. Relevance-based reasoning will lead to accessing the appropriate assumptions that allow the formulation of an eventuality that is a concrete conceptualisation of an already manifest idea: that Bob is presumed to desire at least a drink of some kind. That is, the eventuality $e_i : want'(bob', x)$ is established as part of the immediate context for the interpretation of Mary's subsequent assertion, while the set of alternatives to the item asserted by Mary with respect to e_i can be constructed from manifest assumptions that relate to e_i in the context. As discussed in section 4.5.1, this might be based in this case upon food and drink physically present in the context, or might be restricted to a certain set of available drinks (to give just two likely examples), depending entirely on what assumptions are manifest and how accessible they are in any given context.

In (4.15), which features no *Wh*-question, further inferential steps are involved in establishing the eventuality with respect to which the focus is to be interpreted, as seen in section 4.5.1. Nevertheless, the presupposition of a particular eventuality must be involved and this leads to the identification of alternatives in just the same way. In the case of (4.15), it is clear that the relevant set of alternatives relates to the expectations that the addressee, Liz, has prior to the assertion of the narrow focus. It is manifest that Liz believes that Jake will feed tigers and cheetahs and the purpose of Pete's utterance is to contradict this expectation, via a process of quantity implicature. Expectations are assumptions that may be manifest in context in the same way as any other assumption, so the basic process involved in the interpretation of (4.15) is just the same as that involved in (4.13). That is, the different effects associated with the two examples are all traceable to the act of asserting the participation of a certain entity (in a certain role) within the context of a presupposed eventuality—and hence also in the context of manifest assumptions associated with it.

In contrast, consider the classic 'topic>comment' kind of utterance, in which what is presupposed is merely the existence of some participant and what is asserted is a 'broader' complex of information, involving both participants and verbal meaning(s). With only the identity of a particular participant to go on, and the knowledge that the communicator is asserting some whole new eventuality with respect to this participant, the addressee cannot formulate a closed set of expectations. Indeed, if the very point of a utterance is (manifestly) to convey a new eventuality—a new way of relating the topical entity to other entities and to truth-values—then the addressee's principal expectation is precisely that of gaining hitherto unknown and unpredictable information. Just as importantly, there is no limit in any context on the number of different eventualities that could in principle be predicated of an individual participant, all of different degrees and kinds of relevance to the addressee. There is therefore generally no reason to view different eventualities as alternatives to each other, rather than simply complementary pieces of information that contribute cumulatively to the set of assumptions that constitutes the mutual cognitive environment. As a result, topic>comment (i.e. broad focus) sentences are not usually associated with exhaustivity.

One might question why abstract representations of eventualities as such should be invoked in this kind of explanation of the evocation of alternatives. Given that the specificity of the context for narrow focus seems in many ways to be the essential factor, it might be thought that any mental representation that separates out a narrowly focused expression from a presupposed 'focus frame' is a sufficient basis for this line of argument. For example, simply using lambda-abstraction might be considered appropriate, as in the 'structured meanings' approach of Cresswell (1985) and von Stechow (1991b) (see section 4.2.2) . Alongside the above comments, evidence for the importance of conceptualisation in terms of eventualities is provided by those marked utterances, like (4.25) (repeated from (4.8b)), that show an exhaustive reading with an apparently broad focus (that is, a focus including at least the tensed verb).

(4.25)   János a   cikkeket   olvasta, és nem a   fürdőszobában énekelt.
         János the articles-ACC read   and not the bathroom-in   sang
         'What János did was read the articles (it's not that he sang in the bathroom).'

Such utterances are clearly exhaustive in the very obvious sense of being contrastive/corrective; that is, they clearly involve the assertion of one chunk of information in the context of manifest alternative expectations or prior contrasting assumptions. They do not, however, contrast different eventualities with each other: as argued above, different eventualities do not lend themselves to analysis as mutually exclusive alternatives. Rather, these utterances must be analysed as contrasting alternative characterisations of a single presupposed eventuality. Every communicated contrast requires a fixed point, recognised by both interlocutors, in terms of which the contrast is drawn, and this is provided in these cases by a somewhat abstract eventuality. Thus, there is necessarily a presupposed eventuality involved in the interpretation of such utterances, even though most or all of the participants in it are under dispute. In other words, there must be an abstract eventuality that is 'indexed' for the interlocutors in some way, whose basic content can therefore be questioned without the eventuality losing its identity.

This might be simply a matter of spatial and/or temporal indexing, allowing for discussion of things like 'the eventuality involving János at time t', or may be uniquely identifiable by other means, such as causal relationships with other eventualities: for example, the eventuality manifestly under discussion in (4.25) might be 'eventuality e_{n-1}, the eventuality that caused eventuality e_n, the fact that Mari went into shock'. That this is the correct view of such examples is strongly suggested by the English translation of this kind of sentence, as in *It's not that John sang in the bathroom, but* ..., where the pronoun *it* can be analysed in Davidsonian terms as an anaphor upon an established eventuality referent; that is, roughly, 'Eventuality e_i (the eventuality under discussion) is not correctly characterised as one of John singing in the bathroom' (Davidson 1967; see also Chapter 6, section 6.3.1).

Positing a presupposed eventuality in such cases provides precisely the right kind of abstract entity around which to base the observed exhaustive interpretation; the peg on which to hang different semantic formulae such that they are perceived as contrasting alternatives, rather than separate assertions that do not form any obvious parallel in terms of relevance. The fact that narrow foci in Hungarian interact syntactically with the unmarked position of the main verb, which might be thought of as providing to the core semantic content of an eventuality, is a further indication that eventualities are the appropriate kind of semantic object around which to base the explanation of exhaustivity (as pointed out in section 4.3.2).

The importance of the verb in this respect is made more precise in the system of semantic representation proposed in Chapter 6. Since this is based on neo-Davidsonian semantics, in which every proposition contains an eventuality variable, the verbal predicate is crucial to distinguishing the kind of presupposed eventuality that is significant. Even the representation of a topical entity involves the presupposition of an eventuality in some very general sense, since thematic roles are assigned by functions from individuals to eventualities: a topic such as *Ferenc* therefore contributes the information that 'Ferenc plays a certain role in some eventuality' (which is indeed intuitively part of the information established on encountering such a topic). The eventuality referred to in this case is, however, a mere variable, which effectively leads to the expectation of its being specified with the kind of properties that allow it to link individuals to other individuals and to truth-values. A presupposed eventuality in the sense relevant to narrow foci must already be associated with the kind of predicative material that imbues it with such properties. This material is supplied by verbs (and/or VMs, as will be shown in Chapter 7). This forms a crucial part of the explanation of PV narrow focus interpretation developed in Chapter 6 and, as such, the semantic representations provided there show a very direct link to the structure of Hungarian.

In these representations, the presupposition of eventualities of this kind is not encoded as such. Rather, the linear position and phonology associated with the tensed verb and other expressions determine a certain kind of structuring of semantic representations in the course of their construction, which is based around representations of eventualities and which allows for the recognition of certain information-structural distinctions. In interaction with the left-to-right dynamics of processing, and with the broader context, this allows for the recognition of presupposed eventualities in the sense employed in the present discussion. This in turn leads to the determination of alternatives to narrow foci that are to be asserted—and thus to the kinds of exhaustivity outlined in this chapter.

4.7.1 The costs and benefits of presupposed eventualities

As the above discussion makes clear, a relevant eventuality may be highly salient before a narrow focus construction is used (as in the case of question-answer sequences), but may instead have to be recovered from less salient parts of the cognitive environment or even constructed and accommodated as presupposed. The latter cases clearly may demand considerable processing effort. Does this reduce the plausibility of an account that stresses the role of presupposed eventualities in the derivation of narrow focus readings? It does not. Other things being equal, increased effort reduces the relevance of an utterance, according to RT—but other things are unlikely to be equal. A high demand for processing effort can be off-set by rich cognitive effects and, as mentioned in section 4.5.8, the very fact that a communicator chooses to utilise a construction that, in the context, demands more than the minimum possible processing effort from the addressee may therefore be taken as an indication that relatively rich cognitive effects are to be gained from processing it, thanks to the 'presumption of optimal relevance' that is encapsulated in the Cognitive Principle of Relevance.

The use of narrow focus frequently leads to cognitive effects that involve the elimination of prior assumptions (felt as a sense of contrastiveness in the reading of the focused element). This is particularly likely in cases in which a presupposed eventuality is evoked at the point of utterance, rather than by a preceding question (either by reference to an existing but hitherto low salience assumption or by the accommodation of 'new' material as a presupposition for a further assertion), since this is most likely to involve the contrasting of the narrow focus with manifest beliefs or expectations. As Sperber and Wilson (1986:114) point out, the elimination of a prior assumption can be a particularly significant form of cognitive effect, since it may have knock-on effects. If the assumption in question had served as a premise for the deduction of other assumptions, for example, these too will have to be eliminated. In this way, a chain of cognitive effects could be set in motion, which in some cases could result in significant reorganisation of the cognitive environment. The cognitive effects derived from processing a narrow focus are therefore likely to off-set the extra effort demanded by the need to access or construct an eventuality, even if this involves relatively complex acts of 'accommodation'. Consequently, the analysis of exhaustive focus readings as the effects of processing an assertion made in the context of a presupposed eventuality is entirely consistent with the principles of RT.

4.7.2 Non-exhaustive narrow foci and eventualities

The perspective afforded by the connection of narrow focus readings to presupposed eventualities suggests a novel explanation of the appearance of non-exhaustive narrow foci following a stressed verb, as in Horvath's example (4.17b), repeated here as (4.26).

(4.26) Kit hívtak meg?
'Who did they invite?'

Meghívták   *(például   / többek között) Jánost.
VM-invited-3PL   for-example / others among János-ACC
'They invited JÁNOS, for example / among others.'

My analysis of the PV position as that of narrow foci may seem to create a contradiction here: the *Wh*-question in (4.26) in effect provides a presupposed eventuality of 'them' having invited someone, in the context of which the assertion that they invited János seems logically to be a narrow focus. However, *János* appears not in the PV position but in a post-verbally. According to the view presented above, a stressed post-verbal expression should not be a narrow focus but is interpreted as part of a broader focus containing the verb, in a 'topic>comment' sentence (see section 4.5.5). Such expressions are not related to a presupposed eventuality, but are rather part of the formulation of a new eventuality. In fact, far from undermining this view, such examples support it: the non-exhaustivity of post-verbal foci as in (4.26) is consistent with their being presented by the speaker *as if* part of a new eventuality (whatever the preceding discourse may suggest)[28].

As argued above, the existence of a particular presupposed eventuality provides the fixed point in relation to which an exhaustive/contrastive assertion can be made: sets of alternatives are constructed with respect to some eventuality. The introduction of a new eventuality, through the use of a broad focus (which contains the main verb) does not invite contrast with alternatives because of the fact that different eventualities are of different kinds and degrees of relevance in any given context, and even different eventualities introduced with respect to a single topical entity are not assumed to form sets of alternatives, since the number of eventualities that an entity can participate in is in principle open-ended.

Presenting a combination of verb plus would-be narrow focus as if a new eventuality therefore leaves open the possibility that other eventualities involving the same verbal meaning happened also, these being conceptualised as separate eventualities. For example, if *They invited John* is taken to be a new eventuality asserted with respect to a topical *They*, it is quite possible that other eventualities also occurred with respect to 'them', including other inviting events. If other inviting events are not excluded, then it is clear that *John* cannot be taken as an exhaustive listing of everyone invited by 'them'. Hence, signalling that some statement is to be taken as the assertion of a new eventuality is one way of ensuring that no part of that statement is read exhaustively. This is, in effect, the flip-side of the fact that narrow foci, which do relate presupposed eventualities, are for good pragmatic reasons associated with exhaustive readings, as argued in this chapter.

---

[28] See also Szendrői 2003 for detailed arguments in favour of the idea that some putative examples of post-verbal non-exhaustive narrow focus should be re-analysed as broad foci—'VP-focus', in Szendrői's terms.

According to this reasoning, the post-verbal position of 'non-exhaustive narrow foci' like that in (4.26) shows these foci not to be truly 'narrow' at all, in terms of what the speaker conveys. The form of the assertion in (4.26) suggests the 'topic>comment' meaning 'An eventuality that holds of "them" (as subject) is that they invited János', a non-exhaustive reading that is consistent with the intuitive meaning. This contrasts with the true narrow focus reading 'The eventuality in question (of their inviting someone) was an eventuality of their inviting János', which could be simplified to the more plainly exhaustive 'The one they invited was János'.

Nevertheless, one cannot simply ignore the preceding discourse. If the reading invited by the speaker is really one in which 'They invited someone' is taken to be a new eventuality, then the question-answer sequence would clearly be incoherent without some fairly explicit way of signalling how it is to be taken as relevant. In this sense, this analysis predicts the facts noted by Horvath: that explicit material such as 'for example' or 'among others', or at least rising intonation to signal incompleteness (see section 4.5.5) is necessary to allow a non-exhaustive reading, if the prior context creates the expectation of a narrow focus.

The existence of apparent post-verbal narrow foci like *Jánost* in (4.26) is thus quite consistent with my analysis of the PV position. Such foci are not really narrow foci at all, in terms of the speaker's presentation of the material in the utterance. Consequently, they do not represent counterexamples to the claim that narrow foci appear in the PV position and that it is on the basis of their narrowness that PV foci take on an exhaustive reading.

Note also that non-exhaustive foci like *Jánost* in (4.26) therefore represent a kind of inverse of those cases of accommodation discussed above, in which new information is manifestly presented in order to be used immediately as a presupposition for a further (narrow focus) assertion. In the case of non-exhaustive foci, an eventuality that is in fact already mutually manifest (thanks to the *Wh*-question in (4.26), for example) is effectively abandoned in favour of reworking the information it contains into a 'new' eventuality, which contains also material that would otherwise have been treated as a narrow focus. Such phenomena represent a further illustration of the importance of a psychological view on context and meaning: interlocutors are not constrained by structured representations of information introduced by previous discourse, but are at liberty to manipulate such information, even contrary to its apparently pre-determined status, provided the way in which this is done creates suitably rich cognitive effects for minimal effort.

4.8 SUMMARY

The principal contribution of this chapter is to show (i) that the arguments underpinning the common analysis of the Hungarian 'focus position' are based on a particular, strongly compositional semantic view of the kind of meaning that may be, or must be, encoded in the grammar of a language and (ii) that this analysis leads to incorrect empirical predictions. As such, the data can be used to refute not only the widespread idea that the 'focus position' directly encodes an exhaustivity operator, but also the basic compositional assumptions that require such an analysis to be made.

This argument is clarified by reference to Szabolcsi's (1981) admirably explicit arguments for the exhaustivity operator approach. These rely on the idea that when the use of some grammatical construction can be seen to have an impact upon truth conditions, its effects must be attributed directly to the grammar (rather than to the triggering of inference). This assumption is rejected by post-Gricean pragmatic frameworks and a close look at the focus readings conveyed by the Hungarian 'focus position', as well as consideration of the nature of focus readings cross-linguistically, shows this rejection to be justified. The supposedly encoded exhaustive reading is shown to arise as the unmarked reading of narrow foci in both Hungarian and English, despite their different ways of expressing focus. Non-exhaustive narrow foci require special forms of signalling in both languages. Only on certain uses of the 'focus position' does exhaustivity appear to be a key part of the message conveyed, as opposed to an incidental presumption, in ways that are explicable with reference to context. Furthermore, examples can be constructed which show the exhaustive reading to be entirely absent despite the use of the 'focus position'. This all points to a meaning that is usually, but not necessarily, inferred in use. As part of this argument, the commonly cited parallelism between the use of this position and the English *it*-cleft construction is shown to fall apart: the apparent lack of examples of 'focus position' sentences that equate to less marked English sentence forms is attributable to independent processes of elision which mask the word order used in key contexts in Hungarian.

Another important contribution of this chapter is to show that standard forms of pragmatic reasoning—specifically, 'quantity implicature' (which is shown by Sperber & Wilson 1986/95 to follow from the basics of Relevance Theory)—straightforwardly predict the unmarked exhaustive reading of narrow foci. The relevant notion of 'narrow focus' is considered briefly in this chapter also: as a rough approximation, the kind of focus found in the 'focus position' is one that is set against a richly specified 'presupposed' background that includes the contribution of the verb. Consideration of some of the more unusual uses of the 'focus position' suggest that a more adequate definition should make reference to the existence of a particular presupposed eventuality—an idea that accords with pragmatic reasoning about the derivation of exhaustive readings.

An important consequence of this is that there is no clear criterion for appearance in the 'focus position' of a kind that could be encapsulated in a lexical feature, thus undermining any feature-driven movement analysis of the position as a syntactic phenomenon. Instead, an adequate characterisation seems to demand an analysis based in how the presentation of certain pieces of information at certain key points in the sentence triggers certain readings, via inference. This requires a dynamic approach of the kind argued for in Chapter 2. Such an analysis is pursued in Chapter 6 and it proves to explain also the appearance of items other than foci left-adjacent to the tensed verb.

First, however, there is one further important issue that revolves purely around the use of the PV position for the expression of narrow focus. This is the question of how quantified noun phrases are distributed across PV and the other linearly pre-verbal positions of the Hungarian sentence. Previous analysis has led to theoretically significant claims on the basis of this distribution, but has also found some key facts to be puzzling. In Chapter 5, I investigate the quantificational data and show that such puzzles stem in part from the compositional semantic urge to treat exhaustive focus as a directly encoded phenomenon. As such, this provides further illustration of the negative consequences of conventional assumptions about the syntax-semantics interface and of the concomitant under-use of inferential pragmatics.

5

FOCUS AND QUANTIFIER DISTRIBUTION

5.1 OVERVIEW

One lesson of the previous chapter is that those aspects of focus that are important in the analysis of the immediately pre-verbal position in Hungarian should not be thought of in terms of semantic primitives that are involved in syntactic representations (via the use of features), but rather in terms of the ways in which interpretation proceeds in different contexts (aspects of which may or may not be explicitly indicated by the form of a given utterance). In particular, the nature of the presupposed information involved in a given act of interpretation was shown to play an important role in determining the kinds of interpretation that are associated with the Hungarian pre-verbal 'focus position'. In other words, the perspective taken on different parts of the interpretation of an utterance plays a crucial role, in the sense that the presupposed parts are in a sense a logical preliminary to processing the asserted part in the appropriate context (since they help to construct the appropriate context).

Given this view on the analysis of pre-verbal focus, a promising point of contact emerges with work by Szabolcsi (1997b) on certain categorisations of quantified noun phrases (henceforth QNPs), These categorisations relate to the ability of different QNPs to appear in different pre-verbal positions in Hungarian. Szabolcsi argues for the existence of a syntactic projection 'PredOp' that is superficially indistinguishable from the pre-verbal focus position (that is, it is followed by a destressed verb and causes the post-posing of VMs) and proposes that this comes to host only certain kinds of QNP because it prompts a certain 'semantic assessment procedure'[1]. This is contrasted with another linearly pre-verbal position, 'DistP', which is equivalent

---

[1] In fact, Szabolcsi (1997b, 148) equivocates over the precise syntactic nature of PredOp, suggesting that it could be either (i) a projection separate from Focus or (ii) a syntactically indistinguishable position (PredOp and Focus being 'alternative specifiers of F[ocus]P') that encodes a distinct interpretive strategy. However, the basis of Szabolcsi's overall approach to her proposed LF representations is that each projection relates to a particular interpretive 'process'; an approach that clearly implies the former analysis of PredOp. In any case, Szabolcsi's proposed interpretations of expressions in PredOp and Focus are quite distinct from each other and it is primarily on interpretive grounds that I argue for their unification.

to É. Kiss's (1987) 'quantifier position' (so does not cause VM postposing), and which Szabolcsi argues to prompt a semantic assessment procedure that effectively represents taking the opposite perspective on (quantifier) interpretation to that prompted by PredOp.

In this chapter, I show that Szabolcsi's PredOp position is (under any theoretical assumptions) none other than the same immediately pre-verbal position that hosts pre-verbal foci, and that the assessment procedure that she associates with it is underlyingly just that of the assertion of a narrow focus in the context of a presupposed 'focus frame' (containing a presupposed verbal meaning). It so happens that the narrow focus in these cases is typically on the lexical quantifier, whose semantic contribution is taken to be that of a simple cardinality predicate. This analysis allows not only for the integration of a number of quantificational issues into a broader conception of the significance of Hungarian pre-verbal syntax, but also for straightforward explanation of certain constraints on quantifier distribution that receive only partial explanation under Szabolcsi's 'PredOp' account.

My analysis nevertheless accommodates many of the insights of Szabolcsi's work concerning the relationships between distributional constraints on quantifiers and distinctions drawn in terms of the theory of generalised quantifiers (GQs). In fact, these relationships are in a sense strengthened, since my account re-introduces the importance of one such distinction that is dismissed by Szabolcsi. However, these aspects of GQ semantics are shown to be in effect reflections of some very fundamental procedural distinctions, which must be viewed in terms of the language user's broader cognitive perspective on the act of communication. Identifying Szabolcsi's 'assessment procedures' with the context-based view of focus developed in the previous chapter therefore proves, in a very particular way, to fulfil Szabolcsi's own speculation that a procedural analysis of the quantificational effects in question eventually "may tie together formal and informal lines of research" (1997b, 125).

Since my account is based so closely on Szabolcsi's (1997b) work, I begin in the next section with an overview of the relevant parts of this.

5.2 QUANTIFICATIONAL PROJECTIONS AND PROCEDURES

5.2.1 Szabolcsi (1997b)

Szabolcsi follows Beghelli & Stowell (1997) in assuming that different kinds of quantifier are attracted to different syntactic projections at LF and in thus denying the appropriateness of a single 'quantifier raising' strategy for natural languages. In line with the oft-cited idea that Hungarian is a language that 'wears its LF on its sleeve' (a belief based mainly on the typically left-to-right expression of logical scope in Hungarian), Szabolcsi proposes that what are only abstract LF projections in languages like English are visible in the surface word order of Hungarian. Indeed, it is notable that Beghelli & Stowell's primary source of empirical evidence for the projections they propose for the LF of English is this kind of cross-linguistic analogy. Without this, there seems no particular reason to present their essentially semantic insights in syntactic formalism.

The projections Szabolcsi (1997b) is particularly concerned with are those which she proposes for the pre-verbal positions of Hungarian (which correspond closely, but not exactly, to Beghelli & Stowell's projections). Szabolcsi's proposed structure for these positions is as in (5.1).

(5.1)

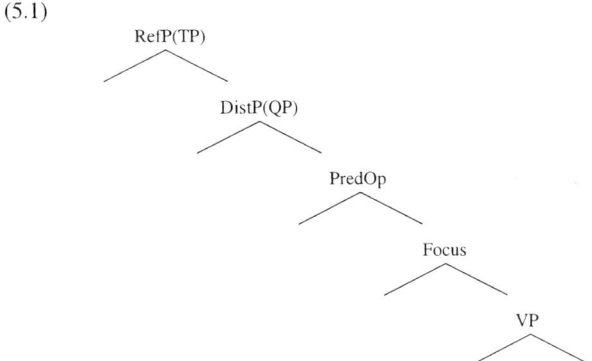

(5.1) includes in parentheses indications of how Szabolcsi's upper projections correspond to the template for the Hungarian sentence assumed in works like É. Kiss (1987), as noted in Chapter 3 and repeated here in (5.2).

(5.2)   (T[opic]P*) (Q[uantifier]P*) (Focus) V (XP*)

In the context of these two important models of the Hungarian sentence, it is necessary to elucidate the terminology that I will employ henceforth. For ease of reference, I maintain the relatively theory-neutral labels 'TP' and 'QP' for the two leftmost positions in (5.2). Recall that in the dynamic approach that I take, interpretations may result from linear position in the course of parsing, given the triggering of different inferences at different points in the parse. Therefore, while I maintain the use of 'TP' and 'QP', it should be borne in mind that this implies no commitment to abstract syntactic positions as such (and certainly the P in these labels should be taken to stand for 'position', in a general sense, rather than 'projection')[2]. 'PV' is retained as a mere label for the status of those immediately pre-verbal expressions that are associated with the postposing of any VM (and are thus distinguished from expressions in the other linearly pre-verbal positions, TP and QP). The label 'Focus' (always with a capital F) is used in reference to Szabolcsi's position of this name—that is, as distinguished from her 'PredOp'.

In terms of these new labels, then, the main aims of this chapter are, first, the reduction of PredOp and Focus to a single position, PV, (at this stage entirely on the basis of its focus-related

---

[2]Similarly, I refer below to certain other conventional entities of conventional syntactic theory, such as the 'N′' within a QNP (i.e. what remains if the quantifier is stripped away) simply because I take this kind of terminology to be suitably clear to most linguists as a label for the kind of sub-strings that I refer to. Such terminology is not an indication that conventional syntactic assumptions are necessary for, or necessarily compatible with, the analysis proposed.

reading) and, second, the explanation of certain quantificational constraints associated with QP and PV.

Szabolcsi in fact has little to say about her Focus position, concentrating on the differences between RefP/TP and DistP/QP (which lie outside the scope of this book) and, in particular, on the significant difference between these two positions, taken together, and PredOp, which is claimed to be the unmarked surface position of certain quantifiers and the only possible pre-verbal position of others. As mentioned above, the diagnostic for inhabitance of PredOp is the same as that for Focus: the obligatory postposing of any VM in the sentence—that is, PredOp and Focus are indistinguishable in surface structure. The principal reason for positing a difference between PredOp and Focus appears in fact to be a matter of interpretation: immediately pre-verbal quantifiers are felt to not necessarily take on the exhaustive reading that is generally associated with the Focus position[3]. The use of the putative PredOp position is exemplified in (5.3).

(5.3) Kevesebb, mint hat diák   értette   félre   a   kérdést.
       fewer   than six student understood aside(VM) the question-ACC
       'Fewer than six students misunderstood the question.'

As (5.3) exemplifies, QNPs commonly found in the relevant position include 'modified numeral' QNPs, such as also *több, mint hat N* 'more than six N' and *legfeljebb három N* 'at most three N'[4]. This has led to the assumption that these form some kind of natural class and that some property specific to them causes their appearance in PredOp/PV (for example, Bende-Farkas 2002, 40, speculates that this may be related to their being "inherently Focus-sensitive, as proposed for English *at least* and *at most* in Krifka (1999)"). However, some modified numeral QNPs can also appear in other positions, so they cannot as a class be required to surface in PV. Furthermore, unmodified numeral quantifiers (e.g. *hat N* 'six N') can also surface in PV. In this case, these take on the reading 'exactly n N' and have phonological stress on the numeral, characteristics which will be explained below. In section 5.5, I show that the common association of modified numeral QNPs with PV follows straightforwardly from nothing more than a very general interpretive procedure that is prompted by PV combined with the simple fact that these QNPs are relatively complex structurally.

The crucial distinction that Szabolcsi draws between QP and PredOp, in explanation of the quantification constraints that each position displays, involves not differences in truth-conditions encoded in the different positions, but rather different procedures for the assessment of truth-conditions. I believe that this procedural perspective holds the key to understanding the nature

---

[3] Szabolcsi does offer some structural evidence for the Focus/PredOp distinction, based on the behaviour of negation with PredOp quantifiers and focused NPs, but the judgements behind this evidence are disputed by a number of other Hungarian speakers—see, for example, É. Kiss (2001)—while the remaining data regarding quantification in immediately pre-verbal positions seem to be uncontroversial.

[4] Note that the use of commas in examples like *több, mint hat N* is merely a matter of Hungarian orthographic convention and should not be taken as an indication of any significant syntactic or semantic structure.

of pre-verbal positions of Hungarian. Szabolcsi, having provided this important insight, fails to exploit it to the full because her analysis nevertheless remains too closely dependent on conventional semantic modes of explanation. This leads to her inability to provide a precise characterisation of one of the quantificational constraints that she identifies. A complete, and in fact strikingly simple, explanation of this constraint emerges once one thinks of the notion of 'assessment procedure' on the more appropriate level of the language user's general cognitive approach to the act of communication; that is, involving the perspective taken on different parts of the information communicated by an utterance, in context.

One of Szabolcsi's (1997b) procedures makes significant use of the idea of witness sets. As Barwise & Cooper (1981) point out, most QNPs which may be assigned truth-conditions as GQs may also be given representations as witness sets (essentially, arbitrarily chosen sets with the properties that correspond to the restrictor N' and a cardinality consistent with the quantifier; see section 5.3.1). While Barwise & Cooper (1981) propose that witness sets may be seen in general terms as a psychologically realistic reanalysis of GQs, Szabolcsi recognises and exploits the potential in maintaining both forms of representation for different functions within a language. Thus, Szabolcsi proposes that QNPs in RefP/TP and DistP/QP are interpreted as witness sets, while QNPs in PredOp receive a 'true generalised quantifier' interpretation. That is, RefP/TP and DistP/QP pick out suitably restricted set referents as logical subjects of predication, and predicating something of these involves checking the members of the respective set for some property (as denoted by the logical predicate part of the sentence). Interpreting PredOp, on the other hand, involves establishing the intersection of the QNP's N' set and the set denoted by the remainder of the sentence (i.e. the 'nuclear scope' of the quantifier in question) and comparing the cardinality of this intersection with the cardinality expressed by the quantifier. The two modes of assessment are schematically represented in (5.4).

(5.4) a. TP/QP:
$[\, [\![\text{DET}]\!]\, [\![N']\!]\,]_{\text{LOGICAL SUBJECT}} \;>\; [\![V(+XP^*)]\!]_{\text{LOGICAL PREDICATE}}$

b. PredOp:
$|\, [\![\text{DET}]\!]\, |_{\text{QUANTIFIER}} \;<\; |\, (\, [\![N']\!] \cap [\![V(+XP^*)]\!]\,)\, |_{\text{'REST OF SENTENCE'}}$

Informally, Szabolcsi describes the two procedures as follows:

(5.5) a. **RefP/DistP**: "start out with a set determined by the quantifier and check its members for some property" (p.125).

b. **PredOp**: "[perform] a counting operation on the property denoted by the rest of the sentence" (p.122).

One contribution of this chapter will be to replace the 'counting operation' to which Szabolcsi refers. The notion of 'counting' is one that Szabolcsi relies on to characterise the set of quantifiers which may appear in PredOp, yet she does not in fact define what distinguishes a 'counting quantifier' from any other. Once PredOp and Focus are recognised as a single position, the procedure described in (5.5b) must be seen as involving something more general than a counting operation and constraints on quantifier distribution prove to emerge from other sources.

5.2.2 Against the PredOp/Focus distinction

As pointed out in Wedgwood (2002), the motivation for unifying PredOp and Focus becomes more obvious once the descriptions of assessment procedures in (5.5a) and (5.5b) are made fully parallel. In order to achieve this, (5.5b) might be re-written as in (5.6).

(5.6)   a.   **RefP/DistP**: "start out with a set determined by the quantifier and check its members for some property"

        b.   **PredOp**: "start out with the rest of the sentence and evaluate the quantifier in terms of this"

Another operation which can be described in terms of 'starting out with the rest of the sentence' is evaluating a narrow focus. In this case the rest of the sentence is a presupposed focus frame (containing a presupposed verbal meaning). This forms the background to the assertion of the focused item. The parallel between this and the proposed characterisation of PredOp suggests that Szabolcsi's 'true generalised quantifier' procedure for PredOp could be just a special case of a more general procedure that requires the expression in PV to be evaluated in the context of the interpretation of the rest of the sentence[5].

The procedural parallel of 'starting out with the rest of the sentence' suggests that Szabolcsi's procedures should be seen not as abstract mathematical procedures, as they could be under a purely semantic analysis, but rather as real-time cognitive processes. The implication is that PredOp QNPs are in fact nothing other than cases of narrow focus on a quantifier. This is the correct parallel, rather than narrow focus on a whole QNP, because the 'true generalised quantifier' mode of semantic assessment evaluates just the contribution of the quantifier—essentially cardinality information—against the context of 'the rest of the sentence', in the form of the value of the intersection of the logical predicate and (the semantic contribution of) the N' from within the QNP.

PredOp quantification should therefore involve QNPs in which the N' material is 'pied-piped' into the focus position. This idea is borne out in native speakers' intuitions regarding the contexts in which PredOp quantifiers are felicitous. For example, a sentence such as (5.7)—Szabolcsi's (1997b, 138) example (59)—requires that there be a manifest contextual assumption that 'some

---

[5]The idea of the PredOp position has been questioned on other grounds elsewhere. É. Kiss (2001) provides argues that PredOp is redundant from a purely denotational semantic point of view. Bende-Farkas (2002) employs some arguments that resemble those of the current section, but is concerned mainly to show that putative PredOp structures share what she sees as the '(semantic) presuppositional structure' of Focus and does not go as far as abandoning PredOp altogether.

number of students fell ill yesterday'. Note that Szabolcsi's own English translation of this example reflects this fact; she turns the whole of the sentence apart from the quantifier into a definite subject NP in the English (contrary to the structure of the Hungarian sentence) in order to get across the presupposed nature of this material.

(5.7)   Tegnap   sok   diákunk   betegedett meg.
        yesterday many student-1PL   sickened   VM
        'The students of ours who fell ill yesterday were many.'

In addition to this fundamental interpretive parallel, there is strong syntactic evidence—beyond the obvious surface relationship to the verb and to VM position—that cases of Szabolcsi's putative PredOp in fact occupy the same PV position as narrow foci; evidence that, in turn, further supports the idea that they perform a similar interpretive function in relation to the rest of the sentence. This evidence draws on the fact that certain classes of expression are generally restricted to appearing only in PredOp/PV (see below, section 5.3). There is only one situation in which these expressions can appear elsewhere in the sentence. This is when PV is occupied by a narrow focus, in which case the restricted expression may appear post-verbally and destressed (in other words, as part of a presupposed focus frame). This is illustrated in (5.8), the monotone decreasing QNP *legfeljebb három N* being one kind of constituent normally restricted to PredOp/PV: in (5.8b), the fact that *Mari* is syntactically focused licenses this QNP post-verbally.

(5.8)   a. *Jánosnak   visszaadott   legfeljebb három könyvet.
                János-DAT back(VM)-gave   at.most   three book-ACC
                Intended: 'To János were given back at most three books.'
        b. Jánosnak   MARI adott vissza   legfeljebb három könyvet.
            János-DAT Mari gave back(VM)   at.most   three book-ACC
            'It was Mari who gave at most three books back to János.'

If PredOp QNPs and foci in Focus are indeed the same kind of object, occupying the same position, it should be the case that a PredOp QNP is sufficient to license the post-verbal appearance of a(nother) decreasing QNP, just as a recognised focus would. This is indeed the case, as exemplified in (5.9). Thus, PredOp QNPs license a distribution which is otherwise only licensed by clear cases of pre-verbal focus—a strong indication that they are actually both examples of a single phenomenon.

(5.9)   Jánosnak   kevesebb, mint hat lány adott vissza   legfeljebb három könyvet.
        János-DAT   fewer   than six girls gave back(VM) at.most   three book-ACC
        'To János, fewer than six girls gave back at most three books.'

Similar evidence for the identity of PredOp and Focus comes from the 'definiteness effect' (DE). As Szabolcsi (1986) first observed, there is a set of Hungarian verbs which are incompatible with definite internal arguments (in some generalised sense). This incompatibility is known to disappear, however, when some other element of the sentence appears as a PV focus, as (5.10a,b) show. Whatever the reason for this may be[6], it provides a test for the similarity of PredOp and Focus: if they really are part of the same phenomenon, PredOp elements should also be able to rescue sentences that are otherwise ruled out by the DE. This turns out to be the case, as (5.10c) demonstrates.

(5.10)   a.   *János hozta a székeket.
　　　　　　　János brought the chairs-ACC
　　　　　　　Intended: 'János brought the chairs.'
　　　　b.   JÁNOS hozta a székeket.
　　　　　　　János brought the chairs-ACC
　　　　　　　'It was János who brought the chairs.'
　　　　c.   Kevesebb, mint hat lány hozta a székeket.
　　　　　　　Fewer than three girl brought the chairs-ACC
　　　　　　　'Fewer than three girls brought the chairs.'

5.2.3 The apparent difference

There are thus good reasons to abandon the idea that PV should be split into PredOp and Focus. Instead, it seems reasonable to maintain that Szabolcsi's semantic procedures for PredOp are in fact a special 'focus-on-quantifier' case of the procedure that underlies the production of narrow focus readings in PV. Indeed, given the clear structural parallels between Szabolcsi's two positions and the connections between their interpretive effects, one might ask why they should ever have been considered to represent separate phenomena. The apparent answers to this are revealing, in terms of the broader theoretical points made in this book. This is because the unsustainable PredOp plus Focus analysis seems ultimately traceable to the belief that the exhaustivity of PV foci must be directly encoded in the syntax of Hungarian. As such, it provides another illustration, to add to those of Chapter 4, of the problems that can be caused by the common tendency simply to match observed meanings to structures, for the reasons set out in Chapters 1 and 2.

As mentioned above, the primary reason given by Szabolcsi for the separation of PredOp and Focus is a perceived difference in interpretation: 'PredOp' quantifiers are not felt to produce the exhaustive/contrastive reading that is associated with PV foci. Given the arguments of the previous chapter, it should be clear that this is not in itself a reason to differentiate any phenomenon from PV focus. Foci in PV have been shown to express the full range of narrow focus interpretations: those that are most felicitously translated into English using unmarked word order, in which exhaustivity often seems virtually incidental, as well as those with a more clearly contrastive impact that correspond to *it*-cleft interpretations.

---

[6]For descriptions of the DE and diverse proposals for its explanation, see Szabolcsi (1986), Kálmán (1995), É. Kiss (1995a), Maleczki (1995, 1996), Bende-Farkas (1995, 2002).

The reason why narrowly focused numeral quantifiers should generally be perceived to be of the former kind (and therefore perceived to be different to PV foci, by those who maintain the parallel with clefts only) is outlined in Chapter 4, section 4.5.4 (see also Wedgwood 2002)[7]. Recall that the set of alternatives invoked by a focused numeral is likely to be an indeterminate, and possibly quite sizeable, sub-sequence of the (ordered) set of natural numbers (indeed, most likely the set of integers). As part of a conventional scale, these are, so to speak, intrinsic alternatives (cf. Krifka 1999); a permanently manifest part of the cognitive environment of any numerate language user. Not being dependent on any particular context, such a set of alternatives typically remains in the background, so to speak. That is, these alternatives to the focused item are not perceived to play an important part in the message that the speaker has to convey, precisely because they are not specially connected to the immediate context—the addressee consequently has no reason to pay particular attention to them. This conforms to RT reasoning: little effort is required to access the 'ever-present' set of numeral values, meaning that there is no particular associated expectation of rich cognitive effects. It is therefore predictable that 'exhaustivity' that results from placing a quantifier in narrow focus is typically of a rather trivial kind that is not felt to be strongly contrastive. Nevertheless, this is a perceptible effect, just as the less strongly contrastive examples of narrow focus in Chapter 4 are nevertheless exhaustive: recall that unmodified numeral quantifiers necessarily take on an 'exactly *n*' reading in PV. The implications of treating the 'exactly *n*' reading as a case of the exhaustivity of narrow focus are briefly investigated below, in section 5.2.4.

Interestingly, in earlier work, Szabolcsi (1981) recognises the connection between PV exhaustivity and the 'exactly *n*' reading. Yet in her 1997b analysis, she claims (without explicit justification) that this reading, which for her is found in PredOp, is necessarily different to that of a numeral quantifier that is uncontroversially in Focus—that is, a clearly contrastive or corrective use. Once inference is properly taken into account, however, the difference between the two is plainly one of context, not of the kind of interpretive operation involved. Specifically, the clearly contrastive kind of focused numeral must relate to a context that manifestly contains a restricted set of possible cardinality values, which are typically connected to the addressee's manifest prior expectations (hence interpretation of the kind 'not five or seven—as you may have thought—but six'). The process of interpretation is underlyingly the same in both cases: assertion of the quantifier as a narrow focus, prompting, via inference, a reading that is exhaustive with respect to whatever set of alternatives the context might invoke. Note that the failure to recognise this, with consequent encoding of the perceived difference between PredOp and Focus at an abstract syntactic level, creates a requirement for PredOp quantifiers to move string-vacuously to Focus in clearly contrastive cases—an operation that pragmatic reasoning shows to be quite redundant.

The reasons for Szabolcsi's position on these matters—indeed, seemingly for the whole 'PredOp plus Focus' analysis—can be traced to the fact that Szabolcsi, like the majority of an-

---

[7]This argument applies directly to the interpretation of unmodified numeral quantifiers: further reasons for the tendency of modified numeral QNPs to appear in PV are discussed below, in section 5.5.

alysts, takes exhaustivity to be encoded as a discrete semantic operator in the Hungarian 'focus position'. In a revision of her 1981 formulation (as referred to in Chapter 4, section 4.4.1), Szabolcsi (1994) argues that any such operator must have essentially the form in (5.11). This is to allow for appropriate entailments: something of the sort would indeed seem necessary to capture the fact that, for example, (5.12) entails that 'they invited Kati' (even though it does not necessarily entail what is conveyed by *Katit hívták meg*, as noted in the quotations from Szabolcsi 1981 in Chapter 4, section 4.4.1).

(5.11) $\lambda z \lambda P[z = \iota x[P(x) \ \& \ \forall y[P(y) \rightarrow y \subseteq x]]]$

(5.12)   Katit   és   Istvánt   hívták   meg.
Kati-ACC and István-ACC invited-3PL VM
'It's Kati and István that they invited.'

As Szabolcsi (1997b, 149) notes, the definition of exhaustivity in (5.11) is only compatible with set (including singular or plural individual) denoting expressions. Any quantifier undergoing Szabolcsi's 'true generalised quantifier' procedure would not be set-denoting, being separated from the semantic contribution of its restrictor N'. Szabolcsi also provides empirical evidence that 'PredOp' (PV) QNPs are not set denoters, in the form of 'others' test in (5.13). This test takes a QNP that is able to appear in either QP or 'PredOp' (PV) and shows that the choice of position determines whether it gets a referential or quantificational reading. When the QNP is in QP, as in (5.13a), it is demonstrably referential—one might say that the speaker has a certain set of students in mind, even if its cardinality is vague—since it is felicitous to refer to 'others' in reply and 'others' could only be understood in relation to a certain set. This is fully consistent with Szabolcsi's proposed 'witness set' interpretation for QP (see further section 5.3.1). With the QNP in 'PredOp' (PV), however, subsequent reference to 'others' is impossible, as shown in (5.13b), reflecting a purely quantificational reading, whereby the quantifier simply indicates the (approximate) cardinality of the set denoted by the rest of the sentence.

(5.13)   a.   A: Több, mint hat diákunk   félreértette   a   kérdést.
more than six student-1PL aside(VM)-understood the question-ACC
B: Lehet,   hogy még   másokat   is   találsz.
is.possible that further others-ACC also find-2SG
A: 'More than six of our students$_{[QP]}$ misunderstood the question.'
B: 'Maybe you will find others, too.'

   b.   A: Több, mint hat diákunk értette félre a kérdést.
#B: Lehet, hogy még másokat is találsz.
A: 'More than six of our students$_{[PredOp]}$ misunderstood the question.'
#B: 'Maybe you will find others, too.'

Immediately pre-verbal QNPs are therefore not set-denoters. It follows that if (5.11) is the semantic contribution made by the Focus position, then such QNPs cannot be in Focus. They must be in a different position where they undergo a different kind of interpretation. This is apparently the principal motivation behind Szabolcsi's postulation of the existence of PredOp as a separate underlying position (see Szabolcsi 1997b, 149, fn.35). However, this move not only ignores significant parallels between the 'PredOp' procedure and the basics of focus interpretation, but also contradicts clear syntactic evidence, as shown above. Encoding the semantics of exhaustivity into the Focus position therefore forces the adoption of an analysis that is conceptually questionable and empirically unsustainable.

Note also how the exhaustivity operator analysis of Focus sits very oddly within the Hungarian pre-verbal field according to Szabolcsi's own (1997b) account. While RefP/TP, DistP/QP and PredOp are all associated with essentially procedural interpretations, Focus alone contributes a declarative set-theoretic constraint on interpretation. While it is of course not impossible that a language could work this way, it does seem at least strange for Focus to be so much the odd one out in the pre-verbal field, even discounting the wealth of other arguments against its separation from PredOp.

Within an approach which allows a greater role for inference, all such complications and inconsistencies are removed. What Szabolcsi takes as evidence for the necessity to separate PredOp from Focus—the distinction between contrastive individual denoters and apparently 'neutral' GQs in the same surface position—can be taken as evidence in favour of a unified PV associated with a single interpretive process: given a single process, different inputs may naturally enough prompt different outputs, provided the process is not overly specific. The ability to produce a variety of effects from more underspecified material is precisely what a more heavily inferential account provides. Once again, serious problems for a conventional, compositional approach can be entirely avoided by simply considering the contributions of extra-linguistic processes. In doing so, the latter approach promises both a significant simplification of the grammar and a more consistent view of the relationship between pre-verbal syntax and the nature of interpretive procedures.

5.2.4 Numerals, narrow focus and scalar implicature

Scalar implicatures, though often analysed with reference to Grice's 'Maxim of Quantity' (see Chapter 4, section 4.5.7), are regularly treated as a separate phenomenon to the exhaustive reading associated with certain kinds of focused expression. However, my explanation, above, of the relatively non-contrastive reading of numerals in PV relies on applying to scalar implicatures exactly the same chain of reasoning (regarding the invocation of sets of alternatives in narrow focus contexts) as I apply to other cases of exhaustive focus. Conversely, my presentation (in Chapter 4, section 4.5.8) of the inferential reasoning that lies behind exhaustive focus readings was based on Sperber & Wilson's (1986/95) analysis of scalar implicature. This section briefly considers some of the issues involved in determining the semantics and pragmatics of cardinal

160 *Shifting the Focus*

numeral interpretation and provides some further justification for the identification of the scalar implicatures associated with numerals as nothing more than a special case of an exhaustive focus. Apparent differences between numerals and other items in this respect are argued to follow naturally from the intrinsic characteristics of numerals, therefore not requiring any difference in the underlying interpretive process.

In the previous section and in Chapter 4, I suggested that the 'exactly n' reading of numeral quantifiers in PV represents simply the process of the exclusion of the set of contextual alternatives to an asserted narrow focus—where this set happens to be the set of other natural numbers (or some indeterminate subset of this). What this means, in effect, is that the semantic contribution of numeral quantifiers is taken to be a simple representation of cardinality—that is, with no built-in 'at least' semantics or other complications. As Scharten (1997) points out, the set-theoretic representation of the cardinality of a set, as in (5.15) effectively makes cardinality a (higher order) one-place predicate, whose term refers to a set.

(5.14) $[\![\text{num}_n]\!] = \{X : |X| = n\}$
E.g. $[\![\text{four}]\!] = \{X : |X| = 4\}$

This observation may be extended into the realms of generalised quantifier representations: in (5.15), the attribution of cardinality is essentially a predicate, whose term in this case happens to be the intersection of two predicate sets (the 'restrictor' and 'nuclear scope'). In section 5.4.1, I show how this is crucial to the constraint on appearance in PV that is required to replace Szabolcsi's inadequate notion of 'counting'.

(5.15) $|\{x : P(x)\} \cap \{y : R(y)\}| = 4$
'the cardinality of the intersection of the restrictor set and the nuclear scope set is four'

This kind of representation is presumably what Szabolcsi has in mind when referring to a 'true generalised quantifier' procedure in which the quantifier 'operates over the rest of the sentence' (the procedure associated with PredOp). Yet the separation of the proposition into a cardinality predicate and its term constructed from the rest of the sentence also helps to elucidate how the quantificational facts can be brought under an informational-structural analysis—the very move that Szabolcsi seeks to avoid by positing PredOp. The grouping together of the 'the rest of the sentence' material into a form that could serve as the term to which a predicate is applied is highly suggestive of a focus frame established in advance of the application of a narrow focus.

Thus, FOUR *students are sleeping* (i.e. with narrow focus on *four*) may be given the set-theoretic generalised quantifier representation in (5.15) (where $P = student'$ and $R = sleep'$), and this could also be seen as one way of capturing the information structure of the sentence. That is, a focus frame that includes sleeping students is accessed (specifically, an eventuality of a set of sleeping students having a certain cardinality) and a narrow focus is then evaluated in relation to this, in the form of the application of a cardinality predicate, thereby creating a complete propositional form. To put it another way, it is the (explicit or implicit) context question 'How many students are sleeping?' that determines that a set-theoretic representation of the interpretation will have the structure in (5.15). There is no need for any specifically quantificational procedure to be encoded.

The treatment of numerals as simple cardinality predicates contrasts with the idea that they have inherently 'at least n' semantics, an analysis that is closely connected to the special status afforded to 'scalar implicature'. This is based upon the observation that each cardinal number appears to entail the value of any number smaller than it. Hence, if I have 20 books, it is also in some sense true that I have 15 books—plus another 5. The entailment is plainly one-way, leading to the idea that the definition of the semantics of a numeral intrinsically involves reference to its place in a scale of unilateral entailments. This means that each numeral must have 'at least n' semantics, since the truth of a statement containing that numeral is in principle compatible with any numeral higher in the scale.

'Exactly n' readings, on this account, are derived by implicature (see, for example, Levinson 1983, Horn 1989). That is, the 'at least n' lexical semantics of the numeral is paired in context with an implicature of 'at most n', which is generally treated as a quantity implicature of some kind. Parallel arguments derive the common readings of items like *many* and *some*—'many/some but not all'—from upper-bounding implicature added to lower-bounded ('many/some and possibly all') lexically encoded semantics. Carston (1998) points out that there has long been known counterevidence to this view where the numerals are concerned, citing arguments such as that of Sadock (1984) to the effect that *Two plus two equals three* is semantically true on this account—if the 'exactly n' reading were the result only of cancellable implicature, it should be possible to create contexts in which this statement is judged to be true (without changing conventional mathematics), but this is not the case. Scharten's (1997, 67–68) example (5.16) gives a particularly clear illustration of the lack of any principled truth-conditional difference between the two readings: (5.16a) intuitively involves the correction of a falsehood in just the same way as (5.16b) does, yet by the 'lower-bounded semantics plus implicature' view (5.16a) involves only the cancellation of an implicature while (5.16b) is the correction of a semantically false statement. It seems clear that this contrast is inappropriate: the two cases are entirely parallel and should be analysed as such.

(5.16)   a. A: How many pupils are there in your class?
           B: 31. No wait, 33.

          b. A: How many pupils are there in your class?
           B: 31. No wait, 29.

For Carston (1998), this kind of evidence leads to the conclusion that numerals are semantically underdetermined in this respect, their truth-conditional properties in any given context being established inferentially. In RT terms, both the 'exactly n' and 'at least n' readings are derived by explicature (and Carston adds that 'at most *n*' may also be inferred, as in *She can eat 2000 calories a day and not put on weight*). Carston proposes that this is prompted by the lexical semantics of numerals containing a special indication of their underdetermined nature—so, informally, they have a form such as [X [THREE]]—in effect a piece of procedural encoding, telling the addressee to establish the lower and/or upper boundedness of the numeric value.

This analysis makes the inference of 'exactly *n*' readings quite distinct from other cases of 'quantity' inference, including non-numeral 'scalar' items like *many* and *some*. The issue is pertinent to current concerns because Carston's position implies that the origin of the 'exactly *n*' reading is distinct from that of the exhaustive reading of non-numeral narrow foci, which bring no lexically encoded trigger for the relevant inference. This means that the 'exactly *n*' reading is by definition a matter of explicature (enrichment up to propositional form), while non-numeral quantity inferences are expected to be regularly non-truth-conditional implicatures. Yet my argumentation regarding both the interpretation and the grammatical behaviour of numeral quantifiers in Hungarian shows it to be an explanatory move in various ways to treat PV numerals as entirely parallel to other cases of narrow focus. Here I wish to show that this is not a mistaken impression, nor is it due to any quirk of Hungarian. Rather, the idea that numerals have a distinct kind of underdetermined lexical semantics results from thinking of the issue in terms of some concrete notion of upper- and lower-boundedness, as in the original notion of 'scalar implicature'. If instead one considers assertions involving numerals from the perspective of exhaustive focus— that is, with an eye to relevant potential alternatives in the context of utterance—the supposed special qualities of numerals prove to be independently explicable. This is not a question of simply imposing the perspective of exhaustive focus due to my present concerns; it is simply a matter of applying relevance-based reasoning. The relevance of an assertion—the point of saying a particular thing—is regularly established with reference to what that assertion implicitly rules out, as argued in Chapter 4. It is therefore natural to ask what is implied by the use of either a numeral or a non-numeral *as opposed to other things*.

Carston, following Horn (1992), justifies the putative special status of numerals with reference to the contrast between examples like (5.17) and (5.18).

(5.17) A: Do you have two children?
 B_1: No, three.
 B_2: ?Yes, (in fact) three.

(5.18) A: Are many of your friends linguists?
 B_1: ?No, all of them.
 B_2: Yes, (in fact) all of them.

The felicitous answer B_1 in (5.17) suggests that the inferred upper bound on the interpretation of *two* in the question is taken to be truth-conditional, while the relative infelicity of a parallel answer in (5.18) is argued to show that *many* does not naturally take on an uncancellable, truth-conditional upper-bounded reading.

Seen from the point of view of the implied alternatives to the crucial expressions, however, these effects seem to have quite independent origins. First consider (5.18): in most conceivable contexts, the intentions behind the question will relate to whether or not the addressee might have access to a suitable number of linguists for some purpose (perhaps the questioner wants an answer to some linguistic question, or to organise some event with the involvement of linguists, or to explain some disturbing habit of the addressee's). In this case, it is unlikely to be relevant to know whether the addressee has *only* linguist friends; all that matters is the existence of some threshold number of linguist friends. In other words, the relevant alternatives to *many* in such contexts do not include *all*; the only truly relevant alternative is *few* (*none* could also be, though the use of *many* in the question implies that the speaker expects the addressee to have some linguist friends). Note that this reflects 'folk linguistic' ideas: people will name *few* as being 'the opposite of' *many*, indicating that *few* rather than *all* is regularly perceived to be the relevant alternative to *many*. If *all* is not a relevant alternative to *many* in the context, it is unsurprising that *many* is not perceived to have an upper-bounded reading. The felicity of reply B_2 in (5.18) shows that speaker B recognises that the situation of all her friends being linguists is compatible with the point of A's question. This information is provided over and above a relevant reply to the question and as such is not made relevant by the question but must rather be considered relevant in some other way (e.g. it is a surprising and therefore interesting fact in itself, which updates A's assumptions about B and quite possibly leads to further contextual implications—which I shall tactfully demure from speculating on here).

In (5.17), on the other hand, different numbers of children, whether higher or lower than two, are very likely to be relevant alternatives—knowing about them would have significant implications. Most issues that make the size of someone's family interesting will be affected by the *precise* size of the family: most people recognise that bringing up three children is a very different matter to bringing up one or two, and so on. *Three* is therefore a straightforward alternative to *two* in such contexts: having three children is a different state of affairs, with different implications, with respect to the (likely) perceived interests and communicative intentions of the questioner. It follows that reply B_2 would be incoherent in this case. The difference between (5.17) and (5.18) is therefore explicable simply by considering what is perceived to be the relevance of the question, as it is understood through the relevant potential alternatives to the quantifying element. As further evidence for this, note that there are nevertheless contexts that would make B_2 an acceptable reply to the question in (5.17) and these are readily explained in terms of contextually relevant alternatives (see below). The above examples therefore provide no motivation to posit a significant lexical difference between the class of numerals and non-numeral quantifiers.

When it comes to comparing numerals with non-quantificational items, the picture is much the same. The essential parallel between numerals and other expressions is shown in (5.19) and (5.20).

(5.19)   a.   John: Who here is a violin teacher?
                     Bill: Mary is.

    b. John: What do you do?
    Mary: I teach violin.
    [The facts: Mary teaches violin in her spare time but has a full-time job as a doctor]

(5.20) a. John: Who here has three children?
    Bill: Mary has.
    b. John: How many children do you have?
    Mary: Three.
    [The facts: Mary has four children.]

The initial point of these examples is that in both cases the (a) example is typically judged unequivocally true and felicitous, given the situation described. The (b) examples, on the other hand, are both decidedly unhelpful, even deceptive, in their failure to provide relevant information. The non-numerals thus parallel the numerals in the production of 'upper-bounded' readings, undermining any account of that relies on a special lexical semantics for the numerals.

Another crucial point illustrated by these examples is the connection between both kinds of 'upper-bounded' reading and the information structure of the utterance (a point emphasised by Scharten 1997 and also implicit in the above discussion of the importance of alternatives). The exhaustive/upper-bounded reading in each case arises when the expression in question is in focus (the (b) examples), while this expression is part of a presupposed focus frame when it felicitously takes on an upward-entailing reading (the (a) examples). The reasons why exhaustive readings are associated with focus should be familiar from Chapter 4: assertion in the context of a presupposed eventuality makes the contextually possible alternatives to an expression relevant. Conversely, making up part of the background to an assertion means that the question of alternatives does not arise—it is in the very nature of background material to be already established and accepted (or at least treated as such), not the focus of the addressee's attention and therefore not inviting inferences regarding what might alternatively have been the case.

It takes a little extra discussion to translate this reasoning into an explanation of why numeral quantifiers typically receive an upper-bounded, 'exactly n' reading when in focus, while regularly maintaining an 'at least n' reading when appearing as background material. This involves reference to precisely the kind of entities and procedures found in the re-formulation of Szabolcsi's (1997b) proposals regarding Hungarian, thus further supporting the reduction of her Focus and specifically quantificational PredOp positions to one position and one encoded procedure.

Let us begin with the question of why the dialogue in (5.20a) can be felicitous, despite the fact that, as mentioned above, the precise size of a family is typically significant, regularly making different cardinalities into incompatible alternatives. The kind of context that makes this reading possible is one in which three children represent a 'threshold' for some purpose; for example, *Anyone with three children qualifies for a special social security benefit. Who here has three children?* What is really being questioned here is the existence of a set of (someone's) children of a certain cardinality. The cardinality itself is presupposed as a crucial part of the characterisation of the relevant kind of set and it is made relevant by the implications of the existence of such a set, not by any contrast with other cardinalities. Any assertion of the existence of a set of a given cardinality is compatible with the existence of sets with higher cardinalities because the smaller set can be simply a proper subset of a larger one. It follows that *three* does not have an upper-bounded reading in this kind of context (though expressed in slightly different terms, this is essentially the analysis of numerals in non-predicative environments from Kadmon 2001; see also Koenig 1993).

In contrast, when the existence of the set is presupposed but its cardinality is in question (that is, the cardinality constitutes the focus of the assertion, as in (5.20b)), it is precisely the choice of one cardinality from among a set of alternative cardinal values that is at stake, so the assertion that a certain cardinality holds implicitly excludes other cardinalities, whether higher or lower. Put in these terms, the parallel to ordinary 'quantity' inference over non-numeral expressions is clear (cf. Chapter 4, section 4.5.8). The link to Szabolcsi's assessment procedures is also plain: when the numeral quantifier contributes to defining some set that forms part of the background of an assertion, it has an 'at least n' reading, just as does in TP and QP, which Szabolcsi gives a witness set interpretation; but when the quantifier is separated from the rest of the sentence and applied as a predicate in its own right, it takes on an 'exactly n' reading, as it does in Szabolcsi's PredOp.

Returning to example (5.17), note that the question *Do you have two children?* could be read in either of two ways, making it predictably compatible with 'exactly n' and 'at least n' interpretations. In many contexts, the natural way to interpret the questioner's intentions would be in effect 'Is the number of your children two?' (the reading that must be assumed by the likes of Horn and Carston in supporting the acceptability judgements in (5.17)), while in other contexts, the intended meaning is closer to 'Does there exist a set of two children of yours?'—for example, in the qualification for benefit context—in which case, the possibility of the existence of a superset of this set is always left open, as argued above. In the former case, the cardinality itself is effectively in focus, being the property that is confirmed or denied by the response to the *yes/no* question (while the 'presupposed nature of the rest of the question is reflected in its paraphrase as a definite NP); in the latter case, the cardinality of the set acts as background to the questioning of an existence predicate. The difference between the upper-bounded and 'at least n' readings thus follows simply from the information structure of the utterance; specifically, whether the numeral quantifier falls within the background or constitutes the focus.

This is not to say that numerals and non-numerals are always entirely parallel in this respect. The following examples both reinforce the broad parallel and show subtle differences ((5.22) is taken from van Kuppevelt 1996, with its original acceptability judgements):

(5.21)   a.   *John*: What does Bob want?
                  Mary: (Bob wants) a coffee. In fact, he wants a coffee and a glass of water.

    b. *John*: Who wants a coffee?
        Mary: Bob (wants a coffee). In fact, he wants a coffee and a glass of water.

(5.22) a. [Harry did a lot of shopping this afternoon.]
            How many books did he buy?
            #He bought four books. In fact he bought seven.
        b. Who bought four books?
            Harry bought four books. In fact he bought seven.

The significance of (5.21) is that *In fact* plays a different role in (5.21a) and (5.21b). In (5.21a), it signals a self-correction by Mary—note that it could be felicitously replaced by more clearly corrective phrases such as *Or rather* or *I mean to say*–while in (5.21b) *In fact* merely signals that Mary is expanding on what she has already said (here *Or rather* would be distinctly odd). The obvious difference between the examples that trigger this contrast in meaning is of course the information structural status of *a coffee*, as indicated by the different *Wh*-questions.

(5.22) shows essentially the same contrast in the case of numerals—except that here the contrast is still clearer, with the (a) example judged to be odd by van Kuppevelt (1996). Should this be taken as evidence in favour of Carston's position, that such inferences are intrinsically of a stronger kind when drawn over cardinalities, owing to some difference in the lexical semantics of numerals? No such conclusion is necessary. Numerals certainly have unique features, but no lexically encoded semantic difference is required to explain their tendency to produce particularly strict upper-bounding inferences. Instead, this comes down once again to the nature of the sets of alternatives that are invoked in response to the focusing of different expressions. Since these alternatives play a key role in the inferential process, they can be expected to affect the outcome of what is a common underlying process.

Sets of cardinal values are special in two ways: first, they are related on a scale; second, they have very precise meanings (even in comparison with other 'scalar' expressions, such as *some, many, all*). Together, these characteristics make numeral values necessarily mutually exclusive in ways that the interpretations of non-numeral expressions generally are not[8]. This statement is not contradictory to the ability of numerals to seem sometimes truth-conditionally compatible, for example in a sentence like (5.23).

(5.23) John has five children, so it is true that he has three children.

This kind of (decidedly artificial) example, in which *five* is read as 'exactly five' but *three* is read as 'at least three', is only truly coherent given a context in which the property of having three or more children is under discussion—otherwise it would, significantly, have at best a distinctly

---

[8] Ariel (to appear) also invokes the 'punctuality' and 'distinctness' of numerals to argue against a special treatment for scalar implicature involving them. Geurts (1998) presents other counterarguments to the Carston/Horn position.

devious rhetorical flavour. This is of course the 'threshold' kind of context described above, in which what is really in question is an existence predicate: the fact that John is asserted to have (exactly) five children licenses the inference that a set of three children (a 'background' notion) can indeed be said to exist with respect to John. Therefore, this kind of example does not involve the assertion of both 'three' and 'five' as the cardinality of the set of John's children. Nor could this be done. While (5.23) may be contextualised, (5.24a) is not clearly acceptable (except possibly in reference to two separate families from different marriages—or, of course, two different men called John) and (5.24b) is nonsense.

(5.24)   a.   ?John has five children and John has three children.

             b.   ??John has five and three children.

These linguistic examples merely reflect a logically necessary fact: it is impossible for any one set to have two different cardinalities simultaneously. Given this, it is inevitable that numerals will be perceived as being strictly, truth-conditionally exclusive (and hence as being asserted exhaustively) whenever they are perceived to constitute alternatives to each other. There is simply no context in which the assertion of any cardinality predicate could be compatible with that of another.

In this respect, relations among cardinality predicates contrast with those among other predicates that may form sets of alternatives in context. The latter are generally not mutually exclusive in principle and therefore the exclusion of alternatives in context can be a weaker kind of inference. It is this, rather than any difference in the interpretive procedure that creates exhaustive readings, that leads to the sense that numerals are 'more truth-conditionally' exhaustive than other expressions in focus.

This excursus on numerals and scalar implicature leaves us with a very simple picture of what is needed to analyse the quantificational phenomena associated with the different pre-verbal positions of Hungarian. Some apparently significant quantificational readings have been shown to be merely special cases of the information-structural readings that are already known to be associated with these positions. The idea developed in Chapter 4 that the PV position hosts narrow foci is all that is required to explain the 'exactly n' reading of numeral quantifiers in that position; no abstract quantificational position such as PredOp need be posited, nor does the semantic contribution of a quantifier need to be anything other than a simple predicate to explain the connection between its appearance there and the reading it receives. This gives a solid basis from which to proceed to the explanation of the constraints on quantifier distribution identified by Szabolcsi (1997b).

5.3 Constraints on TP and QP

5.3.1 The monotonicity constraint

Some quantifiers (mostly, but not all, modified numerals) are restricted to PV; I shall henceforth refer to these as 'PV-only quantifiers'[9]. The nature of PV-only quantifiers may be assumed to relate to the interpretive procedures common to TP and QP, since something about these positions is apparently incompatible with these quantifiers.

Szabolcsi (1997b) (echoing observations of Liu 1997 with regard to modified numerals) identifies the crucial generalisation that distinguishes PV-only quantifiers from those which may appear in TP and QP: in order to appear in TP or QP, a quantifier must be monotone increasing. PV, on the other hand, can host increasing, decreasing or non-monotonic quantifiers—but the important point here is that those that are monotone decreasing or non-monotonic are always PV-only.

For present purposes, monotonicity may be understood in terms of upward and downward entailments. Monotone increasing quantifiers have only a lower bound and are therefore upward entailing: in other words, if a proposition containing the quantifier is true in a world containing n quantified entities of a certain kind, the same proposition remains true in a world containing $n+1, n+2, n+3\ldots$ entities of the same kind. This means that quantifiers like 'at least four' (including *four* on its 'at least n' reading) and 'every' are monotone increasing: 'At least four students smoke' is true in a world containing four students who smoke and equally true in a world containing five, six or a hundred students who smoke. The same holds of 'Every student smokes': here what is truth-conditionally important is that there be no non-smoking students, not how big the number of smoking students is, so the latter may be added to the model *ad infinitum* without affecting the truth value of the proposition.

Monotone decreasing quantifiers have only an upper bound and are therefore downward entailing. This means that worlds that support the truth of a proposition containing a monotone decreasing quantifier are only those that contain some specified number of the quantified entity or fewer than this number. Examples are 'at most n' and 'few': 'At most six students smoke' is only true in worlds containing six smoking students or fewer, while 'Few students smoke' is only true if some (contextually determined) threshold that would constitute 'more than few' smoking students is not exceeded—on the other hand the number of smoking students in the model may be decreased arbitrarily below this threshold (at any rate, as far down as 2, in the special case of 'few', and this arguably by inference) without affecting the truth value of the proposition.

Non-monotonic quantifiers have both an upper and a lower bound and as such do not create

---

[9]That is, QNPs of the relevant class cannot appear in TP or QP, nor can they appear post-verbally and stressed. Outside of PV, they can only appear post-verbally and unstressed, in the presence of a(nother) focus in PV—i.e. when presupposed as part of an open proposition (recall examples (5.8) and (5.9))—or sentence-initially when intonationally marked as 'contrastive topics'. These two positions/readings appear to be available to practically any kind of expression, so are not relevant to the current discussion of constraints on distribution.

entailments either up or down a scale. The obvious example of a non-monotonic quantifier is 'exactly *n*'. The proposition 'Exactly six students smoke' is only true in worlds containing no more and no less than six students who smoke.

Szabolcsi (1997b) notes that the monotonicity-based constraint on QNP distribution in Hungarian can be accounted for by assuming that the particular 'logical subject first' procedure associated with TP and QP is one of establishing and predicating over witness sets. Szabolcsi (1997b, 122) gives the following concise definition of witness sets (see Szabolcsi 1997a for expanded technical definitions).

(5.25) A witness set of a generalised quantifier GQ is a set that is (i) an element of GQ, and (ii) a subset of the smallest set GQ lives on.

A set that a GQ 'lives on' ('a live-on set') is defined as follows (Szabolcsi 1997a, 11).

(5.26) A GQ lives on a set of individuals A if, for any set of individuals X, $X \in GQ$ iff $(X \cap A) \in GQ$.

For practical purposes, the smallest live-on set of a GQ can be taken to be the 'restrictor' set denoted by the N' within a QNP.

In essence, this means that a witness of a QNP is a set made up of (any) members of the denotation of the restrictor N', with the cardinality that is specified by the quantifying determiner. For example, a witness set of *more than two men* might be $\{john, bill, fred\}$, as long as this set is a subset of the set of men in the world. Thus, witness sets—in contrast to generalised quantifier representations—provide a way to establish a denotation for a QNP without having to consider the denotation of the logical predicate of the sentence.

Predication over witness sets is sensitive to monotonicity because it is, so to speak, an act of predication that takes place in isolation from what is true of the rest of the world. This is because, by (5.25), a witness set is necessarily a subset of or equal to the quantifier's live-on set (i.e. the set denoted by the N' of a QNP). This means that there may well exist further members of the live-on set, yet these are not taken into account in assessing the truth of a proposition in terms of predication over a witness set. Witness sets are therefore implicitly monotone increasing, in the sense that predication over witness sets that are not monotone increasing does not guarantee the correct truth-conditions with respect to the world as a whole.

For example, assume that Kenny and Henry are both students and both smokers. The set $\{kenny', henry'\}$ can be taken as a witness set of 'at least two students' and if the proposition 'At least two students smoke' is assessed by predicating of this witness set the property of being a smoker, it will be found to be true—and this will be the appropriate truth value irrespective of how many other student smokers may exist in the world, because 'at least two' is monotone increasing. If the same set were taken as a witness set of the monotone decreasing QNP 'at most two students', then the proposition 'At most two students smoke' would still be judged true as long as Kenny and Henry are students and smokers. This would clearly represent the wrong truth value assignment if there exists any other student smoker in the world.

A more formal overview of this relationship between the monotonicity of quantifiers and the truth-conditions of predication over a witness set is given by Szabolcsi (1997a, 16). This is reproduced in (5.27) (the exemplification of (5.27a) refers of course to the 'at least n' reading of the numeral).

(5.27) Let X be a witness set, and A the smallest live-on set, of GQ. Then:

    a.   If GQ is monotone increasing, then for any X, $X \in GQ$ iff
$\exists W[W \subseteq X]$.
E.g. *Two men run* is true iff there is a witness of $[\![two\ men]\!]$ whose members run.

    b.   If GQ is monotone decreasing, then for any X, $X \in GQ$ iff
$\exists W[(X \cap A) \subseteq W]$.
E.g. *Few men run* is true iff there is a witness of $[\![few\ men]\!]$ which contains all the men who run.

    c.   If GQ is non-monotonic, then for any X, $X \in GQ$ iff
$\exists W[(X \cap A) = W]$.
E.g. *Exactly two men run* is true iff there is a witness of $[\![exactly\ two\ men]\!]$ which equals all the men who run.

Therefore, as Szabolcsi (1997b, 140) points out, the association of Hungarian TP and QP with the creation of witness set denotations provides an explanation for why non-increasing quantifiers turn out to be PV-only. The mode of assessment that relies on setting up witness sets as logical subjects of predication is simply not available with monotone decreasing or non-monotonic QNPs for communicators to convey the propositional meanings that they intend.

5.3.2 Witness set representations and information structure

Szabolcsi concentrates on the formal properties of witness sets, but it is worth noting that they provide a form of semantic representation that is compatible with a number of reasonable assumptions about actual cognitive processes involved in the use of language for communication, in particular with regard to the notion of topicality. Topics are commonly described as being 'the starting point of an utterance' and are also thought of as being necessarily 'given', 'discourse-linked' information (in RT terms, topical information must be mutually manifest before the utterance is produced and generally quite easily accessible, to avoid unnecessarily high processing demands). Both of these characteristics suggest that when a speaker conveys some expression as a topic, it is to be understood by the hearer as directly referring. Direct reference by the NP corresponds to the semantic notion of an NP denotation that is independent of the denotation of the logical predicate. Hence it seems reasonable to suggest that the use of witness sets is not merely a variant of semantic representation which is useful for certain technical reasons of logical syntax, but in fact relates directly to cognitive processes that are involved in relating linguistic structures and context—and therefore to information structure.

Note also how pragmatic inferences supplement witness set representations to overcome the potential vagueness of the latter. Witness sets may in principle be made up of any members drawn from the restrictor noun set, providing the appropriate cardinality is respected; without taking the denotation of the logical predicate into consideration, there is not sufficient information in the sentence to identify specific individual referents in the model as members of the witness set. At this level, witness sets may after all seem to be more a technical semantic 'trick' than a representation with any cognitive reflex. Indeed, there may seem to be a contradiction between the use of arbitrarily constructed witness set representations and the discourse familiarity of topics. In context, however, relevance-theoretic factors (based on salience, encyclopaedic knowledge and so on) will enable the hearer of an utterance to identify the intended members of a witness set. Once such independently necessary inferential pragmatic factors are taken into consideration, there is no conceptual block to viewing witness set representations as having quite direct cognitive and (thereby) information-structural significance.

5.4 CONSTRAINTS ON PV

Just as there are PV-only quantifiers, incompatible with the procedures associated with TP and QP, there is also a class of quantifiers that are unable to appear in PV. Henceforth I shall refer to this class as 'non-PV' quantifiers. This class includes universal quantifiers and *a legtöbb N* 'most N', as well as *NP is* 'also NP' phrases (that is, under the quantificational, but not the 'emphatic' reading of *is*). Uniquely, this constraint holds even if context is manipulated to force a contrastive narrow focus reading of the quantifier, as in (5.28)—even under these circumstances, the universal QNP appears in QP, as the relative order of VM and verb shows (as in Chapter 3, section 3.2.1, the location of pitch accents is indicated by the preceding marker ').

(5.28)   'Minden gyerek megijedt   / *ijedt meg.
         every   child   VM-feared   feared VM
         'EVERY child got frightened (e.g. not just the girls).'

Note that this fact may be taken as a further piece of indirect evidence for a unified PV, as opposed to Szabolcsi's separate Focus and PredOp. If there were one pre-verbal position (and/or interpretive procedure) relevant to quantificational matters (PredOp) and another dealing with focus, one would expect even quantifiers banned from the former to be able to surface in the latter—and hence in the PV surface configuration—given the appropriate information-structural motivation. But this is not the case; rather, there would appear to be a single interpretive process associated with PV (as signalled by V>VM order), with which certain quantifiers are incompatible under any circumstances.

This leaves open the question of how an exhaustive focus reading can be found outside PV, as in (5.28), since the implication is that a quantifier in QP does not undergo the interpretive procedure that produces the appropriate focus reading (i.e. the procedure associated with PV). This question will be addressed in section 5.6. First, in the current section, I deal with the key issue of the proper definition of PV-only quantifiers, which leads to the replacement of Szabolcsi's vague notion of 'counting' with a more straightforward semantic categorisation. Apparent counter-examples to this are explained with reference to inferential pragmatic factors and the need for PV to contain a single predicate; a fact that backs up the analysis of scalar implicatures in section 5.2.4 and that is explained in turn by the explanation, developed in later chapters, of PV as the location of a particular kind of encoded procedure.

5.4.1 Proportionality and PV

What aspect of the procedure associated with PV might be incompatible with those quantifiers that are members of the non-PV class? Looking at the central examples of 'every N' and 'most N', a well-known semantic generalisation (from GQ theory) suggests itself: these quantifiers are proportional—that is, non-intersective.

Proportionality and intersectivity are usually defined roughly as follows (Szabolcsi 1997a, 11):

(5.29) Where DET is a quantifying determiner,

    a.   DET is intersective iff $\text{DET}(A)(P) = \text{DET}(A \cap P)(P)$.

    b.   DET is proportional iff $\text{DET}(A)(P)$ depends on $\text{DET}(A \cap P)/A$.

For example, (5.30) (Lappin & Reinhart 1988, 1028) shows that 'five' is intersective, but 'every' is not.

(5.30)   a.   Five students are radicals
                iff
                Five students who are radicals are radicals.
    b.   Every student is a radical.
                is not equivalent to
                Every student who is a radical is a radical.

Instead, the truth-conditions of 'Every student is a radical' rely on the proportion of the set of students that qualifies as both 'student' and 'radical'—in other words, 'every' is a proportional quantifier.

As Lappin & Reinhart (1988) emphasise, these formal distinctions have practical consequences for the 'approach' involved in assessing the truth value of a proposition. In order to establish the truth value of a proposition containing an intersective QNP, it is necessary only to establish the intersection of the restrictor N' set and the nuclear scope set $(A \cap P)$ and to see whether its cardinality is consistent with that specified by the quantifier. Assessing a proposition containing a proportional QNP, on the other hand, necessitates establishing the cardinality of both the restrictor N' set itself (A) and the intersection of this with the nuclear scope set $(A \cap P)$, in order to calculate whether the proportion of the one to the other is consistent with that specified by the quantifier. This kind of difference in the 'approach' necessary to set-based semantic assessment is reminiscent of the difference in 'semantic assessment procedures' suggested by Szabolcsi as the basis of the contrast between PredOp/PV and the other pre-verbal positions.

However, as Szabolcsi (1997b, 144–145) points out, it cannot be proportionality as such that is incompatible with PV. Some proportional quantifiers are able to appear in PV, and some of these are even PV-only. The examples that Szabolcsi supplies are shown here in (5.31).

(5.31)   a.   *a N-nak több, mint 50 százaléka* 'more than 50% of the N' may appear in PV (cf. the denotationally equivalent, but non-PV *a legtöbb N* 'most of the N').

        b.   Another clearly proportional (quasi-partitive) quantifier apparently found in PV:
A fiúk   közül   több/kevesebb, mint hat emelte fel az asztalt.
the boys among more/fewer   than six lifted up the table-ACC
'More/fewer than six among the boys lifted up the table.'

        c.   *kevés N* '(a) few N' always appears in PV, although it appears to have intersective and proportional readings.

The absence of any consistent criterion for appearance in PV (or PredOp), based on proportionality/intersectivity or any similar semantic distinction, leads Szabolcsi (1997b) to the conclusion that any relevant generalisation must go beyond denotational semantics and to the adoption of the vague notion of a 'counting operation'. I have already argued that the arguments in favour of a unified PV over the use of a PredOp position preclude the analysis of the PV procedure as 'counting' (whatever this may mean). There is also empirical evidence from within the class of non-PV quantifiers which suggests that no operation that matches any intuitive definition of 'counting' can characterise the procedures associated with PV. Proportional quantifiers like *all of the three students*, which include an explicit numeral within the restrictor N', are non-PV in exactly the same way as ordinary universal quantifiers are. Thus, even given a context which forces a contrastive reading of *mind* 'all', this kind of QNP is restricted to QP, as (5.32) shows[10].

(5.32)   Mind a   három diák   megijedt / *ijedt meg (nem csak kettő).
            all   the three student VM-feared   feared VM not only two
            'All of the three students got frightened (not just two)'.

It is not clear how the nature of 'counting' could possibly be understood, if this kind of example does not involve counting.

---

[10]Contrastive focus on *három* or on *diák* would allow the QNP to appear in PV, however, a fact that constitutes important evidence in favour of the approach that I develop. See example 5.33 below and section 5.5.4.

Note that this kind of example also precludes another potential line of explanation; one based on the relative complexity of processing proportional quantifiers by certain procedures, along the lines of Lappin & Reinhart's (1988) analysis of presupposition failure with 'strong' quantifiers. Such an account would run as follows. Proportional quantifiers, unlike intersectives, require that the cardinality of the (logical) subject N' set be established separately to the cardinality of the intersection of the subject and set represented by the rest of the sentence, so that the two can be compared. Iff the sentence is assessed 'subject first', these two cardinality assessments can be performed simultaneously, through the procedure of scanning through the subject set; but if interpretation is approached, as in the case of PV, by assessing the rest of the sentence first, it remains a two stage process. Therefore the PV procedure is blocked for proportional quantifiers on the grounds of relative processing inefficiency. While separate factors might be invoked to explain away some or all of the counterexamples in (5.31) (see below), examples like (5.32) would be truly problematic for such a story, since the explicit numeral makes it unnecessary to put special effort into establishing the cardinality of the subject N'. This effort is in effect taken over from the addressee by the communicator—yet still the QNP is incompatible with PV.

I propose an alternative form of explanation which agrees with Szabolcsi to the extent that a full account must indeed involve non-denotational factors, but within which the intersective/proportional distinction nevertheless plays a role. This role is of the nature of a useful descriptive generalisation rather than being in itself explanatory: the distinction is significant to the extent that it is related to certain inevitable restrictions on the kind of elements that can be involved in narrow focus interpretation.

My account takes its cue from a fact that Szabolcsi does not discuss, which shows the 'non-PV' class of QNPs to be not so strictly barred from PV as has been hitherto stated. It turns out that under certain conditions even a simple universally quantified NP may indeed surface in PV. This happens when the restrictor noun, rather than the quantifier, is given a contrastive focus reading, as in (5.33) (see Bende-Farkas 2002, 35)[11].

(5.33) Minden 'fiú ijedt meg (nem minden 'lány).
        every   boy feared VM not every   girl
        'It was every BOY that got frightened (not every GIRL).'

This fact is a serious problem for the Beghelli/Szabolcsi approach to the pre-verbal syntax of Hungarian, or any other feature-checking approach whereby focused items on the one hand and different classes of quantifier on the other must move to certain positions by Spell-Out (in Hungarian—and by LF in languages like English, according to some approaches). The only

---

[11] The significance of examples like (5.33) has apparently been overlooked for reasons mentioned in Chapter 4: the common view of the role and nature of pragmatics has led to the compartmentalising of different perceived kinds of focus, despite the lack of any linguistic evidence for such distinctions—note Bende-Farkas's (2002) unsupported assertion, in relation to an example similar to (5.33), that "Cases of correction like [this example] are quite different from ordinary focus", going on to note that these "have not been sufficiently studied in the Hungarian literature".

way that an example like (5.33) could be accommodated into such an approach would be to stipulate some form of precedence of focus features over quantificational features, but this would of course fail in the case of focus on the quantifier itself (as in (5.28)). I take this to be an empirical argument in favour of parsing-based frameworks such as Dynamic Syntax. At the very least, this kind of feature conflict calls into question the use of focus features as grammatical primitives[12].

What (5.33) suggests for the analysis of non-PV quantifiers is that it is some property of the quantifier—syntactically speaking, the determiner—rather than the whole QNP that blocks the use of PV in these cases. Furthermore, it is not the mere presence of the quantifier that affects distributional possibilities, but rather the quantifier's relationship to the information structure of the sentence. In order to understand this, it is important to consider once again the way in which the interpretive procedure represented by PV may relate to information structure.

Recall the conclusions of section 5.2.2: the procedure associated with PV is akin to Szabolcsi's 'PredOp' procedure of 'starting out with the rest of the sentence', but must be taken to have the character of a real time cognitive process. This allows it to encompass narrow focus readings wherein the rest of the sentence is in fact a focus frame: mutually manifest propositional material accessed as a unit, which, being presupposed in this way, is literally prior to the newly asserted focus item, at a cognitive level. At the same time, what have been claimed to be unfocused readings of QNPs, in PredOp, turn out to be cases of focus on the quantifier (the intuitive sense of exhaustive focus being relatively weak in the absence of a context that produces an overtly contrastive reading). In these cases, the rest of the QNP must be assumed to appear in PV through some process of 'pied-piping'; that is to say, a syntactic constraint on the linear integrity of NP-sized constituents.

The reason why a QNP in PV is interpreted in terms of focus on the quantifier alone, rather than on the whole QNP, is to be found in the account of the (procedural) interpretive significance of PV that is developed in Chapter 6. This involves the expression in PV being necessarily a single predicate, in order to perform a certain role with regard to the creation of a propositional form. It follows that an individual sub-part of a complex expression such as a QNP must be assumed to be the item in focus, the rest of the expression being pied-piped along with it. This need not in fact be the quantifier—examples like (5.33) show how other sub-parts of a QNP can be treated as the predicate in question, given appropriate intonational signalling—but focus on the quantifier is felt to be the unmarked case, for two reasons. First, the unmarked phrase-initial stress placement of Hungarian causes the main pitch accent to be associated with the quantifying determiner in what is perceived to be the unmarked intonational pattern and, second,

---

[12] As Szendrői (2003) recognises, (5.33) is also a problem for her prosodically-based approach, in which movement to PV is motivated by the need for a focus-stress correspondence at certain interface levels of the grammar. The problem is that *fiú* in (5.33) would be within a naturally stress-bearing syntactic projection within Szendrői's account if it were to stay in QP, requiring just a stress-shift within the QNP to reflect focus on the N' instead of the quantifier. This account therefore contains no motivation for the (downward?) movement of the whole QNP in addition to stress-shift within the QNP.

focus on a numeral quantifier is generally felt to be less interpretively marked, being typically less contrastive than other expressions in PV focus, for the reasons outlined in section 5.2.3.

This not only explains the tendency for PV QNPs to correspond to focus on just the quantifier, but also points the way to an explanation of the existence of non-PV quantifiers: if there is a kind of quantifier that cannot be conceptualised as a discrete predicate, in some crucial sense, then quantifiers of this class will be incompatible with the interpretive procedure encoded by PV. The ability to be treated as a single, self-contained predicate requires that an expression have the status of a discrete constituent of a (significant kind of) semantic representation. In effect, therefore, the account of PV developed in the following chapters in terms of predicates encapsulates a logically necessary fact about items interpreted as narrow foci: they must be representable as discrete semantic entities in order to be separated out from the representation of the contribution of the rest of the sentence (that is, from the focus frame).

This observation provides the basis for an account of quantification in PV that correctly predicts just which quantifiers must be non-PV. In section 5.2.4, I showed that simple numeral quantifiers can be interpreted as straightforward cardinality predicates, so these are predicted to be able to appear in PV. Since they are intersective quantifiers, the intersection of the restrictor and nuclear scope sets is by definition separable from simple numeral quantifiers, and may function as the focus frame for the application of the cardinality predicate as a narrow focus. This is not true of proportional quantifiers (in general, though see section 5.5.3). Their set-theoretic GQ representation shows the semantic contribution of the quantifier to be inextricably connected to the restrictor set (since it is typically with respect to this that they are proportional): the quantifier's contribution is in fact a relation between the restrictor set and the intersection of restrictor set and nuclear scope set. There is therefore no discrete part of the semantic representation that corresponds to the quantifying determiner alone: the whole GQ representation is necessary to establish the contribution of a proportional quantifier. Just as there is no single predicate that can express this, neither (consequently) can 'the rest of the sentence' be represented separately, in order to provide a focus frame. Among the semantically proportional quantifying determiners are some that do not even contain a syntactic or lexical sub-part that is identifiable as a discrete predicative element of the semantic representation. In these cases there is nothing stemming from the contribution of the quantifier that can be taken to be the predicate that is to be assessed as a narrow focus. These cases form the set of non-PV quantifiers.

In order to illustrate the point, consider the difference between the universal quantifier and a simple numeral quantifier. As already discussed, the value of the numeral determiner *four* (or Hungarian *négy*) can be identified as a unitary constituent of a representation like (5.34a), in a way that shows it to be a simple predicate. Meanwhile, the set intersection to the left of the = sign in (5.34a) is available to represent a focus frame that wants only the assertion of such a predicate in order to create a full propositional form. This is not true of a universal quantifier like *every* (or Hungarian *minden*): because of its intrinsic proportionality, no individual part of its truth conditions corresponds to the quantifier alone. Therefore, it cannot be treated simply as a predicate. Instead, the whole GQ representation is necessary to get across the contribution of the quantifier, as in (5.34b) or, in an alternative but equally illustrative representation, (5.34c).

(5.34)   a.   ⟦four/négy⟧:
$|\{x : P(x)\} \cap \{y : R(y)\}| = 4$
'the cardinality of the intersection of the restrictor set and the nuclear scope set is four'

       b.   ⟦every/minden⟧:
$|\{x : P(x)\} \cap \{y : R(y)\}| = |\{x : P(x)\}|$
'the cardinality of the intersection of the restrictor set and the nuclear scope set is equal to the cardinality of the subject restrictor set'

       c.   ⟦every/minden⟧:
$\{x : P(x)\} \subseteq \{y : R(y)\}$
'the restrictor set is a subset of the nuclear scope set' (i.e. there are no members of the restrictor set to which the nuclear scope predicate does not apply)

The constraint against certain proportional quantifiers appearing in PV thus falls out of two existing assumptions: Szabolcsi's (1997b) proposal that (only) PredOp prompts 'true GQ' interpretation and the observation of section 5.2.2 that this in fact represents narrow focus on a quantifier, as in other cases of PV focus.

5.5 THE APPARENT COUNTEREXAMPLES

The previous section explains why the non-PV quantifiers should be proportional, but the exceptions in (5.31)—proportional quantifiers that *do* appear in PV—remain to be explained. This turns out to be a relatively simple matter, once one knows where to look: these exceptions do not represent a complication to the interpretive generalisation associated with PV, but rather behave differently on account of their internal syntactic structure. Szabolcsi seeks a purely semantic (and purely quantificational) generalisation and, on finding none at the denotational level, is forced to appeal to an undefined 'counting operation'; it turns out, though, that it is simply necessary to take notice not only of interpretation but also of the ways in which the semantics of different QNPs are encoded.

The point (already hinted at above) is that some quantifiers are represented by syntactically complex determiners which are partly composed of predicative material, thus allowing for the focusing of certain sub-parts of the quantifier [13]. In these cases, appearance in PV does not have to represent focus on (the contribution of) the whole complex quantifier, so they do not represent a contradiction of the constraint against focusing proportional quantifiers in PV. Focusing on a sub-part of (the semantics of) *minden* 'every' or *a legtöbb* 'most' remains impossible, owing to their

---

[13] See Krifka (1999) for evidence that suggests that things are in fact more complex than this; many 'complex determiners' being more than just determiner material. This issue does not affect the current argument.

178 *Shifting the Focus*

structural simplicity: the meaning of the quantifier is not encoded in terms of sub-expressions that contribute other predicates.

5.5.1 'Counterexample' 1: a complex determiner

It is easy to see that this line of reasoning accounts for one of the pieces of evidence that leads Szabolcsi to deny the relevance of the proportional/intersective distinction, (5.31a). Recall that the apparent problem is the fact that *a N-nak több, mint 50 százaléka* 'more than 50% of the N' is possible in PV, while the denotationally (at least roughly) equivalent *a legtöbb N* 'most N' is non-PV. The denotation common to these QNPs may be represented as a GQ (in abbreviated from) as in (5.35).

(5.35) $|\{x : P(x)\} \cap \{y : R(y)\}| > \frac{1}{2}|\{x : P(x)\}|$
'the cardinality of the intersection of the subject restrictor set and the predicate set is greater than half of the cardinality of the subject restrictor set.'

The explanation for the different distributional possibilities of the two QNPs is that the syntactically complex *több, mint 50 százaléka* allows for the semantic contribution of either '50% /$\frac{1}{2}$' or *több* 'more' to be treated as an individual predicate that is separable from the rest of the sentence and therefore focusable in PV[14]. Under a slightly different representation from (5.35), yet another reading is possible: the contribution of '50' could be treated as a separate predicate, with the contribution of *százaléka* 'percent' included in the presupposed focus frame. The syntactically simpler *a legtöbb N* allows for no such interpretation, since it expresses the proportional quantifier meaning 'most' as a whole, thus making available no 'lower-level' predicates from within its semantic composition (though, as with *minden* FIÚ in (5.33), focus on some part of the N' within the QNP is a possibility and this is associated with the use of PV).

This explanation has significant theoretical consequences. The expressions that appear in a given position do not have to form a natural class according to some semantic or structural definition. What the complex QNP in this section shows is that the common appearance of modified QNPs in PV is not due to any property specific to them, but rather the result of the way they happen to fit with the interpretive process generally associated with PV. They are *able* to appear in PV (irrespective of proportionality/intersectivity), simply because they are structurally complex enough to contain expressions of focusable predicates.

In addition, the pragmatic character of such QNPs helps to explain why they are so commonly found in PV. The desire, on the part of the communicator, to specify such details as 'fewer than *n*', 'exactly *n*' or 'more than 50% of *n*' is typically linked to the contradiction of contextually manifest expectations relating to some presupposed and highly specified eventuality—without

---

[14]The latter possibility of course requires the symbol > in (5.35) to be re-analysed somehow as a predicate. It should be noted that there is nothing in my approach that requires the predicate in PV to be a one-place predicate—see Chapter 6 for further details.

the existence of such expectations, this kind of detail is unlikely to be worth the effort that it takes the addressee to process the extra linguistic material. The regular appearance of these QNPs as narrow foci, and consequently as occupants of PV, is therefore to be expected on pragmatic grounds and requires no further explanation.

5.5.2 'Counterexample' 2: complex QNP-internal information structure

A similar, but in some ways more revealing, example of how the internal syntactic form of the quantifier allows or prevents appearance in PV is provided by (5.31b). For Szabolcsi, this is another example of how the proportional/intersective distinction cannot be the explanation for non-PV quantifiers; it is another clear case of a proportionally quantified QNP (Szabolcsi refers to this structure as "the closest we can get to a partitive in Hungarian"; 1997b, 133) which does seem to appear in PV, given the order of VM and verb. Again, this kind of example will be seen to involve focus on sub-parts of the quantifier, not on the quantifier as a whole. However, rather than pied-piping occurring freely with focus on any of the sub-constituents of the QNP, in this case the form of the QNP suggests a particular partitioning of the information that it conveys. Indeed, a closer look at the syntactic and information structure within this example suggests that the pre-verbal material should not be assumed to be a single QNP in PV at all.

This analysis rests upon the observation that the PP *a fiúk közül* 'among the boys' is 'fronted' within this construction for a reason, playing a particular information-structural role with regard to the following material. This could be seen as following from relevance-theoretic considerations. The motivation to employ the relatively complex construction *a fiúk közül több, mint hat* ($\approx$ 'among the boys, more than six') rather than the (presumably) syntactically simpler *több, mint hat fiú* ('more than six boys') is the set of interpretive possibilities opened up by the former that are unavailable through the latter. In particular, the version with the fronted PP allows for this part of the construction to be viewed as quite separate from the rest and lends itself to a reading in which the PP takes on a kind of 'contrastive topic' reading with regard to what follows—something like "regarding those individuals drawn from the set of boys, as opposed to other individuals from other salient sets ...". This means that there is not a complex proportional determiner in PV in (5.31b), but rather a PP outside of PV and an intersective determiner (*több/kevesebb, mint hat* 'more/fewer than six') in PV. Assuming this, it is immaterial whether the whole of this remaining determiner or a sub-part of it is interpreted as being in focus (this will be determined by context): there is in any case no conflict with the requirements of the PV procedure.

The internal structure of this example in fact parallels another of Szabolcsi's examples of denotationally identical constructions that act differently with regard to appearance in PV. This example does not involve any proportional quantification and therefore the fact that it appears to be entirely parallel to (5.31b) supports the idea that the latter example has no bearing on the question of whether proportional quantifiers can appear in PV—something else is plainly going on, regardless of GQ semantics. The example in question is Szabolcsi's (1997b, 144) (69), reproduced here in (5.36). The apparent puzzle here is that the construction in (5.36a) appears freely in QP or PV/PredOp, while the denotationally equivalent (5.36b) is PV-only (or at least severely degraded in QP).

(5.36) a. Több, mint hat fiú ment el   / elment.
           more than six boy went away(VM) away(VM)-went

       b. Hatnál több fiú ment el   / ??elment.
           six-than more boy went away(VM) away(VM)-went

For Szabolcsi, considering only direct links between denotational semantics and syntax, the contrast in (5.36) can only be seen as an 'idiosyncrasy' of Hungarian (note that neither monotonicity nor Szabolcsi's loose notion of 'counting' is of any obvious help in differentiating (5.36a) and (5.36b))—in other words, it remains unexplained. The puzzle disappears as soon as one admits that other kinds of meaning can be signalled syntactically: like (5.31b), (5.36b) can be analysed as containing a 'fronted' constituent which takes on a 'contrastive topic'-like role with regard to the rest of the pre-verbal material, leaving only *több fiú* truly in PV (in the sense that only this undergoes the PV interpretive procedure). Contrastive topics tend to require the appearance of a narrow focus later in the sentence and it is therefore unsurprising that the fronting of *hatnál* prevents the rest of the QNP material from appearing in TP or QP. Again, this restriction can be traced back to relevance-theoretic considerations: the (by hypothesis) morpho-syntactically more complex (5.36b) should only be used to convey effects that are not available from the use of (5.36a). This comes down to the ability to separate out the idea of 'in relation to six ...' as a contrastive topic, thanks to its lexicalised form in (5.36b). The interpretive function of setting up a simple witness set, on the other hand, can be achieved using the simpler (5.36a).

Native speakers confirm that *hatnál* in (5.36b) has an intuitive 'topic feel', while the intonational possibilities associated with each of the structures in (5.36) provide more concrete evidence that this is the correct analysis. (5.36a) allows for a range of intonational patterns, including the relatively 'neutral' pattern of roughly equal stress on each of the main sub-constituents of the QNP. This is not possible with (5.36b), in which a single stronger stress is always observed on one of *több* 'more' or *fiú* 'boy', corresponding to the necessity for something following *hatnál* to be narrowly focused.

The parallelism between (5.31b) and (5.36b) illustrates the need to recognise that non-denotational factors not only exist but, in affecting syntactic structure in their own ways, may obscure relationships between denotational semantics and syntax. The apparent 'failure' of denotational semantic generalisations in some cases does not necessarily indicate that these generalisations have no relation to syntactic possibilities. Thus, (5.31b) should not be taken as evidence against the descriptive relevance of the proportional/intersective distinction for PV any more than (5.36b) should be seen as counterevidence to Szabolcsi's monotonicity constraint on TP and QP (and the witness set analysis that follows from it). This further reinforces the basic argument of this book:

correspondences between structures and meanings cannot simply be taken to demonstrate direct encoding. Doing so can obscure real structure-semantics connections, as well as creating false ones.

Note, however, that I have argued that apparently denotational semantic constraints such as the one against proportional quantifiers appearing as foci in PV are in themselves derived from more general, cognitively significant procedures; the semantic constraints are not encoded as such, in features or any similar mechanism. Hence, the broader picture that is developing is one of denotational semantic concepts being relevant to the grammar just in so far as they reflect cognitively and communicatively significant distinctions. Such a conclusion might trouble the logician, who relies on strict mathematical principles to define the scope of application of his or her insights, but it should not worry the linguist who professes a genuinely mentalist perspective, to whom the relationships between different ways of characterising linguistic phenomena should be as interesting as the content of any one of those characterisations. Furthermore, as argued in Chapter 2, scientifically-minded linguists need not be as afraid to consider the role of cognitive/communicative factors as they perhaps have been in the past. The perspective of frameworks like RT and Dynamic Syntax shows that the relationship between linguistic structure and the ways it is employed in context is neither a dispensable part of characterising grammatical knowledge, nor a domain about which nothing useful can be said because of its breadth and complexity.

5.5.3 'Counterexample' 3: a different kind of proportionality

The remaining example of a proportional quantifier in PV, (5.31c), obviously cannot be explained in terms of its internal syntactic complexity. Indeed, on the face of it, *kevés N* 'few N' is a counterexample not only to the general idea that proportional quantifiers cannot be focused, but also to the particular explanation that I have been putting forward. It parallels *a legtöbb N* 'most N' and *minden N* 'every N' in being syntactically very simple and therefore offering no possibilities for focus on some non-proportional sub-part of the quantifier. Nevertheless, it not only may appear in PV, but is in fact strictly PV-only, under its more clearly proportional reading ('few N') as much as under its apparently intersective reading ('a few N').

In one way, this situation is in fact predicted by factors which have already been mentioned: *kevés N* is monotone decreasing—in fact most clearly so under its proportional reading—and therefore is expected not to surface in TP or QP. Still, in the absence of any principled motivation to claim that the monotonicity constraint should 'outrank' the proposed proportionality constraint, it remains an apparent counterexample to the latter.

The answer to why *kevés N* is not incompatible with the interpretation of PV lies in the particular kind of proportional reading which this quantifier can take on. Proper consideration of this fact proves it to have two desirable consequences. First, the most useful representation of *kevés N* as a GQ proves (unlike other proportional quantifiers) to include a single constituent—i.e. something construable as a predicate—that corresponds to the quantifier, thus allowing focus on the quantifier in PV. Second, the apparent ambiguity of *kevés N* between a proportional and an intersective reading is reduced to a matter of interaction with context, leaving just one lexical entry, with one basic semantic interpretation, necessary for *kevés*.

Unlike 'most N' and 'every N', 'few N' does not require the quantifier to be read as proportional to its own restrictor set. While *few* in *Few students are taking the exam this year* may be proportional with respect to the contextually salient set of students—'few of the contextually relevant set of students (e.g. those in a particular class) have opted to take the exam'—it may instead be interpreted as being proportional with respect to some other contextually relevant set or amount. An obvious possibility in this example is the number of students typically expected to take the exam in question each year. Hence the sentence may express 'there is only a small number of students taking the exam this year', even in the situation in which every current student is taking the exam—that is, there exist only a few current students (note that there is no contradiction inherent to the sentence *Few students are taking the exam this year, even though none of this year's students have opted not to take it*).

The latter reading is the one that appears to be intersective, but it is in a sense no less proportional than the first reading. 'Few' is always proportional in that it always requires some point of comparison, but this point of comparison may vary. Given that languages like Hungarian make no lexical distinction between the different possible readings of 'few', it is reasonable to assume that the relevant point of comparison can be established from purely contextual information. This means that *kevés* requires only one lexical entry and also—significantly—that the semantics of that lexical entry will make no reference to the quantifier's being proportional with respect to the N' restrictor set of the QNP. Instead, this quantifier can be marked as being proportional in respect of some unspecified part of the context, leaving the precise part to be identified inferentially in the course of processing.

This idea is in fact recognised in many existing semantic analyses of 'few'. Heim & Kratzer (1998), for example, give truth conditions for English *few* essentially as in (5.37) (see also Keenan 1987).

(5.37) $|\{x : P(x)\} \cap \{y : R(y)\}|$ **is small**

The important point in terms of appearance in PV is that this kind of representation, which has been shown to be desirable for independent reasons, includes the contribution of the quantifier alone as a discrete constituent part that makes no reference to another part of the representation. It may therefore be thought of as a predicate and focused in PV.

This is not only true of 'few'. The same reasoning applies equally to 'many' (Hungarian *sok*)—being monotone increasing, this is not PV-only, but it is able to appear in PV. Szabolcsi does not seem to view this as an anomaly, using *sok* without further comment to illustrate the effects of PredOp/PV in her example (59), reproduced here as (5.38).

(5.38) Tegnap   sok   diákunk   betegedett meg.
         yesterday many student-1pl sickened   VM
         'The students of ours who fell ill yesterday were many'

In fact, *kevés* and *sok* should be expected in PV for the same reason: they are both a special kind of proportional quantifier, which is proportional with respect not to the N' restrictor set as such, but to an underspecified contextual set. This allows them the syntactic distribution of an intersective quantifier in Hungarian and a range of interpretations that include both archetypally proportional and more intersective-like readings.

5.5.4 Proportionals in PV and the idea of 'counting'

To summarise the preceding sections, there are constraints on appearance in PV which account for the existence of non-PV quantifiers and which are definable using a combination of structural and semantic factors. One might say that monolexical restrictor-proportional QNPs are barred from PV. However, these constraints are not grammatically encoded, but rather follow from the more general interpretive procedure associated with PV focus—interpretation as a predicate over a term that consists of a presupposed focus frame—and from the pragmatics of QNP use in this context, which leads to focus on the quantifier rather than the whole QNP. The denotational generalisation that proportional quantifiers are non-PV therefore holds to the extent that 'normal' proportional quantifiers are not themselves able to be the narrow focus in PV and, consequently, those proportional quantifiers that are not structurally complex in a way that allows for focus on a sub-part of themselves are completely barred from PV. It also follows that 'normal' proportional quantifiers differ in this respect from the class of quantifiers, including *kevés* 'few', that are proportional with respect to some underspecified aspect of the context.

In the light of this re-assessment of the constraints on PV, what remains of Szabolcsi's observation that the quantifiers which can appear in PV "perform a counting operation"? In the end, this appears to derive simply from the question of the internal complexity of quantifying determiners. The presence of an explicit numeral within a complex determiner implies a degree of internal syntactic complexity that allows for focusing on sub-parts of the quantifier and guarantees the presence of at least one suitable predicate for this, in the form of the numeral itself. It would appear to be simply this incidental structural fact which gives the impression that 'counting' bears some connection to the ability to appear in PV. This seems to be as much substance as the notion of 'counting' can really have; it is difficult to see how any extension of the common intuitive meaning of the word 'counting' could successfully distinguish between the quantifiers 'most' and 'few', for example.

5.6 CONTRASTIVE FOCUS ON NON-PV QUANTIFIERS

One loose end that remains in my account of quantificational constraints is the derivation of sentences like (5.28), repeated here as (5.39), which was used above to demonstrate the complete inability of quantifiers like *minden* 'every' to appear in PV when focus is interpreted as falling on the quantifier. This is consistent with the proposed analysis of the procedure associated with PV, since this kind of quantifier, being proportional, corresponds to no single predicate within its GQ representation, nor does it include any lexicalised predicate that could function as a narrow focus. However, (5.39) does involve a contrastive/corrective focus reading, the applicability of the universal quantifier being asserted to the exclusion of other quantifier values (in this case, in effect, 'every' rather than 'some, but not all'). In the context of the analysis developed in this chapter, this brings up two obvious questions. First, how is a contrastive focus reading of this kind of quantifier possible at all? Second, how is this conveyed through the use of QP, which has been seen to prompt the creation of a witness set and therefore, typically, a topic-like reading?

(5.39) ′Minden gyerek megijedt   / *ijedt   meg.
        every   child   VM-feared   feared VM
        'EVERY child got frightened (e.g. not just the girls).'

It would appear that, even though the presupposed material in such an example is indeed logically 'prior', presupposed information, it is not packaged as such in the grammar—since it cannot be. There is little independent evidence for this to be found in examples like (5.39) themselves, although I take the general coherence and predictive power of the account presented above with regard to quantificational evidence (as well as evidence regarding focus and negation presented in Chapter 8) to provide strong empirical support for this position. It is notable that an utterance like (5.39) is distinctly 'marked', being restricted to contexts in which its contrastive function is made immediately accessible by highly salient alternative quantificational values—such examples almost inevitably have a 'corrective' purpose. This is at least consistent with the idea that such examples involve an unusual manipulation of the procedures encoded in the grammar.

I propose that the derivation of the appropriate reading from this kind of structure does not involve the invocation of a focus frame (containing a presupposed eventuality), with the concomitant determination of possible contextual alternatives, but is rather based on the drawing of a contrast between whole propositions. Within the expression of the asserted whole proposition, the QNP representation may be built up according to the witness sets strategy, reflecting the use of QP. The idea of contrasting whole propositions is consistent with the necessarily strongly contrastive/corrective interpretation of examples like (5.39). As discussed in Chapter 4, section 4.5.4, the presupposed focus frame strategy associated with PV can result in virtually 'incidental' exhaustivity, thanks to potential alternatives being contextually determined, but not necessarily highly salient in the context (and indeed this was argued to be the case with most numeral quantifiers in PV). On the other hand, if a particular whole proposition is required to form the point of contrast with another whole proposition, the former must be highly salient in the immediate context.

Assuming this kind of analysis, the interpretive procedures involved in such instances of 'narrow focus in QP' should be thought of roughly as follows. The syntactic structure encodes a 'logical subject first' reading, as in a standard use of QP, but phonological cues (a pitch accent on only the quantifier) indicate that only the quantifier within the subject witness set is newly asserted information. This serves the double purpose of preventing a sense of excessive redundancy, given the syntactic appearance of the assertion of largely presupposed information, and of indicating how this repetition of 'old' information can be made relevant: by paying special attention to the quantifier. By implication, the addressee should recover from the context a salient proposition that differs only in the value of the quantifier at this point in the proposition and draw a contrast between this and the newly communicated, but largely 'old', proposition.

It might seem that the availability of this strategy as a 'get out' for non-PV QNPs should mean that it is available as an alternative way of creating contrastive readings of any expression. That it is in fact restricted to non-PV quantifiers is explicable in terms of relative processing effort. The dual procedure of setting up the apparent new assertion of a proposition, only to override this by marked phonological strategies, is unnecessarily complex as long as the simpler 'focus frame first' procedure is available through the use of PV[15].

5.7 SUMMARY

The details of quantifier distribution in the Hungarian main clause prove to provide significant support to the arguments developed in Chapter 4, to the effect that the PV position, rather than encoding an exhaustive reading, hosts expressions that are narrowly focused (in the sense that they are interpreted against a background in which the contribution of the rest of the sentence is pragmatically presupposed).

Adding to the arguments of the previous chapter, the analysis of QNPs provides a further illustration of how a compositional encoding account of the exhaustive reading associated with PV leads to an unsustainable analysis. In this case, the problem is that a suitably detailed definition of the exhaustivity reading is incompatible with the interpretation that some QNPs receive when demonstrably in the PV position.

A better analysis follows from re-interpreting Szabolcsi's (1997b) insight that different 'semantic assessment procedures' are encoded in the different pre-verbal positions, such that these

---

[15] An interesting partial parallel exists in English. The *it*-cleft construction does not allow QNPs like *every N* in the clefted position (e.g. **It's every child that got scared (not just the girls)*), but they can be given a contrastive/corrective reading when focus is signalled by purely phonological means (EVERY *child got scared*). In English, purely phonological focus is not restricted to these quantifiers but nor is it a marked operation as it is in Hungarian, which generally has quite rigid stress-placement rules.

procedures are broadened from the purely quantificational domain and instead taken to be reflections of the cognitive perspective taken on different pieces of information conveyed by parts of the sentence. An important linguistic correlate of this is shown to be the concept of predication. The procedure associated with TP and QP proposes a single (Q)NP expression as the logical subject of predication, with the rest of the sentence predicating over it. Under the procedure associated with PV, on the other hand, the contribution of the rest of the sentence is taken to be the logical subject of predication and the PV expression itself predicates over this.

Not only does this provide an intuitively appropriate basis for the derivation of narrow focus readings in the PV position, it also proves to be all that is required to predict the constraints on quantifier distribution that Szabolcsi (1997b) identifies but cannot fully explain with her purely quantificational analysis. It is not quantifier semantics as such, but the availability of a predicate to fulfil the relevant procedure that determines whether a QNP can appear in PV or not. Only this explains why lexically simple proportional quantifiers cannot be focused in PV, but any part of their restrictor N' material may be, while QNPs with internally complex quantifiers are always able to appear in PV. The idea that a 'syntactically focused' expression is in fact a predicate over a logical subject that is formed out of the rest of the sentence provides the basis for a formal analysis of the PV position, which is developed in the next chapter.

6

DYNAMIC STRUCTURED MEANINGS: PREDICATION AND INFORMATION STRUCTURE

6.1 OVERVIEW

In terms of the broader theoretical points argued in this book, the primary purpose of Chapters 4 and 5 was to use the Hungarian PV phenomenon to illustrate the dangers of a theory and/or a methodology that encourages the analyst to assume that identifiable meanings are directly encoded in the structures that appear to convey them. While discussion of pragmatic reasoning showed the way to simpler and more explanatory accounts of the data than can be provided by compositional or quasi-compositional approaches, a full new analysis was not attempted there. In particular, the whole issue of the syntax of the PV position remains to be addressed, including the inversion of VMs and the fact that this occurs not only with pre-verbal focused expressions but also when the negative particle *nem* is used and in the expression of certain apparently aspectual meanings. The present chapter and the following two develop a dynamic, parsing-based analysis that explains all of these phenomena on the basis of one simple encoded procedure. As promised in Chapter 2, this is achieved without recourse to the multiple abstract syntactic positions which are used in a more or less *ad hoc* way in many conventional accounts. By accounting for such a wide range of semantic effects and a complicated set of syntactic data in such a parsimonious fashion, this analysis provides a striking illustration of the overarching theoretical point raised at the very beginning of the book: giving active and thorough consideration to extra-grammatical inferential processes can relieve a huge part of the burden of explanation that is carried by the grammar under conventional approaches. Since such inferential processes are, by hypothesis, intrinsic to normal human cognition, it is fair to assume that the simplified picture of the grammar achieved this way is a more realistic model of linguistic competence.

As mentioned in Chapter 3, my dynamic analysis is similar to a 'single position' analysis of PV phenomena, in the sense that pre-verbal VMs and narrow foci (among other things) are argued to share a single relationship to the tensed verb. To show this requires the argument to be built up in stages. The discussion of VMs is mostly delayed until Chapter 7; in the current chapter the basis of the analysis is put in place through the continued investigation of the information-structural significance of PV. However, the emphasis is no longer simply on the expression of narrow focus, but rather on the connections between this and the creation of 'topic>comment' readings, in which the tensed verb is not preceded by a PV expression (other than any VM) and its denotation is understood to be part of the (broad) focused part of the utterance[1]. As noted in Chapter 4, this combination of factors suggests that the syntactic relationship between the 'focus position', PV, and the tensed verb is not simply an arbitrary structural fact.

The analysis built up in this chapter therefore centres around the role of the verb in relation to the discourse as well as the ways in which other expressions are interpretively 'verb-like' when they bear a certain relationship to the verb's syntactic position—that is, when they are PV foci. This meshes with an observation that formed a key part of the explanation of quantifier syntax in Chapter 5: that narrow focus readings involve the granting of a special status to a single predicate that is made available by the form of the utterance.

The resulting account brings together narrow foci and the 'comment-initial' verbs of topic->comment sentences via the notion of 'main predication', a term that I coin for the act of predication that creates a propositional form out of a non-truth-conditional representation. This idea relies on two basic stages of argumentation, which form the overall structure of the current chapter. First, the predicative nature of focus is established and the idea of main predication motivated. Then a suitable form of representation is developed; one in which the change from a non-propositional to a propositional form is effected by the application of a predicate contributed by explicit linguistic material, rather than by abstract semantic mechanisms.

It is important to note that the idea of main predication is not necessarily the same as the logical predicate (or focus) of the sentence, since the proposition-creating effect of main predication takes place at one particular point in the parse, whereas the creation of the logical predicate can be a relatively complex matter, in the case of a topic>comment sentence (i.e. one with a broad focus). While the logical predicate and main predicate are the same in the case of a sentence containing a narrow focus, in topic>comment sentences, the main predicate is only one part of the broader logical predicate; specifically, the verb. Therefore, while 'logical subject' refers to a concept familiar from the literature (under various names), the use of 'main predicate' is intended in a sense that appears not to have any exact precursor.

---

[1] Recall that I reserve the description 'topic>comment' for the kind of reading that involves a broad focus, ascribing some property to an individual participant entity—and, by extension, also for the kind of sentence that produces this kind of reading. 'Comment' is therefore co-extensive with 'broad focus', but not with 'focus' in general.

6.2 FOCUS AND PREDICATION

6.2.1 Focus and focus frame as predicate and logical subject

The idea that a narrow focus in effect acts as a predicate that takes the rest of the sentence as its term was introduced in the previous chapter, where Szabolcsi's (1997b) 'true generalised quantifier' mode of semantic assessment was shown to be a matter of applying a cardinality predicate to the rest of the sentence. In terms of generalised quantifier theory, it may be the case that the rest of the sentence can be conceptualised as the intersection of two sets, but this is not significant for the overall analysis of PV, which subsumes the QNP examples in the broader matter of the perspective taken on semantic material as presupposed or asserted.

The intersective quantifiers found in PV are thus nothing more than special cases of an interpretive procedure that involves the conceptualisation of a focus frame—made up of 'the rest of the sentence', in Szabolcsi's (1997b) terms—as a term to be predicated over. This is quite consistent with the analysis of a focus frame as a presupposed piece of information: since it is recovered from the cognitive environment as a unitary 'chunk' of information, it seems appropriate to recognise its semantic type as being that of a term of some kind. Given this view, a proposition created by presenting a focus frame and a narrow focus is effectively made up of a single act of predication—the focus as predicate being applied to the focus frame as its logical subject. This provides an elementary link to topic>comment sentences, which are more visibly cases of predication over a logical subject (where the predicate happens often to be fairly complex).

Note that this necessitates the separation of the notion of logical subject from the idea of 'topic', as the latter is applied to expressions found in a particular sentence-initial position in languages like Hungarian (that is, the position referred to in Chapter 5 as 'TP'). I shall refer to such expressions here as 'syntactic topics'. In a topic>comment sentence—that is, one that contains no narrow PV focus—the syntactic topic is typically the logical subject, but in a sentence that contains a narrow focus the logical subject is a broader part of the sentence (everything but the narrow focus), as argued above. This means that the syntactic topic is merely a part of the logical subject in the presence of a PV focus. The function common to all syntactic topics should be thought of more in terms of the traditional idea (to some extent connected to Vallduví's (1992) 'Link') that sentence-initial topics provide a 'starting point' for the assimilation of the information conveyed by the utterance in which it appears.

It may not be necessary to go far beyond this kind of general characterisation within a dynamic, inference-based approach: a variety of inferences might be triggered by the strategy of drawing the addressee's attention to a particular manifest entity as an initial step in setting up the context for interpreting the rest of an utterance[2]. This may well coincide with the status of logical subject, when the point of an utterance is simply to pick out a certain entity and predicate

---

[2] There are nevertheless considerable complexities associated with sentence-initial expressions, especially when 'contrastive topics'—those featuring rising intonation—are taken into account. See, for example, Gyuris (2002).

a relevant property of it, but it may be only the first step in guiding the addressee to the right context for a different kind of act of predication. I do not attempt a more thorough analysis of syntactic topics in this book, but the difference suggested here between syntactic topichood and logical subjecthood should become clearer in section 6.6, below, where my dynamic analysis of Hungarian PV is exemplified.

As Rooth (1996) notes (see Chapter 4, section 4.2.2), the relationship between information-structural distinctions and the partitioning of a sentence into logical subject and logical predicate is not new. Furthermore, the idea that narrow foci somehow carry out a predicative function otherwise associated with the tensed verb is reflected in data from numerous other languages (and in some of the descriptions found in the literature on them). One example with clear parallels to Hungarian is to be found in Paul's (2001) analysis of the focus position of Malagasy. This not only shows a case of syntactically-signalled foci occupying a position that is unarguably related to the usual position of tensed verbs, but also demonstrates other elements of both structure and interpretation that imply that these foci are predicates that take the rest of their respective sentences as their logical subjects.

Malagasy is a strongly verb-initial language, yet it features a focusing construction that involves the focused expression appearing sentence-initially. This leads Paul to analyse such foci as predicates, semantically parallel to intransitive verbs. In addition to the involvement of the unmarked verbal position in the relevant construction, these foci resemble Hungarian PV foci in various other significant ways, including an exhaustive reading and incompatibility with certain quantifiers (including universal quantifiers).

While the position of the focused expression is suggestive of predication, the idea that the rest of the sentence forms a unitary subject of predication in such constructions also has a structural reflex in Malagasy. The particle *no* follows a sentence-initial focus and Paul argues that this is a kind of relativiser, which in effect creates a headless relative from the remainder of the sentence. This, she argues, accounts for the presupposed nature of this material, a headless relative being a form of definite expression. The construction is exemplified in (6.1) (Paul glosses *no* as DET, more or less arbitrarily).

(6.1) I Sahondra no   nanapaka   ity hazo ity.
       Sahondra DET PST.AT.cut this tree this
       '(The one) who cut this tree was Sahondra.'/'It was Sahondra who cut this tree.'

While Hungarian has no such particle, the range of features that the two focus constructions share is sufficient to support the idea that some very similar process of interpretation is involved. It seems reasonable to view this aspect of the Malagasy construction as essentially making explicit something that is inferred in the case of Hungarian PV—that the non-focal part of the sentence forms a presupposed unit that acts as subject of predication for the predicative function of the focus. In the relation between verb position and narrow foci, the parallel between the two languages is clearer, though each manipulates its own particular structural properties to signal this. In Malagasy a focused item takes the independently identifiable sentence-initial position that is normally reserved for the verb. In Hungarian also a focus 'usurps' the expected position of the tensed verb, but in this case this is recognised by virtue of linear position relative to the verb itself, since the verb's 'neutral' position is in any case sentence-medial, as well as by taking over the pitch accent that is associated with the verb in a 'neutral' sentence.

Furthermore, Paul shows that the Malagasy data is far from unique, citing a number of other verb-initial languages that feature comparable focusing constructions. This is in fact merely a particular case of a long established cross-linguistic observation that syntactic foci are frequently found close to the normal verbal position (see, for example, Jo 1995).

6.2.2 Main predication

The implication of such evidence is that there is, at least in languages like Hungarian and Malagasy, one act of predication in the building of each proposition that is particularly significant, in that it either is the focus of the sentence or introduces the focus of the sentence. It is notable that in both cases this predicate takes the presupposed material of the sentence as its logical subject and its application produces at least the basis of a truth-conditional assertion. In dynamic terms, the application of this predicate is the point at which the assertion of a propositional form is brought about, where previously there was only some form of incomplete, non-truth-conditional representation. This can be likened to the application of existential quantification over an eventuality in Davidsonian semantic representations: a mere description of a kind of entity is thus converted into a truth-conditional formula (this parallel is pursued in section 6.4). I refer to this henceforth as the 'main predicate' of the sentence and I propose that the primary effect of the PV position of Hungarian is to signal that its inhabitant has the status of main predicate.

The significance of main predication is only visible from a dynamic perspective on the relation between structure and interpretation that gives inferential processes a broad range of application. This is because the kind of information-structural reading that arises in any given sentence (as well as other kinds of interpretive effect, as shown in the next chapter) depends on the kind of expression that is found in PV. That some item bears the status of main predicate is not something that in itself forms part of the interpretation of a sentence; rather, it is a trigger for the drawing of inferences over the particular predicate that is signalled to have this status. In other words, recognising a predicate as the main predicate causes an addressee to ask "If this predicate is the main predicate, what does this say about how I should proceed in interpreting the sentence as a whole (given the current context)?" It is the answer to this question that ultimately leads to particular information-structural effects. Interpretation of this kind is therefore inherently inferential: the processing of linguistic material in a certain structural configuration does not lead directly to certain kinds of interpretation, but rather the particular linguistic material encountered within the structure in question (as well as its relation to the broader context) leads to different ways of interpreting that structure. The actual nature of the inferences triggered by the attribution of main predicate status to different kinds of expression is outlined in the next section.

6.2.3 Basic inferences over main predicates

The 'main predication' account of PV states that an expression that is found in PV (or the relevant sub-part of this expression, in a case of 'pied-piping') is to be taken as the main, proposition-creating predicate of the sentence. Here I outline the consequences of this for main verbs and for non-verbal expressions, such as referring NPs (the special case of VMs being delayed until the next chapter).

First, consider what happens if a non-verbal expression is encountered in PV. The requirement to interpret this (or an identifiable part of it) as main predicate entails that some term must be contextually available as the logical subject of this predicate. Yet a non-verbal expression cannot be a 'comment', a property ascribed to a topical entity of the kind that thereby creates a proposition. An NP, for example, can be viewed as a predicate in a neo-Davidsonian representation (see section 6.3, below), but only in the sense of a function that relates an entity to an event; it can ascribe nothing to another entity. So for a non-verbal item to be the main predicate, some more complex subject of predication must be found—and since a proposition must result from this, it must be something that is richly specified enough to in effect represent a proposition lacking just the right kind of non-verbal expression. Therefore, the requirement to treat a non-verbal expression as main predicate effectively triggers the search for a presupposed focus frame. The precise identity of this focus frame term may be indicated by explicit post-focal material, in case this is not immediately obvious in the context, but may be recovered directly from the context—foci do of course frequently appear with all presupposed material elided (particularly in answer to explicit context questions, for example).

This contrasts with the situation that typically arises when a verb is encountered in the position that signals main predication. A verb's denotation is a particular kind of predicate, conceivable as a relation between entities and/or between entities and an eventuality. As such, the assertion of a verbal meaning may be taken to involve the introduction of a whole template of argument positions, each of which of course bears its own relation to context. One or more of these may be explicitly introduced as being already manifestly instantiated by contextually identifiable entities, in the form of a pre-verbal topic. Arguments whose identity is presupposed in this sense may of course also remain implicit, to be recovered purely on the basis of contextual factors, in a 'pro-drop' language like Hungarian. Non-presupposed arguments may also exist, if the verb is not intransitive—these are manifested as the 'information foci' of É. Kiss (1998a), which are always part of a broad focus, as argued in Chapter 4. But, importantly, knowledge of the identity of the entities that instantiate such arguments is not necessary for the creation of a propositional form; a mere placeholder will allow the creation of a truth-conditional assertion, whose precise content can be subsequently elaborated by the inclusion of any explicit 'information focus'.

For example, at the point of processing the verb *szereti* 'love' in (6.2a), assuming it bears a pitch accent, a proposition of roughly the form in (6.2b) can be assumed[3].

---

[3] In fact, the existence of the 'definite conjugation' in Hungarian means that the first two words of (6.2a) could

(6.2) a. Ferenc szereti Marit.
Ferenc loves   Mari-ACC
'Ferenc loves Mari.'

b. $love'(ferenc',\textbf{someone/something})$

The topic *Ferenc* provides an explicit subject of predication in this case and the predicate 'love someone', introduced by the verb *love* alone, is sufficient to create a propositional form when applied to this. The subsequent processing of the accusative NP *Marit* represents an act of elaboration of existing material within the proposition. In other words, contrary to common assumptions, a complex logical predicate like 'loves Mari' is not necessarily built up in advance of its application to the logical subject, either on the semantic level or on a syntactic level (that is, there is no motivation to posit anything like a VP node that groups together elements of the logical predicate). This fits well with the prosodic structure of a Hungarian topic>comment sentence: recall that each expression that forms part of a comment—i.e. each 'information focus' expression—bears a pitch accent (Kálmán 1985a, Rosenthall 1992, Roberts 1998), a fact that may be interpreted as indicating that these individual sub-expressions of a comment, or complex logical predicate, are processed separately from each other—certainly, they are not grouped together by prosody as closely as they might be.

For obligatory arguments at least, this kind of process can be handled technically by the use of objects like the 'metavariables' of Dynamic Syntax, which can act as 'placeholders' in a semantic representation. This allows the verb to introduce a whole propositional template (minus tense) at the point at which it is encountered, with metavariables occupying each argument position. This is the approach taken by Kempson *et al.* (2001, 72) in the slightly different context of their analysis of scrambling effects in Japanese. Any existing topic, whether explicitly stated or simply contextually manifest before the verb is encountered, can immediately be substituted for the relevant argument metavariable on processing the verb (case marking guides this process), leaving a propositional representation like (6.3), where **U** is a metavariable. This is essentially equivalent to (6.2b).

(6.3) $love'(ferenc', \textbf{U})$

Non-obligatory elements, such as adjuncts and certain arguments of verbs of variable polyadicity, are no more problematic for the view that the verb alone acts as main predicate. After all, the omission of an optional (or not predictably obligatory) element almost by definition does not prevent a representation from being taken as fully propositional. Optional arguments and adjuncts may be dealt with in terms of 'bridging inference', which Bittner (2001) argues to operate

---

actually have a slightly richer representation: something like $love'(ferenc',\textbf{him/her/it})$. This is not crucial to the point at issue, however. Note that a verb from the 'indefinite conjugation' is still proposition-creating in the relevant sense, such that the first two words of *Ferenc szeret egy diákot* 'Ferenc loves a student' allows for the representation in (6.2b).

at sub-clausal levels, as well as inter-clausally[4]. In other words, the processing of an adjunct following that of a verb leads to a re-assessment of the valence of the main predicate; in effect adding a pronominal argument to the representation, which is immediately substituted by the material that triggers this process. A similar proposal, couched in terms of the structural and interpretive underspecification of Dynamic Syntax plus relevance-theoretic inference, is made by Marten (2002).

Both Bittner's and Marten's proposals are intended to be much more general, covering the whole range of arguments and adjuncts. As such, they fit well with fully 'decomposed' neo-Davidsonian semantic representations, in which all participants are represented alike, as conjoined predicates over events (see section 6.3). For expository reasons I do not follow up this possibility here in the syntactic part of the story, instead restricting the inferential introduction of participants into semantic representations to non-obligatory participants. However, the existence of such forms of explanation demonstrates that the processing of a verb alone can unproblematically provide the kind of predicate over presupposed entities that is sufficient to create a full propositional form. This is the basis of how 'neutral' word order in Hungarian (i.e. when the main verb is not preceded by a narrow focus or negation) produces topic>comment readings. As section 6.6.3 discusses, this is not in fact the only possible reading of such word orderings, but it is the usual one—both of which facts are straightforwardly explicable in terms of the notion of main predication and the influence of context on the interpretation process.

6.3 EVENTUALITIES AND STRUCTURED MEANINGS

It is clear that the notion of main predication requires a dynamic form of representation with certain crucial features. One of these is that it must provide some mechanism whereby a predicate made available by the natural language string may make the difference between a non-truth-conditional description and the assertion of a propositional form. Another is that it must incorporate some suitable form of 'structured meaning' representation, such that distinctions in information structure—that is, in the way in which the propositional form is built up—are reflected in the representation. I address the latter point first, showing how an existing proposal in the literature, Herburger's (2000) theory of focus, point the way to a representation which is suitably structured and which draws together a number of important factors already mentioned in the current analysis of Hungarian PV focus.

Herburger's theory in effect involves the synthesis of two important ideas that arose in the analysis of Hungarian PV focus in Chapter 4: on the one hand, the different possible cognitive

---

[4] In fact, Bittner argues that practically all semantic composition can be viewed in terms of bridging inference; an idea that opens up intriguing, radically inference-based perspectives on grammar and interpretation when allied to a dynamic approach to structure. It is possible that my analysis of Hungarian PV could be re-cast in these terms, though this would require careful consideration of the definition of a full propositional representation for the purposes of identifying main predication. I leave this as a possible avenue for future research.

perspectives on the material in a given sentence, relating to differently structured representations of it in different contexts; on the other, the idea of conceptualising the content of propositions in terms of eventualities. These are brought together in Herburger's work in the sense that it proposes a form of structured meaning representation that is based on the explicit representation of eventualities. Specifically, Herburger proposes that the focus/presupposition distinction[5] should be represented through tripartite structuring of quantification over eventualities. In section 6.3.1, I briefly present the fundamentals of the neo-Davidsonian semantics on which Herburger's proposal is based, and point out the appropriateness of this kind of representation for conveying information-structural effects. Herburger's ideas are then reviewed, in section 6.3.2, in advance of my own, rather different, extension of neo-Davidsonian representations.

6.3.1 Eventuality-based semantics

Neo-Davidsonian semantic representations (Parsons 1990) involve quantification, in most cases existential quantification, over a variable that represents the eventuality expressed by the sentence in question. Parsons (1990) uses different variables, e and s, for events and states, respectively, but my arguments do not make reference to this distinction and therefore I shall use a single kind of variable, e, for 'eventuality'. Following convention, and for the sake of brevity, I shall nevertheless refer to this variable as the 'event variable'. The reification of eventualities as event variables in the semantic representation is suggested by linguistic phenomena such as the pronominal anaphor in (6.4): *it* in the second sentence seems to refer to an entity, but this cannot be understood to be any individual; rather it appears to be the whole eventuality described by the first sentence.

(6.4)   John asked Mary to look after his wallet. He regretted it almost immediately.

Once eventualities are conceived of as entities, which can have any number of properties predicated of them, the properties of a particular eventuality—the detailed content of a proposition—can be expressed as the conjunction of predicates over eventualities. Arguments and adjuncts are conceived of as predicates but still related to verbs, since the functions from entities to eventualities that they denote are essentially thematic roles. Hence (6.5a) can be given a (simplified) representation in the style of Parsons (1990) as (6.5b).

(6.5)   a.   Rosalía wrote a poem.
        b. $\exists e \, (Write(e) \, \& \, Past(e) \, \& \, Agent(e, rosalia) \, \& \, Theme(e, a\text{-}poem))$

As Schein (1993, 331ff.) notes (see also Parsons 1990, 99ff.), the controversial nature of theta-roles need not reflect directly on the legitimacy of such representations. These require only that the functions that relate participants to events be distinguished relative to each verb; they do

---
[5]Herburger in fact refers simply to 'focused' versus 'nonfocused'.

not require that such functions are necessarily consistent across different verbs. For this reason, I later adopt less specific theta-roles in my own representations; see section 6.4.3.

The 'decomposition' of verb phrase meanings into separately applied predicates answers one of the major problems raised by Davidson (1967): how to maintain the common element expressed by a verb like *butter* in sentences like (6.6a) and (6.6b) and thereby reflect the entailment relations between their respective semantic representations.

(6.6) a. Jones buttered the toast in the bathroom with a knife at midnight.

b. Jones buttered the toast.

Davidson points out that to treat the verb *butter* as being of variable polyadicity—that is, as a five-place predicate in (6.6a) and a two-place predicate in (6.6b)—is unsatisfactory in a number of ways. If the verb is treated as being lexically multiply ambiguous, this ignores the clear intuition that *butter* is really the same predicate contributing the same material in each case (and ignores the apparent structure of the language). Furthermore, this ambiguity might have to be infinite, since it is not clear that an upper limit can be placed in any principled way on the number of participants that can be associated with any given verb. This fact also precludes the alternative strategy of assuming that the maximum number of argument positions for a given verbal predicate is present in the logical form of every sentence containing the corresponding verb, whether or not they are linguistically realised (which would also go against intuitions about what sentences like (6.6b) actually convey). Such problems are eliminated by viewing each participant in (6.6a) as a predicate over a single eventuality and taking each to be conjoined in turn to the other material in the sentence. This not only maintains a single predicate $butter'(e)$ in both (6.6a) and (6.6b), but also correctly ensures that the former entails the latter, via a simple operation of conjunction elimination.

Parsons (1990) completes the justification for fully decomposed representations like that in (6.5b) by arguing that even verbs with syntactically obligatory arguments are underlyingly one-place predicates. He points out (1990, 97ff.) that a verb like *stab*, which might be thought of as requiring an Agent and a Theme can be interpreted in the absence of a Theme in sentences like *Brutus stabbed and missed* and, arguably, even in the absence of an Agent. The latter case is illustrated by the fact that an interpretation is readily available for the agentless passive *I was stabbed* even in a context like 'I had a dream last night in which I was stabbed—but there was no one there who could have stabbed me'[6].

The complete decomposition of propositions into strings of conjoined predicates opens up interesting possibilities for representing information structure within semantic formulae. Because such formulae do not require hierarchical structure to express basic predicate-argument relations, their elements may be freely structured for other purposes. This seems particularly appropriate

---

[6]For a range of further justifications for event-based semantic representations, see Davidson (1967), Parsons (1990), Schein (1993), and useful summaries in Rothstein (1998a), Herburger (2000).

in the analysis of a language like Hungarian in which basic word order phenomena like those under discussion in this book show virtually no subject-object (or other role-based) asymmetries. Perhaps surprisingly, this potential has rarely been exploited. The one thorough existing attempt to relate neo-Davidsonian decomposition to information structure, Herburger's (2000) treatment of English, is reviewed below. My proposal, which uses neo-Davidsonian representations to distinguish different instances of main predication, is then developed in section 6.4.

6.3.2 Herburger (2000): structured eventualities

Herburger's principal insight is the recognition that the string of conjoined predicates that specify the properties of the existentially quantified eventuality can be structured in terms of a tripartite quantificational structure, parallel to that given to generalised quantifiers. That is, some predicative material may be considered to be part of the restrictor of the quantification, while the remainder will be in its nuclear scope. The interpretive significance of this, Herburger suggests, is that it can be seen as an indication of the information structure of a sentence at the level of its semantic representation. In Herburger's terms, material that is part of what the sentence is 'about' (a notion that effectively translates as presupposed material, in my terms) is mapped onto the restrictor of the quantification over the event variable. Material that is focused, in the general sense of 'newly asserted' (that is, the kind of focus that is identified by the context-question heuristic) is mapped into the nuclear scope of event quantification.

For example, two of the possible information-structural readings of (6.5a), (6.7a) and (6.7b), are differentiated in Herburger's representations as in (6.8a) and (6.8b), respectively.

(6.7)   a.   ROSALÍA wrote a poem.

        b.   Rosalía wrote A POEM.

(6.8)   a.   [∃e: *Write*(e) & *Past*(e) & *Theme*(e,a-poem)] *Agent*(e,rosalia) & *Write*(e) & *Past*(e) & *Theme*(e,a-poem)

        b.   [∃e: *Agent*(e,rosalia) & *Write*(e) & *Past*(e)] *Theme*(e,a-poem) & *Agent*(e,rosalia) & *Write*(e) & *Past*(e)

Herburger renders the significance of these formulae is as follows:

> The interpretation of [(6.7a)] that is represented in [(6.8a)] states that some relevant event of writing a poem in the past was such that it was a past event of writing a poem and its agent was Rosalía, which amounts to saying that some relevant past event of poem writing had Rosalía as its agent. In contrast, the interpretation of [(6.7b)] given in [(6.8b)] states that some relevant event of writing whose agent was Rosalía had a poem as its theme (and was a past event of writing whose agent was Rosalía). (Herburger 2000, 18)

Herburger concludes that "Focus is not a pragmatic or information structure phenomenon; instead, it has a direct effect on the semantic interpretation of the sentence" (2000, 47). In so doing, she provides a particularly clear example of how the strong kind of compositionality continues to be simply assumed in recent literature. As I have made clear in previous chapters, the fact that something may be expressed at the level of semantic representation does not justify the conclusion that it has nothing to do with pragmatics, since inferential processes must be involved in the creation of a propositional form. In fact, in line with strongly compositional assumptions, Herburger's overall analysis effectively treats focus not merely as a semantic phenomenon, but as a syntactic one, since she assumes that focus triggers a restructuring of LF representations prior to mapping from syntax to semantic translations. The nature of this LF process is unclear; Herburger (2000, 42,47) recognises that there is no syntactic evidence for it. It would presumably have to be sensitive to prosody as well as to syntactic structure as such—or involve some form of prosodically informed syntactic representation about which Herburger is inexplicit—since both may be involved in the signalling of information structure. In any case, it leaves her analysis with the same problems that attend any attempt to encode focus directly, as discussed in previous chapters: it does no more than other 'structured meaning' approaches to address issues of encoding versus inference in this necessarily context-related domain (Herburger's only concession to the role of context is a 'contextual predicate' that is present in every propositional representation; a strategy that is very likely to be rendered redundant by independently justified pragmatic theory, according to the arguments of Chapter 1.

In this sense, Herburger's proposals do not represent a significant departure from other 'structured meaning' approaches (von Stechow 1991a), at least in relation to my aims in this book. That is, the material within the restrictor of event quantification effectively produces an incomplete propositional form to which something is to be added, just as a lambda expression represents a semantic form that awaits some further material to complete its content. Herburger's exploitation of the tripartite structure of generalised quantifiers in the domain of quantification over eventualities is not therefore of particular use to my analysis—the means by which such structured representations are built up being much more germane to my immediate concerns than the details of their form. Nevertheless, certain aspects of Herburger's representations do suggest that the manipulation of neo-Davidsonian semantic formulae in this way holds the potential to provide a more explanatory account.

One useful fact, noted above, is that the use of explicit event variables allows the process of 'meaningful structuring' to be based upon some integral part of the semantic representation (quantification over the event variable), rather than resorting to the more arbitrary mathematical mechanism of the lambda calculus. While this does not yet fulfil the desired goal of performing this task using predicates made available by natural language sentences, it is a step in the right direction. The use of an event-based semantics also allows in a fairly straightforward way for the conceptualisation of different information-structurally significant parts of the semantic formula as objects of the right semantic type. The restrictor part of an existentially quantified event, being at one level an existentially bound entity, is suited to playing the role of logical subject, while material from the nuclear scope is inevitably all predicative material in a neo-Davidsonian representation. Moreover, the simple fact that such representations generalise the notion of predication, such that not only verbs but also arguments and adjuncts are routinely represented as separate acts of predication within a propositional form, is clearly promising with regard to seeking a way of representing the idea of main predication.

What is required is therefore a means of making event-based structured representations dynamic, so that the *process* of creating the relevant kinds of structure is made clear. This should be based in the application of particular predicates explicitly contributed by the natural language sentence, since this is what main predication consists in. A mechanism that achieves these two aims is presented in section 6.4.2, following some further discussion of just what it is that this mechanism must achieve: what it means to create a proposition.

6.4 MAKING STRUCTURED MEANINGS DYNAMIC: EPSILON TERMS

6.4.1 The creation of propositional forms

Recall that main predication is taken to be the point at which a propositional assertion is created. In neo-Davidsonian representations, this is achieved by the application of the existential quantifier over an event variable that is attributed with certain minimum specifications. Davidson (1967, 117) traces this use of the existential quantifier to Reichenbach (1947) and points out its usefulness in addressing the debatable relationship between a sentence and a proposition—and hence between the formula proposed as the semantic translation of a sentence and a proposition. Without existential quantification, a formula can be viewed as a mere description of an event or kind of event—an act of referring rather than asserting. With the addition of the existential quantifier, however, the formula becomes the representation of an assertion; specifically, the assertion that there is an event that makes the formula true. As such, the existential quantification in a formula like (6.5b) is the part that makes it truth-conditional. Therefore this is identifiable as the element that makes it a truly propositional form, rather than a mere description. The connection to my notion of main predication is clear: a main predicate should be definable as the point at which existential quantification over the event variable is introduced, provided the other minimal elements of a propositional form are also present.

Minimally, a proposition must contain two kinds of restriction on the event variable: a kind of eventuality, as typically expressed by verbs, and a temporal anchor point, which is associated with tense. As noted above, the verbal 'kind of eventuality' predicate may be elaborated by further assertions, but it is the application of such a predicate, rather than the details of its content, that is important for the establishment of a propositional form. These minimal restrictions on the eventuality may, in principle, be asserted at the point of main predication or they may be presupposed at this point—in the sense used throughout this book of being manifest in the context and obligatorily so for the required process of interpretation.

A proposition, in skeletal form, may therefore be represented as in (6.9).

(6.9) $\exists e.\ f(e, \mathbf{T}_i)\ \&\ \mathbf{V}(e)$

$\mathbf{V}$ and $\mathbf{T}_i$ may be thought of as metavariables. A metavariable, as used in Dynamic Syntax (Kempson *et al.* 2001), is in essence a requirement to identify and slot into the semantic representation some semantic material of a certain kind. In other words, it is a pro-form-like element, which can draw its content from any part of the context (whether explicit or otherwise manifest in the discourse). One way to think of a metavariable is thus as an invitation to draw relevant inferences of a certain kind. Should the context be enriched by the assertion of material that is made relevant by its substitution for the metavariable, this substitution will take place. Hence, in some circumstances, a metavariable may be little more than a placeholder for some required information; in others, it may pick out information that is manifest prior to any assertions made explicitly in the current utterance. $\mathbf{V}$ and $\mathbf{T}_i$ are particular, sortally restricted kinds of metavariable. $\mathbf{V}$ is intended as an abstraction over kinds of eventuality (verb-like predicates); it effectively requires that a predicate be found that introduces a certain kind of structure (argument and/or conceptual structure) to the eventuality. The representation of the temporal anchor requires some additional explanation.

My assumptions about the relationship between an eventuality and its temporal anchor follow the suggestions made in Kempson *et al.* (2001, 34–35) for the representation of tense information in the Dynamic Syntax framework. There, a propositional formula is treated as a predicate logic formula carrying a temporal 'label', in the form of a metavariable, that represents the index of evaluation for the proposition. Thus, a propositional formula has the form $Fo(\mathbf{T}_i : P)$, where P is a predicate logic formula and *Fo* is simply the 'formula predicate' of Dynamic Syntax, that serves to distinguish the logical representation of interpretation from other, largely procedural, information (such as type specifications and requirements for further information or subsequent steps in a parse)[7]. $\mathbf{T}_i : P$ is true if there is a temporal unit $\mathbf{T}_i$ relative to which P is true.

While this form of labelling relates a temporal index to the predicate logic formula, this index is related to other temporal indices in a separate temporal logic system. A full representation of a propositional form in this version of Dynamic Syntax therefore also includes (among other things) a statement such as $Te(\mathbf{T}_i\ <\ \mathbf{T}_j)$, where *Te* is a temporal logic equivalent of *Fo* (that is, essentially a mere label, in the form of a predicate that constrains the interpretation of the formula that is its argument but does not itself add anything to the propositional meaning of the sentence) and $<$ is a temporal operator (specifically, in this case, precedence).

In my representation (6.9), the function f in effect replaces the colon by which Kempson *et al.* show the relation between the temporal index and the predicate logic formula P. This underspecified function may be considered to range over the different ways of relating an eventuality to a temporal interval, such as overlap and containment (see, for example, Kamp & Reyle 1993,

---

[7] By convention, the metavariable $\mathbf{S}_i$ is used for the temporal anchor in Dynamic Syntax. I use $\mathbf{T}_i$ instead, as a clear reminder that this part of my representations deals with temporal matters.

Chapter 5). The details of temporal information—how the index relates to other times—is still assumed to be dealt with in a separate system. Therefore, while I bring the temporal metavariable $\mathbf{T}_i$ within the description of the eventuality, no temporal information is introduced by the formula $f(e, \mathbf{T}_i)$ other than the minimum necessary to ensure that a proposition may exist: the fact that the eventuality has some temporal anchor. I therefore take this to be the only contribution associated with tense morphology that can be subject to the same processes as those contributions of other elements of the sentence that appear within the description of the eventuality. This is shown in Chapters 7 and 8 to predict important facts about the syntax of Hungarian. Consequently, certain structural properties of Hungarian can be viewed as support for Kempson *et al.*'s (2001) proposals for the analysis of tense.

I claim that the formula $f(e, \mathbf{T}_i)$ is merely 'associated with tense morphology' since this minimal information can effectively be presupposed in advance of the explicit realisation of tense— every sentence is tensed and every proposition has a temporal anchor. Nevertheless, particular grammatical constructions show that this information is contributed by tense (see Chapter 8), so it must be considered to be redundantly associated with tense on most occasions, rather like the content of unstressed pronouns in non-pro-drop languages like English (of course, Hungarian tense is not so fully redundant, as it contributes to the separate temporal logic system).

Having explained the form of (6.9), let us return to the idea that it contains the minimal elements necessary to create a propositional representation. As noted above, it is in fact not the metavariables, but the existential quantification that really makes this description into a proposition: an assertion with truth-conditions. However, the existential quantifier in this context is highly abstract: it has little to do with any element of the natural language sentence and its exact point of introduction into the semantic representation is unclear. It is therefore of little help in representing the idea of main predication, even though it fulfils a parallel purpose.

What is required to convey main predication is therefore a means of achieving the effect of asserting the existence of an eventuality, and in this manner conferring truth-conditions to the formula, but through a more concrete individual act of predication. It so happens that there already exists a form of semantic representation that allows exactly this, though it has not, to my knowledge, been applied to event variables in any comparable way before and therefore its potential to demonstrate the creation of propositions through natural language predicates has not been exploited. The required semantic mechanism is the epsilon calculus of Hilbert & Bernays (1939), as interpreted by Egli & von Heusinger (1995).

6.4.2 The epsilon operator

In the epsilon calculus, when ε binds a variable its effect is to select some referent matching the specifications laid down by any predicates that restrict that variable. That is, it selects a witness of the restrictor set. For example, in (6.10) the epsilon operator selects an individual from the set of cats, assuming that this set is non-empty.

(6.10) $\varepsilon, x \, [cat'(x)]$

Should the variable's restrictor set (the set of cats) prove to be empty, the epsilon operator assigns an entirely arbitrary entity to the variable—so (6.10) as it stands does not represent an existence statement. An epsilon term, whatever its content and internal complexity, is thus not an assertion of any kind, but rather a referring expression. What is required to guarantee existence is an assertion that the referent selected is indeed to be found within the restrictor set—in other words, that the restrictor predicate applied to the variable applies to the whole epsilon term. Hence the equivalence in (6.11a); 'some cat exists' being rendered as in (6.11b).

(6.11)   a. $P(\varepsilon, x \, [P(x)]) \equiv \exists x. \, P(x)$

   b. $cat'(\varepsilon, x \, [cat'(x)])$

(6.11b) may be thought of as follows: '$\exists x. \, cat'(x)$ because an x selected with respect to $cat'(x)$ is a member of the set cat' (not a completely arbitrary entity)'.

As Egli & von Heusinger (1995) recognise, epsilon terms lend themselves naturally to representations of information structure. An epsilon term, being interpreted essentially as a witness set, proposes an entity as a potential argument for some predicate. As argued in Chapter 5, section 5.3.2, if one seeks a cognitively relevant correlate of this kind of object—a referent to which properties may be ascribed—one comes up with the notion of a 'logical subject of predication'. A predicate taking an epsilon term as its argument, on the other hand, represents the act of ascribing a property to an independently established entity, which is close to the idea of the assertion of a 'logical predicate'—and therefore to focus. Egli & von Heusinger themselves refer to these 'outer' predicates as 'rhemes' and to material within an epsilon term as the 'theme'. Note that all of this comes from what may reasonably be assumed about the cognitive impact that certain kinds of semantic object can have when employed in a communicative context (in other words, while Egli & von Heusinger do not say so explicitly, their identification of epsilon terms with 'themes' and outer predicates with 'rhemes' must be based on pragmatic relevance considerations.).

Logical subjects carry a presupposition of their own existence, which also arises from simple relevance-based reasoning: to be proposed as a subject of predication, an entity must exist, at least in some conceptual sense. This is illustrated by the well-known example *The exhibition was visited by the King of France*. Assuming a topic>comment reading, such that the king is not the logical subject, this sentence tends to be judged straightforwardly false when the hearer is aware of the non-existence of French monarchs, while *The King of France visited the exhibition* causes a sense of 'presupposition failure' rather than clear truth or falsity[8].

---

[8] As I suggested in Chapter 4, this is a relevance-based phenomenon. In fact, the most likely effect of uttering the latter sentence in context would be to prompt accommodation of the fact that the communicator refers to some existing individual as 'the King of France' for some contextually relevant reason. Only in cases of failure of communication (i.e. misjudgement of the mutual cognitive environment) or deliberate obscurity of expression (which itself relates to particular cognitive effects) would a sense of 'presupposition failure' actually occur. This illustrates how

The issue of existence readings with epsilon terms therefore involves more than just truth-conditions. Any epsilon term, being communicatively useful as logical subject material, is likely to be *inferred* to denote an existing entity with the properties described, but only an epsilon term that has its own restrictor set predicated of it, as in (6.11b), is *asserted* to exist. Thus, (6.12a) implicates the existence of the cat, while (6.12b) asserts it. (6.12c) shows the usefulness of this distinction and of the epsilon operator's picking out an arbitrary entity in the case of an empty restrictor set: the semantic representation reflects the composition of the natural language sentence and the existence of the topic, being not asserted at any point, is cancellable in line with intuitions—(6.12c) and (6.12d) do not logically contradict each other.

(6.12)   a. $bald'(\varepsilon, x\, [cat'(x)])$ ('The/A cat is bald.')

        b. $cat'(\varepsilon, x\, [cat'(x)])$ ('The/A cat is a cat.')

        c. $\neg bald'(\varepsilon, x\, [king\text{-}of\text{-}france'(x)])$ ('The/A King of France isn't bald.')

        d. $\neg king\text{-}of\text{-}france'(\varepsilon, x\, [king\text{-}of\text{-}france'(x)])$ ('There is no King of France.')

6.4.3 The epsilon operator with event variables

Recall that in a neo-Davidsonian representation, an NP denotes a function (in the form of a theta-role) from an entity to an event variable. Combining this with the epsilon calculus, an NP syntactic topic—as an example, the nominative proper noun *Ferenc*—may be represented as an epsilon term containing such a function, as in (6.13). Since this book does not aim to explicate the nature of theta roles, and since nothing hangs on this (recall the comments to this effect in section 6.3), I do not commit myself here to the use of particular roles like 'Agent' and 'Theme', but simply assume that nominative case contributes a function θ_{NOM}, accusative a function θ_{ACC}, and so on. I also refer to these functions as picking out relations like Subject and Object. This is a mere presentational shorthand (a complete theory would of course have to include an account of how more meaningful functions are mapped from morpho-syntax into the semantic representation)[9].

(6.13) $\varepsilon, e\, [\theta_{NOM}(e, ferenc')]$

---

the notion of 'presupposition' involves not specifiable semantic facts but issues of the compatibility of contextual assumptions with how interpretive *procedures* are indicated by linguistic forms. That is, presuppositions are not encoded; procedures may be (and may be inferred), and it is in the nature of certain procedures to require certain contextual conditions.

[9] As Ronnie Cann has pointed out to me (personal communication), something like the functions θ_{NOM}, θ_{ACC}, etc. might be maintained and thought of as a set of special, partially restricted metavariables that are to be instantiated, via relevance-based reasoning, by the detailed, idiosyncratic participant roles associated with particular verbs. For example, θ_{NOM} would be instantiated by the 'hitter' role in the context of the verbal predicate hit' and the 'thinker' role in the context of $think'$.

However, in a richly inferential dynamic account, this is not all the information available at the point of processing a topic. Since a topic introduces an utterance that is to convey a proposition, it also carries the expectation of the essential elements of a proposition, as presented above in (6.9). The broader conception of a topic is thus of a theta-marked subject of predication which requires a temporally anchored eventuality to be predicated of it. Using the notation introduced above, this is represented as in (6.14).

(6.14) $\varepsilon, e\ [f(e, \mathbf{T}_i)\ \&\ \mathbf{V}(e)\ \&\ \theta_{\text{NOM}}(e, \text{ferenc}')]$

This epsilon term picks out an eventuality from the intersection of the set of eventualities with some verb-like structure, the set of eventualities with a temporal anchor $\mathbf{T}_i$ and the set of eventualities that have Ferenc as Subject—provided that none of these sets is empty, in which case the entity selected will be arbitrary with respect to that set. At this point, the existence of some eventuality, some anchor and Ferenc-as-Subject is therefore implicated, but not asserted; the information represented so far is not propositional.

However, the ground is laid for any subsequently encountered verbal predicate to perform main predication. The application of a verbal predicate, say *walk'*, to (6.14) will create existential quantification over the event variable because $\mathbf{V}(e)$ ('the set of eventualities with some verb-like structure') is effectively a superset of $walk'(e)$ ('the set of walking eventualities'). This means that the latter logically entails the former, so that (6.15a) entails (6.15b). This shows the existential quantification clearly, with the same predicate inside and outside the epsilon term.

While (6.11b) is therefore a kind of propositional form, neither it nor (6.15a) individually has the potential to be an optimally relevant assertion. (6.15b) asserts only that some eventuality presupposed to include Ferenc as Subject exists, which clearly does not justify the effort of processing the specific predicate *walk'*. On the other hand, (6.15a) asserts that this eventuality is in the set of walking events, but leaves open the possibility that the eventuality in question could be entirely arbitrary and hence effectively contentless. Note, however, that these two assertions are in effect made simultaneously, so that applying the predicate *walk'* as in (6.15a) amounts to a single act that asserts both that a certain eventuality is a walking event and that it exists. Taking these two assertions together clearly invites an extra inferential step that creates a potentially relevant assertion: that a walking event exists. Note that this is in any case precisely the result of substituting the now highly accessible predicate *walk'* for the metavariable $\mathbf{V}$ in (6.15a), as in (6.15c), meaning that this inferential step is of minimal processing cost. Though a matter of relevance-based inference, rather than formal necessity, this step is therefore a practical inevitability. It follows that the act of predication in (6.15a) leads not only to the propositional form in (6.15b), but to the more specific and informative assertion (6.15c).

(6.15)   a. $walk'(\varepsilon, e\ [f(e, \mathbf{T}_i)\ \&\ \mathbf{V}(e)\ \&\ \theta_{\text{NOM}}(e, \text{ferenc}')])$
        b. $\mathbf{V}(\varepsilon, e\ [f(e, \mathbf{T}_i)\ \&\ \mathbf{V}(e)\ \&\ \theta_{\text{NOM}}(e, \text{ferenc}')])$
        c. $walk'(\varepsilon, e\ [f(e, \mathbf{T}_i)\ \&\ walk'(e)\ \&\ \theta_{\text{NOM}}(e, \text{ferenc}')])$

Thanks to the presupposed nature of the topic NP and of the idea that there is a temporal anchor (in any case, tense has been processed by the time main predication is recognised), all the ingredients of a proposition are now in place, so main predication has been achieved. (6.15c) is equivalent to (6.16a) as an assertion of existence, but equivalent to the full proposition (6.16b), as long as the sets of eventualities with a temporal anchor T_i and of eventualities with Ferenc as Subject are non-empty, as they are implicated to be.

(6.16)   a. $\exists e.\ walk'(e)$

         b. $\exists e.\ walk'(e)\ \&\ f(e, T_i)\ \&\ \theta_{\text{NOM}}(e, ferenc')$

Topic>comment sentences in a sense have a dual nature, in terms of what constitutes the subject of main predication. At the level of semantic representation, the main predicate is applied to an eventuality, as is inevitable in a neo-Davidsonian semantics. This is an eventuality that is restricted only by certain kinds of material, however, the only fully specified part of which is an individual participant, as in (6.14)—and the nature of main predication by a verbal predicate is such that the relation of this participant to the eventuality is the only presupposed information in the final proposition. The main predicate in such circumstances can therefore be understood to be predicating a property of a particular individual, even though this is not strictly speaking all that stands in the epsilon term that acts as logical subject. Therefore, a topic>comment reading depends on the role of an intermediate representation like (6.14), which in turn follows from inferences triggered during the incremental processing of the sentence.

The relevance of the epsilon calculus to the concept of main predication lies in the possibility of using a predicate from within a natural language string to create existential quantification over the event variable (and hence potentially create a proposition). Since in a neo-Davidsonian semantics even argument NPs denote predicates, the way is open for constituents other than verbs to act as main predicates. This, I propose, is how the notion of main predication can relate topic>comment and narrow focus readings in Hungarian as two possible outcomes of the same basic syntactico-semantic process. All that is required is for main predication to be consistently signalled syntactically (the subject matter of the following section) in order to unify these two kinds of readings.

As argued in section 6.2.3 above, the recognition that some non-verbal expression is to be taken as the main predicate of a sentence triggers the inference that there must exist a suitable subject of predication, in the form of a focus frame that contains everything necessary to create a proposition in combination with this expression. This is reflected in the form of the relevant epsilon-based representations. In effect, a non-verbal main predicate prompts a search for a logical subject that is a presupposed description of an eventuality, in the sense that not only the temporal anchor but also a verb-like predicate must be located within the epsilon term that represents the subject of predication. This must also include an 'open slot' for a participant in the role that the main predicate will fill, given the nature of the epsilon calculus—recall that a predicate can create existential quantification over the eventuality only if it or a superset of itself occurs within the epsilon term that defines the eventuality (just as *cat'* is found inside and outside the epsilon term in the existential statement (6.11b)). Purely inferential processes thus lead from the assertion of a non-verbal main predicate to the conventional idea of a focus frame. These processes are exemplified in section 6.6.2.

This formalisation of the idea of an inferred focus frame fits with the idea that there is an 'existential presupposition' associated with Hungarian PV focus (see, for example, Bende-Farkas 2002). A focus frame, as a logical subject of predication, contains presupposed elements in just the same way as participant topics do in topic>comment sentences. As argued above, this amounts to the inference of the existence of those elements that are necessary to any proposition. This inference is triggered just like any implicature, on the basis of relevance considerations and contextually available assumptions (amongst which is the assumption that an utterance will convey propositional information), but is effectively uncancellable on account of its being indispensable to the creation of a relevant propositional meaning.

The combination of neo-Davidsonian semantics and the epsilon operator therefore gives a clear basis for the processes discussed in section 6.2.3, explaining the contrast between a topic>comment sentence and a sentence containing a narrowly focused constituent, even though both result from a common process of designating a particular expression as main predicate. A focused constituent may be thought of as a predicate with a certain kind of logical subject eventuality, in the sense that a richly specified eventuality, restricted by a verb-like predicate, is conceptualised as a single referring expression that forms the subject of predication. This is in contrast to the logical subject of a topic>comment sentence, which, though necessarily an eventuality in a dynamic Davidsonian representation, is an eventuality whose only real content up to this point is an underspecified relationship to the topical participant. As a result, this kind of sentence is interpretable as the ascription of a property to an individual, as mentioned above (see also section 6.6.1). The difference between these two perspectives on eventualities need not be stipulated by syntactic machinery or semantic primitives, as it falls out from the nature of the items found as main predicates in different sentences and from the context in which an utterance is interpreted.

The notion of main predication and the proposed means of representing this in appropriately dynamic semantic formulae puts in place the basis of the interpretive side of the explanation of Hungarian PV phenomena. To complete this explanation, it is necessary to reconsider the syntactic side of the story and to relate this to the expression of main predication. The basic signalling of main predication in Hungarian is addressed in the following section and shown in the next chapter to provide the means of explaining a range of phenomena associated with PV.

6.5 HUNGARIAN SYNTAX AND MAIN PREDICATION

The principal burden of the current chapter so far has been to show that the interpretive functions of expressions 'in focus' in PV and of tensed verbs in topic>comment sentences can be related through the idea of main predication. It may appear that this fails to provide a fit with the syntactic data. If PV position is defined *relative to* the position of the tensed verb, then the main verb and a PV focus seem to occupy different positions—how could main predication then be considered to relate to some consistent syntactic signal?

A closer look at the syntax of Hungarian, considering a variety of sentences, shows that the usual characterisation of the PV position as a 'pre-verbal' position is in many ways misleading. At any rate, it is clear that main verb position and tensed verb position must be differentiated. It is the latter that PV should be defined in relation to—even if the tensed verb is an auxiliary that effectively expresses nothing but tense and time, as in the case of the future tense auxiliary *fog*. In sentences containing such auxiliary verbs, the main verb appears in its infinitive form. This makes it possible to see the separate influence of tense and the main verb in grammatical constructions—something that is obscured in sentences that lack an auxiliary, in which the verb stem and tense affix depend on each other. In the presence of an auxiliary like *fog*, it becomes clear that the main verb stem does not necessarily follow PV expressions, but rather 'competes' for the PV position with VMs, narrow foci and the negative particle *nem*, just as these 'compete' with each other to appear immediately before the verb stem when there is no auxiliary.

The crucial data are illustrated in (6.17)–(6.20). The word orders marked with # are impossible with the intended readings, although they may be used to produce other, more marked readings (all of which involve special cases of focus; see section 6.6.3 and Chapters 7 and 8).

(6.17) a. Úszik
swim-3SG.PRES
'S/he swims.'

b. Úszni fog. / #Fog úszni.
swim.INF will.3SG
'S/he will swim.'

(6.18) a. Nem úszik.
not swim-3SG.PRES
'S/he doesn't swim.'

b. Nem fog úszni. / #Nem úszni fog.
not will.3SG swim-INF
'S/he won't swim.'

(6.19) a. MARI úszik.
Mari swim-3SG.PRES
'It's Mari who swims.'

b. MARI fog úszni. / #MARI úszni fog.
Mari will.3SG swim-INF
'It's Mari who will swim.'

(6.20) a. Kimegy.
out(VM)-go.3SG.PRES
'S/he goes out.'

b. Ki fog menni. / #Kimenni fog. / *Menni fog ki.
out(VM) will.3SG go-INF
'S/he will go out.'

In each case, the auxiliariless present tense sentence in the (a) example shows the main verb stem remaining in what is thought of as its canonical position, before tense, irrespective of the presence of *nem*, PV focus or a VM. The (b) examples, however, show that when the main verb is morphologically independent of the tense affix, it follows the latter in everything but the VM-less topic>comment sentence (6.17b). The presence of any other item in the PV position proves incompatible with the appearance of the main verb before the tense-bearing auxiliary, a fact that strongly suggests that the main verb effectively 'competes' with other items for the PV position itself. Or, more accurately, when the main verb does precede the tensed auxiliary, as in (6.17b), it enters into the same relationship with tense as does *nem*, a focus or a VM when in PV (as in (6.18b), (6.19b) and (6.20b), respectively).

The picture that emerges from these data is that what I have been calling the 'PV (or Pre-Verbal) position' in fact represents a relationship with tense, rather than with the verb. Given this, it is clear that the main verb itself can in principle be seen, under certain circumstances, as the expression that enters into this relationship with tense—in other words, the verb can be the expression in PV. Simply because of the fact that the expression of tense and the main verb are inseparable in the absence of an auxiliary, the complex [verb+tense] may be taken as equivalent to tense alone when the main verb is finite. Therefore, expressions that enter into the appropriate structural relationship with [verb+tense] can in this case be read as being in PV. On the other hand, the stem of a finite main verb, though always linearly preceding tense, can only be read as holding the relevant relationship to tense when there is no alternative occupant of PV. Note that this is perfectly consistent with the data in (6.17)–(6.20): in the case of infinitives, the main verb visibly precedes tense only in the absence of any other potential occupant of PV. I shall maintain the use of 'PV' as a mere label for the syntactic configuration in question, but it should be borne in mind that this properly refers to a relationship with tense and not to the verb as such[10].

This perspective allows for a maximally simple view of the syntax of PV phenomena. Only one basic syntactic relationship is posited, to correspond to the single interpretive concept of main predication. Complications to the observed word order facts are not actually to be explained by further syntactic mechanisms, but are rather due to the interaction of syntax and quite unrelated morpho-phonological factors.

---

[10] As before, it should also be remembered that 'PV position' refers to a particular structural relationship, signalled partly by phonological means, and not simply to linear precedence. This becomes important when auxiliaries are preceded by no PV item at all; see Chapter 8, section 8.2.

This analysis captures a generalisation about all PV items that is often sacrificed in favour of another generalisation, about VMs. The generalisation captured here is that PV items (including VMs) consistently appear before the tensed verb, whether this is main or auxiliary. Obvious though this is, many syntactic accounts fail to provide a unitary basis for its explanation. Any verb-raising analysis of PV focus (in the style of Bródy 1990) comes up against the serious problems pointed out by Koopman & Szabolcsi (2000) (see Chapter 3, section 3.3.2) and/or assumes that VMs are base-generated to the immediate left of main verbs and is thereby forced into providing a separate explanation for VMs that appear to the left of auxiliaries. Typically, some decidedly idiosyncratic operation of 'VM-climbing' is posited to get VMs that are generated as prefixes to infinitives to surface before an auxiliary (Farkas & Sadock 1989, Szendrői 2003)[11]. Notice that this also implies that VM-less infinitives must be thought of as a kind of VM (Koopman & Szabolcsi 2000, 20; É. Kiss 2002, 207), since such infinitives must 'climb' also, as in (6.17b)—an otherwise unmotivated assumption that is difficult to square with the behaviour of the infinitive in examples like (6.20b).

The assumption of base-generation of VMs to the immediate left of main verbs appears to be based on two observations. The first is the perceived 'neutral' nature of the topic>comment reading associated with VM>V order when the main verb is finite, yet if this were really related to the putatively base-generated VM>V complex, it would be baffling that VM and V are found separated from one another on the corresponding 'neutral' reading of a sentence containing an auxiliary like *fog* (as in (6.20b)). The second reason is the point made by Koopman & Szabolcsi: the fact that a pre-auxiliary narrow focus will cause any VM to surface not in just any post-verbal position, but necessarily to the immediate left of the main verb infinitive. Clearly, this requires an explanation in terms of some other factor, given my analysis of PV effects; Chapter 7, section 7.3 shows how the basis of such an explanation follows from the idea of main predication. In any case, there is no logical necessity to connect the tendency for VMs to precede tense to their tendency to precede the main verb. It seems preferable to recognise this rather than employ more than one mode of explanation for the simple generalisation that PV items always precede the tensed verb.

My analysis of the relationship between the structure and interpretation of PV phenomena in Hungarian therefore boils down to the following. If tense is morphologically independent of the main verb, then the expression that immediately precedes tense is interpreted as the main predicate. If tense and the main verb stem depend on each other morphologically, then the expression that immediately precedes the complex [verb+tense] is interpreted as the main predicate, given appropriate phonological signalling, or the verb itself may be. As things stand, this is in the form of a stipulation—that is, I take main predication to be directly encoded in the structure of Hungarian through left-adjacency to the tensed element (in Dynamic Syntax terms, the procedural

---

[11] All 'VM-climbing' proposals have to appeal to some extra-syntactic factor (morphological in the case of Farkas & Sadock 1989; prosodic in the case of É. Kiss 2002, Szendrői 2003) to motivate the phenomenon, often relying on the inaccurate notion that auxiliaries cannot take primary stress (see Chapter 8, section 8.2).

210 *Shifting the Focus*

semantic notion of main predication could be directly associated with a certain kind of transition between lexical items in the course of parsing). Note, however, that this is a single stipulation of a highly underspecified process, on the basis of which a wide range of interpretive phenomena can be shown to follow. In this respect, this analysis is minimally stipulative, especially in comparison to the kind of syntactic account that posits a string of abstract distinguished syntactic projections to account for the range of PV phenomena.

Furthermore, there are reasons to believe that this particular means of signalling main predication is far from purely arbitrary. After all, tense is the expression of the temporal index on an eventuality and as such is assumed to be an essential part of any proposition. The idea that the signalling of main predication—the conversion of a description of an eventuality into the assertion of a proposition—should be connected to the signalling of another essential part of the proposition is a natural one. Put another way, it makes sense that the identification of an eventuality relative to other eventualities (as achieved by temporal indexing) should be connected to the identification of that eventuality in another sense: locating it in a particular set of eventualities, and thereby effecting existential quantification over it (as achieved by the main predicate). Keeping these two key aspects of a proposition together structurally constitutes a highly efficient way of completing and asserting a proposition and/or triggering the necessary inferential processes to do so. I leave these remarks here, in order to concentrate (in the following chapter) on the explanatory power of treating PV (i.e. immediately pre-tense position) as a signal of main predication, rather than dwelling on the status of this form-meaning correspondence. For the present, I simply note that this may in itself prove to be explicable at some more fundamental level, rather than being an entirely arbitrary property of Hungarian syntax.

6.6 SIMPLE WORKED EXAMPLES

In this section, I work through two simple example sentences to demonstrate how main predication, as represented using neo-Davidsonian formulae and the epsilon operator, accounts for both topic>comment sentences and those containing narrow focus. This brings together the ideas discussed in this chapter, in particular illustrating the dynamic nature of the overall explanation, and prepares for more complex examples in the following chapter.

6.6.1 Topic>comment

In order to show clearly the relationship between the main verb, (other) PV items and tense, I use sentences containing the future auxiliary *fog*. (6.21) is an example of a topic>comment sentence.

(6.21) Ferenc látni fogja Marit
Ferenc see-INF will Mari-ACC
'Ferenc will see Mari.'

Dynamic Structured Meanings: Predication and Information Structure 211

Recall from section 6.4.3 that the parsing of the first word, *Ferenc*, provides the information in (6.22). That is, as the initiation of an utterance that is expected to convey propositional information, the utterance of this expression not only contributes the semantic content of the expression itself—a certain kind of function from an entity into an eventuality—but also posits an eventuality involving a verbal meaning and occurring at some temporal index.

(6.22) $\varepsilon, e \left[f(e, \mathbf{T}_i) \ \& \ \mathbf{V}(e) \ \& \ \theta_{\text{NOM}}(e, ferenc') \right]$

As at every stage in the parse, inferential processes may be triggered at this point. At the very least, inference will be involved in assigning the referent *ferenc'* to the proper noun. Though this may seem trivial, the addressee's cognitive environment may of course include a number of men called Ferenc and it is a relevance-based inferential task to identify the one intended in a given context (that is, one may think of the individual *ferenc'* as chosen over the other possibilities *ferenc2', ferenc3'* ...).

The fact that this expression is sentence-initial and not the main predicate means that it must be assumed to play a key role in setting up the immediate context for an act of main predication. As the literal 'starting point' for the incoming utterance, it signals a link between existing states of knowledge and the anticipated new assertion. This is not due to the existence of some [+topic] primitive, but is a relevant inference over the act of explicitly referring to something in advance of the recognisably asserted part of the utterance. As in Sperber & Wilson's (1986/95) account of word order and information structure in English (see Chapter 4, section 4.2.3), such acts of referring to x may be viewed as setting up the question 'What about x?' (or 'Why have you mentioned x?'). In order for such a question to be coherent and relevant, x must relate to a manifest referent from the context. This has consequences for the readings that syntactic topics receive; in particular, such inferences account for the presupposed nature of topics and their necessarily specific, 'individuated' reading (É. Kiss 1987, É. Kiss 1998b). Other inferences that might already be triggered could relate to the reasons that the communicator may be inferred to have for talking about the man in question. Such inferences could affect the parsing process itself, in cases of ambiguous word order; see section 6.6.3.

Making the assumption that the verb *látni* should be analysed as having two obligatory arguments (*modulo* the comments on arguments and adjuncts in section 6.2.3) the following will serve as a simple representation of its semantic content in the lexicon (that is, with metavariables in its obligatory argument slots)[12]:

---

[12]This might alternatively be represented in a hierarchical fashion (as in Dynamic Syntax, for example), since $\theta_{\text{NOM}}(e, \mathbf{U})$ and $\theta_{\text{ACC}}(e, \mathbf{W})$ represent the external and internal arguments of the verb, respectively. Such structure is undoubtedly required in the analysis of other aspects of the grammar, for example in accounting for the 'Definiteness Effect' (see Chapter 5, section 5.2.2) and in the analysis of VMs, as discussed in Chapter 7, but, for reasons mentioned above, the level of representation relevant for basic word order facts in Hungarian seems to be rather the flat, 'decomposed' kind that contains parallel, conjoined predicates over eventualities. I leave as an open question how different necessary kinds and levels of representation might be related to each other.

(6.23) $see'(e)\ \&\ \theta_{\text{NOM}}(e, \mathbf{U})\ \&\ \theta_{\text{ACC}}(e, \mathbf{W})$

When the predicate *see'* is introduced in the context of the information in (6.22), the internal argument can be immediately identified with the topical nominative expression *Ferenc* that has already been processed and as such is clearly the most relevant substituend for the metavariable U. As the parse proceeds, the infinitival verb is recognised to immediately precede the tense-carrying auxiliary *fog* and therefore to be signalled as main predicate. As a result, the predicate *see'* is applied to the whole eventuality selected by the epsilon operator. Because of the argument structure (6.23), it is effectively a logical necessity that any eventuality to which this predicate applies contains an argument with the θ_{NOM} role and another with the θ_{ACC} role. The metavariable placeholders for these arguments are therefore inserted into the description of the eventuality, within the scope of the epsilon operator.

As a result, the propositional form in (6.24a) is created. Thanks to the metavariable V thereby also finding a substituend (see the discussion of (6.15), above), this is equivalent to (6.24b), which clearly shows the creation of existential quantification.

(6.24)   a. $see'(\varepsilon, e\ [f(e, \mathbf{T}_i)\ \&\ \mathbf{V}(e)\ \&\ \theta_{\text{NOM}}(e, ferenc')\ \&\ \theta_{\text{ACC}}(e, \mathbf{W})])$

   b. $see'(\varepsilon, e\ [f(e, \mathbf{T}_i)\ \&\ see'(e)\ \&\ \theta_{\text{NOM}}(e, ferenc')\ \&\ \theta_{\text{ACC}}(e, \mathbf{W})])$

In other words, a (selected) eventuality of Ferenc doing something (at a separately specified time) to the entity to be substituted for W exists because it is found within the set of seeing eventualities. This contains all the necessary ingredients of a propositional representation, including the assertion of existence, showing that main predication has taken place.

The sentence is completed by the assertion of the object *Marit*. Recall that this is what É. Kiss (1998a) calls an 'information focus', which I take to be part of a broad focus—that is, newly asserted information, but not a main predicate. Prosodically, this is separated from the main predicate by the fact that it bears its own pitch accent. The same pitch accent reflects its status as a logical predicate—a predicate that is to be applied to whatever is perceived to be the contextually most relevant logical subject. In the context of being uttered as part of the same sentence that has already created (6.24), the most relevant potential logical subject is the eventuality represented by the epsilon term in (6.24b). This results in the predication shown in (6.25a). In effect, this involves utilising the output of the process of 'thematising the rheme' proposed by Egli & von Heusinger (1995); that is, the recently applied verbal predicate *see'* is now found inside the epsilon term only. Within a dynamic, incremental parsing based approach this is nothing more than a representation of the fact that material already parsed adds to the context for the interpretation of incoming material[13]. Since *mari'* is now clearly the obvious

---

[13]This brings up an important point regarding what is being formalised. It must be emphasised that the representations used here show the process of constructing propositional forms; they should not be taken to show the form in which propositions are stored, or indeed precisely the form in which they could be evaluated for truth conditions. As discussed above, in these representations the creation of a proposition frequently depends upon the acceptance of im-

substituend for the object metavariable **W**, the full effect of processing the object *Marit* is to create the formula in (6.25b).

(6.25)   a. $\theta_{ACC}((\varepsilon, e\ [f(e, \mathbf{T}_i)\ \&\ see'(e)\ \&\ \theta_{NOM}(e, ferenc')\ \&\ \theta_{ACC}(e, \mathbf{W})]), mari')$

        b. $\theta_{ACC}((\varepsilon, e\ [f(e, \mathbf{T}_i)\ \&\ see'(e)\ \&\ \theta_{NOM}(e, ferenc')\ \&\ \theta_{ACC}(e, mari')]), mari')$

(6.25b) is another existential statement, in terms of the epsilon calculus, $\theta_{ACC}(e, mari')$ being found within the epsilon term as well as predicated of it. This appropriately reflects the fact that the objecthood of Mari in relation to the selected eventuality is newly asserted information (and hence part of the focus). Nevertheless, this is not an act of main predication, since it does not create a proposition for the first time. Rather, the assertion in (6.25b) acts as an elaboration of an existing proposition (although, due to the 'thematisation of the rheme' process between (6.24b) and (6.25b), the propositional status of the epsilon term is not visible in the formula (6.25b)). In some ways, the propositional content of (6.21) should therefore be thought of as the conjunction of (6.24b) and (6.25b). While this may seem formally inelegant in terms of the conventional assumption that each sentence can be algorithmically translated into 'its semantic translation', the proposed conjunction of representations reflects not only the necessarily incremental nature of linguistic processing, but also to some extent the structure of a Hungarian topic>comment sentence, with its apposition of separately stressed participant phrases following the verb[14].

6.6.2   Narrow focus

(6.26) is an example of a sentence that contains both a syntactic topic and a narrow focus.

(6.26)   Marinak   FERENC   fogja adni   a   könyvet.
            Mari-DAT   Ferenc   will   give-INF   the book-ACC
            'It's Ferenc who will give the book to Mari.'

The syntactic topic can be dealt with much as in (6.22), above (assuming a new simplified 'thematic role' function, θ_{DAT}, relating to the dative case marking on *Marinak*). Thus, the state

---

plications of existence in addition to the assertion engendered by main predication (see the discussion of (6.16b), for example). These elements of the representations would have to be converted into fully truth-conditional statements to create a 'usable' propositional form. But since this conversion will always be licensed by inference, other things being equal, it remains true that main predication ultimately I creates a propositional form and I continue to refer to the representations used here as being propositional. I am grateful to Ruth Kempson (personal communication) for stressing the importance of this point.

[14] Nevertheless, it might make sense to incorporate into the semantic representation some way of tracking the propositional status of formulae like (6.24b) as they are manipulated and used in further interpretive processes. I leave this as an idea for future work, since my current concern is simply to illustrate the emergence of information-structural effects in the course of incremental parsing and inference. Including such tracking mechanisms might create the impression of the use information-structural semantic primitives, which is of course something that I expressly avoid here.

of the semantic representation at the point of processing the first word in (6.26) is roughly as in (6.27).

(6.27) $\varepsilon, e \, [f(e, \mathbf{T}_i) \, \& \, \mathbf{V}(e) \, \& \, \theta_{\text{DAT}}(e, mari')]$

This is where the similarity with the interpretation of (6.21) ends, as far as the syntactic topic is concerned. This cannot be the subject of main predication, since the expression subsequently signalled by pre-tense position to be the main predicate is not a verb and therefore not the kind of function that can ascribe a property to an individual. Rather, as noted in sections 6.2.3 and 6.4.3, the designation of $\theta_{\text{NOM}}(e, ferenc')$ as main predicate triggers a search through the context for a suitably specified eventuality—in other words, a focus frame—that can act as subject of predication. Clearly, being already established as part of the eventuality under discussion, the information conveyed by the syntactic topic must be a part of the focus frame. This therefore restricts the search space for the broader subject of main predication. This represents one particular kind of example of the RT notion of how context is constructed in the course of interpretation.

The recovery of the relevant focus frame can be viewed in two ways. If contextual factors ensure that the idea of 'giving Mari the book' is manifestly the only relevant candidate to fulfil this role, it may be slotted into the semantic representation in one go, the destressed post-tense material *adni a könyvet* simply providing confirmation of this decision (this is intuitively quite likely with this particular example, given the material already contributed by the syntactic topic). This amounts to the recovery from context of the eventuality description in (6.28a). As already noted in section 6.4.3, it is a necessary inference from the stipulation of $\theta_{\text{NOM}}(e, ferenc')$ as main predicate that the subject of main predication must include this very function or a superset of it. This requirement is fulfilled by the function $\theta_{\text{NOM}}(e, \mathbf{U})$, the metavariable $\mathbf{U}$ allowing for existential quantification by the main predicate just as the metavariable $\mathbf{V}$ does in (6.24a). As also mentioned in section 6.4.3, the logical necessity of this inferential step can be seen to account for the so-called 'existential presupposition' associated with PV focus.

When the main predicate is applied to (6.24a), the propositional form in (6.28b) is produced. Therefore, if the focus frame is identified immediately from the context, (6.28b) is in effect created as soon as the tense-carrying auxiliary is processed and the main predicate thereby established.

(6.28)   a. $\varepsilon, e \, [f(e, \mathbf{T}_i) \, \& \, give'(e) \, \& \, \theta_{\text{DAT}}(e, mari') \, \& \, \theta_{\text{ACC}}(e, the\text{-}book') \, \& \, \theta_{\text{NOM}}(e, \mathbf{U})]$
         b. $\theta_{\text{NOM}}((\varepsilon, e \, [f(e, \mathbf{T}_i) \, \& \, give'(e) \, \& \, \theta_{\text{DAT}}(e, mari') \, \& \, \theta_{\text{ACC}}(e, the\text{-}book') \, \& \, \theta_{\text{NOM}}(e, ferenc')]), ferenc')$

(6.28a) may be read as 'the selected eventuality such that "it" will give the book to Mari' while (6.28b) asserts that this same eventuality exists in the set of eventualities with Ferenc as Subject. In other words, the eventuality in (6.28a) is asserted to exist insofar as it is asserted to have Ferenc as its Subject. This corresponds exactly to the narrow focus meaning associated with PV foci: 'Ferenc is the one (="it") who will give the book to Mari.'

Alternatively, (6.28b) might be arrived at by a slightly different route: the destressed post-tense material might play a slightly more significant role, if the context alone does not immediately pick out this particular focus frame—in this case meaning that it is not clear which particular eventuality involving Ferenc in the nominative and Mari in the dative is under discussion. In this case, an intermediate, but still propositional, representation might be created by the application of the main predicate, as in (6.29)

(6.29) $\theta_{\text{NOM}}((\varepsilon, e\ [f(e, \mathbf{T}_i)\ \&\ \mathbf{V}(e)\ \&\ \theta_{\text{DAT}}(e,\textit{mari}')\ \&\ \theta_{\text{NOM}}(e,\textit{ferenc}')]),\ \textit{ferenc}')$

Assuming the post-tense word order in (6.26) (this is just one possibility), the destressed main verb infinitive *adni* is encountered next. The predicate *give'* can be simply substituted for the metavariable **V** in this case. This is not an act of assertion as in (6.25)—the destressed expression merely helps the addressee to distinguish between different presupposed eventualities and thus the process involved is still essentially concerned with selecting whole focus frames. That is, the verb is not introduced as a piece of information whose relation to the eventuality in question is assumed to have been previously unknown to the addressee; instead it helps to identify, or confirm, the right eventuality, out of possible contextual candidates. On such occasions, the metavariable is more of a true 'pro-form' than a mere placeholder and the destressed verb in effect ensures that the relevant context is constructed to force the substitution of the appropriate semantic material.

The further specification of the context that is provided by the verb is likely to make manifest the whole focus frame and thus create the completed proposition in (6.28b) directly. It is conceivable that it is still not clear which particular thing to be given to Mari is under discussion, however. Assuming *adni* to require three obligatory arguments, at least at a semantic level, the processing of the verb would then produce the representation in (6.30), with a metavariable occupying the place of the direct object. As presupposed material within a now-identified focus frame, this is once again simply substituted by the appropriate material (*the-book'*) when the destressed post-tense noun phrase *a könyvet* is encountered, creating (6.28b).

(6.30) $\theta_{\text{NOM}}((\varepsilon, e\ [f(e, \mathbf{T}_i)\ \&\ \textit{give}'(e)\ \&\ \theta_{\text{DAT}}(e,\textit{mari}')\ \&\ \theta_{\text{ACC}}(e, \mathbf{U})\ \&$
$\theta_{\text{NOM}}(e,\textit{ferenc}')]),\ \textit{ferenc}')$

6.6.3 Two readings of main predicate verbs

So far, the discussion has assumed that a main verb found in the immediately pre-tense position (as in (6.21)) will be interpreted as the beginning of the 'comment' part of a topic>comment sentence, as in section 6.6.1. It should be noted, however, that another possibility exists: the verb itself may be read as a narrow focus when it signalled in this way as being the main predicate. That is, a verb may, like a non-verbal main predicate, be interpreted with respect to a focus frame, given the right contextual conditions. This would involve post-verbal material such as the object

Marit in (6.21) being fully destressed and would result in a reading with contrastive focus on the verbal predicate itself (as in 'Ferenc will *see* Mari; he won't *hear* her.').

This means that there are in effect two possible parses of a string like (6.21), corresponding to its two prosodic realisations (i.e. with or without post-verbal stress). These both involve the recognition that the main verb is the main predicate, but differ in that one of them involves the verb providing a predication over the pre-verbal (or contextually provided) topical entity, as in section 6.6.1, while the other involves main predication acting as a trigger for the recovery of a whole topical eventuality, or focus frame.

Were this difference identifiable only through the different prosodic patterns, this word order ambiguity might appear to entail the potential for quite inefficient parsing. Not until after the main predicate has been applied does the prosodic difference become apparent, when post-verbal expressions are encountered and seen to be stressed or destressed. This implies that considerable back-tracking would be necessary. For example, if a topic>comment parse is assumed at the point of applying the verb as main predicate, then predication over the topical entity would have to be 'undone' when destressed post-verbal expressions are encountered and predication over an eventuality enacted in its place.

However, prosodic structure is not the only thing that differentiates such readings: by definition, such readings require different contexts and contextual factors are able to influence the parsing process in the kind of dynamic approach that I am assuming (for experimental evidence that context guides parsing, see Crain & Steedman 1985, Altmann & Steedman 1988). Contexts that are compatible with a contrastive or corrective (narrow focus) reading of the verb—that is, contexts containing an eventuality that is manifestly a candidate to act as focus frame for the verb as narrow focus—are unlikely to make a topic>comment reading relevant, and *vice versa*. Moreover, even if extra effort were involved in parsing contrastive uses of verbal main predicates, this would most likely be off-set by the relatively rich cognitive effects associated with contrast.

My dynamic approach to the creation of focus readings thus predicts that the word order of so-called 'neutral' sentences like (6.21) is compatible with another reading involving narrow focus on the verb (given the possible variations of context in which such a sentence may be produced) and does so without any string-vacuous syntactic operations. The wider theoretical significance of such 'ambiguities' with certain linear orderings becomes clear once VMs are considered. The apparent ambiguity of sentences containing pre-tense VMs (parallel to the 'ambiguity' of sentences like (6.21)) has been claimed to be an argument against maintaining a unified position for all PV phenomena, including unmarked VM position (see Chapter 3, section 3.3.1). The notion of main predication in a dynamic approach to grammar and interpretation proves to neutralise this argument. This is addressed in the following chapter.

Dynamic Structured Meanings: Predication and Information Structure 217

6.7 SUMMARY

In this chapter I demonstrated how the association of different kinds of Hungarian sentence with on the one hand topic>comment readings and on the other narrow focus can be derived from a single encoded procedure. As such, the multiple syntactic projections and semantic procedures that are required by conventional theoretical approaches are shown to be unnecessary complications of the grammar. The adoption of a dynamic, inferential perspective is key in explaining how this works in Hungarian, since the explanation makes crucial reference to the effects of the linear presentation of information. Via inference, the crucial procedure has an effect on the interpretation of items that follow the point in the parse at which this procedure is carried out.

The procedure in question is syntactically signalled by left-adjacency to the tensed element, evidence from sentences with auxiliary verbs showing the traditional idea that the 'focus position' is simply pre-verbal to be mistaken. Instead, the main verb in a 'neutral' sentence appears to hold the same relationship with the tensed element that is shown by narrow foci in 'non-neutral' sentences. The procedural semantic nature of this relationship is identified as what I call 'main predication': an act of predication that creates a full (if sometimes skeletal) propositional form. This is unmarkedly carried out by main verbs, whose internal semantic structure is sufficient to create a propositional form in conjunction with tense. Subsequent asserted material ('information focus') simply elaborates the details of the proposition already created in this way. This produces the impression of a 'broad focus' or topic>comment reading. However, when a non-verbal item appears as the main predicate, it requires a term that contains all the necessary material to create a proposition. It therefore triggers the recovery of a contextually available eventuality, a focus frame, resulting in a narrow focus interpretation of the main predicate item.

This procedure is represented using a flat, neo-Davidsonian semantics, in combination with the epsilon calculus. This uniquely allows the conversion of an unquantified eventuality description into a proposition through the application of a predicate gleaned directly from the forms in the natural language sentence. The result is a formal representation that bears a strikingly close relationship to the superficial structure of the Hungarian clause, while maintaining the ability to reflect dynamic processes of interpretation that occur in the process of parsing.

7

VERBAL MODIFIERS AND MAIN PREDICATION

7.1 OVERVIEW

Previous chapters have dealt principally in semantic matters which only become issues for syntax through the kind of compositional reasoning that I aim to call into question—even Chapter 6 is largely concerned with showing that two apparently opposing meanings can be traced to a single interpretive procedure, in order to maintain a simplified syntactic analysis. In this chapter I tackle the key syntactic issue that has influenced accounts of the Hungarian 'focus position' and related phenomena: the distribution of VMs. The notion of main predication developed in Chapter 6, along with the general left-to-right dynamic perspective within which it is defined, proves to provide a simple explanation of this seemingly complex matter. Consequently, the way in which semantic and pragmatic factors are combined is shown to solve an apparently syntactic problem, leaving a minimal explanatory burden on the grammar. Along with the discussion of negation and aspectual constructions in the next chapter, this fulfils the aim stated in Chapter 1 of demonstrating the wide-reaching consequences of assumptions made about the semantics/pragmatics distinction.

As outlined in Chapter 3, the notion of VM encompasses a considerable variety of phenomena, whose only immediately obvious common feature is their syntactic behaviour, in particular their unmarked pre-verbal position that is abandoned for the post-verbal domain in the presence of other PV phenomena such as a narrow focus. A few examples are given in (7.1)–(7.4), recalling those of Chapter 3, section 3.2.4) .

(7.1)   'prefix' VM:

      a. Kati megette az almát.
          Kati VM-ate the appleACC
          'Kati ate the apple (up).'

b. Kati ette meg az almát.
   Kati ate VM the apple-ACC
   'It's Kati who ate the apple (up).'

(7.2) accusative bare nominal:

   a. Pisti levelet írt.
      Pisti letter-ACC wrote
      'Pisti wrote a letter.'

   b. Pisti írt levelet.
      Pisti wrote letter-ACC
      'It's Pisti who wrote a letter.'

(7.3) resultative expression:

   a. Ferenc pirosra festette a kerítést.
      Ferenc red-to painted the fence-ACC
      'Ferenc painted the fence red.'

   b. Ferenc a kerítést festette pirosra.
      Ferenc the fence-ACC painted red-to
      'It's the fence that Ferenc painted red.'

(7.4) locative:

   a. Péter a szobában maradt.
      Péter the room-in stayed
      'Péter stayed in the room.'

   b. Péter maradt a szobában.
      Péter stayed the room-in
      'It's Péter who stayed in the room.'

Conventional, static linguistic frameworks can easily deal with this diversity, on a technical level: the variety of interpretive effects associated with VM-hood can be related to a multiplicity of abstract pre-verbal syntactic positions, each of which may be supposed to relate at LF to a different interpretive effect. I have argued that this sort of approach is of questionable explanatory power, however. On the other hand, if a dynamic account such as my own is to be judged any less *ad hoc*, it should be the case that it is able to appeal to some underlying commonality across the class of VMs, to explain the syntactic similarity of its members.

The main predication analysis of Chapter 6 accounts straightforwardly for the postposing of VMs in the presence of syntactically focused constituents, as illustrated in the (b) examples above. The hypothesis that PV, an immediately pre-tense position, signals the main predicate leads inevitably to the impossibility of a VM intervening between a focus and a tensed verb, since a focused expression is one kind of main predicate. This rests on the reasonable assumption that the syntactic independence of VMs indicates that they make independent contributions to the semantic representation, of a kind that is manifested in a neo-Davidsonian representation as a predicate of the eventuality variable.

The opposite side of VM behaviour is then brought into question, however: what makes the different kinds of VM appear in PV—by hypothesis, as main predicates—in the absence of a focus or negation, and how are they interpretable as an unmarked main predicates—the first element in a broad focus, or 'comment'—rather than being read as narrow foci themselves? After all, the discussion of main predication in Chapter 6 suggests that the main verb is unique in acting as unmarked main predicate in this way. In this chapter, it is shown that VMs share with VM-less verbs the property of introducing certain key elements of structure into the eventuality and that this is the basis of the ability to be an unmarked main predicate. Furthermore, such structure must be introduced at the point of main predication, or, by the logic of main predication as an act of existential quantification, it cannot be introduced at all, other than by presupposition. The behaviour of VMs both in the presence of narrow foci and in 'neutral' sentences is thus shown to follow without further stipulation from the dynamics of the main predication analysis.

7.2 Verbal 'Prefix' Particles and Resultatives

The basis of my analysis of VM behaviour is the fact that VMs create complex predicate structures, on a semantic level, in combination with the lexical verb. As shown in Chapter 3, section 3.2.4, this is supported by a number of pieces of structural evidence, as well as being a logical necessity in the case of certain semantically non-compositional VM+V combinations. The process of complex predicate formation is somewhat mysterious with some VM+V combinations, but is characterisable in every case as a form of modification of the structure of the eventuality, in comparison to what would be produced by the lexical verb alone. This section introduces and illustrates this idea—and the way in which it explains the syntactic behaviour of VMs—using resultative VMs and the closely related telicising prefixes, since these provide the clearest and most easily representable kind of semantic restructuring. This is because in this case the contribution of the VM can be viewed as adding material over and above the contribution of the verb, whereas in the case of many of the other VMs, the relevant modification takes place within the structure of the verbal predicate itself.

Furthermore, the verbal prefix (henceforth VPr) creates some of the most obvious cases of complex predication, frequently featuring non-compositional elements of meaning (see Chapter 3, section 3.2.4) as well as the involvement of semantically highly underspecified items, like the VPr *meg*, which is generally simply described as a 'perfectivising' or 'telicising' prefix (its contribution might most nearly be glossed in English as 'to completion').

It is sometimes claimed that VPrs fundamentally play an aspectual role—indeed, their unmarked, pre-verbal position is characterised by some analysts as an 'Asp(ect)P' projection (e.g. É. Kiss 2002; see Chapter 8, section 8.2.2). It is certainly the case that many VPrs are involved in the creation of certain aspectual readings, though these may vary with the position of the VPr (see Chapter 8, section 8.2). Most commonly, this means the production of telic readings when the VPr appears in PV, as illustrated in (7.5): the VM-less verb in (7.5a) is compatible with a durative adverbial, whereas the addition of the VPr in (7.5b) creates a sentence whose adverbial phrase shows it to be telic.

(7.5)   a.   Mari öt percig sielt a lejtőn.
                 Mari five minute-for skied the slope-on
                 'Mari skied on the slope for five minutes.'

         b.   Mari öt perc alatt lesielt a lejtőn.
                 Mari five minute under down(VM)-skied the slope-on
                 'Mari skied down the slope in five minutes.'

However, as É. Kiss (to appear) points out, the relationship between the presence or absence of a VM in PV and any normal aspectual category is almost certainly too complex and indirect to support a theory whereby aspect is the primary factor in VM position. Thus, in addition to telicising VPrs, there are atelic predicates that involve VPrs or VPr-like particles. These are locative statives and located activities, as exemplified in (7.6a,b), respectively.

(7.6)   a.   János bent maradt a liftben.
                 János within(VM) remained the lift-in
                 'János remained in the lift.'

         b.   A gyerekek lent játszanak az udvaron.
                 the children down(VM) play the courtyard-in
                 'The children are playing down in the courtyard.'

Meanwhile, there are verbs that are telic in the absence of any VM. One class of such verbs is made up of the 'definiteness effect' verbs, which are bounded by the particular result state of a new entity being introduced into the discourse at a particular location (see Bende-Farkas 2002), as in (7.7).

(7.7)   János hozott egy széket.
         János brought a chair-ACC
         'János brought a chair.'

As É. Kiss (to appear) points out, a particular problem for any approach to VMs that relies on movement based on matching aspectual features is the case of accusative bare nominals, since their aspectual character can be affected by the particular context in which they appear, including not only the verb with which they combine, but also other elements of the sentence. Thus, while these nominals typically create atelic meanings in PV, as in the most usual reading of (7.8a), some sentences involving them can result in a bounded reading, as in (7.8b).

(7.8)   a. Éva pulóvert   bontott.
            Éva pullover-ACC broke.up
            'Éva was unravelling a pullover.'
        b. János asztalt   bontott.
            János table-ACC broke.up
            'János rose first from the table.'

Note that this determination of aspectual meaning by the combinations in which different expressions are found is perfectly consistent with an interpretation-based dynamic account, but potentially highly problematic for a conventional generative account of the relationship between syntax and semantics. Different word orders do in some cases demonstrably correspond to different aspectual readings (see section 8.2), which means that aspectual features should be encoded into the syntax under a conventional account, in order that everything occupies the right position at LF to produce the right interpretation at the interface with semantics. Yet this is precisely what the data in (7.8) do not allow for—at least not without such massive complication of the lexicon that the syntactic side of the story practically ceases to express any real generalisations.

Rather than aspectual effects as such being significant, it therefore seems that there is something more basic underpinning the class of VPrs (and, potentially, other VMs). In fact, as has proved to be the case at various points in this book, the truly significant interpretive generalisation is as much procedural as it is a matter of declarative truth-conditional semantics. The feature common to all VPrs is that they enter into complex predicates with the main verb. This very often has aspectual consequences, but the analysis of aspect as such is not the grammatically significant level of generalisation.

For example, *meg* in (7.9) ensures that the verb *olvaszt* 'melt' is interpreted as a telic action—specifically, an accomplishment, in terms of Vendler's (1967) classifications. In practice, what this means is that the Theme argument of *olvaszt* is taken to 'measure' the temporal extent of the melting event (Tenny 1994). This is more obvious in the case of an accomplishment with a count noun Theme, such as *eat an apple*, in which the total consumption of the apple in question is a condition for the eating event to be considered to have been completed. The truth-conditions of (7.9) depend similarly on a change of the state involving the Theme: the quantity of butter referred to must all be in a fully melted state for the event described to be judged to have taken place.

(7.9)   A   háziasszony megolvasztotta a   vajat.
        the housewife   VM-melted   the butter-ACC
        'The housewife melted the butter (completely) / The housewife has melted the butter.'

Given that a change of state appears to be necessarily involved in the characterisation of such propositions, the structure of the accomplishment eventuality that is created by *meg* can be represented in terms of sub-eventuality structure. This can be represented in the manner of Pustejovsky (1991), as in (7.10), showing in a hierarchical representation how the main eventuality expressed by a proposition can be composed of sub-eventualities. Under this kind of approach, an accomplishment is conceived of as a transition (T) from a process (P) to a 'result state' (S)[1]. The transition cannot be judged true unless both the process and the result state are true (and related to each other in the appropriate logical and temporal ways).

(7.10)

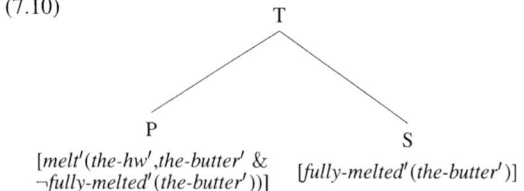

One way to analyse the 'telicising' function of a VPr like *meg* is therefore to view its contribution as the introduction of a sub-eventuality—through an act of predication over the Theme of the main verbal predicate—that represents the result state of a complex eventuality. This analysis is supported by the close parallelism between a sentence like (7.9) and a more transparently 'resultative' construction, as in (7.11). A Pustejovsky-style representation of the interpretation of (7.11) would look like (7.12). Thus, a syntactically and semantically parallel accomplishment sentence is created by simply swapping the VPr for a lexical specification of the result state (as noted also in É. Kiss to appear).

(7.11) A háziasszony folyékonnyá olvasztotta a vajat.
         the housewife fluid-to   melted   the butter-ACC
         'The housewife melted the butter to (a) fluid (state).'

(7.12)

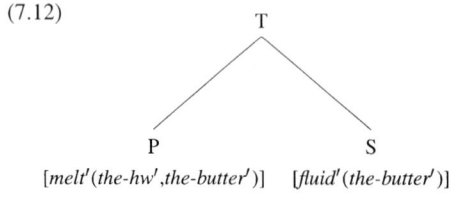

---

[1]Pustejovsky (1991) conceives of processes themselves as sequences of sub-events, but I follow Rothstein's (2001) Davidsonian representations (see below) in treating the process part of a complex eventuality as a single sub-event. At some level, this must be considered a simplification, but it suffices to identify the relevant qualities of VPrs and, importantly, reflects the ways in which complex eventualities are lexicalised. Numerous details of the internal conceptual structure of the verbal contribution are simplified here, relative to Pustejovsky's representations, for presentational purposes.

In order to demonstrate how this aspect of VPr meaning is significant to the issue of main predication, it is necessary to represent sub-eventuality structure in a 'flat' neo-Davidsonian formula. Such formulae already exist in the literature on secondary predication. For example, Rothstein (2001, 159) proposes (7.13b) (adapted slightly for consistency of presentational conventions) as the semantic translation of the English sentence (7.13a), which contains a resultative secondary predicate.

(7.13)   a.   Mary painted the house red.

       b. $\exists e.\exists e_1.\exists e_2.\ e = e_1 \sqcup e_2\ \&\ paint'(e_1)\ \&\ Agent(e_1, mary')\ \&$
           $Theme(e_1, the\text{-}house')\ \&\ red'(e_2)\ \&\ Arg_1(e_2, the\text{-}house')\ \&\ cul(e_1) \sqsubseteq e_2$

Note that Rothstein's formula relates the two sub-eventualities, e_1 and e_2, in two ways. The predicate *cul* is a variant of Parsons' (1990) culmination function, meaning (7.13b) includes the specification that the culmination of the process sub-eventuality (Mary's painting the house) is part of the result state sub-eventuality (the house being red). The 'sum operator' $\sqcup$ separately ensures that the eventuality e consists of these two sub-eventualities (I shall henceforth refer to the eventuality bound by the outermost existential quantifier or epsilon as the 'main eventuality'). The contribution of the resultative expression is analysed as an act of secondary predication. Like any predicate, this requires a logical subject, which is identified by the function Arg_1 (a simple presentational strategy that evades orthogonal questions of the applicability of theta-roles).

The three existential quantifiers in (7.13b) would require a highly complex formula in my epsilon-based means of representation and would cause some difficulty in identifying the true main predicate in (7.13a) (or its Hungarian equivalent). Happily, it is not only unnecessary but undesirable to include all of these acts of existential quantification, in order to be consistent with the approach I have promoted so far. Under my approach, the sub-eventualities e_1 and e_2 should not be asserted to exist, any more than should argument slots subcategorised for by the assertion of a verb. All such elements are entailed by the assertion of some more general aspect of the meaning of the sentence. If it is asserted that an eventuality exists that has the property of being a kissing event, for example, it follows deductively that there must an Agent and Theme of this eventuality. In effect, the existence of these participants is a presupposition (albeit a particularly strict one), since it need not be asserted, but is rather a precondition to the production of any coherent interpretation of a sentence containing the verb *kiss*. Hence placeholders for these participants may be simply inserted into the logical subject of main predication, alongside other presupposed material, within the scope of the epsilon operator (recall the discussion of (6.23) in Chapter 6, section 6.6). Similarly, it only need be asserted that a given eventuality involves a result state in order for it to be a necessary deduction that the eventuality in question is a complex one containing also a process. Hence the existence of the latter need not be asserted.

This gives a first clue as to why Hungarian VMs unmarkedly appear in PV, the position that signals main predication. It is because of the necessary presupposition of their arguments that VM-less verbs are unmarkedly main predicates, as shown in Chapter 6. If VMs introduce structural elements in a similar way, such as the structure of a complex eventuality required by a resultative, then VMs can be unmarked main predicates for the same reason.

Consider what it means for the main predicate of a sentence to assert that the main eventuality, e, has a result state e_2. This boils down to the assertion that e exists, and exists because it is found within the set of complex eventualities that have the sub-eventuality e_2 as their result state. If this is true, it must be the case that there exists a process e_1 that produces the result state, while the assertion in itself presupposes the existence of e_2. In other words, the assertion that e_2 is the result state of e creates the skeletal structure of a proposition containing a complex eventuality in much the same way as the assertion of a verbal predicate encountered in advance of its arguments creates a skeletal proposition containing a simple eventuality. Therefore, the assertion of a resultative VM, just like the assertion of a VM-less verb, effects main predication while leaving the way open for the further assertions that give detailed content to the skeletal structure and thus together produce the effect of a broad focus. As a result, there is no implication that the main predicate is a narrow focus for which a focus frame must exist as logical subject.

The formulaic representation of this can be illustrated clearly using a lexical resultative example like (7.11). In order to clarify the true syntactic relationship between the verb, tense and main predication, I shall once again concentrate on the future time equivalent of this, (7.16a), so that the tensed verb is an auxiliary, and the main verb is morphologically independent. To render the act of main predication as plainly as possible, I propose a number of adaptations to the kind of representation exemplified in (7.13b), such that the Pustejovsky-style conception of complex eventuality structure is directly reflected. Instead of Rothstein's representation of an accomplishment as the 'sum' of two eventualities, I introduce predicates over eventualities that represent the properties of being a transitional eventuality (TRANS), of being the process sub-eventuality (P-SUB) and of being the result state sub-eventuality (R-SUB). I assume these predicates to be defined such that the dependencies between them are inherent to their semantics; in other words, P-SUB and RES are related to TRANS in a way comparable to the relationships between theta-role functions and verbal predicates. In this way sub-eventualities are related to each other only indirectly, via the overarching transition eventuality, as in Pustejovsky's hierarchical representation, yet the different component acts of predication may still be manipulated independently, since they are simply conjoined within a neo-Davidsonian formula.

As with all logical representations of linguistic meaning, there is something arbitrary in positing functions that are defined and inter-related at this particular level of semantic detail. However, the fact that they prove to yield a generalisation that provides the basis for explaining the unmarked nature of main predicate VMs is evidence that representations of this kind have some degree of psychological reality. The sub-eventuality functions P-SUB and R-SUB also have close correlates in the elements of the linguistic string. The former corresponds to a main verb that can be assumed to have some lexical specification of its potential aspectual qualities. A resultative VM is typically an adjective or bare nominal (and therefore predicative) but is also case-marked in such a way that its being the 'goal' of a process is suggested (as in *folyékonnyá* 'fluid-to' in

(7.16a), or *pirosra* 'red-to', which would appear in the translation of (7.13a)). Only the higher-level function TRANS has no overt linguistic correlate, but it seems reasonable to assume that a complex eventuality can be conceptualised as such and assigned this kind of property on the basis of its sub-eventualities.

Ignoring main predication for the moment, the basic structure of the representation of an accomplishment is therefore essentially as in (7.14).

(7.14) $\exists e.$ TRANS(e) & P-SUB(e, e_1) & R-SUB(e, e_2)

A number of details must be added to this basic template. In order to clarify the status of the sub-eventualities, these should be bound by the epsilon operator (in line with my comments above regarding the application of existential quantification only to e) and shown with their inferable structure and content. Just as in Rothstein's formula, a result state predicate must have its own logical subject, which is related to the relevant sub-eventuality by the function Arg_1. It is also necessary for every sub-eventuality to have some content in the form of a 'kind of eventuality' predicate metavariable $\mathbf{V}$. It is therefore one of the consequences of recognising the complex eventuality structure introduced by a resultative VM that the $\mathbf{V}$ metavariable that is presupposed with every utterance becomes 'distributed' among sub-eventualities rather than predicating directly over the 'top level' eventuality e. This is not a purely technical move: it corresponds to the enrichment of the original presupposed $\mathbf{V}(e)$ into a more highly structured kind of eventuality and is therefore an expected part of building a representation of an accomplishment complex predicate.

Putting these observations together, (7.14) can be expanded to (7.15).

(7.15) $\exists e.$ TRANS(e) & P-SUB$(e, (\varepsilon, e_1 [\mathbf{V}_1(e_1)]))$ & R-SUB$(e, (\varepsilon, e_2 [\mathbf{V}_2(e_2) \& Arg_1(e_2, \mathbf{U})]))$

In the case of (7.16a), the $\mathbf{V}_1$ metavariable will in due course be substituted by the predicate *melt'* and $\mathbf{V}_2$ by *fluid'*. The final representation of (7.16a) will therefore correspond to (7.16b).

(7.16) a. A   háziasszony folyékonnyá fogja olvasztani a   vajat.
            the housewife   fluid-to   will melt-INF   the butter-ACC
            'The housewife will melt the butter to (a) fluid (state).'

        b. $\exists e.$ TRANS(e) & $f(e, \mathbf{T}_i)$ &
            P-SUB$(e, (\varepsilon, e_1 [melt'(e_1) \& \theta_{\text{NOM}}(e_1,\textit{the-hw'}) \& \theta_{\text{ACC}}(e_1,\textit{the-butter'})]))$
            & R-SUB$(e, (\varepsilon, e_2 [fluid'(e_2) \& Arg_1(e_2,\textit{the-butter'})]))$

It can now be shown how this representation is built up in the course of parsing (7.16a). As usual, the topical NP *A háziasszony* introduces not only its own denotation—a theta-role function connecting the entity *the-hw'* to an eventuality—but also, by inference, the expectation that this eventuality will have some content in the form of a $\mathbf{V}$-type predicate and some temporal anchor point. This now-familiar stage of interpretation is shown in (7.17a). Next the resultative VM

228 *Shifting the Focus*

folyékonnyá 'to fluid' is encountered and recognised by its pre-tense position as being the main predicate. The basic semantic contribution of this expression is (7.17b) (as can be deduced from (7.15)). When this is applied, as main predicate, to the epsilon term in (7.17a), this has a number of further effects, because the assertion of a result state entails that the eventuality as a whole has a certain structure, as discussed above. The assertion of the predicate R-SUB leads to the deduction that the eventuality in question is of a complex kind, a transition, and thus the structure in (7.15) is introduced (minus the existential quantifier) as an enrichment of the presupposition of a simple $V(e)$ kind of eventuality. The application of (7.17b) as main predicate to the topic material in (7.17a) therefore results in (7.17c).

As usual, any metavariable within the 'top level' epsilon term that corresponds to some part of the main predicate can be substituted with the appropriate content from the main predicate, so that (7.17c) amounts to (7.17d). This shows the existential quantification over e that is caused by the use of the resultative as main predicate.

(7.17) a. $\varepsilon, e\, [f(e, \mathbf{T}_i)\, \&\, V(e)\, \&\, \theta_{\text{NOM}}(e, \textit{the-hw}')]$

b. $\lambda e.\, \text{R-SUB}(e, (\varepsilon, e_2\, [\textit{fluid}'(e_2)\, \&\, \textit{Arg}_1(e_2, \mathbf{U})]))$

c. $\text{R-SUB}((\varepsilon, e\, [\text{TRANS}(e)\, \&\, f(e, \mathbf{T}_i)\, \&\,$
$\text{P-SUB}(e, (\varepsilon, e_1\, [\mathbf{V}_1(e_1)\, \&\, \theta_{\text{NOM}}(e_1, \textit{the-hw}')]))\, \&\, \theta_{\text{ACC}}(e_1, \mathbf{U})])\, \&\,$
$\text{R-SUB}(e, (\varepsilon, e_2\, [\mathbf{V}_2(e_2)\, \&\, \textit{Arg}_1(e_2, \mathbf{U})]))]),$
$(\varepsilon, e_2\, [\textit{fluid}'(e_2)\, \&\, \textit{Arg}_1(e_2, \mathbf{U})]))$

d. $\text{R-SUB}(\varepsilon, e\, [\text{TRANS}(e)\, \&\, f(e, \mathbf{T}_i)\, \&\,$
$\text{P-SUB}(e, (\varepsilon, e_1\, [\mathbf{V}_1(e_1)\, \&\, \theta_{\text{NOM}}(e_1, \textit{the-hw}')]))\, \&\, \theta_{\text{ACC}}(e_1, \mathbf{U})])\, \&\,$
$\text{R-SUB}(e, (\varepsilon, e_2\, [\textit{fluid}'(e_2)\, \&\, \textit{Arg}_1(e_2, \mathbf{U})]))]),$
$(\varepsilon, e_2\, [\textit{fluid}'(e_2)\, \&\, \textit{Arg}_1(e_2, \mathbf{U})]))$

(7.17d) may be read as: 'the eventuality e, selected with respect to the property of being a transition (with a temporal anchor $f(e, \mathbf{T}_i)$) from the eventuality e_1 of the housewife doing something to the resulting state e_2 of some entity having a state of being fluid, exists because it is found within the set of eventualities that involve the result state e_2 of some entity having a state of being fluid'.

While this is a fully propositional assertion, the remaining metavariables in (7.17d) can still be given content by subsequently asserted 'information focus' material, just as such material may follow a main verb when it serves as main predicate in a sentence that contains no VM (see Chapter 6, section 6.6). It is thus the structure-building quality that these VM-less verbs and VMs have in common that makes them able to function as main predicates without triggering a narrow focus reading.

While the lexical resultative in (7.16a) makes for a particularly clear illustration of the main predicating qualities of a secondary predicate VM, the parallelism between (7.10) and (7.12) shows that many VPrs can be analysed in an entirely parallel fashion; the only difference between sentences like (7.9) and (7.11) being the degree of semantic specification associated with the result state sub-eventuality.

Not all VPrs are parallel to resultatives, but it will be shown below that essentially the same kind of proposition-structuring qualities that make resultative VMs unmarked main predicates are associated with all VPrs and other VMs.

It should be noted here that there is another way for a VM as main predicate to be interpreted: as a narrow focus. This way of reading a main predicate is always possible, given a suitable context, though it can only happen when the VM in question has enough conceptual semantic content to allow for contrasts to be drawn with contextual alternatives. The so-called 'dual behaviour' of VPrs in this respect, which has been argued to necessitate multiple abstract pre-verbal positions and which requires string-vacuous movements within most syntactic analyses (see Chapter 3, section 3.3.1) therefore follows without further stipulation from the main predication analysis, as does the fact (noted by É. Kiss 1994, 44) that only VPrs with 'literal' directional semantics can take on a focus reading.

7.3 WHY THE VM, NOT THE VERB, IS THE UNMARKED MAIN PREDICATE

The ability of VMs to be unmarked main predicates is only half the story regarding the syntax of sentences containing VMs. It is also noticeable that the verb itself can only function as an unmarked main predicate—that is, as the first part of a broad 'comment', rather than being a narrow focus—when there is no VM in the sentence. Whenever there is a VM, this is the only possible main predicate that can produce a topic>comment reading, as shown in (7.18).

(7.18)   a.   A színész beszaladt.
                 the actor   in(VM)-ran

          b.   #A színész szaladt be.
                 the actor   ran   in(VM)
                 Intended: 'The actor ran in.'

          c.   A színész be   fog szaladni.
                 the actor   in(VM) will run-INF

          d.   #A színész szaladni fog be.
                 the actor   run-INF will in(VM)
                 Intended: 'The actor will run in.'

In fact, it seems that it is difficult for the verb from within a VM+V complex to be the main predicate at all. Most Hungarian speakers reject sentences in which this kind of verb is placed in PV for the sake of focusing the contribution of the lexical verb—even when the VM+V combination has quite transparent semantics, as in (7.19).

230 *Shifting the Focus*

(7.19) a. #A színész szaladt be, nem lovagolt.
        the actor ran in(VM) not rode
        Intended: 'The actor RAN in; he didn't RIDE in.'
     b. #A színész szaladni fog be, nem lovagolni.
        the actor run-INF will in(VM) not ride-INF
        Intended: 'The actor will RUN in; he won't RIDE in.'

If the verb from within a VM+V combination is to be set in narrow focus, for the sake of contrast, an alternative strategy must be used, in which the VM+V combination is presented as a unit and the verb within it focused by purely phonological means (this is comparable to the phonological contrast of non-PV quantifiers discussed in Chapter 5, section 5.6). This is illustrated in (7.20).

(7.20) a. A színész beSZALADT, nem beLOVAGOLT.
        the actor in(VM)-ran not in(VM)-rode
        'The actor RAN in; he didn't RIDE in.'
     b. A színész beSZALADNI fog, nem beLOVAGOLNI.
        the actor in(VM)-run will not in(VM)-ride
        'The actor will RUN in; he won't RIDE in.'

All of this is predicted by the dynamic main predication account developed above. On first sight, this might not appear to be the case, considering representations like (7.17d). The process sub-eventuality function P-SUB is structurally parallel to the result state sub-eventuality function R-SUB and the latter is able to be a main predicate. So one might expect that the lexical item that relates to the process sub-eventuality—the verb—should be also able to be the main predicate, other things being equal.

Other things are not equal, however: there is an important difference between the linguistic elements that convey P-SUB and R-SUB. Unlike a resultative VM, the verb also has the ability to introduce a predicate over a main eventuality. That is, the contribution of the verb is quite different with regard to the internal structure of the epsilon term when it is part of a VM+V complex, compared to its contribution in a sentence with no VM. In a sense, there are two semantic translations of the verb, though in this case they do not relate to different lexical entries; rather, one is the lexical verb's own semantic contribution, while the other is that same semantic contribution embedded in structure that is introduced by the main predicate. This is why a dynamic approach is crucial to explaining the data in (7.18) and (7.19): achieving the correct interpretation is dependent on ascribing the right semantic status to the verb, but this in turn is dependent on whether the VM is processed before the verb is encountered.

The difference between the two possible contributions of the verb always exists, irrespective of the aspectual properties of the bare verb, since functions like P-SUB are additions to the structure of the verbal predicate, not simply aspectual predicates. Main predication is effected by lexicalised predicates (recall the account of proportional quantifiers in Chapter 5, in which the availability of some lexicalised predicate within a complex quantifier proved sufficient to allow it to appear in PV) and P-SUB is only associated with the lexical main verb when this is recognised to be used in combination with a VM that introduces a certain complex eventuality structure. The verb *olvaszt*, for example, happens to be a process, but this does not mean that it is associated with the function P-SUB in the absence of a VM—its aspectual properties are defined within its own internal semantic structure, below the level at which such a function can apply. Such a verb does not require the addition of special eventuality-structuring predicates like P-SUB in order to apply to the main eventuality variable and create main predication. Similarly, the analysis of resultative VMs should not be taken to imply that all lexical verbs are processes and that accomplishments can only be made by the addition of a VM. Some lexical verbs are accomplishments, as noted above in respect of the 'definiteness effect' verbs, but this is again a matter of their internal structure. Where aspectual structure is internal to the lexical verb, the entire contribution of the verb is conceptualised as a single predicate and none of this structure need be represented within the description of the main eventuality. As a result, when a lexical verb is the main predicate, this always asserts the existence of a simple eventuality, rather than introducing the structure of a complex one.

For example, *melt'* as main predicate would simply produce the propositional form in (7.21).

(7.21) $melt'(\varepsilon, e\ [f(e, \mathbf{T}_i)\ \&\ melt'(e)\ \&\ \theta_{\text{NOM}}(e, \textit{the-hw'})\ \&\ \theta_{\text{ACC}}(e, \mathbf{U})])$

Therefore, if the verb *olvaszt* is encountered on its own in PV, then an eventuality with the form of (7.21) is asserted to exist.

Once an eventuality with a certain structure is asserted to exist, it is too late to assert a different structure. This would be necessary to allow the assertion of a VM at this point: (7.21) is a very different structure to (7.17d)—and there are of course VM+V combinations that are much less compositional than *meg+olvaszt*, for which the difference would be even greater. It follows that the only unmarked reading that can be produced by a verbal main predicate is one with a simple internal structure; that is, one in which the verb is not understood as combining with a VM. This fits with the only observed cases of an apparent VM item appearing as an 'information focus' (i.e. post-verbally and stress-bearing): these items turn out not to have a true VM meaning in this context (see section 8.2).

One might ask why it is too late to re-structure an assertion after the point of main predication. After all, my approach allows quite free inferential enrichment processes during parsing, so why should the post-verbal appearance of a VM not be able to restructure a 'comment', changing a representation like (7.21) into one like (7.17d) by inference? The answer resides in fundamental principles of grammatical processing.

Any attempt to process a VM as part of a 'comment'—in other words, as an 'information focus'—would have to involve the re-structuring of the eventuality as a step within a single parse of the sentence, simply taking an existing partial representation as input and producing the restructured representation. This would amount to destroying information from the representation created by main predication and replacing it with different information. Put in these terms, it becomes clear that the monotonicity of the system of representation is at issue. It is generally held that the monotonicity of any system of building semantic representations should be considered axiomatic (even though in the current approach the inferential processes that *inform* this system may be non-monotonic). This is practically a necessity, since permitting non-monotonic procedures would allow in the possibility of massive computational inefficiency throughout the system. If the monotonicity of the system is assumed, any restructuring of the eventuality after main predication, as part of a single parse, is ruled out in principle[2].

This explains the data in (7.18)—the fact that a 'neutral' (topic>comment) reading cannot be produced by using the verbal part of a VM+V combination as the main predicate. It might still be expected that narrow focus on the verbal contribution should be possible through the use of PV, on the grounds that this would involve the presupposition of the VM+V combination and therefore make the correct form of the verb (i.e. embedded in the P-SUB function) accessible from the context. In this respect, it is notable that there are speakers who find sentences like those in (7.19) acceptable for the purposes of contrastive focus (as Szendrői 2003 also observes)—and one informant who has these intuitions reports that a particularly clear sense of the VM being presupposed is required for this word order to be used, just as the main predication analysis would predict[3]. Even these speakers tend to prefer the phonology-only strategy in most cases, however.

The impossible/dispreferred nature of the PV strategy for focusing such verbs does in fact fit with the dynamic nature of the main predication account. Though it is true that a narrow focus reading involves the presupposition of the semantic structure of the rest of the sentence, it must be borne in mind that the verb has a special status in terms of main predication: it does not normally prompt a narrow focus reading, because of its own structure-introducing properties. It is therefore likely to be the case that the intention to focus the verb cannot be reliably recognised until explicit contrastive material (such as the negative second clause in (7.19a,b)) has been encountered. This means that the simple version of the verb is likely to be applied as main predicate (e.g. (7.21) rather than (7.17d)) before the contrastive focus structure is recognised. This would require the abandonment of the parse initiated with the simple version of the verb and re-parsing using

---

[2] It might be objected that an act of restructuring takes place *at* the point of main predication, in the worked example (7.17), as the simple metavariable V is 'redistributed' among the sub-eventualities that are introduced. V is merely a semantically empty placeholder, however; an indication that some verbal content is expected to be predicated over the eventuality e. This expectation is fulfilled by the structure that is introduced upon main predication. There is no destruction of information involved in such a restructuring; in fact it is enrichment.

[3] Some of these cases may in fact involve the 'progressive aspect' construction, which does not involve true VM+V combinations (see section 8.2): for example, the same informant comments that the difference between (7.20a) and (7.19a) seems to correspond roughly to the difference between the English formulations *The actor RAN in; he didn't RIDE in* and *The actor entered RUNNING; not RIDING*. Other sentences that are judged acceptable in the pattern of (7.19) are not so easily explained in this fashion, however.

the complex predicate form of the verb and a presupposed focus frame. This process does not involve violation of monotonicity within a single parse, so is not ruled out in principle, as a non-focus reading of the verb as main predicate would be, but it is clearly a highly inefficient way to achieve the reading required. A purely prosodic strategy, as in (7.20) allows the VM to precede the verb and thus to assert its structure and ensure that the correct contribution of the verb is understood to be contrasted. Though itself a marked strategy in Hungarian, this purely prosodic focus is presumably less costly than the 'garden path'-like process of asserting the existence of a proposition, only to abort the parse and assert a different proposition. The fact that the use of PV to express narrow focus on the verb from within a VM+V complex is either considered impossible or allowed only in contexts in which the presupposed focus frame is particularly accessible is therefore entirely consistent with the dynamic main predication analysis of PV.

Note that the claim here is that the verb from within a VM-V complex predicate cannot generally be the main predicate; it is not claimed that the verb cannot precede the VM under any circumstances. This does occur; one construction involving V>VM order is discussed in section 8.2. However, there is in fact only one grammatical context in which the verb precedes a VM expression and still results in a clear complex verbal predicate reading (with the exception of those marginal instances of verb-in-focus accepted by some speakers). This is the kind of sentence that triggers all discussions about Hungarian 'focus position': with a finite main verb preceded by some other expression in focus, causing postposing of the VM (as in example (7.1b) from the beginning of this chapter). As established in Chapter 6, this amounts to a situation in which the focused expression introduces the main predicate and in which all other material (including all verbal material) is part of a presupposed focus frame. This means that the structure and the content of the main eventuality are not constructed in the course of processing the sentence in question, but are recovered from context as a whole. There is therefore generally no danger in this case of constructing from the verb alone an inappropriate representation that must be subsequently destroyed in the light of processing the VM. Given the possibility of 'accommodation' of the presupposed material, this does remain a marginal possibility, however—although even in such cases, the broader context is likely to severely constrain the kinds of predicates that are likely to be accessed on the basis of the verb alone. In any case, the order V>VM is restricted to the situation in which it is unavoidable for independent morphological reasons (the mutual dependence of the main verb and tense morphology in the absence of an auxiliary verb). Furthermore, the VM is preferred as close to the verb as possible in this situation (É. Kiss 2002, 85). This supports the claim that the explanation of unmarked pre-tense appearance of VPrs and other VMs depends upon a dynamic approach.

One further detail should be noted, which is broadly consistent with the main predication analysis, despite initial appearances to the contrary. While, as predicted, the verb alone out of a VM+V complex cannot generally appear as the main predicate, even to express contrastive focus, it is in fact possible to treat the whole of the VM+V complex predicate meaning as a narrow focus by placing it in PV, as in (7.22). Note that the word order used in the 'stress-only' strategy for verb focusing (as in (7.20b)) implies this also.

(7.22)   A   háziasszony megfagyasztani fogja a   vajat   (nem kidobni).
         The housewife VM-freeze-INF will the butter-ACC not out(VM)-throw-INF
         'The housewife will FREEZE the butter, not THROW IT OUT.'

This is somewhat unexpected, since all other aspects of the PV focus phenomenon have strongly indicated that the main predicate analysis is right in requiring only a single predicate to appear in PV and, within this, the syntactic behaviour of VMs suggests that they should be treated as separate lexicalised predicates from the verbs which they modify (albeit different kinds of predicate), such that the VM alone occupies the PV position unmarkedly. The explanation of examples like (7.22) must therefore be that VM+V complexes can under certain circumstances be conceptualised as a single lexicalisation of a complex predicate meaning and may consequently appear in PV as a single predicate for the purposes of singling out this composite meaning—that is, to create a narrow focus reading of the VM+V complex.

This assumption is not so *ad hoc* as it may seem, nor does it introduce unconstrained and empirically unattested new possibilities of complex predicate formation for the purposes of focusing. This is because it is in any case necessary to assume that VM+V complexes have a complicated relationship to the lexicon. The frequently non-compositional, quasi-idiomatic semantics of such complexes demands that they must relate to individual lexical entries (Ackerman & LeSourd 1997), even as their syntactically independent component parts must have their own separate lexical entries (at least in a dynamic analysis). It is therefore not so surprising that VM+V complexes can be conceptualised as single predicates for the purposes of narrow focus readings like that in (7.22). Notably, this reading is available only under certain structural conditions: the VM must precede the verb, preventing the initial selection of the simple semantic form of the verb as main predicate, and the complex must bear only a single pitch accent, falling on the VM and thus indicating a compound-like structure[4].

---

[4]One might ask whether the VM>V structure in the case of a 'neutral' sentence with a finite verb, as in (7.9), does not also involve the contribution of the whole VM+V complex in PV, rather than the VM, as argued above. The two analyses of the contribution of the VM—as an individual predicative element or as a part of a complex lexeme—are structurally indistinguishable here because of the inseparability of the verb stem and the tense morpheme. It would not in fact affect the present analysis greatly if the VM+V complex were taken to be a single predicate in such cases, though it seems preferable to maintain a parallel analysis for all VMs, not all of which can be analysed as having partially lexicalised relationships with particular verbs. Notice one thing that this *doesn't* mean: the whole [VM>V>TENSE] complex could still not be treated as equivalent to tense alone, in the manner of the [V>TENSE] complex with finite main verbs. If it could, VMs should be able optionally to fail to invert in the presence of a focus. However, the treatment of [V>TENSE] as equivalent to tense exists because of independent *morphological* constraints and has nothing to do with semantic constituency. There is no such constraint on the attachment of VM to verb—and because the VM *can* be a syntactically and semantically independent predicate, it must be assumed to be intended to be in PV whenever it occupies the immediately pre-tense position (and shows the relevant prosodic marking).

7.3.1 VMs as unmarked main predicates: empirical support

The idea that a VM in PV is, on its own, the main predicate of the sentence, and that it is able to be so unmarkedly because of its role in determining the structure of a complex eventuality, is supported by a further piece of empirical evidence, which shows a clear parallel between certain VMs and VM-less verbs. This is the ability of these expressions to express an entire proposition, given a suitably rich context.

Hungarian is a 'pro-drop' language with regard to both subjects and objects, meaning that a single tensed verb, say *Csókolta*, can be a whole sentence, expressing a whole proposition—in this case, 'He/she kissed him/her/it'. This is consistent with the notion that the main verb here performs main predication, since main predication is precisely a matter of one predicate creating a propositional assertion. According to my arguments in Chapter 6, the main verb is an unmarked main predicate because it can introduce the structure of the whole proposition, with metavariables as placeholders in as yet unmentioned elements of the proposition. Given this, if the context is sufficiently rich, these metavariables may all function anaphorically, being substituted by contextually salient entities, in which case only the main predicate need be phonetically realised at all.

It is therefore notable that some VMs can stand alone as grammatical assertions in a certain context, which contains rich, salient presupposed material, yet does not produce a narrow focus reading of the VM. This is the case of answering a 'yes-no' question with a VPr alone, as in the use of (7.23b) in reply to (7.23a) (É. Kiss 2002, 59).

(7.23)   a.   Hazamegy?
                home-go.2SG
                'Are you going home?'

         b.   Haza.
                home
                'Yes (I am going home).'

Note that it is not simply the relatively specific meaning of the VPr *haza* and the compositional semantics of the VM+V combination in (7.23a) that allow this: for example, *Megtaláltad?* 'Have you found it?' can be given the positive answer *Meg* (Bende-Farkas 2002, 139).

The context of the 'yes-no' question introduces complexities of information-structural interpretation that are beyond the scope of this book and I do not offer a full account of the interpretation of (7.23b) and similar sentences here. Nevertheless, the ability of some VMs to stand alone in this fashion is mysterious in the absence of an interpretive generalisation that brings VM-less main verbs together with just the VM part of VM-V complexes. The notion of main predication provides such a generalisation; one that sheds some light on the phenomenon exemplified in (7.23). The idea that VMs are unmarked main predicates because they can introduce the skeletal structure of a complex eventuality, with metavariables as placeholders, is entirely consistent with

236 *Shifting the Focus*

the fact that the utterance of a VM alone can be sufficient to assert a whole proposition, provided that the context is such that it provides substitutes for every metavariable in the skeletal propositional structure[5]. Only this kind of basis to the parallel between VMs and VM-less main verbs can account for the fact that it is the VPr rather than the verb that is the minimal utterance in such a context.

7.4 OTHER VMs

The analysis of resultative VMs, including telicising VPrs, shows how the syntactic properties of VMs can be derived from the idea of main predication in PV, within a dynamic, incremental processing approach to the creation of propositional forms. For such an account to be explanatory it clearly must be applicable to other members of the diverse class of VMs; that is, the other items that share precisely the syntactic properties in question. A detailed analysis of every sub-class of VM would require a lengthy study in itself and would take the present work into areas that lie well beyond its scope, but there are at least preliminary reasons to believe that each kind of VM can be treated in a manner that is parallel in significant ways to that proposed above for resultatives and telicising VPrs. These reasons are presented in this section.

It is worth noting that the very diversity of the expressions that qualify as VMs is an indication that the ultimate explanation of their behaviour must lie in something like the present account. Since this class does not conform to any conventional syntactic or semantic category, it is unlikely that conventional syntactic or semantic approaches could ever uncover the basis of what makes its members behave alike in certain ways. On the other hand, a perspective that transcends such categories, looking rather at the broader character of the contributions that different expressions can make at different points in the construction of a propositional form, has the potential to draw together otherwise unexpected groupings of linguistic items.

7.4.1 Bare nominals

Singular bare nominals (henceforth BNs) show the syntactic behaviour of VMs, although they produce quite different aspectual effects to resultatives and perfectivising VPrs. Thus, BNs appear unmarkedly before the tensed verb, but are postposed in the presence of negation or a narrowly focused expression, as in (7.24) (see also Chapter 3, section 3.2.4).

(7.24) a. Ferenc fát   vágott.
            Ferenc wood-ACC cut
            'Ferenc was cutting wood.'

---

[5] Note that the point here is to emphasise the parallelism between VMs and verbs, given that Hungarian is a 'pro-drop' language. The analysis here is not intended to explain the pro-drop phenomenon itself.

b. Ferenc vágott fát.
   Ferenc cut   wood-ACC
   'It's Ferenc who was cutting wood.'
c. Ferenc nem vágott fát.
   Ferenc not cut   wood-ACC
   'Ferenc wasn't cutting wood.'

The aspectual interpretation produced is typically atelic. This is in line with Tenny's (1994) notion that internal arguments 'measure out' the eventuality, since BNs do not introduce a discourse referent, but rather seem to denote a property. This is shown by the difficulty with which BNs support anaphoric reference. As É. Kiss (1994, 52) shows, though the anaphoric reference within a sentence like (7.25a) is marginally acceptable (the 'definite conjugation' of the verb *elvesztette* acts like an object pronoun), this must be analysed as the result of 'bridging inference': the existence of book(s) that Mari bought is implied by the fact that she went book-buying, even though no particular book is actually referred to[6]. In other contexts, such reference is not possible, as shown in (7.25b)[7]. This is a strong indication that a BN, at least in this kind of construction, does not introduce a discourse referent in the way that a full NP would.

(7.25) a. ??Mari könyvet$_i$ vásárolt, majd elvesztette$_i$.
          Mari book-ACC bought then lost(DEF)
          'Mari book$_i$-shopped, then she lost it$_i$.'
       b. *János iskolába$_i$ ment, majd felrobbantotta$_i$.
          János school-to went then blew.up(DEF)
          Intended: 'János went to school$_i$, then he blew it$_i$ up.'

It would appear that the combination of determiner and nominal is necessary to introduce a discourse referent, a situation that implies that a possibility mentioned by Kempson *et al.* (2001, 240), that the determiner may introduce individual referents, applies at least in Hungarian[8]. The important point in the current context is that this leaves BNs denoting a property rather than an individual. This has led to suggestions (e.g. McNally 1999) that the PV appearance of BNs is an instance of syntactic and semantic incorporation, in the sense of Van Geenhoven

---

[6] The improvement of an otherwise unacceptable sentence through bridging inference is fully in line with a view of the syntax-semantics interface that allows for inferential pragmatic enrichment in the course of interpretation

[7] This section is primarily concerned with accusative nominals, whereas (7.25b) involves a 'goal' locative, which functions like a resultative. Nevertheless, it is presumably the determinerless nature of the nominal in (7.25b) that makes anaphoric reference impossible, so I take É. Kiss's reasoning to be relevant here.

[8] As Bende-Farkas (2002, 70) points out, plural bare nominals do license pronominal anaphora, suggesting the possibility that alternatively plural morphology can introduce a (plural) discourse referent. This may be quite consistent with the general idea that determiners introduce discourse referents: Bende-Farkas also points out that the Hungarian plural suffix on nominals is in complementary distribution with all determiners other than the definite article, *a(z)* (2002, 75).

(1998), who develops an idea originally due to Carlson (1977) that existential quantification over BNs is supplied by the verb into which they incorporate. This means that many verbs must be assumed to have two semantic translations. For example, the English verb *see* would have a non-incorporating version, whose arguments are individuals (as in (7.26a)), and an incorporating version, whose internal argument is a property (as in (7.26b)), which appears in phrases such as *see spots*.

(7.26) a. $\lambda y.\lambda x.see'(x,y)$
 b. $\lambda P.\lambda x.\exists y\ [P(y)\ \&see'(x,y)]$

Cohen & Erteschik-Shir (2002) argue that such lexical ambiguity can be replaced by a generalised type-shifting operation for verbs, of the kind introduced for NPs by Partee (1987). Cohen & Erteschik-Shir propose that this operation is triggered by the type mismatch between verbs and property-denoting BN arguments, but offer little discussion of the precise grammatical circumstances under which such ways of 'rescuing' type mismatches should be permitted. In any case, the 'incorporation' of BNs in Hungarian is clearly linked to particular syntactic configurations (and is to a degree lexically restricted; see É. Kiss 1998b), so something other than a simple type mismatch must be involved in the interpretation of Hungarian BNs. In this context, it is notable that the notion of main predication in PV provides just the kind of syntactically manifested interpretive procedure that is missing from Cohen & Erteschik-Shir's account: one that could act as the trigger for something akin to their type-shifting operation.

Bende-Farkas (2002, 70ff.) points out that the interpretation of Hungarian BNs differs from that of Van Geenhoven's 'semantically incorporated' nominals, since the latter support anaphoric reference, via the existential quantifier in representations like (7.26b) (Van Geenhoven (1998) deals primarily with incorporation in languages like West Greenlandic, in which this is appropriate)[9]. Rather than using the kind of representation in (7.26b), Bende-Farkas assumes that it is in the nature of all verbs that combine with VMs that they require to be associated with some extra property and she represents them as in (7.27) (within a DRT analysis). While this kind of verbal contribution must interact with other VMs in more complex ways, a property-denoting BN simply substitutes directly for the property-type placeholder P.

(7.27) $\lambda P.\lambda x.\ P\text{--}VERB(x)$

Bende-Farkas is concerned primarily with the representation of interpretations, however, and does not attempt to explain the grammatical origins of these interpretations, beyond the general idea that the appearance of VMs in their pre-verbal position is associated with the formation of

---

[9]Cohen & Erteschik-Shir (2002, 153ff.) wish to prevent English BNs also from being interpreted as relating to particular discourse referents, despite the form of (7.26b). Their solution to this involves appealing to the relative ordering of the type-shifting operation and Erteschik-Shir's (1997) discrete level of 'focus structure'. In Chapter 4, section 4.2.2, I questioned the appropriateness of the latter, on general theoretical grounds and for Hungarian in particular.

complex verbal predicates. This is in no way a fault with Bende-Farkas's particular approach, but rather a virtually inevitable situation with any analysis which assumes that static syntactic representations provide the input to interpretive processes. The notion of main predication within a dynamic approach to both structure and interpretation, on the other hand, provides the potential to explain *how* a variety of effects follow from certain structural facts.

I adopt in the following discussion a schematic form of representation like that in (7.27) which suffices to demonstrate why BNs typically must appear in PV, in advance of the verb. As this kind of representation implies, I assume that a BN in PV forms a complex verbal predicate with the verb that it precedes and that it simultaneously saturates an argument position associated with that verb. I leave aside the question of precisely how these operations are effected, as this involves a raft of complex issues that are not immediately relevant to the present argument, at levels of analysis that are not straightforwardly representable with the formal techniques I employ here (for example, the details of argument structure and aspectual interpretation).

When a BN, for example *fát* 'wood', is encountered in PV, it is signalled that a property-denoting non-verbal predicate ($wood'$) is involved in predicating directly over the main eventuality. This involvement must be sufficient to effect main predication, yet this kind of predicate is not of a type that can predicate directly over eventuality variables—it is rather expected to restrict a nominal variable. The only way in which it can predicate over an eventuality variable and thereby create main predication is via complex predicate formation with a verb. The complex predicate required for main predication can be given a simplified representation as in (7.28). The subscript CP, for 'complex predicate', serves to distinguish the restricted kind of verbal contribution required here from the V that is presupposed in every eventuality prior to main predication.

(7.28) $wood'$–V_{CP}

As ever, for this to effect existential quantification over the eventuality variable, some equivalent predicate must be inferred to exist within the epsilon term that is to serve as the subject of main predication. There are two ways in which this can happen. One is the familiar case of the production of a narrow focus reading via the recovery of a focus frame: a whole presupposed eventuality that lacks specification only of the predicate in question—for example, the context makes manifest a presupposition that 'Ferenc was cutting something [such that this kind of cutting is a recognised complex verbal predicate]'—say, via inference from a salient assumption that 'Ferenc was cutting grass'. In terms of the simplified representations employed here, this can be shown as (7.29).

(7.29) $\varepsilon, e\ [P\text{–}cut'_{CP}\ \&\ \theta_{NOM}(e, ferenc')]$

Since this is presupposed, cut'_{CP} can be inferred to be the contextually favoured substitute for the V_{CP} metavariable part of (7.28). Providing this substitution is made, predicating (7.28) of (7.29) will create main predication, since $P\text{–}cut'_{CP}$ is a superset of $wood'\text{–}cut'_{CP}$ and, as such, entailed by it. This yields the representation in (7.30), with the reading in (7.31).

(7.30) $wood'\text{-}cut'_{CP}(\varepsilon, e\ [P\text{-}cut'_{CP}\ \&\ \theta_{NOM}(e, ferenc')])$

(7.31) Ferenc fát   vágott.
        Ferenc wood-ACC cut
        'It's wood that Ferenc was cutting.'

However, the accessibility of this kind of focus frame is restricted to rather rare contexts. The second, more common, way in which processing (7.28) could effect main predication is via the inference that the initially presupposed $V(e)$ predicate must be restructured to produce a metavariable of the form $P\text{-}V_{CP}(e)$. Recall that this merely stands for a more complicated representation of the complex predicate: the effects of this restructuring include the saturation of the lexical verb's internal argument slot and the imposition of certain relations between sub-eventualities and temporal structure. Since a property takes the place of the internal argument, there can be no 'measuring out' of a telic eventuality, so, in effect, an unbounded series of eventualities is asserted to exist. Thus, this restructuring represents the introduction of particular elements of complex predicate structure, as a result of applying the contribution of the BN alone.

In fact, given the form of the main predicate (7.28), the **P** within this inferred $P\text{-}V_{CP}(e)$ structure will instantaneously be substituted by $wood'$, so that main predication by (7.28) produces the representation in (7.32) (assuming, for the sake of completeness, that *Ferenc* has already been encountered as a topic).

(7.32) $wood'\text{-}V_{CP}(\varepsilon, e\ [wood'\text{-}V_{CP}(e)\ \&\ \theta_{NOM}(e, ferenc')])$

Since $wood'\text{-}V_{CP}$ is a development of **V**, this fulfils all the conditions for the status of full proposition, so main predication is achieved in advance of encountering the lexical verb.

The structure of the eventuality having been determined in this way, the contribution of the verb, when it is processed, must fit into this structure—that is, it must be of the kind represented by cut'_{CP}, rather than cut'. The consequent non-introduction of an internal argument slot and the realignment of the aspectual elements of the verb's meaning can be seen as parallel operations to Cohen & Erteschik-Shir's (2002) verbal type-shifting operation. Like the type mismatch that they take to trigger type-shifting, the proposed restructuring operation results from the fact that one lexical element is interpreted in the context provided by the interpretation of another, but in this case the precise kind of context involved is given more definition and motivation through the overall dynamic approach and the particular operation of main predication.

If the verb, rather than the BN, is the main predicate, this restructuring cannot take place. This is because an eventuality with the usual internal structure of the lexical verb is thereby asserted to exist. In this case, the usual internal argument slot associated with the verb will be projected and the BN will only be able to appear if it can somehow be coherently interpreted as a full argument, rather than a mere property. This interpretation can only arise in a context that supports certain inferences. This analysis thus explains the 'perfective' aspectual interpretation of V>BN ordering in the absence of a PV focus and known lexical and contextual restrictions on this (Kiefer 1994), without further stipulation. These latter points are discussed further in section 8.2.

At one level, my account entirely parallels the 'semantic incorporation'-based approach, in that in a sense two forms of the verb are posited, with two internal semantic structures, only one of which enables it to combine with the BN. The dynamic main predication account simply reverses the direction of explanation, deriving the particular semantic form of the verb from the linguistic context at that point in the parse. As a result, the relationship between BN interpretation and the syntactic phenomenon of PV is explained, rather than stipulated.

In fact, the dynamic analysis shows that, in effect, both orderings of BN and verb in Hungarian involve some equivalent or other of Cohen & Erteschik-Shir's type-shifting. This is because of the necessity to seek an individuated reading of the BN if it is encountered after the main verb. Whether it is the verb or the nominal that 'shifts' in some way depends on which determines the context for the interpretation of the other—each will do this whenever it performs main predication. This provides strong evidence in favour of the present approach: if the simple fact of type-mismatch within a static representation were the trigger for restructuring/type-shifting, one would not expect linear order or occupancy of the PV position to make a difference to the kind of 'shift' that takes place.

The explanation of the unmarked PV position of the BN is therefore somewhat similar to that of the PV position of resultative VMs: the interpretation of the BN+V combination that is considered to be unmarked is determined by the introduction of certain structure to the main eventuality, and this structure can only be asserted if the BN precedes the verb and provides main predication. It should again be noted that such linear signalling is not required if the interpretation of the whole BN+V combination is presupposed rather than asserted, so that the V>BN order that arises in the presence of a PV focus or negation when the verb is finite does not contradict this analysis.

7.4.2 Adverbs

The distribution of different adverbs in the Hungarian sentence involves complex and little-researched associations between different classes of adverb and the use of different pre-verbal positions. Certain adverbs can represent asserted material only in PV (so they are 'PV-only' items, in the sense used in Chapter 5), and certain *readings* of others also seem to be strictly associated with appearance in PV. Other adverbs or readings of adverbs are more commonly associated with the position known as QP; that is, they appear before VM>V order. In both cases, this description refers to what is perceived to be a non-focused reading of the adverb; most adverbs can also be given a contrastive focus reading in PV (though there are some non-PV adverbs; see below).

A full classification of these adverbs and the characterisation of their particular lexical properties would be a major research topic in itself. With currently available knowledge, many of these adverbs are problematic for any approach to Hungarian pre-verbal syntax (typically, syntactic features are postulated in an openly *ad hoc* fashion to ensure the correct distribution). The following discussion is therefore of necessity somewhat general and speculative. Nevertheless, there are a number of indications that the behaviour of adverbs is consistent with the main predication analysis of PV.

One identifiable interpretive correlate of the syntactic distinction between adverb-in-QP and adverb-in-PV is the difference in the 'scope' of certain manner adverbs; a subset of what Ernst (1984) calls Agent-oriented adverbs, as in cases like (7.33a,b)[10].

(7.33) a. Mari udvariatlanul kiment.
Mari rudely   out(VM)-went
'Rudely, Mari went out.' [i.e. it was rude of Mari to leave]

b. Mari udvariatlanul ment ki.
Mari rudely   went out(VM)
'Mari went out rudely.' [e.g. she slammed the door]

It is important to note that this pattern is not repeated with all such adverbs; for example, *okosan* 'cleverly' does not cause postposing of the VM under a reading parallel to (7.33b) (É. Kiss 2002, 21). This may be an example of a curious general tendency in Hungarian for adverbs with some form of 'negative' meaning, in a very broad sense, to associate with PV more unmarkedly than those that relate to qualities that are generally perceived as being positive. I offer no explanation of this fact here, beyond a few comments below on the class of so-called 'exclusive' adverbs. It remains significant, in any case, that the difference in interpretation for those manner adverbs that do surface in PV is precisely the one shown in (7.33).

The adverbial interpretation obtained with the adverb in QP is sometimes described as the 'sentential reading', but clearly involves modification of the Agent participant, as the alternative translation in (7.33a) suggests. While it is the eventuality that makes Mari rude, the nature of the eventuality itself is unaffected by the adverb: the reading amounts to saying 'Mari did something and she did it rudely; and what she did was go out'. This way of rendering the reading in question corresponds closely to the structure of the Hungarian sentence.

(7.33a) involves a use of QP (that is, the linear position between a syntactic topic and PV) which, for reasons of simplicity in presentation, was not mentioned in Chapter 5: this position here introduces an assertion, but, significantly, not one that does not constitute main predication. The appearance of *udvariatlanul* in QP asserts Mari's rudeness with respect to some eventuality, but does not create a true propositional form, since the eventuality at this point in the parse has no internal structure of the kind associated with verbal predicates, so it cannot be said that some particular eventuality has been asserted to exist before the VM is encountered. This analysis is further supported by the fact that the same kind of reading results from encountering the adverb

---

[10]For discussion of the semantics of this kind of adverb in English, see Jackendoff (1972), Thomason & Stalnaker (1973), McConnell-Ginet (1982), Ernst (1984, 2000).

in the position of an 'information focus': post-verbally and carrying a pitch accent, as in (7.34). This kind of example, described by one native speaker informant as having an 'appositive feel', has essentially the same 'scope' reading for the adverb and demonstrates that this reading is one in which the internal structure of the eventuality is unaffected by the adverb.

(7.34) Mari kiment   udvariatlanul.
        Mari out(VM)-went rudely
        'Mari went out, and it was rude of her to do so.'

When the adverb is in PV, this produces what is sometimes called the 'VP reading', or, in McConnell-Ginet's (1982) terminology, the 'Ad-V' reading of the adverb. From the current point of view, this is more helpfully viewed as one in which the adverb modifies the whole eventuality. In (7.33b), it is the particular event in question of Mari going out that is asserted to have the property of rudeness, in comparison to other events of Mari going out. In other words, the event in question is effectively interpreted as a unit that forms the logical subject of the predicate introduced by the adverb. This is precisely what one would expect from the appearance of the adverb in PV, given the notion of main predication.

In this sense, the so-called 'Ad-V' reading of this kind of adverb is inherently a narrow focus. The reason that this does not always result in an exhaustive interpretation is the nature of adverbial meanings: one way of going about something does not tend to preclude many other ways of describing it, while contrast is also unnecessary to make this kind of narrow focus relevant, since the assertion that some eventuality proceeds in a particular way is likely to have significant cognitive effects without direct contrast to existing assumptions about how it happens (this is nevertheless always a possibility—e.g. when the addressee of (7.33b) manifestly believes that Mari left politely—while in any case there is certainly a generalised sense of contrast with other ways of going out). As Jackendoff (1972, 70) points out, the paraphrases that most nearly convey the appropriate reading of such adverbs are parallel to simpler structures that clearly show an 'identificational' meaning (which is just what is commonly attributed to Hungarian syntactic focus). Thus, the relationship between (7.35a) and (7.35b) is the same as the relationship between (7.36a) and (7.36b), when *John* is read as a narrow focus.

(7.35) a. Mary went out rudely.

        b. The manner in which Mary went out was rude.

(7.36) a. I met John.

        b. The person whom I met was John.

On the other hand, one might ask whether this could not be 'information focus' in the case of the adverb. After all, a sentence like (7.33b) is not necessarily felt to presuppose a focus frame (here, that Mari went out in some manner), being just as felicitously taken as a complex 'comment' about the topical Mari; a newly reported thing that she has done. On this basis, one might imagine that an adverb on its 'Ad-V' reading should be able to surface as an information focus—the addition of further information to an already-established eventuality—yet it cannot, as (7.34) shows: the so-called 'sentential reading' will always result from this. There must, therefore, be another reason why the 'Ad-V' reading is only associated with PV.

This reason is also hinted at in Jackendoff's (1972) analysis: the 'Ad-V' reading (as suggested by McConnell-Ginet's name for it) is analysable as one in which the adverb and verb form a complex predicate. If (7.33b) is taken as being essentially a topic>comment sentence, for example, then it is clear that the topical Mari is asserted not simply to have gone out but rather to have performed a more complex act of going-out-rudely. This is more than mere elaboration of what happened, as specified by the verb's meaning. For this complex predicate to result compositionally from the lexical items in (7.33b), it must be the case that the semantics of the adverb is able to modify some aspect of the internal structure of the verbal predicate (note that the precise interpretation of different combinations of verbs and 'Ad-V' adverbs will depend on the particular internal structure of the verb.). The adverb therefore performs a form of re-structuring operation on the verb, at a semantic level, in order to produce this reading (cf. McConnell-Ginet's 1982 account, wherein an 'Ad-V' adverb in effect changes the argument structure of the verb so that the adverb itself becomes one of the verb's arguments). The explanation of the obligatorily PV position of 'Ad-V' adverbs therefore parallels that of the unmarked PV position of resultative VMs and BNs: were the verb to be the main predicate, the eventuality would be asserted to exist with the structure determined by the internal semantics of the unmodified verb, after which point it would be too late to perform the necessary modification, in a monotonic system. It follows that any appearance of the relevant kind of adverb after the point of main predication will result in the so-called 'sentential' reading, in which the existence and internal character of the eventuality is unaffected by the ascription of the adverbial property to the Agent participant.

The case of 'sentential' versus 'Ad-V' adverbs thus brings together the two central cases of main predication: narrow focus and items that enter into complex verbal predicates with the lexical verb, by affecting the internal semantic structure of the latter. At one level, 'Ad-V' adverbs are always narrow foci, but this very characteristic is related to the fact that at another level of analysis these adverbs operate on some element of the internal structure of the verbal predicate. Thus, (7.33b) expresses that 'Mari's going out was rude', but at another level this cashes out as 'Mari's going out was an eventuality with a certain internal structure that defines it as an eventuality of going-out-rudely'.

All of this of course brings up the question of why other adverbs, like *okosan* 'cleverly', gain the 'Ad-V' reading without appearing in PV and therefore without entering into any kind of complex predicate relationship with the verb. I leave this as an open question, pending a detailed survey of the data, noting only the speculative idea that the negative element perceived in the meaning may lend such adverbs a certain marked semantic 'weight' that causes them to take on a marked pragmatic reading (i.e. narrow focus) and/or requires some particular form of combination with the lexical verb.

There is at least one more class of adverbs whose reading can vary systematically with appearance in QP or PV (for reasons other than contrastive focus). These are depictive adverbs, which correspond to what are often non-adverbial secondary predicates in languages like English. This suggests that, again, an explanation along the lines of that given above for resultative VMs is likely to exist also for depictive adverbs—that is, in terms of the depictive in PV restructuring the verbal predicate. The details remain relatively unclear, however: the data are more complex than in the case of Agent-oriented adverbs and have not been subject to a great deal of research so far.

Some depictives are restricted to either QP or PV. When a depictive may appear in either, one factor that relates systematically to the choice of position is the difference between subject- and object-oriented readings, though this is not a simple one-to-one relationship. Ágnes Bende-Farkas has suggested one relevant generalisation in relation to this (personal communication): it appears that when an adverb is capable of either a subject- or object-oriented reading, only the subject-oriented reading is available when the adverb appears in QP, as in the example (7.37a), whereas both readings can result from the adverb's appearance in PV, as in (7.37b).

(7.37) a. Az őr   részegen   lecsukta   a foglyokat.
           the guard drunkenly down(VM)-shut the prisoners-ACC
           'The guard locked up the prisoners (while he was) drunk.'

       b. Az őr   részegen   csukta le   a foglyokat.
           the guard drunkenly shut   down(VM) the prisoners-ACC
           'The guard locked up the prisoners (while he was) drunk.'
           or:
           'The guard locked up the prisoners (while they were) drunk.'

The fact that the object-oriented reading is made available in such cases by the use of PV is reminiscent of the way that other VMs have been seen to interact with internal arguments; for example, the absorption of the verb's internal argument slot by BNs in PV and predication over the 'measuring' internal argument performed by resultative VMs. Conversely, the QP reading of an Agent-oriented adverb like *udvariatlanul* 'rudely' appears to associate strictly with the external argument, as in (7.33a). Clearly, there is a good deal to be said about such phenomena at levels of semantic analysis that are not easily related to the kind of representations that I employ to show main predication. In the absence of a thorough semantic analysis of Hungarian depictive adverbs, it must suffice to note that they have significant points of connection with other kinds of VM whose behaviour is explained by the main predication analysis.

A still less well understood class of adverbs is that of so-called 'exclusive adverbs' (É. Kiss 1987, 90). This is made up of adverbs that typically have some form of negative meaning, in a fairly broad sense. Some of these, including *alig* 'hardly', *hasztalan* 'in vain', *későn* 'late', *ritkán* 'rarely' and *rosszul* 'badly', appear to be restricted to the PV position (when asserted), while others, such as *bonyolultan* 'in a complicated manner' and *erőtlenül* 'weakly', appear regularly in PV, without the sense of being a contrastive focus, but may also appear in QP (that is, before VM>V order), in certain contexts. Syntactic analyses have so far provided no better way of accounting for these adverbs than to declare them 'inherent foci' (É. Kiss 2002, 89ff.) (the latter group being presumably 'unmarkedly foci', in some sense)—not for any interpretive reason, but in the sense that they necessarily carry a formal feature [+focus]. É. Kiss (2002, 90) notes that some semantic property must be ultimately responsible for their being endowed with this feature, but does not identify what this might be.

One problem with this approach is that these adverbs can appear also with a clearly contrastive focus interpretation, as in (7.38) (one might imagine a context in which Ferenc's wife is correcting the addressee's manifest assumption about why she is upset with Ferenc).

(7.38)   Ferenc későn jött   haza,   nem részegen.
          Ferenc late   came home(VM) not   drunkenly
          'Ferenc came home LATE, not DRUNK.'

In general, the syntactic approach to 'focus position' rests on the premise that a non-contrastive pre-verbal expression cannot be in the focus position, FP, and that it can be deduced from this that the contribution of FP at the LF interface is consistently the addition of a contrastive (or 'exhaustive', or 'exclusive') reading (hence the notion that contrastive focus on a VPr, for example, must involve string-vacuous movement to Spec,FP). Arguments against this approach were given in Chapter 4; here it suffices to note that it is also incompatible with the notion of 'inherent foci', especially if a contrastive element of meaning can be added over and above the usual reading of these expressions.

In the context of the main predication analysis, two possible explanations of the distribution of these adverbs suggest themselves. One is suggested by the analysis of constraints on quantifier distribution from Chapter 5. A number of the PV-only adverbs have a clearly quantificational element to their semantics—for example, *alig* 'hardly' and *ritkán* 'rarely' seem to quantify over instances of a certain kind of eventuality. The 'negative' aspect of the meaning of PV-only adverbs might therefore be related to the factor that keeps quantifiers like *few* restricted to PV: they are monotone decreasing. This would go along with the existence of another parallel between quantifying adverbs and quantifiers; there are 'non-PV' adverbs, typically with an element of universal quantification in their semantics, that mirror the 'non-PV' quantifiers of Chapter 5 in being excluded from PV even in a contrastive context, as illustrated by *mindig* 'always' in (7.39) (É. Kiss 1987, 91).

(7.39)   a.   János mindig megijed.
                János always VM-gets.frightened
                'János always gets frightened.'

b. *János mindig ijed   meg, nem csak néha.
   János always gets.frightened VM not only sometimes
   Intended: 'János ALWAYS gets frightened, not just sometimes.'

Nonetheless, there is another possibility, which is more likely to apply to all of the 'exclusive' adverbs. This is suggested by a fact noted by É. Kiss (2002, 90): *csúnyán*, the adverb derived from the adjective *csúnya* 'ugly' is restricted to PV only when it has the meaning 'in an ugly manner' (see (7.40a,b)). It can also be used as a degree adverb, corresponding roughly to English *badly* on a degree reading, and it appears in QP on this usage, as in (7.40c).

(7.40)   a.   János csúnyán írta   meg a   leckét.
              János "uglily" wrote VM the lesson-ACC
              'János wrote the lesson in an ugly way.'
         b.   *János csúnyán megírta   a   leckét.
              János "uglily" VM-wrote the lesson-ACC
         c.   János csúnyán elvágta a   kezét.
              János "uglily" VM-cut the hand.3SG-ACC
              'János badly cut his hand.'

This suggests that there may be a sense in which the PV-only adverbs are all in some sense inherently eventuality-oriented, 'Ad-V' adverbs of the kind represented by *udvariatlanul* in (7.33b) and are therefore of necessity main predicates, as argued above. A degree adverb, on the other hand, like a subject-oriented depictive, has no effect on the internal structure of the eventuality. Indeed, one speculative possibility is that the degree reading is actually somehow conceptualised as a property of the agentive individual, such that the underlying semantics of (7.40c) would be 'John's performance of an action was to a bad extent and that action was cutting himself', rather than 'John's cutting himself was bad'. In any case, linking the 'exclusive' adverbs to 'Ad-V' adverbials at least gives a potential explanation of the syntactic behaviour of these adverbs in terms of a general interpretive mechanism. Note that this even leaves open the possibility that certain adverbs could become 'grammaticalised' diachronically as PV-only adverbs, without the need to resort to purely syntactic features like [+focus], since details of lexical semantics such as specifications of inherent eventuality- or subject-orientation filter through in this way to affect syntactic distribution.

7.4.3 Locatives

One of the least well understood aspects of the whole PV phenomenon in Hungarian is the inclusion of non-Goal locative phrases in the class of VMs. Here, as with the PV adverbs, only a few initial observations on this phenomenon are attempted, but these suffice to indicate that locative VMs are consistent with the reasoning developed above.

That at least some locatives must be considered VMs is shown both by their unmarked PV appearance, as in (7.41a), and by the fact that the post-verbal appearance of a locative phrase in this kind of sentence is compatible only with an overt PV focus, as in (7.41b), or some other marked reading, such as the 'existential aspect' discussed in section 8.2 (and in fact analysed as a particular kind of narrow focus in section 8.3), as in (7.41c) (using the ′ marker to distinguish the location of the main pitch accent in the latter two examples)[11].

(7.41) a. Péter a   szobában maradt.
           Péter the room-in   remained
           'Péter stayed in the room.'

      b. ′Péter maradt   a   szobában.
          Péter remained the room-in
          'It's Péter who stayed in the room.'

      c. Péter ′maradt   egyedül a   szobában.
          Péter remained alone   the room-in
          'Péter has been left on his own in the room before.'

Locatives are unusual among VMs, in that they can be full NPs (though they can also be BNs; cf. (7.25b)). Normally the appearance of a full NP in PV results in narrow focus on that NP. This is one possible reading of the word order in (7.41a)—given a suitable context and the prosody characteristic of narrow focus structures—but the unmarked reading of (7.41a) is as a 'neutral', topic>comment sentence.

The VM status of locative phrases is therefore on the face of it somewhat unexpected. There are nevertheless a number of indications that they fit into the class of expressions that must be main predicates in the unmarked case.

First, locatives are not always structurally unlike other VMs in this way. In addition to determinerless locative nominals, there are locative VPrs (or at least VPr-like particles), as mentioned in section 7.2. (7.42) illustrates these (see also the examples in (7.6)).

(7.42) a. A szobor ott   található   a   parkban.
           the statue there can.be.found the park-in
           'The statue can be found in the park.'

      b. János kint nyírja a   füvet.
         János out cuts   the grass-ACC
         'János is cutting the grass outside.'

---

[11] The adverb *egyedül* 'alone' is added to (7.41c) simply to create a pragmatically more probable sentence. Hungarian *marad* translates as *stay* only in the sense of 'remain', and this is virtually incompatible with presuppositions that are involved in the 'existential' reading; see section 8.2. The basic structural point illustrated in (7.41) is unaffected—only (7.41a) can be a 'neutral' reading.

As (7.42a) shows, the locative VPr may be co-referential with a full locative NP, in a fashion reminiscent of clitic-doubling structures in other languages, but it may also appear on its own, as in (7.42b).

The unmarked use of locatives as main predicates is consistent with some general facts about the nature of location. Main predication creates the assertion of the existence of an eventuality, and the connection between location and existence is not only a matter of logical inference—if something is located, it must exist—but also attested to be often manifested in linguistic phenomena (Lyons 1977, 722). Some similar reasoning presumably lies behind É. Kiss's brief comments on locative VMs: "Intuitively, they serve to anchor spatiotemporally the state denoted by the base verb" (2002, 66). However, this alone does not explain the distribution of locatives, with or without the idea of main predication. For one thing, the use of locatives as real VMs is somewhat restricted, as outlined below. More generally, this reasoning suggests that locatives should be similar to tense, since both locations and times 'anchor' the eventuality and thereby imply its existence. But whereas locations are both regularly focusable and often unmarkedly found in PV, times cannot be put in contrastive focus by focusing tense (see section 8.3) and tense cannot appear unmarkedly in PV.

What has emerged so far from the argumentation of this chapter is that VMs tend to restructure the verbal predicate in some way, whether by adding semantic structure above and beyond that introduced by the lexical verb or by in some way accessing the verb's internal structure and adapting it. Either way, the dynamic predication account predicts that the VM rather than the verb must appear in PV, so that the unmodified structure of the verb alone is not introduced. The existence of locatives that behave as VMs implies that these must introduce complex predicate structures, an idea that is given some structural support by the existence of locative VPrs.

True VM-like behaviour—obligatory PV position, on an unmarked reading—is restricted to certain combinations of locatives and verbs. As (7.41) illustrates, a full NP locative is generally a true VM in combination with a stative verb. Locative BNs act as VMs also with non-statives, as shown in (7.43) (as the translations show, the intended meaning does not involve focus on the subject, which would rescue the linear orders in (7.43b and d)).

(7.43)   a.   Ferenc ágyban olvas.
                Ferenc bed-in reads

          b.   #Ferenc olvas ágyban.
                Ferenc reads bed-in
                For: 'Ferenc reads in bed.'

c. Kati gyárban dolgozik.
   Kati factory-in works

d. #Kati dolgozik gyárban.
   Kati works factory-in
   For: 'Kati works in a factory.'

Full NP locatives with most non-stative verbs appear to be able to appear unmarkedly in a post-verbal position, however, as in (7.44a). Notably, unlike the case of some adverbs, a full NP locative cannot appear in PV in the presence of a VPr without producing a reading of narrow focus on the locative, as shown in (7.44b,c).

(7.44) a. Kati dolgozik a kertben.
       Kati works the garden-in
       'Kati is working in the garden.'

   b. Mari a kertben ette meg az almát.
      Mari the garden-in ate VM the apple-ACC
      'It's in the garden that Mari ate the apple.'

   c. Mari megette az almát a kertben.
      Mari VM-ate the apple-ACC the garden-in
      'Mari ate the apple in the garden.'

Some non-stative verbs do seem to require locative full NPs to act as VMs (for example, (7.45)), while others do under certain readings; compare (7.44a) with (7.46).

(7.45) a. Réka Budapesten született.
       Réka Budapest-in was.born

   b. #Réka született Budapesten.
      Réka was.born Budapest-in
      For: 'Réka was born in Budapest.'

(7.46) a. Kati egy gyárban dolgozik.
       Kati a factory-in works
       'Kati works in a factory.'

   b. Kati dolgozik egy gyárban.
      Kati works a factory-in
      'Kati is working in a factory (right now).'
      [also contrastive focus related readings]

The locative in (7.45) shows obvious VM behaviour, in that the word order in (7.45b) could only be associated with some form of clearly contrastive narrow focus reading. In (7.46), on the other hand, either word order is possible with an apparently 'neutral' information structure, but with clearly different readings: with the locative in PV (suggesting that the locative is a VM), a habitual reading is produced; the version involving the locative as an information focus, post-verbally, produces a progressive reading[12].

What crucial feature do statives like 'stay', achievement verbs like 'be born' and the habitual reading of the process 'work' share? I propose that this is a kind of informational 'lightness', that requires the locative to be read as the main informative part of the utterance. In effect, these verbs (on these readings) cannot be anything but 'background' to assertion of the location. To treat the verbal meaning as an independent part of the assertion contained in the utterance is in some way uninformative—the fact that any living person was born is a tautology; the fact that someone 'stays' is uninformative without a specification or presupposition of their location; the fact that an adult human being has some paid occupation is a default cultural assumption—and the grammar of Hungarian appears to reflect this.

What this means is that when such verbs co-occur with a locative phrase, they act as 'light verbs', in something like Bende-Farkas's (2002) sense: they can only participate in an act of assertion by 'incorporating' the location, via some modification of their own internal semantic structure, and forming a complex predicate with it. This comes through on an intuitive level most clearly with the 'work' sentences: the habitual reading is intuitively about 'doing factory-work' as a single concept, whereas the progressive reading is more obviously an assertion of both what someone is doing and where they are doing it. In other words, in the latter reading the locative is more intuitively an adjunct to a 'heavy', stand-alone version of the verb—as a referent related to the main eventuality by a 'theta-role' function and introduced by conjunction into the neo-Davidsonian propositional form. It is unsurprising that locative BNs are restricted to the former strategy, since these are property-denoting and (unlike some accusative BNs) they cannot even be contextually enriched to have a referential meaning (of a kind that would not be available without such enrichment processes by using a full NP).

As in the case of accusative BN incorporation, this may be a partially lexicalised property, but the trigger for any individual act of complex predicate creation also involves the relation of linguistic form to context, as the dynamic approach predicts. This is likely to be the basis of an interesting grammatical contrast involving the verb *dolgozik* 'work': replacing *egy gyárban* 'a factory' with *a gyárban* 'the factory' in (7.46) is reported to remove the VM-like properties of the locative phrase under either word order. This is possibly related to the lexical properties of the 'modified' version of the verb, but may simply come down to contextual factors: if the factory in question is not mutually manifest as uniquely relevant, and hence needs to be introduced as a new discourse referent using the indefinite article, this implies a context in which Kati's (habitual) occupation is being reported, and in which the concept of working is therefore backgrounded. On the other hand, sufficient manifestness of the factory to cause the use of the definite article favours

---

[12]Despite the common terminology, this is not the same reading as that associated with the 'progressive construction' discussed in section 8.2

a context in which the fact that Kati is working is newsworthy on its own, so that the locative is naturally read as an adjunct to the 'heavy' version of the verb's semantics. The complex predicate reading thus disappears as a result of inferences regarding the contextual relevance of the particular combination of verb and locative.

Further support for the idea that a verb like *dolgozik* forms complex predicates because of its informational 'lightness' in combination with certain locatives comes from the behaviour of locatives with more specific verbs of working. Even on a habitual reading, a more specific verb, such as *táncol* 'dance' does not cause even an indefinite locative to show VM behaviour (that is, to achieve the relevant reading only in PV). Thus, (7.47) allows a habitual, topic>comment reading although it contains an indefinite and post-verbal locative (cf. (7.46b)). This is because the verbal meaning itself, being not so predictable as 'work', is informative enough to be an independent part of the assertion itself, not merely background to the information in the locative phrase—and hence can be the main predicate.

(7.47) Ildi táncol egy bárban.
        Ildi dances a   bar-in
        'Ildi dances in a bar.'

If this analysis is on the right lines, then once again the explanation of VM behaviour is to be found in the fact that complex predicate formation involves modification of the contribution of the verb, so that allowing the verb alone to be the main predicate would block certain readings and in some cases make any subsequent VM expression uninterpretable. As with the analysis of certain adverbs, locatives also represent a case where the focusing function of main predication and its role in creating complex predicates find a point of contact[13].

7.5 SUMMARY

This chapter has demonstrated that not only the postposing of VMs in the presence of focus but also the unmarked pre-tense position of VMs in 'neutral' sentences follows from the main predicate analysis of PV. This depends on only minimal, relatively uncontroversial assumptions about the nature of VMs, concentrating in particular on the tendency of VMs to enter into complex predicate relationships with the main verb. This explains why any VM that is present, rather than the main verb with which it is associated, must be the main predicate in a 'neutral' sentence. In essence, this is due to the need to recognise the appropriate reading of the verb—one that is able to enter into a complex predicate relationship—at crucial points in the parse.

The heterogeneous class of VMs brings up many poorly understood issues, but the signs are that each major kind of VM is amenable either to some analysis in terms of complex predicate

---

[13] The discussion of the relative informativeness of verbs in relation to a construction associated with focus invites comparison with the much-discussed English phenomenon of 'early' stress placement even in 'out of the blue' contexts, in examples like *NIXON died*. See Ladd (1996, 188ff.) and references therein.

formation or to re-analysis as a kind of focus reading. Clearly, there is scope for much interesting research in these areas, to which the success of the main predicate analysis, in broad outline, might help to give direction. In other cases, such as VMs with resultative meanings, it is already possible to give fairly precise characterisations of the interpretive processes involved in VM use. These mesh well with the adoption of neo-Davidsonian representations, as proposed in Chapter 6.

The explanation of VM distribution depends on the dynamic nature of the analysis, being fundamentally a matter of the order in which different expressions are processed, relative to each other and to crucial points of procedural encoding. This creates a unified explanation of VM behaviour in all sentences, whether the main verb or an auxiliary is finite, and therefore does away with the need for any special processes like 'VM-climbing'. Note also that the syntactic behaviour of VMs follows as a prediction of the main predicate analysis, given well supported assumptions about the complex predicate forming nature of most VMs. Once again, therefore, a processing-based, inferentially informed approach proves to allow for a strikingly parsimonious and genuinely explanatory analysis and as such to introduce greater clarity into a model of linguistic competence.

There remain a few important questions surrounding VM distribution. Having explained their unmarked PV position, two particular constructions must be explained in which VMs appear post-verbally, despite the apparent lack of any narrow focus. Also, the postposing of VMs in the presence of negation must be accounted for. These matters are the subject of the following chapter.

8

'ASPECTUAL CONSTRUCTIONS' AND NEGATION

8.1 OVERVIEW

The Hungarian PV position provides three further illustrations of how conventional syntactico-semantic approaches create unnecessary complications of the grammar, through their inability to account adequately for the influence of linear ordering and, in particular, inferences that are triggered thereby. At issue are two constructions that are often claimed to encode aspectual semantics and the issue of the distribution of the negative particle *nem*. These phenomena have been argued to require a raft of specialised grammatical machinery, in the form of dedicated syntactic projections, silent operators and corresponding features. These all prove to be straightforwardly explicable in terms of the main predication analysis of PV; the 'aspectual' constructions being in fact predicted by the analysis in Chapter 6, while the explanation of negation requires the addition of just one very simple assumption about *nem*. In tackling these phenomena, this chapter also ties up the last remaining major issues concerning the syntax of PV and VMs.

The analysis in Chapter 7 of the relative positions of VM and verb brings up the question of why VMs follow the verb in two particular constructions that on the face of it do not involve narrow foci. One of these expresses a certain kind of progressive reading, the other the so-called 'existential' or 'evidential' reading. Section 8.2 deals with these constructions in terms of main predication, showing that one of them does not involve true VMs at all, but rather alternative readings of expressions that can be VMs, while the other does in fact involve a certain kind of narrow focus, despite there being nothing in the PV position, immediately preceding the tensed verb.

The other remaining puzzle involving the distribution of VMs is why they should postpose in the presence of the negative particle *nem* when it performs 'sentential negation', but co-exist pre-verbally with *nem* in certain other contexts. This boils down to the general ability of *nem* to appear pre-verbally with a PV focus, but this in itself remains to be explained. These issues are discussed in section 8.4, where it is shown that the main predication analysis avoids the syntactician's *ad hoc* solution of stipulating two positions for *nem*, given the maximally simple (if unconventional) assumption that *nem* introduces a consistently narrow scope negation operator.

8.2 THE 'EXISTENTIAL/EVIDENTIAL' AND 'PROGRESSIVE' CONSTRUCTIONS

As mentioned in Chapter 3, É. Kiss's (1987,1994) original 'single position' analysis of Hungarian PV (see Chapter 3, section 3.3.1) includes two phonologically null objects that can fill the relevant pre-verbal position (Spec,VP in É. Kiss 1994). These are the operators PROG and EXIST that are claimed to create certain aspectual readings by taking scope over the verb and subsequent material. The reason for positing these operators in the PV position is that the relevant readings occur when a VM is postposed to a post-verbal position, as in (8.1) (examples due to É. Kiss 1994, 49ff.). Note that word order does not tell the whole story here: the two constructions are distinguished prosodically (as previously, a stress mark simply signifies the presence of a non-topic pitch accent on the following word).

(8.1)   a.   János 'nyitotta 'ki   az 'autóját,   amikor 'odaérkeztem.
               János   opened   out(VM) the car-his-ACC when   there-arrived.1SG
               'János was opening his car when I got there.'

         b.   János 'nyitotta ki az autóját   kulcs nélkül.
               János   opened out the car-his-ACC key   without
               'János has opened his car without a key (before).'

(8.1a) exemplifies the so-called progressive construction (henceforth PC), in which É. Kiss (1994) posits a pre-verbal silent PROG operator. This features a pitch accent on the verb and on each major constituent that follows it, including the verbal prefix (VPr). As Kiefer (1994) points out, this is only possible when the combination of verb and VPr maintains some of the VPr's underlying directional semantics (e.g. *ki* 'out' supplying the 'outward' part of the action of opening a car door in (8.1a)): if the VPr merely serves a telicising function when it is pre-verbal, it cannot serve a 'progressivising' function post-verbally.

(8.1b) illustrates the construction in which É. Kiss (1994) posits the operator EXIST in Spec,VP. This is variously known as the 'existential', 'experiential' or 'informing' aspect (or tense, according to Piñón to appear). I shall simply refer to it as the EC, for 'existential construction'. This conveys that the eventuality described has already occurred, or, given a morphologically present tense verb or future auxiliary, that it will occur at some future time. In either case, as Piñón (to appear) details, it must be the case that the eventuality in question can re-occur at least once. Hence, the EC is impossible in a sentence like (8.2), assuming it does not occur in a conversation about reincarnation (note that the English translation with '*have ... before*' is also anomalous, giving an initial clue as to the basis of this reading)[1].

(8.2) #Réka 'született Budapesten.
Réka was.born Budapest-in(VM)
Intended: 'Réka has been born in Budapest (before).'

8.2.1 The 'abstract operator' analysis

Treating these constructions as the result of abstract pre-verbal operators is problematic in a number of ways, yet has been widely accepted in the syntactic literature until recently. Not the smallest of the problems with this approach is the general theoretical point on which Piñón (1995, 168) quotes Harlig (1989, 59): "the positing of invisible aspectual operators ... to fill these positions, which in every other case must be filled by lexical material, solely to generate the necessary word order, [is] completely ad hoc"[2]. As in the case of encoded exhaustivity, the silent operator approach artificially assumes that the observed interpretation must directly reflect the contribution of some syntactico-semantic primitive, betraying the limits of analytical frameworks that do not easily admit significant underspecification. As a result, connections to other kinds of construction, though strongly suggested by the prosodic characteristics of the PC and EC and by the effects of V>BN orders, are ignored, alongside the possible contribution of inferential processes.

At the empirical level, the problems with the operator-based approach relate to the close parallelism that it implies between the PC and the EC. Whether under a single position analysis of PV, as in É. Kiss (1987, 1994), or under the assumption that EXIST and PROG (and foci and VMs) each occupy different abstract pre-verbal projections, as in Piñón's papers, the implication is that the syntactic parallelism seen in (8.1) results from parallel derivations. For É. Kiss (1994), this means the occupancy of Spec,VP in each case forces the VM to remain post-verbal; for Piñón, V-movement in the manner of Bródy (1995), to functional projections above VP, strands the VM in both the PC and EC.

This presumed parallelism is not sustainable. The striking prosodic contrast is one indication of this. While within a conventional syntactic approach the prosodic structure could be argued simply to be triggered by the presence of the operators themselves, this leaves the nature of the particular prosody associated with each construction entirely unexplained. A further asymmetry is that the EC can be found in VM-less sentences (again with the verb stressed and all post-verbal material destressed), whilst it makes little sense to speak of the PC in the absence of a VPr: if the aspectual possibilities of a simple verb may be related to abstract operators, there seems no way to prevent the supposition of as many abstract operators as there are aspectual readings of

---

[1] The acceptability judgement here (due to Piñón to appear) refers only to the intended EC reading. The word order and stress pattern in (8.2) is possible on another reading: that of contrastive focus on the verb.

[2] Despite showing some sympathy with this argument, Piñón develops analyses of both the PC and EC in terms of abstract operators (1995 and to appear, respectively), though not under a 'single position' analysis of PV.

verbs—a situation that no-one would consider explanatory.

However, the crucial counter-evidence comes (not for the first time in this book) from the nature of sentences containing tensed auxiliaries. The EC with the future time auxiliary *fog* is discussed in Piñón (to appear) and works as one might predict from other 'non-neutral' sentences, with the VM appearing immediately before the infinitival main verb, in the post-auxiliary domain; see (8.3a). Examples with auxiliary constructions are not found in the literature where the PC is analysed, however. This is perhaps because such an example requires a rather unusual context: predicting that someone will be in the middle of doing something when something else happens in the future. But it is not impossible. When such an example is elicited, the resulting sentence, for example (8.3b), proves to destroy the apparent parallelism between the EC and the PC.

(8.3)   a.   **EC:** Mari ′fog lesielni   a   lejtőn.
                   Mari will down(VM)-ski-INF the slope-on
                   'Mari will ski down the slope (still).'

         b.   **PC:** Mari ′sielni   ′fog ′le   a   ′lejtőn, amikor...
                   Mari ski-INF will down(VM) the slope-on when
                   'Mari will be skiing down the slope, when ...'

Furthermore, as (8.4) shows, the PC shows V>VPr order even when both verb and VPr are post-auxiliary, in the presence of a PV focus—in spite of the general belief that PV focus neutralises the grammatical expression of aspectual distinctions (É. Kiss 1994, 47)[3].

(8.4)   ′Mari fog ′sielni   ′le   a   ′lejtőn, amikor...
           Mari will ski-INF down(VM) the slope-on when
           'It's Mari that will be skiing down the slope, when ...'

(8.3b) and (8.4) indicate that there must be a fundamental difference between the relationship between structure and interpretation involved in the PC to that involved in the EC. This runs contrary to all existing syntactic analyses, but is predicted by the dynamic account of VM behaviour worked out in Chapter 7.

8.2.2 The AspP analysis

É. Kiss's more recent analysis (2002, 62–67) avoids many of the problems associated with abstract operators by replacing PROG and EXIST with a pre-verbal AspP projection, whose head may be specified as carrying different aspectual features (e.g. [+/−eventive], [+/−perfective]). As mentioned in Chapter 3, this is no longer a 'single position' analysis of PV: VMs are claimed

---

[3] Here the need to keep the verb and VPr prosodically distinct for the sake of the PC appears to lead to the suspension of the usual destressing of post-verbal material in the presence of a focus. The tensed verb remains destressed, however, so the essential prosodic signal of the PV relation is maintained.

to be generated post-verbally and move to Spec,AspP in 'neutral' sentences. The verb is also assumed to move to the Asp head position to check aspectual features. When the features of the Asp head do not match those of any VM, the VM is omitted entirely, or, if the directional semantics of the VM is essential to the meaning of the intended verbal predicate, it remains *in situ*—below the verb, which still moves to Asp. Since É. Kiss assumes that material within the VP is always referential, the VM in such cases is not read as part of a complex verbal predicate but rather as a referential directional adverb. This account therefore has the virtue of deriving the word order of the PC in a way that explains Kiefer's (1994) observation that the VPrs involved in the PC always maintain 'literal' directional semantics.

On the matter of this 'literalness' constraint, the evidence is that the conclusion reached by É. Kiss is the right one. As Kiefer points out, VPrs in the PC are interchangeable with a form bearing the suffix *-felé*, which uncontroversially produces an adverbial form (rather in the manner of changing *down* to *downwards* in English). For instance, the examples in (8.5) are essentially equivalent in meaning and appear to involve the same grammatical construction.

(8.5) a. ′Ment ′le   a   ′lépcsőn, amikor ...
           went down the   stair-on when

       b. ′Ment ′lefelé   a   ′lépcsőn, amikor ...
           went downwards the   stair-on when
           'S/he was going down (on) the stairs, when ...'

The interchangeability of VPr and VPr-*felé* supports the idea that VPrs themselves have a purely adverbial function in the PC.

Another feature of É. Kiss's (2002) account with which my own analysis concurs (see section 8.3, below) is that it connects the EC to PV focus, thereby at least partially breaking the previously assumed parallelism of the EC and the PC and also explaining the prosodic character of the EC. É. Kiss argues that the EC must involve raising of the verb to F, the head of FP—although she does not explain how the interpretation of the EC relates to the interpretation of focus[4].

É. Kiss (2002) could be said to predict the data in (8.3b) and (8.4) (which she does not discuss), though only via some rather arbitrary assumptions about the conditions under which AspP is projected, which in some ways raise more questions than they explain. É. Kiss posits the projection of AspP in the post-auxiliary domain when the sentence contains a PV (i.e. pre-auxiliary) focus or negation, in order to account for the fact that VMs precede the main verb infinitive under these circumstances. The would be consistent with the data from the PC with an auxiliary.

---

[4]Besides the prosodic evidence, É. Kiss's stated reasons for connecting the EC to the FP projection are purely syntactic. She assumes that the verb in the EC must move to a higher position that AspP because she assumes that an adverb like *már* 'still', which may appear between the verb and VM in the EC, is adjoined to AspP. Note, however, that this contradicts É. Kiss's claim elsewhere in the same work that FP and AspP do not co-occur, which is her explanation of the post-verbal position of VMs in the presence of PV focus (see Chapter 3, section 3.3.3).

260 *Shifting the Focus*

However, the assumption of the presence of AspP in these circumstances seems otherwise quite *ad hoc*: there exists no reason independently of the data why AspP should be projected beneath tense in just these circumstances. After all, there is no AspP assumed beneath tense when PV focus appears before a finite main verb, nor can the projection of AspP be connected to the position of the main verb, since the verb is said to move to Asp, not *vice versa* (and this would in any case contravene É. Kiss's generally Minimalist approach).

Thus, while the use of AspP and FP in the analysis of the PC and EC represents a considerable improvement on the 'abstract operator' approach in terms of empirical coverage, it falls short of truly explaining the relationship between the structures involved and their interpretations. To the extent that É. Kiss's (2002) analysis does have explanatory value, this can be viewed as a technical reflection of certain insights that are more fully explicated through the dynamic account of the behaviour of VMs, as developed in Chapter 7.

8.3 THE MAIN PREDICATION ANALYSIS

The existence of both the EC and the PC and their associated interpretations follow, without further stipulation or the introduction of any new machinery, from the analysis of VM behaviour in terms of main predication. Moreover, further data discussed by Kiefer (1994), involving postverbal occurrences of bare nominals (BNs), are explicable by the same reasoning that accounts for the PC with VPrs.

8.3.1 Explaining the 'progressive construction'

Before turning to the PC itself, consider what happens when a BN follows the main verb, and both carry a pitch accent. The sentence that results has a perfective aspectual reading, as shown in (8.6), despite the durative reading normally associated with the combination of a BN and a verb (in BN>V order).

(8.6)   Jancsi ′vágott ′fát.
        Jancsi cut   wood-ACC
        'Jancsi has cut wood.'

Thus, such sentences appear structurally similar to the PC, yet have practically the opposite aspectual effect. Under the 'abstract operator' approach, there is no alternative but to posit the existence of a further, perfective operator (Bende-Farkas 2002, 135). Note that the prosodic similarity of this perfective operator with the PC but not with the EC would be unexplained in this case.

É. Kiss's (2002) AspP analysis potentially fares better: assuming an AspP carrying the feature [+perfective], a BN would not be expected to raise to Spec,AspP, so this word order is in a sense predicted. On the other hand, the AspP account suggests that BNs are inherently non-perfective, since this must presumably be the reason for their unmarked pre-verbal position, in which case it is unclear how there can be a BN in a sentence like (8.6) at all. There is an alternative motivation for the usual raising of BNs—in fact the one proposed by É. Kiss (2002, 70), who is vague on the aspectual properties of BNs—which is their non-referentiality (given É. Kiss's association of VP-internal positions with referential expressions). This faces essentially the same problem: the position of the BN in (8.6) should be an impossibility. Note that the reasoning applied by É. Kiss to post-verbal VPrs cannot be employed in this case: the BN as such cannot be said to contribute an indispensable part of the semantics of the verbal predicate—even if the nominal were somehow essential, this would give no reason why it should be unquantified.

In fact, I show below that part of É. Kiss's reasoning here captures an important insight: the BN in sentences like (8.6) does have to take on a kind of referential reading. However, the process by which it does so can only be coherently expressed within a dynamic, interpretation-based approach and with inference over extra-linguistic context. The relevant correspondence between word order and meaning could of course be forced using the tools of a modern generative framework, but not without the entirely *ad hoc* move of adding some feature like [+referential] to a bare nominal (within a language in which (non-)referentiality seems generally to be determined compositionally inside the NP), in addition to features relating to complex contextual constraints.

The basic matter that the AspP approach seems implicitly to reflect is whether or not the VM and verb form a complex predicate in a given construction. As mentioned in Chapter 7, the conditions for interpreting a VM+V combination with the structure of a complex predicate of the appropriate kind include prosodic phrasing that ensures that VM and verb are grouped together as a unit that carries a single pitch accent, rather than each carrying a separate accent, and the VM preceding the verb where possible (that is, *modulo* independent morphological constraints). Both of these facts follow from the main predication analysis. As outlined in Chapter 6, every non-topical expression that carries a pitch accent (that is, every 'information focus') is treated as a separately asserted predicate, even though only one of these is the main predicate. Furthermore, it is shown in Chapter 7 that the necessary semantic structure for the combined meanings of VM+V combinations are introduced by the VM and that if the verb's semantic contribution is assessed first, this structure cannot be subsequently created. It follows that if a VM appears post-verbally and accented, it cannot be interpreted as part of a VM+V complex. Therefore, the only VMs that do appear in this kind of construction will be those particular cases that, due to elements of their lexical semantics and/or their relation to extra-linguistic context, are capable of taking on an independent reading.

This accounts for the progressive aspect and the adverbial reading of VPrs in the PC. A PC sentence like (8.7a) (cf. É. Kiss 1994, 47) turns out to be nothing more than (8.7b) (i.e. (7.5a) repeated with indications of stress added) with an extra adverbial expression. The verb contributes the same semantic material, not being a part of any complex verbal predicate. It is therefore unsurprising that (8.7a) and (8.7b) show compatibility with the same durative adverbial phrase.

(8.7) a. Mari öt percig 'sielt 'le a 'lejtőn.
Mari five minute-for skied down the slope-on
'Mari skied downwards on the slope for five minutes.'

b. Mari öt percig 'sielt a 'lejtőn.
Mari five minute-for skied the slope-on
'Mari skied on the slope for five minutes.'

The same argumentation also accounts for, and by extension helps to define, a complex and rather obscure kind of constraint on post-verbal accented BNs. The PC therefore encapsulates these cases and can henceforth be understood as both 'progressive construction' and 'perfective construction'. The constraints in question are described by Kiefer (1994), who notes that sentences like (8.6) or (8.8a) are possible, while judging (8.8b) unacceptable (the asterisk is Kiefer's).

(8.8) a. 'Szedett 'szilvát.
plucked plum-ACC
'S/he has picked plums.'

b. *'Nézett 'tévét.
watched television-ACC
'S/he has watched television.'

In addition, some V>BN structures require certain contexts to make them acceptable. For example, Kiefer comments that "the acceptability of [(8.9a)] depends on whether—in the given context—the sentence can be interpreted as having made available grass for some purpose" and notes that this accounts for the more marginal status of (8.9b), since "the contexts in which hair is needed are less obvious than the ones in which grass is needed" (1994, 447).

(8.9) a. 'Vágott 'füvett.
cut grass-ACC
'S/he has cut grass.'

b. 'Vágott 'hajat.
cut hair-ACC
'S/he has cut hair.'

Simply making the object available for some purpose cannot be the condition on the PC with BNs, however. Kiefer notes that (8.10ab) are also acceptable.

(8.10) a. 'Mosott 'kezet.
washed hand-ACC
'S/he has washed his/her hands.'

b. ′Tisztított ′cipőt.
   cleaned shoe-ACC
   'S/he has cleaned his/her shoes.'

It is also noticeable that the PC brings about some kind of 'individuation' of the BN. The hands and shoes in (8.10a,b) are inferred to be the particular ones belonging to the subject of the sentence. Similarly, (8.11a) and (8.11b) show that the BN is interpreted as referring to an individual cake or letter, despite having a property reading only when in PV.

(8.11) a. ′Sütött ′tortát.
            baked cake-ACC
            'S/he has baked a cake.'
        b. Pisti ′írt ′levelet.
            Pisti wrote letter-ACC
            'Pisti has written a letter.'

Kiefer concludes that all the acceptable examples involve changes of state, and suggests that the objects of change of state verbs can always be individuated. Hence the unacceptability of describing television-watching using the PC, as in (8.8b): this is an activity that doesn't change the state of anything in the world. Further consideration of the role of context supports the broad outlines of this generalisation, but suggests that the relevant notion of 'change of state' cannot be too strictly extensional, but must be broad enough to accommodate activities that bring about what is conceptualisable as a change of state only in some internal, cognitive sense.

For example, Kiefer's rejection of (8.8b) itself appears to be too categorical, at least for some speakers. Certain kinds of context can rescue even this example. For example, imagine that János is living in a remote part of the countryside and Mari concludes that János can't possibly have heard about some momentous event that has occurred in Budapest. Under these circumstances, Ferenc may contradict Mari by uttering (8.8b): János will know the news, because he's watched television. The change of state involved here is one of János becoming informed as a result of 'sufficient' television watching.

This state of affairs is precisely what is expected from a dynamic perspective: grammatical procedures create a point in the parse at which only a certain kind of interpretation of an incoming expression can contribute to a coherent overall interpretation of the sentence. If the encoded semantics of the expression interact with the extra-linguistic context in such a way that the appropriate reading can be inferred, a coherent and relevant propositional form is created and the sentence is judged acceptable. In other cases, the sentence may appear quite impossible.

The nature of VPrs in the PC has already been accounted for in these terms. The details of the interpretation of BNs in the PC are as follows. When the verb appears before the BN, the argument-absorbing operation referred to in section 7.4 cannot take place and no complex predicate interpretation is possible. Instead, the normal predicate-argument and temporal structure associated with the verb in question is projected—and this structure cannot be destroyed in a monotonic system. In the case of the transitive verbs in examples (8.6)–(8.11), this includes the introduction of an object metavariable linked to the verb by the θ_{ACC} function. Thanks to the semantic type of the metavariable, this means that an individuated object referent is presupposed to exist. Therefore, when an accusative-marked BN is subsequently encountered as 'information focus' material, it can only be integrated into the eventuality by substitution for the metavariable, and this is only possible if it can be taken to introduce a referent.

Given that the lexical semantics of the BN only introduces a property, the quantification and consequent individuation of the BN can only come from some element of the extra-linguistic context, on the basis of relevance-theoretic inference. The fact that a certain quantity of grass or hair is required—say, for hay- or wig-making—gives a suitable quantification, for example. Similarly, there is a sense in which someone has to watch a certain amount of television before they can be reliably assumed to be informed about current affairs on this basis, so again a kind of quantity is inferable in just this kind of context. One may imagine semantic material being added to the propositional representation on the basis of this kind of contextual enrichment. For example, a quantifying predicate such as 'an amount appropriate for hay-making' may be introduced along with a variable that the predicate *grass'* can serve to restrict. The BN is thus able to contribute to a propositional form as if it were a full NP, if the grammatical context forces this as the only possible reading, and only if the extra-linguistic context provides the semantic material to complete this kind of contribution.

One final point remains to be explained (as it would have to be under any analysis of this phenomenon). Given that an individuated reading is required by the grammatical context in this way, one might ask why these forms exist, when a full NP could be used instead, requiring no inferential enrichment processes of this kind. There appear to be two (related) reasons for using a BN in this way, both of which are justified by the production of particular cognitive effects. One is the accurate communication of vagueness: no quantifier or determiner could adequately express the highly context-dependent quantities conveyed, which tend to be of the nature of 'some sufficient quantity for purpose x', rather than any numerically definable amount. Indeed, there need not be a clearly definable amount even in principle (as in the television-watching case), as long as the context makes the existence of some degree of quantification a relevant factor. This leads on to the other reason: the relative unimportance of precise quantification. Even in cases like (8.11a,b), in which the stereotypical production of one object at a time leads to the inference of a strict quantity, this quantity is not important to the meaning of the sentence as a whole: the important message is that the action in question (e.g. letter-writing or cake-baking) took place up to some point at which it could be inferred to be a completed action—i.e. an accomplishment. It so happens that in most contexts this is when a single letter or cake has been produced, so these examples appear to have the translations that Kiefer gives them, but this could not be said to be the main point of the utterance. The communicator thus chooses to employ an unquantified NP in order to emphasise the purpose of the action described rather than simply 'measuring' it.

8.3.2 Explaining the 'existential construction'

As made clear in the discussion of É. Kiss (2002) in section 8.2.2, the structural properties of the EC point quite clearly to its being a species of PV focus. Remarkably, this possibility has been largely ignored in the literature, the generally held assumption apparently being that the EC must be viewed as a quite independent, irreducible phenomenon, whence the treatment of it as the result of an EXIST operator in some pre-verbal position. The most recent and thorough account of this construction, Piñón (to appear), retains this strategy, without entertaining any possible link at an interpretive level to the nature of PV focus (Piñón mentions the structural similarity to focusing only to mount a purely syntactic argument against É. Kiss's (1994) locating the EXIST operator in the same position as focus—an issue that does not arise from a dynamic perspective). As noted above, such analyses therefore fail to account for the prosodic character of the EC in particular.

The general unwillingness to link the EC and focus is presumably related to a perception that the former involves a quite unique kind of interpretation, and indeed there are aspects of the meaning of the EC that seem quite idiosyncratic—in particular, the constraint against its occurrence with 'one-time-only' eventualities, as illustrated in (8.2). Yet there are also many clear parallels on the interpretive side between focus and the EC. Most importantly, the EC involves the presupposition of an eventuality as the background for an assertion. Recall the description of the EC from section 8.2 (which is based on that in É. Kiss 2002): the EC asserts that an eventuality of a certain kind has occurred already or will occur at some point in the future (with the possibility of recurrence in both cases). In effect, the existence of an instance of the eventuality in question is asserted. For this to be the assertion, the nature of the eventuality must be presupposed. Indeed, the relevance of such an assertion is typically established in relation to a manifest assumption that such an event has not happened and/or can't happen. In other words, the EC regularly has the 'corrective' sense that is often associated with the use of PV focus.

Thus, it seems quite accurate to describe the EC sentence in (8.1b), repeated here as (8.12), as containing the focus frame 'an eventuality of János opening his car without a key' and the assertion that an instance of such an eventuality exists at a temporal index (which is separately established as a past time referent within the temporal logic system). This gives a natural explanation to the prosodic structure of the EC: the unstressed post-verbal material simply has the same phonological characteristics as any other presupposed focus frame.

(8.12)   János 'nyitotta ki   az autóját   kulcs nélkül.
         János opened out the car-his-ACC key   without
         'János has opened his car without a key (before).'

Another piece of evidence that supports the analysis of the EC as a kind of focus comes from its interaction with 'definiteness effect' verbs. As mentioned in Chapter 5, section 5.2.2, the definiteness effect is known to be neutralised by PV focus on a constituent other than the internal argument. That is, in the presence of focus the internal argument is able to be a definite NP (with the verb as usual appearing in the 'definite conjugation' when it has a definite object) even with verbs that normally require an indefinite internal argument. An example of such a verb is *hoz* 'bring', as shown in (8.13a,b,c). The EC also allows for the appearance of a definite internal argument with verbs like *hoz*, as shown in (8.13d).

(8.13)   a.   János ′hozott   egy ′széket.
               János brought(INDEF) a   chair-ACC
               'János brought a chair.'

       b.   *János ′hozta   a   ′széket.
               János brought(DEF) the chair-ACC

       c.   ′János hozta   a   széket.
               János brought(DEF) the chair-ACC
               'It's János who brought the chair.'

       d.   János ′hozta   a   széket.
               János brought(DEF) the chair-ACC
               'János has brought the chair (already).'

This is a strong indication that the EC not only bears structural similarities to PV focus, but involves the same kind of interpretation.

If the EC involves focus, what is in focus? That is to say, what is the main predicate that takes on this focus reading? A syntactically focused expression is expected to be found to the immediate left of a destressed tensed verb, but the EC construction shows the tensed verb lacking any such PV expression and carrying stress itself. Is it possible that the verb itself is in focus? The future version of the EC, with auxiliary *fog*, shows that, despite the appearance of examples like (8.12) and (8.13d), the EC cannot boil down to focus on the main verb, since here, uniquely, the auxiliary is stressed (as in (8.3a))[5]. The 'early' position of the main verb in (8.12) and (8.13d) is therefore once again down to independent morphological necessity. The most obvious hypothesis is therefore that it is the tensed verb that is structurally 'in focus' in the EC and that this corresponds to temporal information itself being the main predicate.

This idea explains many properties of the EC. As outlined in Chapter 6, section 6.4, according to Kempson *et al.* (2001), the contribution of tense to the description of any eventuality provides the essential 'anchor' point, but the remaining semantic content of tense is processed quite separately. This means that the temporal anchor is uniquely suited to asserting the existence of an eventuality whose descriptive content is entirely presupposed: if an eventuality obtains at an index T_i, it must exist—and if this is all that is asserted of the eventuality at the point of main predication, all of its content must be retrievable from context.

---

[5] As noted in Chapter 3, this is problematic for Szendrői's (2003) stress-based analysis of PV effects, which claims that VM>*fog*>V$_{[-FIN]}$ order is due to *fog* and similar auxiliaries having an inherent inability to carry a primary stress (see also É. Kiss 2002, 206).

Nevertheless, one might expect a different reading from placing the contribution of tense morphology in narrow focus. On the face of it, this idea is suggestive of contrast between one tense with another; readings such as 'It's not that he WILL eat the apple, but that he DID eat the apple'. In fact, not only is this not the reading associated with $V_{+TENSE} >$VM structures; it is not expressible using PV focus at all. Indeed, native speakers profess some puzzlement at how such a meaning should be expressed in Hungarian, the least awkward option apparently being that in (8.14).

(8.14) (?) János nem meg ′fogja enni   az almát,   hanem meg ′ette az almát.
János not VM will eat-INF the apple-ACC but   VM ate the apple-ACC
'It's not that János WILL eat the apple, but that he DID eat the apple.'

In other words, a purely phonological strategy, using unmarked word order, is the only way to convey such a meaning—just as in the case of contrastive focus on a universal quantifier, discussed in Chapter 5, section 5.6. As in that case, the reason for this is that the would-be focus simply cannot be the main predicate. In the case of tense, this is for reasons indicated in Chapter 6, section 6.4: the contribution of particular tenses or of the future auxiliary *fog* is not introduced into the semantic representation as predication over the main eventuality variable, but rather affects temporal variables via a separate logical system.

While the material associated with particular tenses and times does not predicate over the main eventuality, there is one semantic entity introduced by every tense morpheme that does. This is a function from eventualities to a temporal index, schematically represented in Chapter 6, section 6.4 as $f(e, \mathbf{T}_i)$. This function is therefore able to perform main predication as a result of a structural signal to interpret the tense morpheme as providing the main predicate. Recall that the meaning of this function on its own is simply that the eventuality e has a temporal index $\mathbf{T}_i$; in other words, the simplest possible indication that the eventuality occurs.

This is the most general way possible of asserting that an eventuality exists, in effect allowing for a propositional form with entirely presupposed content. In section 8.4, it will be shown that this has important consequences for the analysis of negation. The current point, however, is that a structural indication of focus on tense naturally yields a truly 'existential' reading that provides a clear basis for the interpretation of the EC.

In terms of the epsilon-based main predicate representations, the simple EC sentences (8.15a,b) both correspond to the formula in (8.16) (the difference between them being determined in the separate temporal logic system in which $\mathbf{T}_i$ is given some definition, relative to other times).

(8.15)   a.   Réka ′lakott (már)   Varsóban.
                 Réka lived   already Warsaw-in(VM)
                 'Réka has lived in Warsaw (before).'

          b.   Réka ′fog (még) lakni   Varsóban.
                 Réka will still   live-INF Warsaw-in(VM)
                 'Réka will live in Warsaw (still).'

(8.16) a. $f((\varepsilon, e\, [f(e, \mathbf{T}_i)\, \&\, \textit{live}'(e)\, \&\, \theta_{\text{NOM}}(e, \textit{reka}')\, \&\, \theta_{\text{LOC}}(e, \textit{in-warsaw}')]), \mathbf{T}_i)$

The structure of the EC is therefore related to the 'existential' part of its interpretation without further stipulation by the main predicate account: an eventuality with entirely presupposed content is asserted to exist by virtue of having some temporal anchor. Other elements of the interpretation follow to some extent by inference on this basis. The constraint on the repeatability of the eventuality (as illustrated by (8.2))—which Piñón (to appear) encodes in the truth-conditional semantics of his EXIST operator—results from one way of making relevant the assertion of the existence of an instance of an eventuality. The reasoning involved is the following: the fact that the eventuality is known to have one occurrence may be taken as evidence for its being not impossible and therefore as evidence that it may happen again. Thus, the EC has an encoded 'existential' part and an inferred 'evidential' part to its meaning, corresponding to its two most common names in the literature. For example, in (8.12), the fact that János has opened his car without a key before means that it is reasonable to believe he could do so again—and any previous expectations that he could not manage this are thereby contradicted. Similarly, (8.15a,b) provide evidence that Réka is always capable of living in Warsaw (despite the addressee's doubts about her dealing with a Polish-speaking environment, say), in the form of the knowledge that she has lived there before or is known to be going to live there. If this is the way in which the EC assertion of the existence of an eventuality achieves relevance, it is clearly incompatible with eventualities that are intrinsically limited to one occurrence, such as that in (8.2).

It is not clear, however, that this is the only kind of inference that could be drawn from the existence of an instance of a given eventuality. It may be that this construction has become to some extent conventionalised to perform its 'evidential' function, as has apparently also happened to the English construction *x has V'ed before* (compare (8.2) with the English sentence ??*Réka has been born in Budapest before*, which is intuitively infelicitous for similar reasons.). Indeed, the EC shares a number of features with kinds of perfective aspect manifested in many languages, as detailed by Piñón (to appear), suggesting that it may express some universal aspectual function, in some sense. Even if this is the case, the current analysis suggests that everything beyond the basic existential element of the interpretation should be viewed as some higher-level constraint on the use of the construction, rather than a matter of direct syntactico-semantic encoding. This might be comparable to the association of certain syntactic constructions with particular registers. Encoding further detail into the interpretation of the construction as such is undesirable since the restriction of the encoded meaning to the 'existential' assertion is consistent with the explanation of so many other aspects of the syntax of PV. These include the involvement of tense in the syntax and interpretation of negation, as shown below.

8.4 NEGATION

Chapter 7 shows why VMs tend to be main predicates and hence appear in PV. This in turn provides an explanation for the postposing of VMs in the presence of syntactically focused constituents: since these foci are also main predicates, and main predication must be associated with PV, no VM can appear between the focused expression and the tensed verb.

Focus in PV is not the only thing that causes VMs to postpose. As mentioned in Chapter 3, the negative particle *nem* appears immediately before the tensed verb in cases of 'sentential negation' and this causes any VM to appear post-verbally, as shown in (8.17a). Does this mean that *nem* is also a main predicate? It appears not, for the syntactic parallelism between *nem* and narrow focus is not complete. Unlike a focused expression, *nem* may in fact, under certain circumstances, co-occur pre-verbally with an item that can be a VM. Also, only one narrow focus may appear pre-verbally, as the main predication analysis predicts, but *nem* can appear pre-verbally alongside a PV narrow focus.

This may occur in either of two ways, with *nem* either preceding or following the PV item with which it co-occurs. In the latter case, this means that *nem* appears between the PV item and the tensed verb. A PV item that precedes *nem* in this way is necessarily interpreted as a narrow focus. The negative particle in such cases is destressed, and is interpreted as part of the focus frame, even though it appears before the tensed verb. This use of negation is illustrated in (8.17b)[6].

When *nem* precedes a co-occurring PV item, the scope of negation is felt to be different: the reading is one of 'constituent negation' of the expression to the right of *nem*, rather than sentential negation. In this case too the co-occurring PV item must be read as a narrow focus, even if it is a VM. This is as expected: it is in the nature of constituent negation that it is an assertion about an individual expression in the context of a presupposed eventuality—specifically, the assertion that the denotation of that expression does not participate in the specified way in the eventuality in question. This is exemplified in (8.17c,d).

(8.17) a. Kati 'nem mászott fel   a fára   öt perc   alatt.
            Kati not climbed up(VM) the tree-on five minute under
            'Kati didn't climb up the tree in five minutes.'

        b. Kati a 'vadgesztenyefára   nem mászott fel   öt perc   alatt.
            Kati the horse-chestnut.tree-on not climbed up(VM) five minute under
            'It's the horse-chestnut tree that Kati didn't climb in under five minutes
            [i.e. she did climb all other trees/things in under five minutes].'

---

[6] Another reading is possible when a VM precedes *nem*; the so-called 'emphatic' reading which has roughly the impact of 'Indeed I didn't/won't P' (see, for example, Piñón 1992). I take this to require a somewhat more complex analysis than the case of simple narrow focus on the VM, and note here simply that it broadly fits into the predicted pattern: a negative eventuality is presupposed and the VM introduces an assertion with regard to it.

c. Kati nem ′felmászott   a   fára   (hanem ′lemászott   a   fáról)
    Kati not up(VM)-climbed the tree-on but   down(VM)-climbed the tree-from
    öt   perc   alatt.
    five minute under
    'Kati didn't climb UP the tree, but DOWN it, in five minutes.'
d. Kati nem a ′vadgesztenyefára   mászott fel   öt perc   alatt.
    Kati not the horse-chestnut.tree-on climbed up(VM) five minute under
    'It's not the horse-chestnut tree that Kati climbed in under five minutes [but something else].'

As noted in Chapter 3, the behaviour of *nem* has been argued to be incompatible with any 'single position' analysis of PV phenomena. Piñón (1992), for example, makes explicit the nature of the problem, which is widely assumed in more recent work: if foci and *nem* may co-occur before the tensed verb, and in either order, as in (8.17b,c,d), then it cannot be the case that there is a single syntactic position that represents the pre-verbal location of foci, *nem* and VMs, nor could such a position be said to explain the postposing of VMs in the presence of either *nem* or a focus. A common syntactic solution in recent work is to posit two positions for negation in the pre-verbal domain, in the form of two NegP projections, one above an FP projection for foci and one below it (e.g. Koopman & Szabolcsi 2000, É. Kiss 2002; É. Kiss attributes the idea to Olsvay 2000). Generally, the postposing of VMs with negation is derived by some parallel mechanism to that which is used to cause postposing in the presence of focus, such as movement of the verb to the left of any VM, in the manner of Bródy 1990, 1995, whenever either FP or the lower NegP is filled (see, for example, Puskás 2000. É. Kiss 2002, 131, on the other hand, gives syntactic arguments against verb-movement to NegP, in line with her analysis of focus).

This apparent problem with negation is an artifact of conventional syntactic approaches and does not arise within the kind of processing-based approach that I assume (while the analysis involving NegPs and FP is neither necessary nor even available). Rather than assuming that VMs, foci and negation target a single syntactic position, my approach is based on interpretively significant relationships between such items and the expression of temporal information—and between each other. As such, whether two items can co-occur in a particular linear configuration depends not on the existence of certain abstract positions, but on the interpretive contribution of each item and whether their combination, in conjunction with any pertinent elements of procedural syntactic encoding, produces a coherent interpretation.

The fact that negation is able to co-occur with a PV focus therefore does not necessarily preclude the idea that a single meaningful relationship explains the pre-verbal position of VMs, narrow foci and *nem*. Rather, it is important to consider what the precise contribution of *nem* is and how this relates to the meaningful relationship in question—that is, to main predication. It is clear that negation is not in itself a predicate, in any sense that could make it parallel to the various functions over eventualities that perform main predication. It is therefore not in itself ever a main predicate and it is predictable from this that *nem* does not have precisely the distribution of narrow foci, VMs or main verbs. Its close association with main predication nevertheless follows straightforwardly from common conceptions of what negation is.

8.4.1 Negation and main predication

One connection between negation and uses of main predication is the involvement of presupposed eventualities. As Horn (1989) discusses at length, a negative proposition in some sense always presupposes the corresponding positive proposition. Horn comes to the conclusion that the relevant notion of 'presupposition' is a pragmatic one, rather than the logical conception of presupposition; a position that is of course consistent with the perspective taken on presupposition throughout the present work (indeed, Horn presents a neo-Gricean account that closely parallels Relevance Theory, in its concentration on the balance between effort and informative reward). This reflects a reasonable supposition about the nature of negative propositions in cognition: it is hard to see how we could conceptualise specific statements about non-existence and/or non-occurrence other than in relation to what we take to exist or occur. It also allows for a coherent treatment of negative propositions within the kind of extensionalised treatment of eventualities that I employ in this book: an eventuality bound by negative existential quantification being extensionally simply the empty set, this could only achieve relevance in relation to positive assumptions.

As a result, negation bears a close conceptual parallel to narrow focus, which also exists in the context of a presupposed eventuality. Since negation is treated in my analysis as a purely local operator (see section 8.5), the negated predicate, whether in the production of sentential or constituent negation, has a unique status in the propositional form, just as a narrow focus does. The parallel is not always obvious, since sentential negation frequently involves accommodation of the presupposition, giving the impression of a high degree of contextual 'newness', in contrast to the 'corrective' reading most commonly thought to be associated with PV foci, in which the presupposed focus frame is very obviously 'given' information (however incomplete this characterisation may be, as argued in Chapter 4). Nevertheless, it is intuitively clear that a dialogue cannot begin with a negative sentence, unless the addressee manifestly holds some relevant assumptions relating to the positive proposition to which this sentence corresponds.

As for the precise semantic contribution of linguistic negation, it is most commonly encountered in semantic representations as an operator, which may perhaps be applied to a variety of semantic objects, but with a certain structurally-defined scope. This allows for a maximally transparent correspondence between linguistic and semantic form, the contribution of a negative particle like *not* or *nem* being regularly represented directly in semantic formulae as the operator ¬. There is another significant way of thinking about the contribution of negation, however, that is recognised in certain key parts of the semantic literature: the idea that negation is in itself a mode of predication. This is encapsulated in Montague's (1973) syncategorematic analysis of negation (see also Horn 1989). There is a fairly obvious sense in which these two views coincide: the negation of any element by the application of an operator typically involves the negation of some predicate applied to a variable, and this may just as well be thought of as an act of negative predication. This is particularly clear in neo-Davidsonian representations, in which cases of the 'constituent negation' of an individual-denoting argument or adjunct (as in (8.17c)) are straightforwardly represented—using a single negative operator (rather than requiring the use of $\neq$, for example)—as the negation of a predicate that relates an individual to an eventuality. The distinction between 'constituent negation' and 'sentential negation' therefore involves no difference in the manner of negation, but rather a simple distinction in the kind of predicate that is negated— just as 'identificational focus' versus 'neutral' (topic>comment) interpretation has been shown to reduce to the kind of predicate that performs main predication.

In the epsilon calculus, this view of negation has further significance, since the expression of existence here involves an act of predication. The use of negation in this context was illustrated in passing in (6.12c,d) of Chapter 5, section 6.4.2; parallel examples are given in (8.18).

(8.18) a. $\neg hungry'(\varepsilon, x\,[cat'(x)])$
       b. $\neg cat'(\varepsilon, x\,[cat'(x)])$
       c. $\neg \exists x.\,cat'(x)$

(8.18a) states that 'The/A cat is not hungry'. That is, it merely denies that a presupposed logical subject has a certain property; the x selected with respect to the set of cats not being found within the set of hungry things. (8.18b), on the other hand, is equivalent to (8.18c). If the x selected with respect to the set of cats is not found in the set of cats, then this x must be a completely arbitrary object and the set of cats must be empty.

Applying this observation to the mixture of neo-Davidsonian decomposition and the epsilon calculus that I have proposed, it is clear that main predication can be negative as well as positive. That is, just as the application of a positive main predicate asserts the existence of an eventuality, a main predicate preceded by the negative operator asserts the non-existence of an eventuality with respect to the predicate in question. This is illustrated throughout section 8.5.

The epsilon- and eventuality-based form of representation thus has the potential to encapsulate the attractive features of both major views on negation. The operator $\neg$ exists in the representation as an explicit element corresponding to the linguistic negative particle, while the idea that negation is a mode of predication has clear significance in terms of the idea of negative main predication. When the word order facts in (8.17) are considered in the light of this idea, they receive an explanation of striking simplicity and generality—especially in comparison to the *ad hoc* stipulation of NegP projections in the conventional syntactic account[7].

---

[7] One notable alternative to more stipulative syntactic approaches is Payne & Chisarik's (2000) Optimality Theory account. While this is some ways more insightful, it shares the problems of OT in general: in many ways it only pushes back the stipulative aspect of the analysis one stage. A suitable series of violable constraints may produce the right word order effects, but one would like to know where these constraints come from and what status they really have. While OT constraints are hypothesised to be innate, they often have apparent functional bases, as Haspelmath (1999) points out—which leads back to more concrete issues like the cognitive impact of linear order and of certain kinds of phonological phrasing in different contexts.

8.5 THE HOMOGENEITY OF NEGATION

The essence of this explanation is that *nem* contributes a negative operator whose effect is always strictly local: it negates just the predicate that immediately follows it. In other words, *nem* corresponds to a strictly narrow scope operator. This proposal contradicts common assumptions about how negation must work, since sentential negation is generally taken to involve wide (at least VP-)scope application of the negative operator and only constituent negation is thought of as involving narrow operator scope.

This is typically assumed to be consistent with a general tendency for scope to be expressed in left-to-right terms in languages like Hungarian (hence the claim that Hungarian 'wears its LF on its sleeve'). The data in (8.17) are often dealt with in these terms, under the assumption that focus is also an operator, in some general sense. It is then possible to say that the lower operator has scope over all the material to its right, while the higher operator has scope over the lower one. This, it is assumed, is what leads to the sense of narrow-scope negation when *nem* precedes and, by assumption, c-commands a focused expression—while negation has wide scope, but comes within the focus frame, when the precedence/command relation is reversed (see É. Kiss 1987, 54, citing Hunyadi 1981).

I will show, however, that narrow scope application of negation to a main predicate, in precisely the way suggested by the surface syntactic evidence, leads, via inference, to an interpretation equivalent to sentential negation. This creates a more parsimonious explanation of negation in Hungarian than that allowed for by the assumption of varying scope. If the semantic scope of the negative operator is consistently narrow, there is no need to invoke an independent explanation (that is, in terms of syntactic mechanisms) to account for the narrow scope of *nem* when it appears before a focused expression—that is, in cases of 'constituent negation'. In the kind of scope-based account outlined above, this is at least explained in terms of a fairly general principle claimed about the syntax of Hungarian, but the basis of the crucial assumption that focus should be treated as an operator-like object has been shown, in Chapter 4, to be unsustainable. Furthermore, as will be shown below, it proves unnecessary to specify the possible syntactic positions of *nem* when the effects of a consistently narrow scope operator are considered in the context of different kinds of predicate. This removes the need for essentially *ad hoc* NegP projections.

In the rest of this section, I discuss each of the principal word order possibilities involving *nem*, illustrating how each follows from the idea of pre-tense main predication developed in Chapter 6, in conjunction with the maximally simple assumption that the semantic contribution of *nem* is a consistently local operator over predicates of eventualities.

8.5.1 'Constituent negation'

The narrow scope, 'constituent negation' reading of the order *nem* > focus > V falls out naturally in my approach as an example of negative main predication involving a participant-denoting expression. This is exemplified in (8.19) (once again I use a sentence containing *fog* and an

274 *Shifting the Focus*

infinitival main verb to clarify the encoding of main predication).

(8.19)   Ferenc nem Marit   fogja látni.
         Ferenc not Mari-ACC will see
         'It's not Mari that Ferenc will see.'

The interpretation of (8.19) proceeds much as the interpretation of any sentence containing a narrow focus, as discussed in detail in Chapter 6. The accusative NP *Marit* is recognised, by virtue of its pre-tense position and the destressing of subsequent material, to be the main predicate. This is just the same procedure as in a positive sentence containing narrow focus: the assertion of a non-verbal predicate as the main predicate causes a search through the context for a presupposed, 'focus frame' eventuality that can act as the logical subject of this act of predication, such that a full propositional form is created thereby. The only difference is that in the case of (8.19) the presupposed, 'focus frame' eventuality of Ferenc seeing someone is asserted to *not* exist within the set of eventualities with Mari as Object. This is a truth-conditional assertion with all the necessary elements of a proposition and thus main predication is achieved by means of this negative predication, just as in the positive cases already encountered. It is represented as in (8.20a).

(8.20)   a. $\neg\theta_{ACC}((\varepsilon, e\ [f(e, \mathbf{T}_i)\ \&\ see'(e)\ \&\ \theta_{NOM}(e, ferenc')\ \&\ \theta_{ACC}(e, \mathbf{U})]),\ mari')$
         b. $\neg\theta_{ACC}((\varepsilon, e\ [f(e, \mathbf{T}_i)\ \&\ see'(e)\ \&\ \theta_{NOM}(e, ferenc')\ \&\ \theta_{ACC}(e, mari')]),\ mari')$

As usual, the metavariable $\mathbf{U}$ can be substituted by *mari'*, yielding (8.20b), which denies the existence of any eventuality of Ferenc seeing Mari[8]. It is the intermediate representation in (8.20a) that makes the word order in (8.19) relevant, however. Were the intention simply to deny the existence of such an eventuality, a 'neutral' word order could be employed (see below), without putting the addressee to the effort of seeking a focus frame that would make the main predicatehood of $\theta_{ACC}(e, mari')$ relevant. The cognitive effects of (8.19) are therefore signalled to be based in the presupposition that Ferenc will see someone and the fact that this will not be Mari.

Note that the combination of the epsilon calculus and inferential reasoning delivers the right truth-conditions here: the eventuality of Ferenc seeing someone at $\mathbf{T}_i$ is not asserted not to exist; it simply does not exist in the set of eventualities with Mari as Object. Indeed, establishing the relevance of (8.19) necessarily involves the recovery of an eventuality of Ferenc seeing someone at $\mathbf{T}_i$, thus leading to the sense that this is strictly presupposed information. The survival of this 'existential presupposition' under negation has been taken to be evidence that constructions like Hungarian PV focus involve a 'semantic presupposition' (e.g. Bende-Farkas 2002), but the

---

[8]Once again it must be emphasised that all representations are used in context, meaning that only relevant eventualities come into question. The representation in (8.20b) need not be deemed inappropriate if future eventualities that are not relevant in the current context include Ferenc seeing Mari.

present analysis shows that the interpretation in question follows from general processes of inference over a particular kind of predication. Furthermore, no auxiliary assumptions about the interaction of the scope of negation with the 'scope of focus' are required: the correct interpretation follows from a single act of predication.

The fact that *nem* can precede a narrow focus in PV is therefore straightforwardly explained as a special case of main predication. The operator introduced by the occurrence of *nem* does not need to have its scope determined by syntactic means; it simply converts an act of predication from a positive one into a negative one. It is less immediately obvious how this can be the basis of an explanation of how *nem* can intervene between a PV focus and the tensed verb. This requires an extra inferential step that relates to what it means for an eventuality to be negated. Discussion of the order focus > *nem* > V is therefore delayed until simpler cases of sentential negation have been accounted for.

8.5.2 Simple sentential negation

Sentential negation is signalled by the appearance of *nem* immediately before the tensed verb. Recall that this effectively means that *nem* precedes tense, rather than the verb as such, as is clear when the tensed verb is the purely temporal auxiliary *fog*, so that an item that precedes a finite main verb can be interpreted as preceding tense whenever a linear relationship to tense is significant. This is important for my analysis of sentential negation, given that I make the assumption that the negative operator introduced by *nem* always operates locally over the predicate to its right. Putting this assumption together with the data, it seems that a sentence containing what is thought of as sentential negation in fact involves the negation of the temporal predicate that is contributed by tense. This is seen clearly in a future time sentence such as (8.21).

(8.21) Ferenc nem fogja látni   Marit
        Ferenc not will see-INF Mari-ACC
        'Ferenc will not see Mari.'

Unlike in (8.19), there is nothing here in between *nem* and the tense-carrying verb that could be construed as the main predicate; there is no narrowly focused constituent which may be interpreted as a locally negated expression, to be interpreted in the context of a presupposed focus frame. Note that, unlike in the case of a positive sentence, even the main verb would necessarily be interpreted as a narrow focus were it to precede the auxiliary in this case, being locally negated. But this is not the case in (8.21). What remains as the negated main predicate here is tense itself. The propositional form that results is therefore as in (8.22).

(8.22) $\neg f((\varepsilon, e\, [f(e, \mathbf{T}_i)\, \&\, see'(e)\, \&\, \theta_{\text{NOM}}(e, ferenc')\, \&\, \theta_{\text{ACC}}(e, mari')]), \mathbf{T}_i)$

In effect, (8.22) says that a selected eventuality of Ferenc seeing Mari does not exist, since it is not found in the set of eventualities with the temporal anchor $\mathbf{T}_i$ (which is restricted to future times by the separate temporal logic system). This amounts to a simple negation of the existence of the eventuality, because of the nature of the temporal anchor.

In section 8.3, positive narrow focus on tense was shown to produce not contrast between different time frames, but a simple assertion of the existence of a presupposed eventuality. This follows if specifications of how a time referent relates to other times are determined by a separate logical system and so cannot possibly perform main predication[9]. The part of the semantic contribution of tense that can perform main predication is a function linking the eventuality to a time that is not specified with respect to a time frame by this function. This means that focus on tense can only assert the existence of the eventuality by virtue of its having a time of occurrence. In section 8.3 it was argued that this assertion of existence leads to the 'existential/experiential' reading conveyed by the EC.

It follows that applying the negative operator to tense, in the absence of any other main predicate, will produce an assertion of the non-existence of the eventuality, without producing a sense of contrast with regard to any of its semantic content. That sentential negation should be the negative equivalent of the EC may seem a surprising result, given that the latter is thought of as a highly marked construction, while sentential negation seems intuitively quite basic. This impression, however, is explicable simply by reference to the contexts in which the meaning associated with each would be relevant. Both constructions work in relation to presuppositions of the opposite polarity—the EC achieves relevance in relation to the assumption that the eventuality in question has not happened (perhaps because it cannot), while sentential negation must relate to an assumption that a corresponding positive eventuality is at least a possibility, as noted above. The former is clearly a much more restricted kind of context; one may have any number of general assumptions that imply that a variety of manifest eventualities are more or less possible, but the assumption that some particular eventuality will not happen or has not happened is much more specific. This is inevitably the case, given the reasoning outlined above that negative propositions are effectively parasitic on positive ones. Note that this is reflected in the form of representation developed in Chapter 6: the existence of a temporal anchor is a default presupposition to any eventuality. At a technical level, then, a tense-negating negative sentence always has the presupposition required to give it relevance, while the negative presupposition required by the EC is the marked case.

The analysis of sentential negation as narrow scope negation of tense accounts for the PV-related position of *nem* on this reading. The idea that sentential negation must be strictly pre-tense for this reason in turn predicts the postposing of main verbs (as in (8.21)) when 'sentential'

---

[9]Again, the level at which meanings are lexicalised makes a difference: explicit time adverbials can be contrastively focused. The precise content of these adverbials and how they form links between different logical systems is a matter for future research; it is not, however, unreasonable to speculate that some of these, at least, may involve some form of relation between sub-eventualities, rather than between time referents as such. In any case, there is a clear intuitive difference between the way in which tense introduces and organises temporal information and the way this is done by lexical temporal expressions, which always accompany tense in any case, and this intuition is captured by the present analysis.

nem precedes an auxiliary like *fog*, and also the postposing of VMs, given the analysis that they have received in the previous chapter. To illustrate, consider (8.23), the negative sentence corresponding to (7.11).

(8.23) A háziasszony nem olvasztotta folyékonnyá a vajat.
       the housewife not melted   fluid-to   the butter-ACC
       'The housewife didn't melt the butter to (a) fluid (state).'

The basic representation of this would be as in (8.24) (cf. (7.17d)).

(8.24) $\neg f((\varepsilon, e\ [\text{TRANS}(e)\ \&\ f(e, \mathbf{T}_i)\ \&\ \text{P-SUB}(e, (\varepsilon, e_1\ [melt'(e_1)\ \&\ \theta_{\text{NOM}}(e_1, \textit{the-hw}')\ \theta_{\text{ACC}}(e_1, \textit{the-butter}')]))\ \&\ \text{R-SUB}(e, (\varepsilon, e_2\ [fluid'(e_2)\ \&\ Arg_1(e_2, \textit{the-butter}')])))]), \mathbf{T}_i)$

The close link between negation and tense has been noticed before. For example, Puskás (2000, 321) proposes that the pre-verbal position of sentential *nem* is attributable to the head of NegP requiring "to be construed with a tense feature", following work by Zanuttini (1996) on Italian. As it stands, this represents little more than a stipulation of adjacency to the tensed verb within a particular formalism. The present analysis, with its basis in interpretive procedures, provides a more genuinely explanatory foundation to the observations modelled syntactically in this way. Furthermore, it does so by means of exactly the same procedures as those that are responsible for constituent negation.

Note that the least marked main predicate differs in positive and negative sentences, but is in both cases one of the essential elements of a full proposition. In positive sentences, a VM or VM-less main verb is able to create existential quantification without producing a narrow focus reading, since these expressions introduce significant kinds of semantic structure, thereby linking a topical entity to other entities and asserting the existence of an eventuality containing the topical entity in a relevant fashion. In a negative sentence, on the other hand, the fact that the verbal or VM main predicate has specific semantic content forces it to take on a constituent negation reading, because it is processed in the context of the presupposed eventuality that accompanies negation for independent pragmatic reasons. For this reason, only the temporal anchor is semantically general enough to perform negative main predication without triggering a constituent negation reading.

8.5.3 Focus > *nem* > V

Above, I argue two crucial points in relation to the interpretation of *nem*: that its semantic contribution is simply an operator that applies locally to an act of predication and that the production of apparent wider scope negation involves inferences over the negation of temporal information. Note that there is nothing in this analysis of *nem* that links it necessarily to the main predicate. At a semantic level, there is nothing to prevent negation from appearing within the logical subject

278 *Shifting the Focus*

of main predication. However, pragmatic considerations demand that any such act of negation would have to be of an unmarked kind, corresponding to an apparently wide scope reading, since constituent negation can otherwise only achieve relevance in relation to a presupposed eventuality; that is, by assuming that the negated expression is a narrow focus. The current analysis therefore correctly predicts that negation is typically only found within a focus frame when it applies to the temporal predicate contributed by tense. This corresponds to the word order focus > *nem* > V, with *nem* unstressed, as part of the focus frame.

The appearance of *nem* before the tense-carrying verb does not block the signalling of main predication, since *nem* does not itself contribute a predicate, but only an operator that effectively changes the application of the tense function from positive to negative predication. This means that [*nem*+tense] is just a kind of temporal predicate, so that whatever precedes this complex can be considered to precede tense for the purposes of signalling main predication. Thus, the incremental interpretation of (8.25a), for example, will produce the representation in (8.25b), which by now-familiar steps of substitution and inference is equivalent to an existential proposition.

(8.25)   a.   FERENC nem fogja látni   Marit.
             Ferenc   not will   see-INF Mari-ACC
             'It's Ferenc who won't see Mari.'

         b. $\theta_{NOM}((\varepsilon, e\ [\neg f(e, \mathbf{T}_i)\ \&\ see'(e)\ \&\ \theta_{ACC}(e, mari')\ \&\ \theta_{NOM}(e, \mathbf{U})]), ferenc')$

Because of the negation of the temporal predicate within the epsilon term (i.e. within the logical subject of main predication), (8.25b) asserts the existence, in the set of events with Ferenc as Subject, of an event that is characterised by the presupposition that it does *not* to obtain at $\mathbf{T}_i$ (a time specified elsewhere to be a relevant future time). That is, a non-occurring event exists with respect to Ferenc-as-Subject. This almost self-contradictory assertion can be made relevant only via certain inferential steps. First, it is reasonable to assume that a non-occurring eventuality can only be conceptualised in contrast to a related eventuality that does occur—otherwise all non-occurring eventualities are the same, being extensionally the empty set. Consequently, the assertion that an event does not occur with respect to some particular individual in a certain participant role implicates that such an event does occur with respect to other individuals in that role. This is why (8.25b) receives the interpretation that Ferenc is contextually unique in not seeing Mari.

This pragmatic analysis correctly predicts a number of facts that are normally taken to require independent explanation by special syntactic mechanisms. One of these facts is that the order VM > *nem* > tense is only possible when the VM is to be given a focus reading. Despite the fact, as argued above, that the complex [*nem*+tense] is equivalent to tense alone for the purposes of main predication, a VM appearing before *nem* cannot produce a topic>comment reading as it normally can when it is the main predicate. This is once again due to the pragmatics of negating tense. Recall that applying a main predicate to an event whose presupposed temporal anchor point is negated is equivalent to asserting the existence of a non-occurring event. As discussed in relation to (8.25b), this can be made relevant in relation to a focus by the implicature that a parallel event does obtain at the anchor time with regard to contextual alternatives to the entity in focus. There is no similar way to make sense of the presupposition that an event does not occur within a topic>comment sentence, the very purpose of which is to newly ascribe a property to a presupposed entity. For purely pragmatic reasons, ascribing the *lack* of some property to an entity can only be relevant in a contrastive context, meaning that more than just the topic and the temporal anchor must be presupposed. This in turn means that whatever appears to the left of [*nem*+tense] will acquire a focus reading.

8.5.4 Why *nem* is pre-verbal

In addition to explaining the interaction of *nem* PV elements, the analysis developed in this section also accounts without further stipulation for the general lack of post-verbal instances of *nem*. As mentioned above, there is no formal reason why predicates other than the temporal anchor should not be negated within a 'focus frame' logical subject. That is, nothing in the technicalities of my approach rules out the post-verbal appearance of *nem*. Nevertheless, this is generally accepted to be ungrammatical, as (8.26) illustrates.

(8.26)   *János megette nem az almát.
         János VM.ate not the apple.ACC

Far from being a gap in the analysis, this represents the correct division of labour among different parts of the process of interpretation. Those applications of *nem* that prove impossible, as in (8.26), are ruled out by pragmatic considerations, making it is unnecessary to complicate the grammar with any further machinery to this end.

Just as a negated eventuality (in the form of an eventuality with a negated temporal anchor) is only made relevant in relation to an eventuality that is assumed to obtain, so the non-participation of a particular entity in a given eventuality can only be made relevant in terms of a contrast with at least one other entity that does participate in the relevant way. Otherwise, the list of entities that do not participate in a given way in a given eventuality is in principle infinite and irrelevant. For example, the information that 'the apple' is not the Object of the eating event in (8.26) could only be taken at the pragmatic level to signal the relevance of something else that does fill this role. But this reading requires the rest of the sentence to be the background to this contrast; it must be a focus frame, with the negated constituent in focus (that is, the main predicate). This is incompatible with the word order in (8.26), which is that of a 'neutral',topic>comment sentence; by definition, this cannot contain a narrow focus. Similarly, a focus frame itself cannot contain an expression that must be taken to be a narrow focus. It follows that non-temporal predicates cannot in general be negated following the main predicate and it follows in turn from this that negation does not surface to the right of the tensed verb. This does not need to be stipulated by grammatical mechanisms such as the proposal of NegPs, nor does *nem* have to be considered anything other than a local operator over predicates.

The argument in favour of the present analysis is thus principally one based on Occam's Razor, inferential pragmatic reasoning being independently necessary in any model of human linguistic abilities. There is, however, also some empirical evidence that supports the view that post-verbal negation is ruled out on pragmatic grounds only—albeit evidence from sentences whose acceptability is distinctly marginal. This comes from the phenomenon of 'double focus', whereby a sentence contains two contrastive foci, the second of which appears post-verbally, indicated purely by pitch accent. A full account of these pragmatically highly marked sentences is beyond the scope of this book, but their existence implies that post-verbal constituent negation should be possible in a similarly marked sense, in the presence of another, pre-tense focus.

This expectation seems to be borne out. The considerable complexity of adding the semantics and pragmatics of negation to an already highly marked construction means that examples are restricted to very unusual contexts and therefore elicit very marginal acceptability judgements, but according to the judgements of at least some native speakers, 'double focus' sentences show that post-verbal negation is not in fact impossible following the tensed verb, when the main predicate is a narrow focus. For example, (8.27) may, like its English translation, appear quite unacceptable at first sight, but, according to an informant, is possible in a special context such as the following.

The results of the annual chess tournament are being discussed. Mari is by far the strongest player and beat most of the people she played. All but one of the other matches were drawn. This means that only one player was beaten by an opponent other than Mari. If the identity of this person is questioned, (8.27) might be uttered.

(8.27) Jánost verte meg nem Mari.
János-ACC beat VM not Mari
'It's János who was beaten not by Mari.'

The marginal possibility of such examples supports the approach taken here: rather than stipulating the positions of negation by syntactic means, it is more revealing to ask in which positions negation can contribute to a coherent meaning in a given sentence. In addition to explaining the positions in which *nem* does and does not normally occur, on the basis of a very simple set of assumptions, this approach even predicts the circumstances under which negation may occasionally surface in otherwise blocked positions[10].

---

[10]É. Kiss (2002, 133) (citing Olsvay 2000) also gives examples like (8.27), with negation in the post-verbal domain, but her point is based on their non-existence where one theoretical approach would predict that they should be possible. However, she notably hedges her grammaticality judgement here—"ungrammatical, or very marginal"— and marks her examples in such a way that a cline in (un)acceptability is indicated. This is more consistent with an analysis in which the inaccessibility of the necessary context is responsible for the intuitive judgement than with one based on strict technical constraints.

8.5.5 Negation and the interpretive relevance of lexicalisation

As a final thought, it is worth noting that the facts from negation lend support to the analysis of resultative VMs in section 7.2, in terms of the relevance of the level at which aspectual information is lexicalised. As such, they provide a useful last illustration of the value of the basic theoretical points made in Chapters 1 and 2. A sentence like (8.23), repeated here as (8.28), is ambiguous between a reading in which the whole activity is not even initiated (e.g. 'The housewife didn't melt the butter to fluid. It was already rancid, so she just threw it out') and one in which the process part is initiated but the result state is not achieved (e.g. 'The housewife didn't melt the butter to fluid; she just made it soft enough to spread').

(8.28)　A　háziasszony　nem olvasztotta folyékonnyá a　vajat.
　　　　the housewife　not　melted　　fluid-to　　the butter-ACC
　　　　'The housewife didn't melt the butter to (a) fluid (state).'

This ambiguity is compatible with the means of representation exemplified in (8.24)—in a more fully worked out account, the different presupposed eventualities to which the different readings relate could differ in their internal structure, thanks to the possibility of manipulating the separate sub-eventuality predicates.

As Tóth (2001) points out, this ambiguity contrasts with the case of an accomplishment that is lexicalised in a VM-less verb. Thus, (8.29) is not ambiguous; unlike its English counterpart, it can only mean that János did not begin to eat an apple, not that he began but failed to finish one.

(8.29)　János nem evett egy almát.
　　　　János not ate　an apple-ACC
　　　　'János did not eat an apple (at all).'
　　　　not: 'János did not finish eating an apple.'

This is accounted for by the kind of semantic representation proposed, in which lexicalisation has an influence on the representation of meaning at cognitively significant levels. The appropriate relation between form and meaning is thus captured without the need to complicate the syntax with machinery that has only string-vacuous effects (as Tóth 2001 is forced to by the assumptions of her conventional syntactic framework). Nor does this involve any spurious redefinition of a structural representation as a semantic one. As argued in Chapters 1 and 2, investigating what linguistic forms actually encode cannot be simply a matter of defining truth-conditions and matching them to representations of linguistic structure (which will inevitably get more and more abstract as interpretation is considered in more detail). Only consideration of how the semantics of individual forms interact with each other and with context can tell us what kinds of meaning representation are in fact introduced at different levels of processing.

This short section thus serves to emphasise the importance of the perspective advocated in this book. The forms of natural languages us just what we need to guide 'pro-active' interpretation, which exploits a variety of human cognitive faculties. If we attempt to trace all identifiable (e.g. truth-conditional) meaning directly to grammatical objects, we stand only to duplicate the work of different cognitive modules and thereby to distort our model of linguistic competence.

8.6 SUMMARY

This chapter has accounted for issues concerning the syntax of VMs which remained from the discussion in Chapter 7 and has done so in terms of the main predicate analysis of PV. Indeed, the so-called 'progressive construction' (PC) proves to be a straightforward prediction of this analysis. Not only is this phenomenon accounted for without any further stipulation, so is its structural similarity to, yet interpretive difference from, the postposing of bare nominals. In effect, the PC involves main predication by the main verb. As predicted in Chapter 7, this means that complex predicate readings of the verb and VM are impossible, a fact that explains in turn a set of restrictions on the nature of post-verbal verbal prefixes and bare nominals, as noted in Kiefer (1994).

The other supposedly aspectual construction connected to VM position, the 'existential' or 'evidential' construction (EC), is shown to follow from the main predicate analysis, given the assumption made in Chapter 6 (after Kempson *et al.* 2001) that tense morphology introduces only an underspecified temporal anchor into the main propositional representation, other details of temporal semantics being dealt with in a separate temporal logic system. Narrow focus on this temporal anchor, through its serving as main predicate, therefore asserts the existence of a proposition that has entirely presupposed content. This provides a suitable basis for the inferential derivation of the meaning associated with the EC.

The last major question about VM syntax is why VMs typically postpose in the presence of sentential negation, despite the fact that the negative particle *nem* is compatible with other PV elements, in the shape of narrow foci. The negative particle cannot be a main predicate in itself, but is rather an operator that operates over predicates. The postposing of VMs in the case of sentential negation is explained if *nem* must be adjacent to the tensed element in order to create sentential negation. This requirement is predicted if *nem* is a consistently local (narrow-scope) operator and 'sentential negation' is created by negating a main predicating temporal anchor. Given the aforementioned assumptions about the semantics of tense, this kind of negation does indeed yield the reading associated with sentential negation (thus creating the impression of 'wide-scope negation' from the application of a narrow-scope operator). Inferential reasoning concerning the pragmatic utility of locally negating other elements of a sentence explains the restriction of *nem* to certain syntactic positions and to pre-verbal co-occurrence with only certain kinds of expression.

With an absolute minimum of additional assumptions, which are closely related to the surface evidence provided by the language, the main predication analysis thus proves to explain VM behaviours that relate to a wide range of interpretive effects. This removes the need to posit numerous abstract syntactic objects and a lot of complex encoded semantics. As in the previous analytical chapters of this book, a dynamic, inferentially informed approach results in a much more parsimonious and more explanatory account of the data.

9

SUMMARY AND CONCLUSIONS

9.1 THEORETICAL CONCERNS

While the larger part of this book is concerned with a fairly detailed analysis of the Hungarian syntactic position that is commonly thought of as the 'focus position', this has been presented expressly in the service of illustrating some quite fundamental theoretical arguments of broad applicability.

The overarching concern is with the need to identify which aspects of linguistically conveyed meaning should be attributed directly to the grammar of a language and which may instead be determined at least in part by inferential pragmatic processes. Chapters 1 and 2 argued (i) that this distinction is crucial if we are to produce good models of syntactic and semantic competence and (ii) that the distinction can only be accurately drawn through active consideration of extra-grammatical influences on meaning, in particular inferential pragmatics, so that their effects can be removed from the burden of explanation on the grammar. This argument develops a position already held within post-Gricean pragmatic frameworks like Relevance Theory (Sperber & Wilson 1986/95, Carston 2002), but points to the importance of going further, to investigate the implications of this position for syntactic as well as semantic theory.

Two fundamental assumptions of conventional approaches to syntax and semantics were argued to represent particular obstacles to the process of delineating the proper *explanandum* of a grammatical theory. One is the assumption of truth-conditional semantic compositionality. Though in principle not necessarily advocated in its strong form by all analysts, it was argued to have a considerable influence on both theory and practice in analysis of the syntax-semantics interface (indeed, the standard assumption of such an interface in itself betrays the pervasiveness of strongly compositional thinking). Furthermore, I argued in Chapter 1 (following Stanley & Szabó 2000) that conventional forms of syntactic and semantic analysis are in effect undermined by anything other than strong compositionality, despite the willingness of many analysts to accept a degree of pragmatic influence on truth-conditional semantics while pursuing conventional analytical frameworks.

The second problematic assumption comes from the syntactic side, and is no less fundamental. This is the idea that the structure that provides the input to semantic interpretation is defined statically over entire sentences (in a sense that applies equally to Montagovian frameworks and to those that assume that some more abstract Logical Form structure provides the input to interpretation). This not only encourages a highly compositional view of semantics (reflecting what Cann *et al.*, forthcoming, call a 'jigsaw view of language'), but also precludes the identification of some potentially highly significant contributions to meaning: inferences triggered by the state of a partial representation of meaning at some point during the parsing of a string. In order for such contributions to be recognised, so that their effects may be properly accounted for outside the grammar, a dynamic approach to linguistic structure and its relationship to meaning must be adopted, as argued in Chapter 2. I suggested that Dynamic Syntax (Kempson *et al.* 2001, Cann *et al.* forthcoming) provides a suitable perspective, though I did not adopt the existing technical tools of this framework in the present work, because of the particular nature of the data to be analysed. Relevance Theory was advanced as a well-grounded pragmatic theory which could be invoked to discuss inferential processes.

The resulting picture is one of linguistic forms acting as instructions for, or constraints on, the construction of propositional meanings—a process that is also informed by pro-active relevance-based inferential reasoning—rather than encoding them compositionally. This is consistent with what we know about parsing, which shows people exploiting considerations of relevance to context from the very beginning of the process of interpretation (Crain & Steedman 1985, Altmann & Steedman 1988).

9.2 EMPIRICAL ILLUSTRATIONS

The Hungarian data was used to illustrate problems with fundamental aspects of conventional approaches to linguistic analysis and the ability of the dynamic, inferential approach that I advocate to produce highly explanatory alternative accounts of linguistic data.

On one level, the rather *ad hoc* nature of many aspects of conventional syntactico-semantic accounts of the Hungarian 'focus position' (as briefly reviewed in Chapter 3)—multiple abstract syntactic projections to deal with different expressions sharing one surface position, discrete semantic operators posited to account for each possible interpretive effect, and so on—gives good reason on its own to question the theory and the methodology applied, but I also provided more concrete and decisive demonstrations of how the basis of conventional approaches leads to problems in dealing with the data. The central argument in this respect concerns the expression of 'exhaustive focus'. In Chapter 4, I discussed how the assumption of truth-conditional semantic compositionality leads inevitably to the conclusion that the exhaustive reading of 'focus position' foci is directly encoded in that position (there existing an unusually explicit exposition of the reasoning involved, in the form of Szabolcsi's 1981 analysis) and showed empirically that this conclusion is both undesirable and unsustainable. Despite its relatively obscure basis in a single syntactic phenomenon of Hungarian, this argument is highly significant from a broader perspective, as it represents a case in which linguistic data contradicts not just a single analysis but a fundamental assumption that underpins an entire family of analytical approaches.

It is also worth noting that while the decisive evidence (from section 4.6) depends on carefully constructed example sentences, there are plenty of indications from common usage of the 'focus position' and from the general pragmatic markedness of *non*-exhaustive focus that the encoded exhaustivity analysis is inappropriate. The fact that this style of analysis has been accepted throughout decades of scholarship, in spite of all this evidence, may be taken also as an illustration of the argument of Chapter 1 that a strong version of compositionality tends to underlie aspects even of analyses that purport not work to any such assumption.

In addition to demonstrating these theoretical points, Chapter 4 also provided some initial indications of the true nature of the focus reading. The exhaustivity of 'focus position' foci was argued to follow by simple and inevitable inferential processes from the assertion of a narrow focus. 'Focus position' foci are narrow in a certain sense, which was identified as interpretation in the context of a presupposed (and typically richly specified) eventuality.

This idea was developed in Chapter 5 into an explanation of quantified noun phrase (QNP) distribution in the pre-verbal field of Hungarian, which includes the so-called 'focus position'. No more than the assumption of two very basic interpretive procedures (with a close connection to information-structure) proved necessary to predict an apparently quite idiosyncratic distribution of QNPs, which an analysis in terms of quantifier semantics could not characterise adequately. The issue of QNPs also provided another demonstration of how compositional analysis of natural language can lead to unsustainable results: Szabolcsi's (1997b) otherwise highly insightful analysis of the QNP distribution is saddled by the need to fit with her semantic operator account of the 'focus position', which happens to be incompatible with cases of quantifier-in-focus. This forces the presumption of a purely quantificational position that superficially resembles the focus position, thus over-complicating the grammar and precluding the kind of simple procedural analysis that is required.

The successful analysis of QNP distribution developed in Chapter 5 rests upon the notion of predication. The observed constraints on quantification in the 'focus position' proved to be consistent with an analysis whereby expressions in that position are predicates that apply to a term constructed from the rest of the sentence. This idea was developed in Chapter 6 to produce an account of the broader relationship between the linear position associated with syntactic focus—left-adjacency to the tensed element—and the information-structural readings of a variety of Hungarian sentences. Assuming the immediately pre-tense element to effect 'main predication', defined as the creation of a propositional form through the application of a single predicate, proved to account for the largely overlooked generalisation that pre-tense main verbs are typically the beginning of the asserted material in a sentence (being followed by other asserted material and thus creating a 'broad focus', or 'topic>comment', reading), while non-verbal expressions in this position are followed only by non-asserted or 'presupposed' material (thus creating a 'narrow focus' reading of the pre-tense element). The essential insight is that main verbs provide crucial elements of the structure of a proposition. As a result, combining a main verb with a temporal anchor in itself produces a propositional form, albeit a skeletal one (an idea that has a syntactic analogue in the ability of a tensed verb alone to be a sentential utterance in a 'pro-drop' language). A non-verbal expression, on the other hand, can only create a propositional form on its own if the rest of the proposition can be recovered from the extra-linguistic context (just as a non-verbal expression can only be a complete contribution to discourse if a 'focus frame' precedes it in the form of a *Wh*-question). This is why the requirement for a non-verbal expression to effect main predication can only be fulfilled when the remaining material in the sentence can be taken to be 'presupposed'.

Moreover, this analysis predicts the apparent postposing of main verb infinitives in the presence of syntactically focused expressions: the focus reading only emerges when the non-verbal element occupies the crucial immediately pre-tense slot. If an infinitive is found in this slot, it follows that no other expression will be treated as main predicate and hence as a narrow focus. This aspect of the syntax of infinitives is not easily accommodated into conventional syntactic accounts, which tend to locate the 'focus position' relative to the position of a finite main verb, in order to account for the behaviour of 'verbal modifiers' (VMs), many of which look like separable prefixes to main verbs. Chapter 7 showed that the syntactic behaviour of VMs is predicted by the 'main predication' analysis. Just as with the infinitival verbs, any VM that is left-adjacent to the tensed element prevents any other expression from occupying this position and being the main predicate.

This is perhaps a good time to re-emphasise the nature of the explanation of syntactic phenomena under a dynamic approach, as described in Chapter 2, section 2.5.1. Unlike in conventional generative models, the well-formedness of a string of words and the interpretive effect of some expression occupying a certain position are not pre-defined by constraints defined over whole sentences or their generative derivations. Instead well-formedness is defined in terms of the ability to produce a complete propositional representation in a way that satisfies all of the requirements that may be introduced during parsing. The need for the immediately pre-tense expression in Hungarian to effect main predication is an example of such a requirement (a particularly significant one, as it happens); one that demonstrates how the dynamic approach not only makes predictions about well-formedness but does so in a way that truly explains, not stipulates, how some word orders are well-formed only on certain readings. It also illustrates how the ability to fulfil requirements, and therefore well-formedness, can depend on extra-linguistic context: some word orders can only satisfy the main predication requirement if certain assumptions are mutually manifest to communicator and addressee (such that important information can be taken to be 'presupposed').

One advantage of this mode of syntactic explanation is that expressions do not have to be inherently specified as being suitable to occupy some position or undergo some interpretive process (through the use of syntactic features, for example); instead, the interaction of the basic properties of expressions with the nature of the processes they must undergo and the nature of extra-linguistic context determines whether the appearance of some particular expression in a particular syntactic position will be well-formed. As a result, the dynamic mode of explanation promises a greatly simplified lexicon, among its other advantages. For example, no lexical process of assigning [+ focus] features is required in Hungarian. The relevant reading simply emerges in the course of interpretation, when it is required to produce a successful parse.

This kind of analysis demands innovative formalism. In Chapter 6, I introduced the idea of epsilon terms binding eventuality variables as a way of representing main predication. In neo-Davidsonian terms, the creation of a propositional form can be viewed as the creation of existential quantification over an eventuality with certain minimal properties. The use of the epsilon calculus allows this to be achieved through the application of a single predicate derived directly from a natural language expression—and this is precisely what a formalisation of main predication should represent. The epsilon calculus was also argued to provide an appropriate analogue of the distinction between presupposed and asserted material, in terms of the material bound by an epsilon versus material that predicates over an epsilon term, respectively.

Chapter 7 explained why the usual position of VMs in 'neutral' sentences (i.e. sentences containing no pre-tense narrow focus or negation) is the immediately pre-tense, 'main predicate' position. VMs not only introduce important structure into the proposition created, meaning that they can perform main predication without requiring a presupposed 'focus frame' term, but also form complex predicates in conjunction with the contribution of the main verb. If the main verb, rather than the VM, occupies the main predicate position, a proposition with a certain structure is created, as determined by the verb. Any attempt subsequently to create a complex predicate reading of the verb would mean a re-structuring of the whole proposition, thus violating the monotonicity of the construction of interpretations (and in any case introducing a highly inefficient parse). Unlike more conventional generative approaches, the parsing-based dynamic perspective naturally accommodates the fact that the semantically diverse class of VMs behaves more or less homogeneously in syntactic terms, because it allows for the identification of a process to which they bear the same significant relationship.

In Chapter 8 the main predication analysis was shown to account for some remaining phenomena connected to the Hungarian 'focus position' which have previously tended to receive particularly stipulative, *ad hoc* forms of analysis. These are (i) the supposedly 'aspectual' effects that are connected with the lack of any clear 'pre-verbal' expression and (ii) the interaction of the negative particle *nem* with the tensed element. The two 'aspectual' constructions were shown in Chapter 8 to be syntactically quite different from each other, as revealed in examples featuring a tensed auxiliary. This rules out the most common form of syntactic explanation, whereby these constructions are both explained by the presence of silent operators appearing in something akin to the 'focus position'. The 'progressive construction' was shown to be a simple case of main predication by the main verb, under which analysis the necessarily referential interpretation of a post-verbal VM is predicted without further stipulation: according to the reasoning of Chapter 7, no complex predicate meaning can be formed from the verb and VM once the verb has effected main predication. The 'existential construction', on the other hand, involves tense itself acting as main predicate. On the assumption that the principal contribution of tense is simply to introduce a temporal anchor to the proposition, this has the effect of communicating that some eventuality with entirely presupposed content exists (because it has some temporal anchor). This is consistent with the perceived interpretation of such sentences: an assertion that something can happen (contrary to expectations) on the grounds that it has happened before or is known to be going to happen.

The negative particle *nem* was given a new analysis as a consistently local (narrow scope) operator, in effect simply converting an act of predication into one of negative predication. Via the use of the epsilon calculus introduced in Chapter 6, this asserts the non-existence of some eventuality with respect to some particular set when applied to the main predicate. The only case in which this will not invoke a sense of contrast is when the negated main predicate is the predicate that provides a temporal anchor, as this in effect simply asserts that the eventuality in question does not exist (i.e. it does not occur). This explains why a 'sentential negation' reading only arises when *nem* appears immediately before the tense-bearing element, while 'constituent negation' is produced by the appearance of *nem* to the left of any other expression. The full range of possible positions for *nem* was shown in Chapter 6 to follow from this analysis, along with the particular readings associated with each. Conventional syntactico-semantic analyses typically require a series of dedicated syntactic projections and other abstract entities to account for the distribution of *nem*. Thus, once again, this phenomenon demonstrates how the dynamic, pragmatically informed approach to linguistic analysis produces less *ad hoc*, more parsimonious analyses than are achieved through the combination of static syntax and compositional semantics.

9.3 IMPLICATIONS AND FURTHER RESEARCH

As noted in Chapter 2, in addition to providing empirical backing for my criticisms of conventional syntactico-semantic assumptions, the analysis of Hungarian data is intended as a kind of 'existence proof' for genuinely explanatory, predictive and in crucial ways formalisable linguistic analysis that includes active consideration of 'performance' issues like inferential pragmatics and the influence of time-linear processing. Despite the fears of the structuralist linguists, which continue to influence the assumptions of modern mainstream generative linguistics, approaching linguistic structure in terms of the meanings it may or may not produce, and explicitly taking into consideration the inferential and contextual elements of these meanings, does not lead into a morass of unanalysable and idiosyncratic data, nor inevitably to the inability to make more than *ad hoc* and unexplanatory declarations about coincidences of form and meaning. One of the particularly striking things about the procedure that I have identified as being at the heart of a surprisingly wide range of phenomena in Hungarian is its 'fundamental' nature, in the context of semantic theory, the notion of creating a propositional meaning being about as basic a component of semantics as could be imagined. That matters of considerable structural complexity and superficial semantic diversity can be shown to follow predictably from such a fundamental process is an indication of how far from *ad hoc* description this approach can be.

Indeed, the production of complex effects from the interaction of very few, very simple elements is a feature of the analysis. Thus, the basic notion of main predication is complemented by the simplest possible analysis of the negative particle *nem*: it simply negates the predicate to its right. The contribution of tense is also stripped down to its simplest possible form within the representation of the asserted content of an eventuality, as a simple anchor point or index. The ability to produce complex and diverse effects on the basis of maximally simple encoded information and independently necessary inferential abilities has clear implications for wider issues of concern to linguists, such as learnability.

This also brings up the question of universality. While the theoretical lessons of the linguistic analysis presented in this book are intended to reach well beyond Hungarian, the details of the analysis itself are not—at least not necessarily. One feature of a dynamic, inferential approach, in which knowledge of language is characterised in terms of procedures for achieving an interpretation (rather than as abstractly represented declarative information on how to relate static syntactic structures to static semantic structures) is that the means of triggering particular interpretive effects are in principle many and various. The analysis of Hungarian developed here therefore makes no predictions that other languages should look the same. Languages employ many kinds of resource to trigger different interpretations, whether syntactic, morphological or phonological, all of which may interact in subtle ways. Furthermore, one cannot discount the possibility of the 'grammaticalisation' of certain phenomena even in a radically dynamic approach, effectively creating rule-based behaviour out of what was previously the result of inference (at the syntactic level, this might be a matter of changing procedural parsing information in the lexicon, or might even involve changes at levels of the fine detail of lexically encoded semantic material, which could cause visible structural effects via chains of inference).

Having said this, one would expect to find other languages employing recognisably *similar* strategies to Hungarian, given the apparent fruitfulness of a single, very basic encoded procedure in this language. Certainly, a number of interesting comparisons do exist cross-linguistically, not only in the basic matter of discourse-related word order phenomena[1] but also in superficially unexpected interactions between different elements, such as between foci and many VM-type elements, as Jo (1995) points out. Indeed, a number of significant-looking parallels arose in the course of this book between Hungarian and English, despite the stark typological contrast between the two. Structural universals do of course potentially offer an alternative form of explanation for these cross-linguistic similarities, but, as Culicover (1998) suggests, the degree of fine parameterisation necessary to capture the detail of cross-linguistic variation might in many

---

[1] As well as obvious cases like Basque and Turkish, areally and typologically quite removed cases like Papago/Tohono O'odham, as described by Payne (1987), appear to show striking similarities, once the descriptive preferences of different linguists are picked through. Recall also the comments on Malagasy from Chapter 6.

cases reduce the proposed structures to being just about equally learnable or unlearnable with or without any presumed universal basis. An approach that recognises from the outset the possibility of using quite widely varying tools to achieve similar goals therefore seems to be preferable from this perspective too—and this is in the nature of any approach that gives inference a significant role.

A number of directions for future research arise both from points of detail arising in the analytical parts of this work and from the overall approach. Two ideas that arise almost incidentally in the course of the analysis in this book but which seem worthy of considerable attention in their own right are the treatment of the contribution of tense morphology and the related analysis of sentential negation.

The idea, taken from Kempson *et al.* (2001) (who in turn follow Finger & Gabbay 1992), that tense introduces only an underspecified temporal anchor into the main representation of propositional meaning, with the details of temporal interpretation dealt with in a separate temporal logic system, proved to be fruitful in my explanation of Hungarian syntax, particularly in relation to the phenomena analysed in Chapter 8. However, the idea is obviously decidedly unconventional and while this book includes evidence that appears to support it, approaches like that of DRT (Kamp & Reyle 1993) suggest that considerable progress can be made by thinking of temporal meanings in exactly the same ways as elements of basic predicate-argument structure. Clearly the idea demands further research, to seek further linguistic evidence for this logical possibility.

The idea that the 'wide-scope' reading of negation is in fact derived from the local negation of the existence of a temporal anchor to a proposition is an intuitively plausible one that holds the promise of simplifying grammar considerably. This proved to the case in the analysis of Hungarian and it seems worth pursuing this with respect to other languages also. One burden relieved from the grammar in this way is the need to represent scope syntactically, where negation is concerned. This brings up another significant question: to what extent does the notion of logical scope belong in the grammar at all[2]? There are a number of suggestive connections between the kind of interpretive procedures discussed in this book and 'scope readings'. Connections between wide scope and such notions as 'topicality' and specificity have been noted before (e.g. Erteschik-Shir 1997, Ebert & Endriss 2004) and these notions are closely connected to that of 'logical subject of predication' (as noted in Chapter 5). Conversely, expressions in the Hungarian 'focus position' are typically associated with 'narrow scope' readings (see, for example, Bende-Farkas 2002, 30ff.), while the appearance of syntactic focusing has been argued in this book to derive entirely from an encoded predicative procedure. This suggests that we may need to think of scope in somewhat different, perhaps more fragmented, terms than the conventional picture of homogeneous syntactically-expressed scope implies, with many elements of what have been

---

[2] A purely syntactic notion of scope, defined in terms of some structural relation such as c-command, is obviously not available in a dynamic approach. Dynamic Syntax employs 'scope statements' at key stages of derivation, simply assuming these to somehow fixed by inference in an extra-linguistic context (Kempson *et al.* 2001, Cann *et al.* forthcoming). My comments on scope here are intended to point to possible ways of understanding and explaining the relevant processes of inference.

thought of as scope readings reducing to other factors[3].

Other questions that merit investigation have been indicated at various points in the preceding chapters. Among these are numerous questions involving the precise contribution of different kinds of VMs, including some basic descriptive work that remains to be done to establish the circumstances under which certain kinds of expression show truly VM-like behaviour (in particular adverbs and locatives). Some promising ideas in this regard were mentioned in Chapter 7, though they depended on rather vague notions like the relative 'semantic weight' (in terms of informativeness) of verbs with and without locative or adverbial adjuncts. Further work could help to give substance to such notions and to indicate the precise interaction of encoded semantics and pragmatic inference that might underpin them. The interaction of narrow focus with the 'definiteness effect' verbs mentioned at various points in the book is another matter that might be approached in the light of the analysis of focus readings developed here—which, one would hope, might lead towards an explanation of the definiteness effect phenomenon itself. Numerous other issues inevitably arise from the kind of wide-ranging analysis presented in the preceding chapters, within which it would be impossible to tie up every detail. What can be concluded from the analysis as it stands is that such issues should be approached not via the methodology of matching representations of meaning to perceived structures (nor *vice versa*), but through the active consideration of how inferences triggered in context interact with the encoded contributions of linguistic forms themselves, as they are integrated into a dynamic process of interpretation.

---

[3]Note that the likes of Beghelli, Ben-Shalom & Szabolcsi (1997), Reinhart (1997), Szabolcsi (1997b) already point towards a more heterogeneous notion of scope. Meanwhile, Erteschik-Shir (1997) proposes to derive scope readings directly from the information-structural status of different expressions. While my general approach is not compatible with her analysis of information structure, there are clearly important questions to be asked about why information-structural interpretation and scope readings seem so closely related and to what extent one might reduce to the other.

BIBLIOGRAPHY

Abraham, W. & de Meij, S., eds (1986). *Topic, Focus and Configurationality: Papers from the 6th Groningen Grammar Talks, Groningen, 1984*. John Benjamins. Amsterdam.

Ackerman, F. & LeSourd, P. (1997). Toward a lexical representation of phrasal predicates. In: *Complex Predicates*, (A. Alsina, J. Bresnan & P. Sells, eds.). pp. 67–106. CSLI Publications. Palo Alto, CA.

Altmann, G. T. M. & Steedman, M. (1988). Interaction with context during human sentence processing. *Cognition* **30**, 191–238.

Ariel, M. (1999). Mapping so-called 'pragmatic' phenomena according to a 'linguistic-extralinguistic' distinction: The case of propositions marked 'accessible'. In: *Functionalism and Formalism in Linguistics*, (M. Darnell, E. Moravcsik, F. Newmeyer, M. Noonan & K. Wheatley, eds.). pp. 11–38. John Benjamins. Amsterdam.

Ariel, M. (2002). Privileged interactional interpretations. *Journal of Pragmatics* **34**, 1003–1044.

Ariel, M. (to appear). A 'just that' lexical meaning for *most*. In: *Where Semantics Meets Pragmatics*, (K. Turner & K. von Heusinger, eds.). Elsevier Science. Oxford.

Asher, N. & Lascarides, A. (2003). *Logics of Conversation*. Cambridge University Press. Cambridge.

Bach, K. (1999). The semantics-pragmatics distinction: What it is and why it matters. In: Turner (1999). pp. 65–84.

Bach, K. (2000). Quantification, qualification, and context: A reply to Stanley and Szabó. *Mind and Language* **15**(2–3), 262–283.

Bach, K. & Harnish, R. M. (1987). Relevant questions. *Behavioral and Brain Sciences* **10**, 711–712.

Barwise, J. & Cooper, R. (1981). Generalized quantifiers and natural language. *Linguistics and Philosophy* **4**(2), 159–219.

Beghelli, F., Ben-Shalom, D. & Szabolcsi, A. (1997). Variation, distributivity and the illusion of branching. In: Szabolcsi (1997c). pp. 29–69.

Beghelli, F. & Stowell, T. (1997). Distributivity and negation: The syntax of *Each* and *Every*. In: Szabolcsi (1997c). pp. 71–107.

Bende-Farkas, A. (1995). Prefixation and discourse. In: Kenesei (1995b). pp. 193–219.

Bende-Farkas, A. (2002). Verb-object dependencies in Hungarian and English: A DRT-based account. Ph.D. thesis, IMS, Stuttgart University.

Bittner, M. (2001). Surface composition as bridging. *Journal of Semantics* **18**(2), 127–177.

Blakemore, D. (1987). *Semantic Constraints on Relevance*. Blackwell. Oxford and New York.

Blakemore, D. (1992). *Understanding Utterances: an Introduction to Pragmatics*. Blackwell. Oxford.

Breheny, R. (1998). Interface economy and focus. In: *Current Issues in Relevance Theory*, (V. Rouchota & A. H. Jucker, eds.). pp. 105–139. John Benjamins. Amsterdam.

Breheny, R. (2002). The current state of (radical) pragmatics in the cognitive sciences. *Mind and Language* **17**(1/2), 169–187.

Bródy, M. (1990). Some remarks on the focus field in Hungarian. *UCL Working Papers in Linguistics* **2**, 201–225.

Bródy, M. (1995). Focus and checking theory. In: Kenesei (1995b). pp. 29–44.

Brunetti, L. (2003). A unification of focus. Ph.D. Thesis, University of Florence.

Cann, R., Kempson, R. & Marten, L. (forthcoming). *The Dynamics of Language*. Elsevier. Oxford.

Carlson, G. N. (1977). *Reference to Kinds in English*. Doctoral dissertation, University of Massachusetts, Amherst. Published in 1980. New York: Garland.

Carr, P. (1990). *Linguistic Realities: an Autonomist Metatheory for the Generative Enterprise*. Cambridge University Press. Cambridge.

Carston, R. (1988). Implicature, explicature, and truth-theoretic semantics. In: *Mental Representations: The Interface between Language and Reality*, (R. M. Kempson, ed.). pp. 155–181. Cambridge University Press. Cambridge.

Carston, R. (1998). Informativeness, relevance and scalar implicature. In: *Relevance Theory: Applications and Implications*, (R. Carston & S. Uchida, eds.). pp. 179–236. John Benjamins. Amsterdam.

Carston, R. (1999). The semantics/pragmatics distinction: A view from Relevance Theory. In: Turner (1999). pp. 85–125.

Carston, R. (2002). *Thoughts and Utterances: The Pragmatics of Explicit Communication*. Blackwell. Oxford.

Carston, R. (2004). Explicature and semantics. In: *Semantics: A Reader*, (S. Davis & B. Gillon, eds.). pp. 817–845. Oxford University Press. Oxford.

Choe, H.-S. (1989). Restructuring parameters and scrambling in Korean and Hungarian. In: *Configurationality*, (L. Marácz & P. Muyskens, eds.). pp. 267–292. Foris. Dordrecht.

Chomsky, N. (1959). A review of B. F. Skinner's *Verbal Behavior*. *Language* **35**(1), 26–58.

Chomsky, N. (1965). *Aspects of the Theory of Syntax*. M.I.T. Press. Cambridge, Mass.

Chomsky, N. (1977). *Essays on Form and Interpretation*. North-Holland. New York.

Chomsky, N. (1988). *Language and Problems of Knowledge: The Managua Lectures*. M.I.T. Press. Cambridge, Mass.

Chomsky, N. (1995a). Language and nature. *Mind* **104**, 1–61.

Chomsky, N. (1995b). *The Minimalist Program*. M.I.T. Press. Cambridge, Mass.

Chomsky, N. (2001). Derivation by phase. In: *Ken Hale: A Life in Language*, (M. Kenstowicz, ed.). pp. 1–52. M.I.T. Press. Cambridge, Mass.

Cohen, A. & Erteschik-Shir, N. (2002). Topic, focus and the interpretation of bare plurals. *Natural Language Semantics* **10**, 125–165.

Crain, S. & Steedman, M. (1985). On not being led up the garden path: The use of context by the psychological syntax processor. In: *Natural Language Parsing: Psychological, Computational, and Theoretical Perspectives*, (D. R. Dowty, L. Kartunnen & A. M. Zwicky, eds.). pp. 320–358. Cambridge University Press. Cambridge.

Cresswell, M. J. (1985). *Structured Meanings*. M.I.T. Press. Cambridge, Mass.

Culicover, P. & McNally, L., eds (1998). *The Limits of Syntax*. Vol. 29 of *Syntax and Semantics*. Academic Press. San Diego.

Culicover, P. W. (1998). The minimalist impulse. In: Culicover & McNally (1998). pp. 47–77.

Dalmi, G. (1998). Last resort: PF-incorporation of prefixes and other heads in Hungarian. *TLP Yearbook 1998: Budapest Department of Theoretical Linguistics Working Papers in the Theory of Grammar* **6**(3).

Dalmi, G. (2000). Wackernagel-effect in the Hungarian focus field. In: *Proceedings of ConSOLE 8*, (C. Czinglar, K. Köhler, E. Thrift, E. J. van der Torre & M. Zimmermann, eds.). pp. 61–75. SOLE. Leiden.

Davidson, D. (1967). The logical form of action sentences. In: *The Logic of Decision and Action*, (N. Rescher, ed.). pp. 81–95. University of Pittsburgh Press. Pittsburgh. Reprinted in Davidson (1980).

Davidson, D. (1980). *Essays on Actions and Events*. Oxford University Press. Oxford.

Dessalles, J.-L. (1998). Altruism, status, and the origin of relevance. In: *Approaches to the Evolution of Language: Social and Cognitive Bases*, (J. R. Hurford, M. Studdert-Kennedy & C. Knight, eds.). pp. 130–147. Cambridge University Press. Cambridge.

Downing, P. & Noonan, M., eds (1995). *Word Order in Discourse*. John Benjamins. Amsterdam.

É. Kiss, K. (1987). *Configurationality in Hungarian*. D. Reidel. Dordrecht.

É. Kiss, K. (1994). Sentence structure and word order. In: Kiefer & É. Kiss (1994). pp. 1–90.

É. Kiss, K. (1995a). Definiteness effect revisited. In: Kenesei (1995b). pp. 63–88.

É. Kiss, K. (1998a). Identificational focus versus information focus. *Language* **74**(2), 245–273.

É. Kiss, K. (1998b). On generic and existential bare plurals and the classification of predicates. In: Rothstein (1998b). pp. 145–162.

É. Kiss, K. (1999). The English cleft construction as a focus phrase. In: *Boundaries of Morphology and Syntax*, (L. Mereu, ed.). pp. 217–229. John Benjamins.

É. Kiss, K. (2001). Focussed number phrases. In: *Audiator Vox Sapentiae*, (C. Féry & W. Sternefeld, eds.). pp. 259–266. Akademie Verlag. Berlin.

É. Kiss, K. (2002). *The Syntax of Hungarian*. Cambridge University Press. Cambridge.

É. Kiss, K. (to appear). First steps towards a theory of the verbal particle. To appear in *Approaches to Hungarian, Vol. 9*, ed. by István Kenesei and Christopher Piñón.

É. Kiss, K., ed. (1995b). *Discourse Configurational Languages.* Oxford University Press. Oxford.

É. Kiss, K. & Gyuris, B. (2003). Apparent scope inversion under the rise fall contour. *Acta Linguistica Hungarica* **50**(3–4), 371–404.

Ebert, C. & Endriss, C. (2004). Wide scope indefinites as aboutness topics. In: *Proceedings of the Conference "sub8 – Sinn und Bedeutung", 8th Annual Meeting of the Gesellschaft für Semantik, Johann-Wolfgang-Goethe-Univerität, Frankfurt am Main, 2003,* (C. Meier & M. Weisgerber, eds.). Konstanzer Arbeitspapiere Linguistik. pp. 95–109. Universität Konstanz, FB Linguistik. Konstanz.

Egli, U. & von Heusinger, K. (1995). The epsilon operator and e-type pronouns. In: *Lexical Knowledge in the Organization of Language,* (U. Egli, P. E. Pause, C. Schwarze, A. von Stechow & G. Wienold, eds.). pp. 121–141. John Benjamins. Amsterdam.

Ernst, T. (1984). Towards an integrated theory of adverb position in English. Ph.D. thesis, Indiana University.

Ernst, T. (2000). Manners and events. In: *Events as Grammatical Objects: The Converging Perspectives of Lexical Semantics and Syntax.* pp. 335–358. CSLI Publications. Stanford.

Erteschik-Shir, N. (1997). *The Dynamics of Focus Structure.* Cambridge University Press. Cambridge.

Farkas, D. (1986). The syntactic position of focus in Hungarian. *Natural Language and Linguistic Theory* **4**, 77–96.

Farkas, D. & Sadock, J. (1989). Preverb climbing in Hungarian. *Language* **65**, 318–338.

Finger, M. & Gabbay, D. (1992). Adding a temporal dimension to a logical system. *Journal of Logic, Language and Information* **1**, 203–233.

Fodor, J. A. (2001). Language, thought and compositionality. *Mind and Language* **16**, 1–15.

Fodor, J. A. & Pylyshyn, Z. (1988). Connectionism and cognitive architecture: A critical analysis. *Cognition* **28**, 3–71.

Gazdar, G. (1979). *Pragmatics: Implicature, Presupposition and Logical Form.* Academic Press. New York.

Gazdar, G. & Good, D. (1982). On a notion of relevance. In: Smith (1982). pp. 88–100.

Geurts, B. (1998). Scalars. In: *Lexicalische Semantik aus kognitiver Sicht,* (P. Ludewig & B. Geurts, eds.). pp. 95–118. Gunter Narr. Tübingen.

Glanzberg, M. (2005). Focus: A case study on the semantics/pragmatics boundary. In: Szabó (2005). pp. 72–110.

Grice, H. P. (1975). Logic and conversation. In: *Syntax and Semantics 3: Speech Acts,* (P. Cole & J. Morgan, eds.). pp. 41–58. Academic Press. New York. Reprinted in Grice (1989): 22–40.

Grice, H. P. (1989). *Studies in the Way of Words.* Harvard University Press. Cambridge, Mass.

Gyuris, B. (2002). Contrastive topics and alternatives in event semantics. In: Kenesei & Siptár (2002). pp. 187–216.

Harlig, J. (1989). The interaction of verbal aspect and noun phrase determination in Hungarian. Ph.D. thesis, University of Chicago.

Haspelmath, M. (1999). Optimality and diachronic adaptation. *Zeitschrift für Sprachwissenschaft* **18**(2), 180–205.
Heim, I. & Kratzer, A. (1998). *Semantics in Generative Grammar*. Blackwell. Malden, Mass. and Oxford.
Herburger, E. (2000). *What Counts: Focus and Quantification*. M.I.T. Press. Cambridge, Mass.
Hilbert, D. & Bernays, P. (1939). *Die Grundlagen der Mathematik II*. Springer. Berlin, Heidelberg, New York. Second edition. Reprint 1970.
Horn, L. (1981). Exhaustiveness and the semantics of clefts. In: *Proceedings of NELS 11*. pp. 125–142.
Horn, L. (1989). *A Natural History of Negation*. The University of Chicago Press. Chicago and London.
Horn, L. (1992). The said and the unsaid. In: *Ohio State University Working Papers in Linguistics 40 (Proceedings of SALT II)*. pp. 163–192.
Horvath, J. (1981). Aspects of Hungarian syntax and the theory of grammar. Ph.D. thesis, UCLA, Los Angeles.
Horvath, J. (2000). Interfaces vs. the computational system in the syntax of focus. In: *Interface Strategies*, (H. Bennis, M. Everaert & E. Reuland, eds.). pp. 183–206. Royal Netherlands Academy of Arts and Sciences. Amsterdam. Proceedings of the Colloquium, Amsterdam, 24–26 September 1997.
Hunyadi, L. (1981). A nyelvi polaritás kifejezése a magyarban. Dissertation for the Candidate's Degree, Kossuth L. University, Debrecen.
Jackendoff, R. (1972). *Semantic Interpretation in Generative Grammar*. MIT Press. Cambridge, Mass.
Jackendoff, R. (1997). *The Architecture of the Language Faculty*. MIT Press. Cambridge, Mass.
Jackendoff, R. (2002). *Foundations of Language: Brain, Meaning, Grammar, Evolution*. Oxford University Press. Oxford.
Jo, M.-J. (1995). The theory of syntactic focalization based on a subcategorization feature of verbs. In: É. Kiss (1995b). pp. 335–374.
Kadmon, N. (2001). *Formal Pragmatics: Semantics, Pragmatics, Presupposition, and Focus*. Blackwell. Malden, Mass. and Oxford.
Kálmán, L. (1985a). Word order in neutral sentences. In: *Approaches to Hungarian*, (I. Kenesei, ed.). Vol. 3. pp. 13–23. JATE University. Szeged.
Kálmán, L. (1985b). Word order in non-neutral sentences. In: *Approaches to Hungarian*, (I. Kenesei, ed.). Vol. 3. pp. 25–37. JATE University. Szeged.
Kálmán, L. (1995). Definiteness effect verbs in Hungarian. In: Kenesei (1995b). pp. 221–242.
Kamp, H. & Reyle, U. (1993). *From Discourse to Logic: Introduction to Model-Theoretic Semantics of Natural Language, Formal Logic and Discourse Representation Theory*. Kluwer. Dordrecht.
Karttunen, L. & Peters, S. (1979). Conventional implicature. In: Oh & Dineen (1979). pp. 1–57.

Keenan, E. L. (1987). A semantic definition of "indefinite NP". In: *The Representation of (In)definiteness*, (E. Reuland & A. ter Meulen, eds.). pp. 286–317. M.I.T. Press. Cambridge, Mass.

Kempson, R. (1988). Grammar and conversational principles. In: *Linguistics: the Cambridge Survey*, (F. Newmeyer, ed.). pp. 139–163. Cambridge University Press. Cambridge.

Kempson, R., Meyer-Viol, W. & Gabbay, D. (2001). *Dynamic Syntax: The Flow of Language Understanding*. Blackwell. Oxford.

Kenesei, I. (1986). On the logic of word order in Hungarian. In: Abraham & de Meij (1986). pp. 143–159.

Kenesei, I. (1995a). On the syntax of Focus. Ms., JATE, Szeged.

Kenesei, I. (1998). Adjuncts and arguments in focus in Hungarian. *Acta Linguistica Hungarica* 45(1–2), 61–88.

Kenesei, I., ed. (1995b). *Approaches to Hungarian V: Levels and Structures*. JATE. Szeged.

Kenesei, I. & Siptár, P., eds (2002). *Approaches to Hungarian, Volume 8: Papers from the Budapest Conference*. Akadémiai Kiadó. Budapest.

Kiefer, F. (1994). Aspect and syntactic structure. In: Kiefer & É. Kiss (1994). pp. 415–464.

Kiefer, F. & É. Kiss, K., eds (1994). *The Syntactic Structure of Hungarian*. Vol. 27 of *Syntax and Semantics*. Academic Press. San Diego.

King, J. C. & Stanley, J. (2005). Semantics, pragmatics, and the role of semantic content. In: Szabó (2005). pp. 111–164.

Koenig, J.-P. (1993). Scalar predicates and negation: Punctual semantics and interval interpretations. In: *CLS27: Papers from the 27th Regional Meeting of the Chicago Linguistic Society, 1991. Part Two: The Parasession on Negation*, (L. Dobrin, L. Nichols & R. Rodríguez, eds.). pp. 140–155. Chicago Linguistic Society. Chicago.

Komlósy, A. (1992). Régensek és vonzatok [heads and arguments]. In: *Strukturális Magyar Nyelvtan: Mondattan [Structural Grammar of Hungarian 1: Syntax]*, (F. Kiefer, ed.). pp. 299–527. Akadémiai Kiadó. Budapest.

Koopman, H. & Szabolcsi, A. (2000). *Verbal Complexes*. M.I.T. Press. Cambridge, Mass.

Kratzer, A. (1991). The representation of focus. In: Wunderlich & von Stechow (1991). pp. 825–834.

Krifka, M. (1991). A compositional semantics for multiple focus constructions. In: *Proceedings from Semantics and Linguistic Theory I (Cornell Working Papers in Linguistics 10)*, (S. Moore & A. D. Wyner, eds.). pp. 127–158.

Krifka, M. (1999). At least some determiners aren't determiners. In: Turner (1999). pp. 257–291.

Ladd, D. R. (1996). *Intonational Phonology*. Cambridge University Press. Cambridge.

Lappin, S. & Reinhart, T. (1988). Presuppositional effects of strong determiners: a processing account. *Linguistics* 26, 1021–1037.

Larson, R. & Segal, G. (1995). *Knowledge of Meaning: An Introduction to Semantic Theory*. M.I.T. Press. Cambridge, Mass.

Levinson, S. (1983). *Pragmatics*. Cambridge University Press. Cambridge.

Levinson, S. (1987). Minimization and conversational inference. In: *The Pragmatic Perspective*, (J. Verschueren & M. Bertuccelli-Papi, eds.). pp. 61–129. John Benjamins. Amsterdam.

Levinson, S. (2000). *Presumptive Meanings: The Theory of Generalized Conversational Implicature*. M.I.T. Press. Cambridge, Mass.

Lewis, D. (1979). Scorekeeping in a language game. *Journal of Philosophical Logic* **8**, 339–359.

Lewis, D. (1983). *Philosophical Papers, volume I*. Oxford University Press. Oxford.

Liu, F.-H. (1997). *Scope and Specificity*. John Benjamins. Amsterdam.

Ludlow, P. (1992). Formal rigor and linguistic theory. *Natural Language and Linguistic Theory* **10**, 335–344.

Lyons, J. (1977). *Semantics*. Cambridge University Press. Cambridge.

Maleczki, M. (1995). On the definiteness effect in Hungarian (a semantic approach). In: Kenesei (1995b). pp. 261–284.

Maleczki, M. (1996). Semantic relationships between verbs and their arguments. *Language Sciences* **18**(1–2), 449–442.

Marten, L. (1999). Syntactic and semantic underspecification in the verb phrase. Ph.D. thesis, University of London.

Marten, L. (2002). *At the Syntax-Pragmatics Interface: Verbal Underspecification and Concept Formation in Dynamic Syntax*. Oxford University Press. Oxford.

McConnell-Ginet, S. (1982). Adverbs and logical form: A linguistically realistic theory. *Language* **58**(1), 144–184.

McNally, L. (1999). Review of A. Szabolcsi, ed. Ways of Scope Taking. *Linguistics and Philosophy* **22**, 563–571.

Montague, R. (1970). Universal grammar. *Theoria* **36**, 373–389. Reprinted in Montague (1974).

Montague, R. (1973). The proper treatment of quantification in ordinary English. In: *Approaches to Natural Language*, (J. Hintikka, J. Moravcsik & P. Suppes, eds.). pp. 221–242. Reidel. Dordrecht and Boston. Reprinted in Montague (1974).

Montague, R. (1974). *Formal Philosophy*. Yale University Press. New Haven.

Moore, T. (1982). Comments on Sperber and Wilson's paper. In: Smith (1982). pp. 111–112.

Neale, S. (1999). Coloring and composition. In: *Philosophy and Linguistics*, (K. Murasugi & R. Stainton, eds.). pp. 35–82. Westview. Boulder.

Neeleman, A. & Reinhart, T. (1998). Scrambling and the PF interface. In: *The Projection of Arguments: Lexical and Compositional Factors*, (M. Butt & W. Geuder, eds.). pp. 309–353. CSLI Publications. Stanford.

Nunberg, G. (2002). Do you know what it means to miss New Orleans?. *Linguistics and Philosophy* **25**, 671–680.

Oh, C.-K. & Dineen, D. A., eds (1979). *Syntax and Semantics 11: Presupposition*. Academic Press. New York.

Olsvay, C. (2000). Negative quantifiers in the Hungarian sentence. M.A. thesis, Eötvös Loránd University, Budapest.

Parsons, T. (1990). *Events in the Semantics of English: A Study in Subatomic Semantics*. M.I.T. Press. Cambridge, Mass.

Partee, B. H. (1987). Noun phrase interpretation and type-shifting principles. In: *Studies in Discourse Representation Theory and the Theory of Generalized Quantifiers*, (J. Groenendijk, D. de Jongh & M. Stokhof, eds.). pp. 115–143. Foris. Dordrecht.

Paul, I. (2001). Concealed pseudo-clefts. *Lingua* **111**(10), 707–727.

Payne, D. (1987). Information structuring in Papago narrative discourse. *Language* **63**(4), 783–804.

Payne, J. & Chisarik, E. (2000). Negation and focus in Hungarian: an Optimality Theory account. *Transactions of the Philological Society* **98**(1), 185–230.

Pelletier, F. J. (1994). The principle of semantic compositionality. *Topoi* **13**, 11–24.

Pelletier, F. J. (2003). Context dependence and compositionality. *Mind and Language* **18**(2), 148–161.

Piñón, C. (1992). Heads in the focus field. In: *Approaches to Hungarian, Volume 4: The Structure of Hungarian*, (I. Kenesei & C. Pléh, eds.). pp. 99–121. JATE. Szeged.

Piñón, C. (1995). Around the progressive in Hungarian. In: Kenesei (1995b). pp. 155–189.

Piñón, C. (to appear). The existential tense in Hungarian. In: *The Nature of the Word*, (K. Hanson & S. Inkelas, eds.). M.I.T. Press. Cambridge, Mass.

Puskás, G. (2000). *Word Order in Hungarian: the syntax of Ā-positions*. John Benjamins. Amsterdam/Philadelphia.

Pustejovsky, J. (1991). The syntax of event structure. *Cognition* **41**, 47–81.

Récanati, F. (2002). Does linguistic communication rest on inference?. *Mind and Language* **17**, 105–126.

Récanati, F. (2004). *Literal Meaning: The Very Idea*. Cambridge University Press. Cambridge.

Reichenbach, H. (1947). *Elements of Symbolic Logic*. Macmillan. New York.

Reinhart, T. (1995). Interface strategies. *OTS Working Papers* (TL-95-002).

Reinhart, T. (1997). Quantifier-scope: How labor is divided between QR and choice functions. *Linguistics and Philosophy* **20**, 335–397.

Rizzi, L. (1997). The fine structure of the left periphery. In: *Elements of Grammar*, (L. Haegeman, ed.). pp. 281–337. Kluwer. Dordrecht.

Roberts, C. (1996). Information structure in discourse: Towards an integrated formal theory of pragmatics. *Ohio State University Working Papers in Linguistics* **49**, 91–136.

Roberts, C. (1998). Focus, the flow of information, and universal grammar. In: Culicover & McNally (1998). pp. 109–160.

Rooth, M. (1985). Association with focus. Ph.D. thesis, University of Massachusetts, Amherst.

Rooth, M. (1992). A theory of focus interpretation. *Natural Language Semantics* **1**, 75–116.

Rooth, M. (1996). Focus. In: *The Handbook of Contemporary Semantic Theory*, (S. Lappin, ed.). pp. 271–297. Blackwell. Oxford.

Rosenthall, S. (1992). The intonation of simple sentences in Hungarian. In: *Papers from the Third Annual Formal Linguistic Society of Midamerica Conference*, (L. Smith Stvan et al., ed.). pp. 297–310. IULS. Bloominton, Indiana.

Rothstein, S. (1998a). Introduction. in *Events and Grammar* (Rothstein 1998b). pp. 1–11.

Rothstein, S., ed. (1998b). *Events and Grammar*. Kluwer. Dordrecht.

Rothstein, S., ed. (2001). *Predicates and their Subjects*. Kluwer. Dordrecht.

Rubovitz, T. (1997). The relevance of relevance theory to syntactic phenomena: Relevance theory and extraction from relative clauses. In: *Proceedings of the University of Hertfordshire Relevance Theory Workshop*, (M. Groefsema, ed.). pp. 120–130. Peter Thomas and Associates. Chelmsford.

Sadock, J. (1984). Whither radical pragmatics?. In: *Meaning, Form and Use in Context: Linguistic Applications*, (D. Schiffrin, ed.). pp. 139–149. Georgetown University Press. Washington.

Scharten, R. (1997). Exhaustive interpretation: A discourse-semantic account. Ph.D. thesis, Katholieke Universiteit Nijmegen.

Schein, B. (1993). *Plurals and Events*. M.I.T. Press. Cambridge, Mass.

Seuren, P. (1993). Why does 2 mean "2"? Grist to the anti-Grice mill. In: *Functional Description of Language: Proceedings of the Conference (Prague, November 24–27 1992)*, (E. Hajičová, ed.). pp. 225–235. Faculty of Mathematics and Physics, Charles University, Prague. Reprinted in Seuren (2001).

Seuren, P. (2004). *Chomsky's Minimalism*. Oxford University Press. Oxford.

Skinner, B. F. (1957). *Verbal Behavior*. Copley. Acton, MA.

Smith, N., ed. (1982). *Mutual Knowledge*. Academic Press. London and New York.

Sperber, D. & Wilson, D. (1986/95). *Relevance: Communication and Cognition*. Blackwell. Oxford. (First published 1986, second edition 1995).

Sperber, D. & Wilson, D. (1987). Précis of Relevance: Communication and Cognition. *Behavioral and Brain Sciences* **10**(4), 697–710.

Stalnaker, R. (1974). Pragmatic presuppositions. In: *Semantics and Philosophy*, (M. Munitz & P. Unger, eds.). pp. 197–214. New York University Press. New York.

Stanley, J. (2000). Context and logical form. *Linguistics and Philosophy* **23**, 391–434.

Stanley, J. & Szabó, Z. G. (2000). On quantifier domain restriction. *Mind and Language* **15**(2–3), 219–261.

Steedman, M. (2000). *The Syntactic Process*. M.I.T. Press. Cambridge, Mass.

Szabó, Z. G., ed. (2005). *Semantics versus Pragmatics*. Oxford University Press. Oxford.

Szabolcsi, A. (1981). Compositionality in focus. *Folia Linguistica Societatis Linguisticae Europaeae* **15**, 141–162.

Szabolcsi, A. (1983). Focussing properties, or the trap of first order. *Theoretical Linguistics* **10**, 125–145.

Szabolcsi, A. (1986). From the definiteness effect to lexical integrity. In: Abraham & de Meij (1986). pp. 332–360.

Szabolcsi, A. (1994). All quantifiers are not equal: the case of focus. *Acta Linguistica Hungarica* **42**, 171–187.

Szabolcsi, A. (1997a). Background notions in lattice theory and generalized quantifiers. in *Ways of Scope Taking* (Szabolcsi 1997c). pp. 1–27.

Szabolcsi, A. (1997b). Strategies for scope taking. in *Ways of Scope Taking* (Szabolcsi 1997c). pp. 109–154.

Szabolcsi, A., ed. (1997c). *Ways of Scope Taking*. Kluwer. Dordrecht.

Szendrői, K. (2001). Focus and the syntax-prosody interface. Ph.D. thesis, University College London.

Szendrői, K. (2003). A stress-based approach to the syntax of Hungarian focus. *Linguistic Review* **20**(1), 37–78.

Tenny, C. (1994). *Aspectual Roles and the Syntax-Semantics Interface*. Kluwer. Dordrecht.

Thomason, R. & Stalnaker, R. (1973). A semantic theory of adverbs. *Linguistic Inquiry* **4**, 195–220.

Tóth, G. (2001). Some notes on propositional negation in Hungarian. In: *Working Papers in the Theory of Grammar, Theoretical Linguistics Programme, Budapest University (ELTE)*. Vol. 9. pp. 37–48. Research Institute for Linguistics, Hungarian Academy of Sciences. Budapest.

Tsiplakou, S. (1998). Focus in Greek: Its structure and its interpretation. Ph.D. thesis, School of Oriental and African Studies, University of London.

Tugwell, D. (1998). Dynamic syntax. Ph.D. thesis, University of Edinburgh.

Turner, K., ed. (1999). *The Semantics/Pragmatics Interface from Different Points of View*. Elsevier Science. Oxford.

Uriagereka, J. (1999). Multiple Spell-out. In: *Working Minimalism*, (S. D. Epstein & N. Hornstein, eds.). pp. 251–281. M.I.T. Press. Cambridge, Mass.

Vallduví, E. (1992). *The Informational Component*. Garland. New York.

Vallduví, E. & Engdahl, E. (1996). The linguistic realization of information packaging. *Linguistics* **34**, 53–78.

Vallduví, E. & Vilkuna, M. (1998). On rheme and kontrast. In: Culicover & McNally (1998). pp. 79–108.

Van Geenhoven, V. (1998). *Semantic Incorporation and Indefinite Descriptions: Semantic and Syntactic Aspects of Noun Incorporation in West Greenlandic*. CSLI Publications. Stanford.

van Kuppevelt, J. (1996). Inferring from topics: Scalar implicatures as topic-dependent inferences. *Linguistics and Philosophy* **19**(4), 393–443.

van Riemsdijk, H. (1982). *A Case Study in Syntactic Markedness: The Binding Nature of Prepositional Phrases*. Foris. Dordrecht.

Vendler, Z. (1967). Verbs and times. In: *Linguistics in Philosophy*. pp. 97–121. Cornell University Press. Cornell.

von Heusinger, K. (2002). Information structure and the partition of sentence meaning. In: *Travaux du Cercle Linguistique de Prague / Prague Linguistic Circle Papers*, (E. Hajičová, P. Sgall, J. Hana & T. Hoskovec, eds.). Vol. 4. pp. 275–305. John Benjamins. Amsterdam amd Philadelphia.

von Stechow, A. (1991a). Current issues in the theory of focus. In: Wunderlich & von Stechow (1991). pp. 804–824.

von Stechow, A. (1991b). Focusing and backgrounding operators. In: *Discourse Particles: Descriptive and Theoretical Investigations on the Logical, Syntactic and Pragmatic Properties of Discourse Particles in German*, (W. Abraham, ed.). pp. 37–84. John Benjamins. Amsterdam.

Wedgwood, D. (2002). 'Focus position' and quantification: The relevance of pragmatic theory. In: Kenesei & Siptár (2002). pp. 241–260.

Wedgwood, D. (2003). Predication and information structure: A dynamic account of Hungarian pre-verbal syntax. Ph.D. thesis, University of Edinburgh.

Wilson, D. & Sperber, D. (1979). Ordered entailments: An alternative to presuppositional theories. In: Oh & Dineen (1979). pp. 299–323.

Wilson, D. & Sperber, D. (1993). Linguistic form and relevance. *Lingua* **90**(1/2), 1–25.

Wilson, D. & Sperber, D. (2002). Truthfulness and relevance. *Mind* **111**, 583–632.

Wilson, D. & Sperber, D. (2004). Relevance Theory. In: *The Handbook of Pragmatics*, (L. Horn & G. Ward, eds.). pp. 607–632. Blackwell. Oxford.

Wunderlich, D. & von Stechow, A., eds (1991). *Semantik: ein internationales Handbuch der zeitgenössischen Forschung [Semantics: an international handbook of contemporary research]*. Walter de Gruyter. Berlin.

Zanuttini, R. (1996). On the relevance of tense for sentential negation. In: *Parameters and Functional Heads: Essays in Comparative Syntax*, (A. Belletti & L. Rizzi, eds.). pp. 181–207. Oxford University Press. Oxford.

INDEX

Ackerman, F., 234
adjunct, 193–195, 199, 211, 251, 252, 272, 293
adverb, 84, 86, 222, 241–248, 250, 252, 259, 276, 293
    adverbial reading of VM, 259, 261–262
    scope of, *see* scope
Altmann, G., 216, 286
ambiguity, 18, 19, 24, 26–27, 53, 56, 103, 182, 196, 211, 215–216, 238, 281
Ariel, M., 13, 21, 23, 24, 31, 166
Asher, N., 6
AspP [Aspectual Projection], 91, 92, 258–261
auxiliary verb, 77, 86, 90, 91, 93, 207–210, 212, 214, 217, 226, 233, 253, 256, 258, 259, 266, 267, 275, 277, 289
    stressed, 93, 208, 266

Bach, K., 35, 49, 50
bare nominal, 81, 83, 220, 222, 226, 236–241, 244, 245, 257, 260–264, 282
    locative, 248, 249, 251
Barwise, J., 153
Basque, 291
Beghelli, F., 27, 150, 151, 174, 293
Ben-Shalom, D., 293
Bende-Farkas, Á., 75, 83, 152, 154, 156, 174, 206, 222, 235, 237–239, 251, 260, 274, 292
Bernays, P., 201
Bittner, M., 193, 194
Blakemore, D., 24, 41, 57, 58
BN [abbreviation introduced], 236
Breheny, R., 34, 55, 102–104
bridging inference, 193, 237

Bródy, M., 11, 89, 90, 92, 112, 209, 257, 270

Cann, R., 7, 8, 58, 69, 286, 292
Carlson, G., 238
Carr, P., 66
Carston, R., 3, 13, 17, 19–20, 24, 26, 30, 34, 35, 37, 41, 45, 48, 52, 53, 55, 69, 113, 161, 162, 165, 166, 285
Chisarik, E., 272
Choe, H., 89
Chomsky, N., 1, 11, 14, 51, 55, 59–61, 63, 64, 71, 113
cleft construction, *see* it-cleft
cognitive effects, 43–44, 46, 50, 52, 102, 103, 105, 106, 120, 121, 133, 138, 139, 143, 145, 202, 216, 243, 264
cognitive environment, 42, 50, 157, 211
    mutual, 42, 43, 50, 68, 105, 106, 117, 119, 122, 133, 135, 138, 141, 143, 189
Cohen, A., 238, 240, 241
complex predicate, 82–84, 86–88, 221, 223–253, 282, 289, 290
computational linguistics, 13, 50, 72
connective, 19–20, 24, 57
contextual effects, *see* cognitive effects
contextual implication, 43, 103, 121, 124, 139, 163
Cooper, R., 153
'counting' quantifier, 153–154, 160, 172–173, 177, 180, 183
Crain, S., 216, 286
Cresswell, M., 141
Culicover, P., 291

308 *Shifting the Focus*

Dalmi, G., 91–92, 112
Davidson, D., 142, 196, 199, 224
definite conjugation, 107, 192, 237, 266
definiteness effect, 155–156, 211, 222, 231, 265–266, 293
discourse configurational, 6, 76, 85, 99
Discourse Representation Theory, 6, 7, 238, 292
DistP, *see* Quantifier position

Ebert, C., 292
EC [abbreviation introduced], 256
Egli, U., 201, 202, 212
É. Kiss, K., xiv, 75, 76, 79–81, 83–88, 90, 91, 94, 97, 98, 104, 110–112, 114, 123, 127, 129, 150–152, 154, 156, 192, 209, 211, 212, 222, 224, 229, 233, 235, 237, 238, 242, 245–247, 249, 256–261, 265, 266, 270, 273, 280
ellipsis, 88
elliptical character of human languages, 24, 45
Endriss, C., 292
Engdahl, E., 9
epsilon calculus, 201, 217
    and existential quantification, 201–203, 239
    and information-structural meaning, 202–203, 210–216
    and negation, 272, 274, 275, 277, 278
    combined with event variables, 203–206, 225, 227–228, 230, 231, 239–240, 267, 272
Ernst, T., 242
Erteschik-Shir, N., 98–100, 238, 240, 241, 292, 293
eventuality
    'main eventuality', 224–226, 230, 231, 239, 241, 251, 267
    relevance to exhaustive focus, 110, 118, 138–145, 164
    sub-eventualities, 224–232, 240, 276, 281
    variable bound by epsilon operator, *see* epsilon calculus
    variable in neo-Davidsonian semantics, 191, 195–197, 221

Farkas, D., 80, 87, 209
functionalism, 4, 76, 98, 99

Gabbay, D., 7, 8, 57, 58, 193, 200, 201, 237, 266, 282, 286, 292
Gazdar, G., 16, 50
van Geenhoven, V., 237, 238
generalised quantifier theory, 150, 153–154, 158, 160, 189
    monotonicity, *see* monotonicity
    proportional vs. intersective, 172–186, 189, 231
    tripartite quantificational structure, 153–154, 160, 173, 176–177, 197–199
    witness set, 153–154, 158, 165, 169–171, 180, 184, 185
Good, D., 50
Grice, H.P., xiii, 3, 16, 45, 130, 132, 159
    Gricean pragmatics, 3, 16, 20, 24, 34, 45, 48–49, 54, 113, 114, 116, 125, 130–132, 136, 159
    neo-Gricean pragmatics, 17, 132, 271
    post-Gricean pragmatics, xiii, 3, 12, 17, 33, 34, 38–39, 41, 47, 50, 69, 72, 73, 100, 137, 146, 285
Gyuris, B., 76, 189

Harlig, J., 257
Harnish, R., 50
Haspelmath, M., 272
Heim, I, 54
Heim, I., 182
Herburger, E., 105, 124, 194–198
von Heusinger, K., 8, 98, 201, 202, 212
Hilbert, D., 201
Horn, L., 135–137, 161, 162, 165, 166, 271

Horvath, J., 85, 101, 108, 110, 112, 124–126, 128, 143, 145
Hunyadi, L., 273

incorporation analysis
　noun incorporation, 237–239, 241, 251
　of VMs, 90, 92
informativeness, 126, 130–135, 204, 251–252, 271, 293
intersective quantifier, *see* generalised quantifier theory
is [Hungarian particle], 77, 78, 80, 171
it-cleft, 10, 79, 110, 114, 116–118, 120, 127–129, 135–137, 146, 156, 185

Jackendoff, R., 5, 24, 28, 59, 60, 66, 100, 242–244
Jo, M., 85, 91, 191, 291

Kálmán, L., 78, 111, 156, 193
Kadmon, N., 165
Kamp, H., 7, 200, 292
Karttunen, L., 113
Keenan, E., 182
Kempson, R., 7, 8, 57, 58, 69, 193, 200, 201, 213, 237, 266, 282, 286, 292
Kenesei, I., 79, 108, 110, 112
Kiefer, F., 75, 241, 256, 259, 260, 262–264, 282
King, J., 20, 25, 26, 33, 35, 54
Koenig, J.-P., 165
Komlósy, A., 93
Koopman, H., 90–92, 209, 270
Kratzer, A., 54, 100, 101, 182
Krifka, M., 28–34, 101, 152, 157, 177
van Kuppevelt, J., 165, 166

Ladd, D.R., 97
lambda, *see* operator
Lappin, S., 172, 174
Larson, R., 19

Lascarides, A., 6
LeSourd, P., 234
Levinson, S., 132, 161
Lewis, D., 32, 106
Liu, F., 168
locative, 81, 82, 220, 237, 247–252, 293
locative 'prefix', *see* verbal 'prefix' particle
Ludlow, P., 71
Lyons, J., 249

Malagasy, 190–191, 291
Maleczki, M., 156
Marten, L., 3, 7, 8, 56, 58, 69, 194, 286, 292
McConnell-Ginet, S., 242–244
McNally, L., 237
Meyer-Viol, W., 7, 8, 57, 58, 193, 200, 201, 237, 266, 282, 286, 292
Minimalist Program, 1, 56, 59–61, 63, 87, 91, 260
monotonicity
　of generalised quantifier, 155, 168–170, 180–182, 246
　of grammar, 232, 233, 244, 264, 289
Montague, R., 23, 271
　Montagovian compositionality, 23, 61, 62, 87, 112, 286
　Montague grammar, 112, 113, 116
　syncategorematic analysis of negation, 271
Moore, T., 50
mutual knowledge, 42

Neale, S., 24
Neeleman, A., 60
neo-Davidsonian, *see* eventuality
neo-Gricean pragmatics, *see* Grice, H.P.
neutral sentence, 10, 11, 77–79, 81–83, 89–91, 93, 125, 126, 180, 216, 221, 232, 234, 248, 251, 252, 258, 259, 272, 274, 279, 289
non-exhaustive focus, 86, 124–127, 134, 138, 143–146, 287

Nunberg, G., 17

Occam's Razor, 14, 66, 280
Olsvay, C., 270, 280
operator, 31, 87, 91–92, 119, 130, 200, 225, 255, 286
~ [focus interpretation operator], 29, 118
'associating with focus', 28, 101
epsilon, *see* epsilon calculus
exhaustive focus, 93, 125, 126, 145, 158, 159, 273, 287
EXIST, 83, 91, 256–258, 260, 265, 268, 289
lambda, 23, 100–102, 141, 198
negation, 20, 256, 271–283, 290, 292
scope of, *see* scope
perfective, 260
PROG, 83, 91, 256–258, 260, 289
scope, *see* scope
overspecification, 18

Papago, *see* Tohono O'odham
Parsons, T., 195, 196, 225
Partee, B., 238
particle climbing, *see* VM-climbing
Paul, I., 190, 191
Payne, D., 291
Payne, J., 272
PC [abbreviation introduced], 256, 262
Pelletier, F.J., 21–23, 26, 27, 35
Peters, S., 113
Piñón, C., 87, 88, 256–258, 265, 268–270
pitch accent, 10, 76, 78, 91, 92, 96–98, 104, 108, 111, 124, 127–129, 137, 171, 175, 185, 191–193, 212, 234, 243, 248, 256, 260–262, 280
post-Gricean pragmatics, *see* Grice, H.P.
Principles and Parameters, 1, 59, 71
pro-drop, 106, 192, 201, 235, 236, 288
procedural meaning, 3, 7, 23, 24, 57–58, 67, 68, 70, 72, 73, 81, 93, 99, 101, 102, 139, 149–154, 156, 159, 160, 162, 164, 165, 168, 169, 171–176, 181, 183–185, 187, 200, 202, 209, 217, 219, 238, 253, 270, 287, 290–292
pronominal, 194, 195, 237
pronoun, 58, 129, 142, 201, 237
proportional quantifier, *see* generalised quantifier theory
Puskás, G., 75, 81, 270, 277
Pustejovsky, J., 224, 226
PV [abbreviation introduced], 77

Quantifier position, 76, 84, 149, 151–154, 158, 159, 165, 168–173, 175, 180, 181, 184–186, 230, 241–247

Récanati, F., 45
reference assignment, 18–21, 29, 43
RefP, *see* Topic position
Reichenbach, H., 199
Reinhart, T., 6, 60, 172, 174, 293
Reyle, U., 7, 200, 292
van Riemsdijk, H., 89
Rizzi, L., 6, 76
Roberts, C., 29, 48, 98, 101, 102, 111, 125, 193
Rooth, M., 28–30, 98–101, 118, 119, 123, 124, 190
Rosenthall, S., 10, 76, 111, 193
Rothstein, S., 196, 224–227
RT [abbreviation introduced], 7
Rubovitz, T., 3

Sadock, J., 161, 209
Scharten, R., 160, 161, 164
Schein, B., 195, 196
scope
logical scope and syntax, 1, 18, 26–27, 76, 150, 256, 273, 275, 292–293
of adverb, 86, 242–247
of epsilon operator, 212, 225
of focus reading, 88, 107–110, 275

of negation operator, 256, 269, 271, 273, 275–277, 282, 290, 292
of syntactic explanation, 42, 59, 60, 62–67, 98
of VM, 83, 87
Segal, G., 19
Seuren, P., 113
Skinner, B., 51
Sperber, D., xiv, 3, 7, 32, 35, 36, 41–46, 49, 54, 55, 58, 69, 102–104, 131–135, 138, 146, 159, 211, 285
Stalnaker, R., 42, 105, 242
Stanley, J., 20, 22, 25, 26, 33–37, 46, 54, 114, 285
static representation of syntax, 7, 39, 54, 57–62, 67–70, 94, 220, 239, 241, 286, 290, 291
von Stechow, A., 98, 100, 101, 141, 198
Steedman, M., 1, 62, 216, 286
Stowell, T., 27, 150, 151
syntactic movement, 81, 86, 91–93, 101, 125, 126, 135, 146, 175, 222, 229, 246
verb movement, 11, 89–92, 257, 270
Szabó, Z., 22, 25, 26, 33–37, 46, 54, 114, 285
Szabolcsi, A., xiv, 11, 27, 79, 80, 90–92, 112–116, 118, 122, 129, 146, 149–160, 164, 165, 167–175, 177–180, 182, 183, 186, 189, 209, 270, 286, 287, 293
Szendrői, K., 60, 91–94, 108, 144, 175, 209, 232, 266

Tóth, G., 281
telicity, 81, 221–224, 236, 237, 240, 256
Tenny, C., 223, 237
theta-role, 195, 203–204, 212, 213, 225–227, 251, 264
Thomason, R., 242
Tohono O'odham, 291
topic, 76, 81, 99, 102, 103, 108, 127, 142, 144, 170, 171, 180, 184, 189–190, 192, 193, 203–205, 213, 214, 216, 227, 228, 240, 242, 244, 277, 279, 292
contrastive topic, 76, 108, 168, 179, 180
Topic position, 76–77, 85, 151–154, 159, 165, 168–171, 180, 181, 186, 189
topic>comment sentence, 76, 79, 82, 93, 103, 106, 109, 110, 126, 127, 140, 141, 144, 145, 188, 189, 193, 194, 202, 205, 206, 208–213, 215–217, 229, 232, 244, 248, 252, 272, 278, 279, 287
Tsiplakou, S., 85
Tugwell, D., 8
Turkish, 291
Turner, K., 1

underspecification, 3, 4, 7, 11, 18, 23, 24, 27, 28, 31, 33, 35, 53–56, 72, 81, 85, 112, 159, 183, 194, 200, 206, 210, 221, 257, 282, 292
Uriagereka, J., 60

Vallduví, E., 8, 9, 79, 81, 98, 99, 110, 135, 189
Vendler, Z., 223
verbal 'prefix' particle, 78, 81–83, 87, 90, 106, 209, 219, 221–236, 246, 250, 256–263, 282, 288
locative, 222, 248–249
Vilkuna, M., 79, 81, 110
VM [abbreviation introduced], 10, 78
VM-climbing, 91, 92, 209, 253
VPr [abbreviation introduced], 221

Wh-question, 9, 97–98, 101, 104–107, 109, 111, 120, 124, 125, 128–129, 140, 144, 145, 166, 288
Wh-word, 85
Wilson, D., xiv, 3, 7, 32, 35, 36, 41–46, 49, 54, 55, 58, 69, 102–104, 131–135, 138, 146, 159, 211, 285
witness set, see generalised quantifier theory

Zanuttini, R., 277